CANADA'S
SMALLEST
PROVINCE

A HISTORY OF P.E.I.

This book is dedicated to the
people of Prince Edward Island,
their forebears and heirs.

Canada's Smallest Province

A HISTORY OF P.E.I.

Edited by
Francis W. P. Bolger

FOR

ALAN DICKIE

Best Wishes

Francis W P Bolger

December 12, 1991.

NIMBUS
PUBLISHING LTD

Nimbus Publishing Limited
P.O. Box 9301, Station A
Halifax, Nova Scotia
B3K 5N5

Design: Arthur Carter, Halifax

Canadian Cataloguing in Publication Data

Main entry under title:

Canada's Smallest Province

Reprint. Originally published: [Charlottetown, P.E.I.: Prince Edward Island 1973 Centennial Commission], 1973
      Includes bibliographical references and index.
      ISBN 0-921054-91-2

1. Prince Edward Island -- History. I. Bolger, Francis W. P., 1925-

FC2611.C36 1991   971.7   C91-097591-4
F1048.C36 1991

Printed in Canada by John Deyell Company.

Contents

Illustrations

Preface

This book is published by the Prince Edward Island 1973 Centennial Commission to commemorate the 100th anniversary of the entry of Prince Edward Island into the Canadian Confederation. It relates in appropriate detail, the French and British colonial periods, the protracted story of the Island's entry into Confederation, and its political, economic and social development to the present.

The history of the Aborigines, the colorful years of the French Regime and the establishment of British rule are examined by John H. Maloney, Minister of Development and Minister of Industry and Commerce for Prince Edward Island, Nicolas de Jong, Provincial Archivist, and Douglas B. Boylan, Clerk of the Executive Council and Secretary to the Provincial Cabinet. The beginnings of Prince Edward Island's independence, the proprietary land tenure question and its effects on the political, social and economic development of the Island between 1767 and 1842 are described by the editor. Political advance and social reform between 1842 and 1861 are covered by W. S. MacNutt of the History Department of the University of New Brunswick. Nation Building in Charlottetown and the Island's resistance to Confederation until political and economic forces led it into union with Canada on July 1, 1873, are again my concern.

Mary K. Cullen, Historical Researcher, National Historic Sites Service, Ottawa, deals with the transportation question from 1873 until the present. Frederick L. Driscoll of the History Department of the University of Prince Edward Island analyses Dominion-Provincial relations in the post-Confederation period. Marlene-Russell Clark, Research Officer, Executive Council Secretariat of Prince Edward Island, describes the Island's electoral system and Island politics since Confederation. Finally, Lorne C. Callbeck, Research Scientist, Agriculture Canada Research Station, Charlottetown, reviews the economic, social and cultural history of the past century.

This book was made possible through the efforts of the History Committee of the Prince Edward Island 1973 Centennial Commission, which assumed responsibility for its publication and distribution. On behalf of this Committee, the editor thanks the above authors for their outstanding contributions, and for their co-operation in conforming to the editorial demands of co-ordinating the project as a whole. It is sincerely hoped that this volume will afford its readers an appreciation of some of the important themes and issues in the history of Canada's smallest province.

Francis W. P. Bolger
University of Prince Edward Island
July 1, 1973

HISTORY COMMITTEE OF THE PRINCE EDWARD ISLAND 1973 CENTENNIAL COMMISSION.

Frederick L. Driscoll	Department of History, University of Prince Edward Island, Committee Chairman
Francis W. P. Bolger	Chairman, Department of History, University of Prince Edward Island
Douglas B. Boylan	Clerk of the Executive Council and Secretary to the Cabinet of the Prince Edward Island Government
Nicolas de Jong	Provincial Archivist, Government of Prince Edward Island
Douglas Mayne	Functional Committee Co-ordinator, Prince Edward Island 1973 Centennial Commission
Hugh H. Simpson	Alderman of the City of Charlottetown, and President of H. M. Simpson Ltd.

CANADA'S
SMALLEST
PROVINCE

A HISTORY OF P.E.I.

Chapter One

The First Centuries

I

"And in the Beginning..."

By JOHN H. MALONEY

July 1, 1534, is the great dividing line in Prince Edward Island history. On that day Jacques Cartier, more than two months out of St. Malo, hove to off the North Shore, landed, and claimed the land for the King of France, Francis I. An ancient era had ended; the modern era had begun. Our theme in the next few pages is the prehistory of Prince Edward Island, that is the story of its beginnings and of the peoples who lived here in peace and contentment for thousands of years before the coming of the white man.

This Island is part of the great sedimentary land mass that underlies the Gulf of St. Lawrence. Into this area, about 200 million years ago, poured the waters of a huge drainage system comprising New Brunswick, Nova Scotia, Quebec, Labrador and Newfoundland. Possibly some of the drainage waters were from Northwest Africa, for at that time the American continental land mass had not yet separated from the European. At that time also, the great salt beds underlying Prince Edward Island at a depth of 12,000 to 13,000 feet were laid down. On top of these were laid layer upon layer of sediments to be pressed upon and made into the bedrock of what would become Prince Edward Island.

The next great landmark in Prince Edward Island's history is the last ice age. The Wisconsin ice age began about 75,000 to 100,000 years ago. Almost all of Canada, Prince Edward Island included, was covered by a mantle of ice as thick as two and a quarter miles at its center over Hudson Bay. How thick it was over this province is unknown, but from the amount of earth moved and formed into kames and eskers, as seen in King's County, it must have been considerable. Further proof is given by granite boulders, found scattered over Prince and western Queen's Counties, which were brought here by the glaciers spreading east from New Brunswick.

Some 25,000 years ago the ice mass had begun its last great retreat, and approximately 13,000 years ago this province was ice-free with the

1

grasses beginning to green its gently rolling contours. It was into such a land that the first inhabitants came. To understand who they were and whence they came, one must look briefly at the whole question of how man came to North America in the first place. Of one thing we are certain — man did not originate in North America.

The first inhabitants of the New World are referred to as Paleo-Indian. These people crossed into the American continent from Asia by way of the Bering land bridge from 35,000 to 15,000 years ago, more probably about 25,000 years before the present. The Paleo-Indian had spread down the Pacific coast, across what is now the southern United States and possibly even into Central and South America at least 12,000 years ago. They were big game hunters using a fluted, lance-shaped point, known as Clovis or Folson spear points, which are unique among stone weapons and are a certain identification of Paleo-Indian occupations.

About 13,000 years ago Maritime Canada became ice-free and habitable, although still cooler than the present day. Eventually, the Paleo-Indian spread to the East Coast of North America and up into Maritime Canada with a small population which was finding survival increasingly difficult. The northern migration occurred in pursuit of the caribou herds which multiplied rapidly upon the newly available grasslands.

A Paleo-Indian site in Debert, Nova Scotia, was carbon dated by archaeologists some 10,600 years before the present with an error margin of forty-seven years. The fluted, lanceolate projectile point was present at Debert and has also been found at Basin Head on Prince Edward Island, indicating that the Paleo-Indians may have lived or foraged on the Island. This is made even more likely by the existence of a land bridge between Prince Edward Island and New Brunswick until at least 7,000 years ago and possibly longer. For a time after the glacial retreat the water level was about two hundred feet lower than today, more than sufficient to make the Northumberland Strait into dry land.

The Paleo-Indians fished, hunted and gathered plants, but apparently did not make use of the shellfish which abound in Maritime Canada. These small, inbred bands of nomadic hunters had a high fat and protein diet and used the spear primarily; it is highly unlikely that they had the bow and arrow. When the herds of large game animals were pushed north by the forests, the Paleo-Indians were forced to hunt smaller animals. What happened to the Paleo-Indian culture is unknown; they may have died out or merged into the new people moving into Maritime Canada.

About 3,500 B.C. a new people moved gradually northward from what is now the Eastern United States into present-day New Brunswick, Nova Scotia, and Prince Edward Island; for several thousand years the eastern coast of North America had been experiencing a steady growth in population, the development of regional adaption into tribes, and growing trade between regions for such rare materials as obsedian, a workable glass-like stone.

This new Maritime people depended largely on shellfish for food and have thus come to be known as the Shellfish People. Characteristic of their former camp sites are mounds of decaying shells. Erosion of Prince Edward Island's North Shore often reveals one of these shell heaps in the bank. Like the Paleo-Indian, the Shellfish People lacked pottery, a form of utensil whose design and decoration would have revealed much of their culture.

Without salt these people could not cure fish; so, during August and September, clams, or even better, oysters were smoked and dried for winter stores. Lime from the shell has preserved bones of fish, birds, and animals and shows a diet possibly more varied than our own. Evidence of thirty different birds used for food includes such species as the Great Auk, the Loon and the Canada Goose. The tools of the Shellfish People, especially those of ground stone, show excellent workmanship and an attention to detail which often surpasses in skill those of the more complex later cultures.

About the time of Christ, a group of Eastern Algonquins moved out of central Canada and into the Maritimes. These first Micmac supplanted the Shellfish People and established their own domination. Although conclusive information is lacking, it is likely the Shellfish People were conquered by a combination of warfare and adoption. It is highly probable that the women and children were adopted by the Micmac, for life was precious and not to be wasted. Assimilation is further suggested by the Micmac occupation of Shellfish sites and the continuity of the tools used by women. Intermariage and the adoption of lifestyles produced a new race of people, different from the Algonquins and uniquely Micmac.

Eventually the Micmac spread out to cover the Maritimes from the coast of Gaspé to Nova Scotia, including Prince Edward Island. The St. John River valley became the home of the Maliseet, a tribe akin to the Micmac. It is said that the word Maliseet means 'one who speaks Micmac poorly'.

Knowledge of these early Micmac people is derived largely from interpretation of archaeological sites, the analysis of folklore and the accounts of explorers and missionaries. The most famous and extensive of these accounts are the *Jesuit Relations,* written in the early 1600's. From the Jesuits, particularly Biard, and such men as Denys and Lescarbot, we can construct a picture of Micmac life before the presence of the white man. A people highly skilled in the art of survival, the Micmac were also able to develop a rich and humane culture.

This Micmac Island of Abegweit was a forested land of rivers and beaches. Fish filled the waters, shellfish the shores, and the forests were the home of countless birds and animals. Berries, roots and herbs completed the list of Micmac food resources. Former Micmac campsites can often be located by the presence of the so-called "Indian Orchards"; clusters of fruit trees and berry bushes that have grown from seeds discarded by the Micmac years ago. Many of these orchards can be seen along the bays of the North Shore of Prince Edward Island, a favorite Micmac camping area. Even the earth itself was used in the struggle for survival. Women worked clay, coiled it in a spiral, and baked it in hardwood coals to make pots, while the men made tools by chipping stones.

The Jesuit, Biard, described the Micmac as "of lighter build than we are; but handsome and well-shaped, just as we would be if we continued in the same condition in which we were at the age of twenty-five. You do not encounter a big-bellied, hunchbacked or deformed person among them: . . . Any of our people who have some defect, such as the one-eyed, squint-eyed and flat-nosed, are immediately noticed by them and greatly derided, . . . for they are droll fellows and have a word and a nickname very readily at command." Intermarriage with Europeans over the last several hundred years has clouded the original Micmac physical characteristics. Usually blackhaired and blackeyed, they had little body hair and "no beards, the men no more than the women, except some of the more robust and virile." Swift runners in the hunt and excellent swimmers, the Micmac formed a particularly athletic and handsome race.

To achieve any understanding of these early people one must always remember the greatest good — plentiful food, and the greatest fear — starvation; neither extreme was uncommon. Whether at work, travel or relaxation, each member of the family kept at least one eye out for food. Because of starvation, a harsh life, and a high rate of infant mortality, the Micmac were fortunate to maintain their own numbers. The early population has been variously estimated and seems to have been three to four thousand, at the most, for the whole Maritimes.

Constant fear of starvation might be expected to produce a dour and hostile people. Yet the Micmac laughed easily and made loyal friends. Indeed, the very survival of the early French explorers was often due to Micmac kindness. Completely dependent upon Europe for food, the French were unlikely to survive a delay of the supply ship. One such episode is described in the *"Jesuit Relations"*: "Poutrincourt having had with him twenty-three people, without sufficient food to nourish them, had been obliged to send some off among the Savages, to live with them: the others had had no bread for six or seven weeks, and without the assistance of these same Savages, I do not know but that they would all have perished miserably".

Humor and a good sense of fun were part of a people who knew how to enjoy what they had. "In order to thoroughly enjoy this, their lot, our foresters start off to their different places with as much pleasure as if they were going on a stroll or an excursion." Tabagie or feasts with singing, dancing, speeches and usually general hilarity were held on many occasions — from weddings to funerals to a boy's first successful hunt.

Time was a cyclic thing to those early Micmac, each year being a round of activity concerned with the constant search for food. In January it was seal, a great delicacy whose oil provided a sauce which was stored and used year-round. During February and into March the hunting was for beavers, otters, moose, bears and also caribou which has been described as "an animal half ass and half deer." The fish started up-river to spawn in mid-March, in such plentitude that you could not "put your hand into the water without encountering them." Spring was also the time for the return of many species of birds whose flesh and eggs provided a welcome change from the winter menu.

May to September were the best months with many varieties of fish, shellfish, roots and berries readily available. The surplus was enough to make possible the summer ingathering. Summer was the period for large camps along the beaches of Prince Edward Island's North Shore. A bay with protective sand-bars across the mouth was a favorite location. Sites are found on Cascumpec Bay, Malpeque Bay, New London Bay, Rustico Bay, Tracadie Bay, Savage Harbour, North Lake and many others. Some of these campsites were inhabited every summer for thousands of years. Wigwams were placed in a single row just above the high water mark. The men had plenty of time in the summer to fill their lobster claw pipes and enjoy games of Waltes, a game played with six double-sided bone dice. Visiting, gossip, storytelling and courtship were also the order of the day. Meetings between chiefs also took place with decisions reached on matters of war, peace and inter-tribal relations. Gathering together in the warm summer months is an ancient Micmac custom still preserved in the annual St. Anne's Day celebrations at Lennox Island.

Mid-September was the time to leave the beaches and the cold north wind and move to the rivers where the eels were fat. In October and November hunting was again of first importance, and in December they collected a fish called 'Ponamo', probably a kind of cod. Winter camps were smaller so as to better distribute the available resources; one family or a few related families usually comprised the camp. In about six weeks the family would fish and hunt out an area and move on to return when the wildlife had replenished itself.

For these nomadic people travel was easy along the many waterways in their light bark canoes caulked with spruce gum and fat. The portage or overland hike between bodies of water was a common part of travel, particularly between the North and South Shores of Prince Edward Island. The usual crossing from the mainland was from Cape Tormentine into Bedeque Bay, and up the Wilmot River, from where a portage of a few miles brought the travellers into Weber's Cove on Malpeque Bay. From Rocky Point the Micmac canoed up the Hillsborough River and then, near Glenroy, portaged about two miles to Tracadie Bay.

Ingenuity and the ability to improvise combined in the Micmac to make a highly portable culture. Within a few hours or less the Micmac family could construct a comfortable home. Upon arrival at an attractive location near good water, a fire was started and camp made immediately. While the men cleared ground with an adze or stone axe, the women gathered poles which were placed in a circle and lashed at the top leaving a smokehole for the fire directly underneath. The poles were then covered with hides, bark or mats of finely woven reeds. Inside the wigwam evergreen boughs formed a floor with beds of mats and soft furs; "And, what no one would believe, they are very warm in there around that little fire, even in the greatest rigors of the winters."

Missionaries such as Father Biard and the many other dedicated Jesuits were men of good will who treated the Micmac fairly and had a sincere desire to help them. However, it must be remembered that the priests and other French of the early 1600's regarded the Indian as basically a heathen savage, whatever the virtues he might have possessed. There is definite surprise in Biard's statement; "You will see these poor barbarians, notwithstanding their great lack of government, power, letters, art and riches, yet holding their heads so high that they greatly underrate us, regarding themselves as our superiors." Biard reflected the simplistic European belief in its own cultural superiority. The Micmac had good reason to feel superior to those early expeditions manned as many of them were by the "sweepings of the jails and gutters of the old world." Biard's false claim that the Micmac lacked government, power, art, letters and riches, is worthy of further consideration.

Tribal government was administered by a combination of public opinion and the power of the chief, who usually represented one large family or more, depending upon the extent of his power. The chief or Sagamore concerned himself with the general welfare of the village and had such duties as the assignment of hunting territories. During the summer-gathering the chiefs held council to make political decisions. The chief's power rested to a considerable degree on the respect he gained from his people for wisdom and courage, since in a small community the leader is more directly accountable to his people.

Small offenses were arbitrated by the chief or common friends, although these offenses were rare. ". . . They are hardly ever offended long, as far as we know . . . for we have never seen anything except always great respect and love among them." Serious crimes such as murder or wife stealing were judged by public opinion and punishment was often left to the revenge of the victim or his family. If the offender repented, and wished to make amends, he was usually forgiven.

Occasionally a crime was committed of such horror that it demanded a punishment more severe than death. Cannabilism, a great temptation in time of hunger, was such a crime, for it threatened the welfare of the whole tribe. Ostracism or expulsion from the tribe cast the now homeless, friendless criminal alone into the forest where he was the prey of wild animals and evil spirits. Insanity, death and eternal dishonor were the result of ostracism.

Communal life could breed great tension, so the Micmac had a complex etiquette and status system to reduce the opportunities for discord. It was so beneficial that "no one would dare to refuse the request of another, nor to eat without giving him a part of what he had." The wigwam usually had a hunter's entrance and a girl's entrance. Each person had a special place within the wigwam depending upon sex and generation. One side of the fire was reserved as the boy's place; the other side was occupied by the grandparents near the girl's entrance, the parents in the center, and the girls near the hunter's entrance. The wife assigned each person to his proper place while her husband maintained the central fire.

Children were taught early to conform to the mode of suitable behavior. Unusual talents or ability were discouraged; belief held that a child who was too bright in his youth would have no sense at all when he grew up. Males and females treated each other formally and with great discretion, especially brothers and sisters. A brother would never speak or act rudely before his sister, nor would he contradict her. A woman would not enter the wigwam of a man whose wife was absent nor would a man enter the wigwam of a woman whose husband was absent.

Biard was correct in stating that the Micmac lacked 'letters'; but only to the extent that they did not have a method of writing. The Micmac preserved their history and wisdom in songs, stories and in the skills of the Medicine Man. Gifted storytellers passed on the tribal lore from generation to generation.

The Medicine Man or Automain was the doctor, psychiatrist, mystic, priest and historian of Micmac life. In a world populated by spirits, some of great evil, the Automain's charms were indispensible for protection and the gaining of favors. A considerable portion of the Automain's act may have been deception or fraud, as the Jesuits insist; however he did possess a very real knowledge of human psychology and basic medicine. The Automain was respected and influential in village life. He foretold the future, fought evil spirits in order to cure the sick, helped choose the best hunting spots, passed judgement on war plans and was consulted on anything of importance.

Little is known of the Micmac religion save that it centered around worship of the sun, the provider of light and warmth. Each morning at dawn the sun was greeted and at sunset another ceremony was held. At the command of their creator sun, the Micmac tried to find contentment and to be happy in their often harsh world. The afterworld, much like this one, was occupied by the souls of the dead, who ate, drank and hunted in a very mortal fashion. Reward for virtue and punishment for sins existed only as a vague concept; "farther than this they do not seek nor care for the causes of these things."

The world of the Micmac was populated by many beings, some of which, like the Skadegamutc, were much feared. The Skadegamutc, which delighted in evil, was usually the ghost of a dead person but on occasion might be that of a still living person. Gluscap, a mythical but mighty hero, gave many things, including the canoe, to his people. He lived beyond the clouds and, if visited, would grant any favor except eternal life.

Some humans were 'ginap' (had possessed supernatural powers) and possessed great strength and endurance used for good purposes. Stories are told of ginap children who have defeated whole bands of raiding Mohawks. An individual of great evil power was 'buoin' and could be so dangerous as to have made a person sick by merely looking at him. Keskamzit was a kind of magic which came suddenly as a talent or ability but only if it was kept secret. If a man caught a fish with two or more heads and threw it back, telling no one, he would have Keskamzit and from then on caught many fish From childhood, the importance of dreams was stressed as was the necessity for proper interpretation. Danger could be avoided and good fortune foretold with the help of dreams.

Art was another aspect of Micmac life too easily dismissed by Biard. Yet the women created clothing and ornaments of remarkable beauty from hides, paint, shells and brightly dyed porcupine quills. Finely cured leathers were trimmed with lacing and painted with lace-like designs. The introduction of tiny coloured beads by traders was welcomed by the Micmac whose beadwork was a true art form. Wood or sone was carved to make pipes, amulets, toys for the children, or simply to please the eye.

We are now able to re-evaluate Biard's claim that the Micmac lacked government, power, letters, art and riches. It is true that the Micmac had few formal political structures. However, custom and public opinion was enough, for among them, each man was his own master and his own protector. Letters and art the Micmac had, but in a form unrecognized as such at the time. A people occupying an area the size of Maritime Canada cannot be said to have lacked power or riches. Indeed, exploration and colonization of this area had as its basis the desire for one of these riches, namely, fur pelts.

Children were very much desired and cherished. A childless marriage was usually dissolved by mutual agreement. Immediately after birth the infant was washed in a nearby stream, whatever its temperature, and then given seal oil or bear grease to drink. Wrapped in warm, soft furs the new child was placed in the cradleboard in which he was carried by his mother while she worked digging clams or picking berries. If the baby cried, his mother would dance and sing, while still working, to soothe him. Powdered wood, moss or seaweed served as a diaper in the cradleboard which supported the baby, facing out, on his mother's back. Painstaking decorations of paint, quillwork and wampum on the child's clothes and cradleboard reflected the great love felt for children. As the nomadic Micmac woman could not feed or transport more than one baby at a time, she would breastfeed her children for three or more years. Nursing reduced a mother's fertility rate by about eighty-five per cent.

In contrast to the affection and tenderness shown to children, men and women rarely displayed their affection to one another. The young lad courting a girl "does not dare look at her, nor speak to her, nor stay near her . . . otherwise he would be the laughingstock of all, and his sweetheart would blush for him." The suitor gave presents to the girl's father in proportion to his prestige and his daughter's beauty. If the young man found favor with the maiden, her relatives gathered to discuss the match. The man's age, character, family and ability as a hunter all came under consideration. Often, the young man lived in the wigwam of his future bride's parents for a year before marriage. Divorce was acceptable and widows were encouraged to remarry for it was considered that one should not mourn the dead too long. Some men, such as chiefs, had more than one wife as they had large households to be supervised.

As is true of most people dependent upon hunting and gathering for food, men were very much the masters and women the followers. Being obligated to remain at home with the children, the women did most or all of the camp work. It was the woman who made the utensils of bark and clay, dug clams and picked berries, skinned, cleaned and cooked her husband's catches, tanned hides and made clothes and robes, strung snowshoes, and put up and took down the wigwam. When the band moved camp the women carried everything, including children, while the men went ahead to break the trail. Despite her inferior status the Micmac woman was spirited and, within her sphere, an authority. It was rare for a Micmac husband to question his wife's management of the household or her distribution of the food he had provided.

The important pursuits of hunting and fishing were the principal duties of the men. When not engaged in these activities, the men stayed around the camp talking and, perhaps, carving wood. All woodwork was done by the men, who made bows, arrows, spear and knife handles, cradle-boards, snowshoe frames and toys for the children. During a hunt small game was left where it fell and later brought in by the hunter's wife. Large game, such as caribou, was too heavy to transport so the whole family simply moved the camp to the caribou.

In old age, the Micmac was looked after by his children or relatives with respect and kindness. In council the experience and words of the aged commanded attention. Instruction of the young was another area of grand-parental influence. Those who were helpless with age, were supplied with meat and carried from camp to camp, either by canoe or on the backs of the young.

For about 1500 years the Micmac hunted and fished quietly in Prince Edward Island. All this changed with the coming of the white man. Fur traders paid high prices for pelts with the result that the Micmac devoted more and more time to trapping, buying his necessities from the traders, Within fifty years (circa 1650) the original Micmac lifestyle had altered to the extent that stone tools were no longer made.

The story of the Micmac is one of a nomadic people in an environment demanding constant struggle. They were people who were able to develop those qualities which make man humane. The white man should always remember the words of a Micmac chief to Colonel Cornwallis in 1765: "The land you sleep on is ours. We sprang out of the earth like the trees, the grass and the flowers."

II

The French Regime, 1534-1758

By NICOLAS de JONG

I THE EARLIEST DOCUMENTARY EVIDENCE

Jacques Cartier provided posterity with its first documented account of Prince Edward Island - (Ile St. Jean) in 1534.[1] However, his account created no immediate European interest in the Island. The earliest record of continuous occupation postdates Cartier's visit by one hundred and seventy-five years.

The first mention of Ile St. Jean, as a name given to a specific location, is attributed to Samuel de Champlain.[2] Although Champlain does not include the Island in his map of 1604 he does make reference to it in *Des Sauvages* which was published in the same year. It may, therefore, be assumed that he was aware of its existence in 1603. However, it was not until his map of 1632 that the Island was reasonably portrayed and distinctly named. D. C. Harvey, in discussing the derivation of the name, stated, that "the name Saint John was doubtless derived from the supposititious St. John's Island shown inside and outside Cape Breton at intervals on all maps subsequent to Reinal's map of 1505."[3] The Island retained its name of St. Jean, or the English equivalent, until February, 1799, when the name of Prince Edward Island received Royal Assent.

A further descriptive account of Ile St. Jean was included by Nicholas Denys in his work *Descriptive and National History of Acadia* published in 1672.[4] However, this account is no more complete than Cartier's. It seems very probable that its incomplete nature represents a conscious effort to supress information. Denys did not wish to stimulate the interest of his competitors.

Ile St. Jean, in the sixteenth and the first half of the seventeenth centuries, was visited only irregularly by fishermen and traders. These were men concerned with the demands of their immediate interests which

11

required no permanent base of operation. Consequently, the amount of extant documentation from this period, pertaining to Ile St. Jean, is limited. As A. H. Clark states: ". . . beyond reference to specific grants of the area to individual enterpreneurs for one purpose or another, our records are bare."[5]

II INDIVIDUAL AND COMPANY GRANTS

Ile St. Jean was included in a number of grants during the seventeenth century. The first of these was secured by Nicholas Denys on December 3, 1653, from the company of New France and Miscou, in return for a payment of 15,000 livres.[6] The area covered by this grant extended between "La grande baie Saint-Laurent," beginning at "Cap Canseau," and "Cap des Rosiers." Also included were the Iles de Terre-Neuve, Iles du Cap Breton, de Saint-Jean and other adjacent Islands.[7] The conditions attached to the grant required that Denys locate "at least two settlements each of forty families of Catholic, Apostolic, and Roman French, or a single one of eighty families, maintain a sufficient number of good and virtuous ecclesiastics for holding divine service, aid the said families, and labor for the conversion of the Indians."[8] This grant was confirmed by Letters Patent dated January 30, 1654.

Denys, however, failed to fulfill these conditions satisfactorily. Consequently, in 1663, part of his concession was revoked and granted to Sieur François Doublet. This grant, dated January 19, 1663, included both the Magdalen Islands and Ile St. Jean. In return for the fishing rights around the coasts of these Islands, Doublet agreed to establish a colony, to clear and cultivate land, and to make a small annual payment to the Company of New France and Miscou.[9] Doublet inaugurated his sedentary fishery in the Magdalens during the summer of 1663. In the winter of 1663-1664, he formed an Association with François Gon, Sieur de Guincé and Claude de Landemare in order to establish a firmer financial base so that the concession could be more fully exploited.

These arrangements, however, were to no avail as Doublet's death in the spring of 1664 spelt the end of the Association. Whilst there is no extant formal statement to this effect, the Association's failure may be assumed from a statement Denys makes in reference to Doublet: "He went away at the end of two years, as I had predicted to him, his Company being disheartened by the losses in which this clever man had involved them."[10]

In 1686, two years prior to the death of Denys, Sieur Gabriel Gauthier was granted the sealing concession in the Magdalen Islands and the right to establish a sedentary fishery in Ile St. Jean. Although Gauthier claimed that establishments were set up in all the Islands, his venture failed. Of the three ships sent out by the company between 1686 and 1688 not one succeeded in landing its cargo in France. A second society was formed but it met with a similar fate.

Early European interest in Ile St. Jean made but a slight impression. The effects of any commercial activity on the physical environment were inconsequential. No attempt was made by Denys, Doublet or Gauthier to centralize their fishing or fur-trading interests on the Island. Other un-documented excursions to the Island undoubtedly took place. However, these would have reflected the seasonal variations associated with the econo-mic activities carried on in the Gulf of St. Lawrence rather than a concern for the economic potential of the Island itself. D. C. Harvey furnishes the correct prespective when he writes that "in the meantime, France was concentrating upon the St. Lawrence Valley and her ships sailed serenely by to Quebec and Montreal."[11]

III ACADIAN MIGRATION AND THE BEGINNINGS OF PERMANENT SETTLEMENT

At the time Port Royal fell to the British in 1710 there were an estimated 2,000 Acadians scattered through the settlements to the east of their Capital. By the terms of the Treaty of Utrecht, 1713, France retained both Ile Royale and Ile St. Jean, whilst peninsular Acadia and New-foundland were ceded to the British. Those Acadians who were unwilling to become British subjects were granted the right to leave British territory within a stated period of time.

Thus, a position was created in which the French urged the Acadians to migrate to Ile Royale whilst the British preferred that they remain in Acadia. The French, with no desire to antagonise the English, relied upon the Acadian fear of the English and upon the influence of their mission-aries to effect this end. The Acadians, however, had formed a strong attachment for the area and also retained the hope that Acadia would subsequently be recovered by France. Consequently, they remained in-decisive. As Harvey states: "Had the Acadians been convinced that their colony would never be reconquered by France they would probably have made the sacrifice expected of them and migrated en masse. Had they really wanted to migrate, all that the few English in the colony could have done would not have prevented them."[12]

Ile St. Jean was not considered as an alternative reception area until it became clear to French officialdom that their attempts to attract the

Acadians to Ile Royale had failed. However, the movement of Acadians to Ile St. Jean commenced prior to this realization when, in 1710, an undisclosed number crossed the Northumberland Strait. The migrants soon discovered that the entire Eastern coast, to a depth of six leagues, had been granted in the same year to Sieur de Louvigny. The Acadians were thus largely unsuccessful in their efforts to obtain land grants. De Louvigny's concession was revoked in May, 1716, on the grounds that he had made no capital outlay on the concessions. It may also be accepted that the Acadians' aversion to a feudal structure of land tenure was an additional consideration behind the Council's decision. However, extant documentation indicates that the decision to reunite Ile St. Jean to the Royal Domain came too late to encourage these Acadians to remain. Governor Caulfield at Annapolis in a report to the Lords of Trade dated May 16, 1716, stated that "the Island of St. John is completely abandoned by the people of Annapolis who went to settle there."[13]

The French in 1719, frustrated in their efforts to attract the Acadians to Ile Royale, accepted an offer from Comte de Saint Pierre to establish a settlement in Ile St. Jean. In conjunction with this arrangement, French officials at Ile Royale were instructed to do all in their power to favor the inclination of the Acadians to settle on the Island.

IV   LE COMTE DE SAINT PIERRE

In August, 1719, a proprietary grant of Ile St. Jean, Miscou and adjacent Islands was made to Comte de Saint Pierre. The terms of this grant were specified as follows:

The administration of justice was reserved by the Crown; and of economic rights, the Crown also reserved the products of mines which were to be used for the good of the colonists, such lands as might be necessary from time to time for the erection of Public buildings or fortifications, and woods suitable for ship-building, although the Count was free to build vessels on the Islands and to erect sawmills for the manufacture of lumber. The grantee was required to retain or indemnify any habitants who might be already settled, to locate 100 settlers the first year and fifty each succeeding year until the Islands were populated and supplied with necessary livestock, and to construct such roads as were necessary for the public service.[14]

It was further stipulated that the Islands would be reunited with the Royal Domain if these conditions were not met. This concession was extended without addditional conditions on January 18, 1720, to include the Magdalen and Brion Islands. In these latter areas, however, the Comte's interests were associated with the sedentary fishery.

On April 15, 1720, three small ships, carrying three hundred passengers with provisions and supplies, sailed from Rochefort. The responsibility for the new government was given to Sieur de Gotteville de Bellisle. He was accompanied by Denys de la Ronde who joined the expedition at Louisbourg, and together they selected as their headquarters the site of Port La Joie, inside what is now called Charlottetown harbour, which continued as the capital throughout the entire French period.

Two Sulpician priests, Rev. René-Charles de Breslay and Rev. Marie-Anselme Metivier, accompanied the colonists. These were the first priests to come to Prince Edward Island. The first entry in the parish registers of the church, St. Jean L'Evangeliste, is dated April 10, 1721.[15] In addition to the church, other buildings were erected to house the garrison of thirty men, the workmen and the colonists. These structures, despite their temporary nature, remained in use at Port La Joie until they were destroyed by the New Englanders in 1745.

Once the housing requirements were met, De Gotteville attended to the company's business. In November, 1720, De la Ronde was sent to Bay Verte and Beaubassin with instructions to acquire Acadian carpenters and other workmen to assist in the winter shipbuilding program. A total of three ships were built under the program. The largest, (100 tons) was designed to carry cod to Europe, the second, (60 tons) was to be used in the West Indian trade and the third, (25 tons) was intended for the walrus and seal fishery around the Magdalens. The priorty put on these vessels is illustrative of the most important areas of French commercial interest.

Also in this year, a preliminary report was submitted by De Gotteville to the Regent of France. This report gives a straightforward account of the Island's natural state and the chief objects of French interest. The fine timber, the occasional meadows, the abundance of codfish, the size of harbours and the friendly attitude of the Indians are all emphasized.

A second and more detailed report, dated November 6, 1721, was submitted by De la Ronde to the Minister of Marine and Colonies. De la Ronde makes specific reference to Port La Joie and also considers the harbours at Tranche Montagne, St. Pierre, Savage Harbour, Tracadie, Quiquibougat (Rustico), Malpeque and Cascampeque. He also states that settlements had been established at Tranche Montagne, Tracadie, St. Peter's and Port La Joie. The population of the latter he estimated at one hundred being comprised of 16 families from France and 4 from Acadia.[16] From these figures it is clear that the stated Acadian preference for Ile St. Jean was merely an excuse to avoid going to Ile Royale. As Clark notes:

The Acadians were deterred perhaps not so much by the "dryness" of the soil, of which a complaint is recorded, as by the kind of labor, and the amount of it, involved in clearing the Island's forests. These people had become closely adjusted to an agricultural economy based on the treeless Fundy tidal marshes; similar sites were extremely limited in Ile St. Jean.[17]

Comte de Saint Pierre applied for an interpretation of both his 1719 and 1720 grants on account of interlopers, from Ile Royale, engaging in the fisheries of Ile St. Jean. As a result, it was determined that he had exclusive rights to fishing and commerce within a league of the coasts of all the Islands within his concession. The Comte received this interpretation in March, 1722, only after he had made a direct application to the King.

The complications led the King to appoint Sieur Robert Poitier Dubuisson as sub-delegate of the Intendant of New France in Ile St. Jean on March 10, 1722. Dubuisson was responsible for the administration of both civil and criminal justice, and had the authority to appoint a recorder, a prosecutor and a notary.

The affairs of the company, however, were not progressing sufficiently to retain the interest of the shareholders. Saint Pierre made no financial contribution during 1722. His partners assumed greater responsibilities but they in turn failed to meet their commitments in 1723 and 1724. The company was subjected to increasing criticism over the manner in which the monopoly was being exercised, and the company's financial director was beset on all sides by creditors. On November 27, 1724, De Mezy, Commissaire at Ile Royale, reported to the Minister in Paris:

that all the settlers of Ile Saint Jean had been obliged to abandon the colony and had come to Ile Royale, and that he had embarked all those who would have been at the charge of the King and sent them with their families back to France; that the effects of the company were seized and taken to Louisbourg, where they were sold at auction (including their ship, *La Chimene*) and the proceeds were divided among the creditors in proportion to their claims. M. Aubert, the financial director of the company, returned to France and this marked the last incident in the affairs of the company of Saint Pierre.[18]

In the six years, 1719-1725, the company spent a total of some 1,200,000 livres on the enterprise. On October 13, 1725, the exclusive rights of Comte Saint Pierre were revoked. His charter was finally annulled in 1730.[19]

The weakness of the company's position stemmed primarily from an inability to compete with the fishing interests of Ile Royale and the continued lack of enthusiasm exhibited by the Acadians for moving across the Northumberland Strait. Settlement during the first two years was limited, and almost entirely from France. The collapse of Saint Pierre's enterprise was a severe blow to the Island's economy, but a few Acadians and independent fishermen continued to cling tenaciously to their new homes.

V   *REUNION TO THE ROYAL DOMAIN*

On November 14, 1724, St. Ovide de Brouillan, Governor of Ile Royale, informed the Council in Paris that the English at Canseau were preparing boats to engage in the sedentary fishery. In July of the following year he wrote suggesting that a detachment of twenty-five to thirty men should be sent to Ile St. Jean to formalize the French interest. The Minister of Marine and Colonies responded in the autumn of 1725. St. Ovide was instructed to send a captain and ensign with twenty-five to thirty men to take formal possession of the Island and thus deprive the English of the erroneous notion that they could establish a foothold.

De Pensens was instructed to lead this expedition in the spring of 1726. He was subsequently appointed Commandant in the Island on July 2, 1726. Upon his arrival, he found the remnants of Saint Pierre's establishment scattered, and the inhabitants discouraged and quarrelling among themselves. The company buildings at Port La Joie were in a state of disrepair, although settlement continued in the area. Blanchard provides the following contemporary description of Port La Joie:

From the valley, its slopes and heights on either side, the forest had well nigh completely disappeared. Some families had settled along the West River. Thus the settlement at Port La Joie was a community of farmers and soldiers. An eyewitness declared that the fields of wheat he saw at Port La Joie were equal to any he had seen in France, Spain, or Italy. A government report of that time shows the yield of grain around Port La Joie was set at two thousand bushels. The staple crops were wheat, barley, oats, peas and rye.[20]

St. Ovide visited the colony in the late summer and De Pensens, discouraged by his appointment, accompanied him on his return to Louisbourg. St. Ovide's ensuing report reveals a two-fold policy towards the Island. Firstly, Acadians were to be encouraged to migrate from Nova Scotia to the Island, and secondly, their services were to be utilized in the interests of Louisbourg. To further these aims Father Felix was sent to the Island. It was his duty, not only to attend to the spiritual needs of the community, but also to encourage the Acadian migration. This facet of French policy incurred the resentment of the English and "did much to account for their exasperation which culminated in the expulsions of 1755 and 1758."[21] It was, therefore, the intention of the French to utilize Ile St. Jean as a resource area for Louisbourg. The colony was not to be considered as an end in itself. Consequently, the position of Ile St. Jean, as opposed to that of Louisbourg was continuously downgraded.

De Pensens returned to the Island in the spring of 1727. Also in this year a total of six Acadian families, encouraged by the increased interest of official France, crossed over to the Island. They were permitted to select land, wherever they wished, in proportion to the size of their families. Amongst other developments in this year the fishing operations out of Cascumpek (Cascumpeque) and St. Peter's were expanded, and additional manpower was obtained from Louisbourg to cut masts for the Navy.

The first census of the Island's population was undertaken in the following year. A total of 76 men, 51 women, 156 children and 14 domestics were enumerated for an aggregate of 297 persons. To these should be added some 125 fishermen. A total of 54 houses was recorded and in addition, it was noted that 8 schooners and 19 shallops were engaged in the fishery. The total catch for the year was estimated at 4,874 quintals of cod.[22]

Other significant events occurred in this year. Firstly, a further one hundred settlers arrived fom Acadia, and secondly, the crops were devastated by a plague of field mice. The loss of the crop was a serious blow to the colonists' aspirations. They were compelled to plough under their crops and to seek subsistence from the fisheries. Despite the hardships of the winter months, they sowed again in the spring of 1729 after De Pensens had obtained some thirty hogsheads of seed wheat from Acadia.

The poor physical condition of the garrison may be judged from De Pensen's communication of October, 1728, to the Minister. It reads in part as follows: . . . "it will be impossible to live longer on Ile Saint Jean if your Excellency does not order the erection of new dwellings. Those left here by the Comte de Saint Pierre are so completely rotten that the soldiers and myself run every moment the risk of being crushed under their ruins."[23]

Records pertaining to the events of 1729 are few. It is evident that an English vessel was pillaged and burnt by the Indians, and that Debuisson, who continued as sub-delegate to the Intendant, was granted a salary of 600 livres. The garrison, during the winter of 1729-1730, was under the command of Lieutenant Du Haget and De Pensens. The Commandant, De Pensens again wintered at Louisbourg.

The harvest of 1730 was a good one. At Port La Joie, over two hundred hogsheads of grain were gathered, at Malpeque forty, at Savage Harbour thirty and at St. Peter's over fifty. Fishing was also good and only a shortage of salt prevented the fishermen at St. Peters from preserving 300 quintals for each of the 20 shallops engaged in the industry.

Reports of this success encouraged some 60 Acadians to journey to the Island to view areas of potential settlement. Thus, they were not all included in the census of 1730. This second census recorded 76 men, 55 women, 182 children and 12 domestics for a total of 325 persons. There were a further 140 fishermen who now owned 4 schooners and 23 shallops. In the two-year period, 1729-1730, a total of 37 new settlers arrived on the Island. However, because of out-migration the actual population increase was only 28.[24] In this year also the grant to Comte de Saint Pierre was finally annulled and the Island was reunited to the Royal Domain as a dependency of Louisbourg.

In his report, dated March 5, 1732, De Pensens stated that a total of 28 habitants had settled at Port La Joie and along the Northeast River. These locations were always preferred, as cultivation here was at its most extensive. A further seven had settled at the head of the Northeast River whilst somewhat smaller numbers went to Malpeque and Tracadie. St. Peter's, the centre of the fishery, remained the most heavily settled area on the Island. De Pensens described the settlement in detail:

Most of the inhabitants were deep sea fishermen or masters of shallops of whom there were twenty-five. Only eight habitants were engaged in clearing land suitable for wheat. Although the fishing was good and much less costly than at Ile Royale, the fishermen had all they could do to make ends meet for lack of equipment. In spite of the fact that a ship had come from France each of the last two years the fishermen had been under obligation to merchants in Louisbourg and compelled to buy their provisions there at an increased cost of 50 per cent. This made it difficult for them to pay their debts and at the same time to provide for their families during the winter.[25]

The total population of these settlements together with two fishermen's families at East Point numbered 347. New areas of settlement were not opened up until 1750 when Acadian migration, after the founding of Halifax, made it necessary to locate new outposts at the river mouths to the southeast and southwest of the Island. In the intervening period the policy of the French government was one of consolidating these settlements through the process of lateral expansion.

VI DE ROMA AT THREE RIVERS

A little over a year after the Island had been united to the Royal Domain a large area was granted to the Company of the East. On July 17, 1731, a grant of 3,500 arpents frontage and forty arpents depth was made to Srs. Cottard, du Bocage, Narcis and de Roma. Excluded, however, were any lands already conceded to inhabitants. This area approximated the watersheds of what are now the Brudenell, Montague and Cardigan

Rivers. In effect a large feudal estate was created, held in hommage to Louisbourg but free from all Royal dues. The following terms for the grant were specified:

The only obligation placed upon the corporation was the conservation of oak suitable for shipbuilding, the report of mines to the King or his officers, and the grant of such lands as the King should need for forts or public buildings. Justice was also reserved to the King and to be administered by the sub-delegate of the Intendant of New France in Ile Saint Jean. . . . The company was to take out eighty settlers in 1732, and thirty each subsequent year, with the necessary stock to establish hearth and home. It was to encourage these settlers to clear lands, and to build such roads as were necessary for public use. True to the French policy of uniting the interests of the state and of religion, the company was to build one or more churches in return for which they would be honored as patrons. On failure to carry out these conditions the land was to revert to the crown. On the other hand, the company was to be permitted to establish stores and drying places on the North Coast of the colony outside their concession, where they would be treated generously with grants of land in proportion to the number of shallops which they should employ in the fisheries.[26]

Settlement was begun in 1732 under the direction of the colorful Jean Pierre de Roma. He selected Brudenell Point as his centre of operations and immediately began an ambitious construction program. Blanchard provides a description of the buildings at Three Rivers:

The settlement consisted of nine solidly built log houses; the two largest were each eighty feet in length. One was called the house of the company, where de Roma and his family resided; the others acommodated the company's fishermen. A building sixty feet long received the labourers employed and strangers, while another of the same dimensions was reserved for the officers and crews of ships. The overseers and tradesmen had a roomy dwelling of sixty-nine feet. One building of fifty feet was partitioned off for stores, and a bake-house, a forge and a stable, each forty feet, completed the edifices of the establishment.[27]

De Roma was also interested in overland communication. Consequently, a number of roads (in fact, they more closely resembled bush trails) were constructed. These roads extended from Brudenell Point to Cardigan, to Sturgeon River, and to St. Peter's some eight leagues distant. In the interests of security a further road was built, with the co-operation of the garrison, to Port La Joie. The company also owned five vessels which were employed not only in a four-cornered trade between Ile St. Jean, the West Indies, Quebec and the garrison at Louisbourg but also between the Island and France.

However, these somewhat grand designs were not well received by De Roma's partners. In the first year of operation they advanced goods and equipment to the value of 91,000 livres. The company in return shipped fish, valued at 45,000 livres to France, purchased 15 to 20 shallops and two batteaux and also constructed a fishing base at St. Peter's. Despite these promising indications the partners refused further financial support. They were finally bought out by De Roma in May, 1737.

In the years 1737-1745 De Roma continued to display great energy and enthusiasm in his undertakings. However, luck continued to run against him. After a small harvest in 1737 prospects appeared good for the following year. But in common with other areas of the Island, his settlement was ravaged by field mice. In 1741 he lost a vessel and all its cargo. This setback compelled him to seek credit from the Minister against which he could only pledge his uncertain returns of the following year. The settlement managed to exist between 1741 and 1745 only through strict economy.

However, these efforts were to no avail, for on June 20, 1745, a detachment of New Englanders sent from Louisbourg, arrived at Three Rivers. They met with no resistance from the settlers. De Roma wih his family and servants managed to escape to St. Peter's and eventually to Quebec. The buildings which had been set out with such care and detail were destroyed. His losses were estimated at 100 bushels of wheat, 4 horses, 10 cows, 50 sheep, 20 swine and 100 poultry.[28]

Thus the labor of thirteen years was obliterated in just a few hours. De Roma's enterprise was ruined and his small settlement was dispersed. Prior to recent archaeological investigations of the area, which revealed many other structures, all that remained were two large depressions, two half-filled wells, and some of the chimney bricks.[29]

VII   THE COLONY, 1732-1744

Meanwhile, De Pensens spent the year 1732 in France. His command in Ile St. Jean was assumed by De la Perelle who was instructed to encourage settlement, to offer assurance to the Acadians that they were secure in the title of those lands that they selected, and to prevent the destruction of timber.

On the other hand, De Pensens, whilst in France, did manage to stimulate some official interest in the Colony. He reiterated his request that 1,500 livres be provided for the upkeep of his boat and as insurance against accident. He also requested that he be appointed Lieutenant de Roi if and when such an office were created. Both these requests were granted, and he was duly appointed Lieutenant de Roi on June 2, 1733.

Upon his return to the Island De Pensens found little change in the general condition of the inhabitants. A few Acadians had arrived and three soldiers had settled under the plan of granting discharges, for no more than eight soldiers a year who wished to leave the garrison at Louisbourg and to take advantage of three years' pay, clothing and rations. Also in this year the road connecting Port La Joie and Three Rivers was completed. Thus, it became possible to make the journey in a day and a half.[30]

De Pensens returned to the Island with specific orders to open a road between Malpeque and Port La Joie, to erect new barracks and a new powder vault, and to provide new quarters for the Lieutenant de Roi, the surgeon and the chaplain. To ensure the completion of this program in 1734, St. Ovide provided a full company of soldiers to assist in the collection of lumber. In fact, the powder vault and the establishments for the surgeon and chaplain were not completed until 1735. The construction of the barracks was not undertaken.

A census was taken in 1734 and again in 1735. The returns of 1734 recorded a population of 396 and 176 fishermen for a total of 572. The corresponding figures in 1735, 432 and 131 fishermen for an aggregate of 563 are indicative of the fluctuating nature of the fisheries and the trend towards increased settlement on the land. In both these years the colonists' point of origin was also noted. In 1734 four persons came from Spain, 16 from Canada, 162 from Acadia and 214 from France. The respective figures in 1735 were: 3, 15, 198, and 216. These figures illustrate the increasing importance of the Acadian migrations.

The inclusion of agricultural statistics in these returns provides the first indication that the agricultural resources of the colony were assuming a position of importance similar to that accorded the fisheries. It is clear from these compilations that the new colonists tended, where possible, to transport their livestock with them. The respective figures for 1734 and 1735 were 332 and 433 head of cattle and 119 and 190 sheep.[31]

De Pensens, who had suffered bouts of sickness since his departure from France in 1733, was retired with a pension in April, 1737. Du Haget was appointed to command the new garrison of forty men. Briefly, his instructions were to ensure that the barracks and military stores were in good order. He was to maintain discipline among the troops and to provide for the sick. His authority did not extend to the King's magazine over which Dubuisson had charge. He was also expected to assemble his detachment whenever Dubuisson should wish to hold a review. His only concern with the administration of justice was the provision of assistance to the sub-delegate of the Intendant in executing his judgments.

The winter of 1736-1737 was one of great hardship for certain of the colonists as a forest fire, in August 1736, destroyed crops and several homes.[32] In response to this crisis seed grain was sent from Louisbourg and Du Haget provided subsistence rations from the King's stores. The colonists were to become even more familiar with this pattern of external assistance and internal subsistence in the future.

The appointment of Duchambon as Lieutenant de Roi on May 17, 1737, did little to alleviate the hardships of the inhabitants. The plague of field mice that ruined De Roma's expectations was equally as destructive in other areas of the Island. The results were similar to the calamity of 1728. Le Normant, Commissaire in Ile Royale, made arrangements to have seed wheat shipped from Acadia, and he also sent provisions from Ile Royale. The quantities were small, 112 quintals of flour, 8 quintals of peas, 36 quintals of shot, 10 quintals of powder and 25 guns.

Official statements of Acadian reaction to these deprivations are contradictory. Duchambon reported that the habitants were elated by the assistance they received. However, Dubuisson, who was in closer touch with the people, stated that the years 1736-1738 were "years of great suffering, the habitants coming to him in a crowd dying of hunger."[33]

Conditions, however, improved in 1739. Duchambon reported that 666¾ bushels of wheat and 150 bushels of peas had been sown and that cleared land was available for sowing half as much again. Summer rains, which were general throughout Canada in this year, accounted for a poor growing season. However, yields were sufficient to make the colony self-sufficient.

The quality of the building stock at Port La Joie remained unimproved. The French were reluctant to expend resources at a questionable location. Duchambon, soon after his appointment, stated that St. Peters was to be preferred over Port La Joie. This opinion was endorsed by Bigot who reported, in 1740, that St. Peter's should be considered since it was the most thickly populated, the richest in commerce and the most varied in fishing. He also pointed out that if the King wished to fortify the Island in the hopes of attracting settlers, then Three Rivers should not be excluded. These reports stimulated no official reaction and Port La Joie continued as the neglected centre.

A total of 450 persons were enumerated in the census of 1740. They were located at the following centres: 81 at Port La Joie, 147 at St. Peter's, 48 along the Northeast River (Pisquid), 63 at Savage Harbour, 44 at Tracadie, 53 at Malpeque and 14 at Three Rivers. The livestock numbered 166 oxen, 337 cows, 402 sheep and 14 horses. The record also indicates that 819 bushels of grain were sown and that 7 schooners and 22 fishing boats were operated from the Island.[34] In the five-year period, 1735-1740, the recorded population increase was slight. It should be noted that the figure of 450 excludes fishermen. However, it is evident that the livestock base was becoming more firmly established. The increased number of sheep is particularly pertinent in this respect.

Immigration under Duchambon commenced in 1741 when five Acadian families crossed from Beaubassin and settled at Malpeque. Duchambon also negotiated with several other Acadian families. The agreements he established guaranteed provisions for a single year to any family moving from Acadia to the Island. As a result of these negotiations eleven families migrated in the spring of 1742. In the following year, a further eight families moved from Acadia and settled in Malpeque. By 1744, therefore, after three successive years of reasonable prosperity, Acadian migration was proceeding at a manageable if unspectacular rate.

VIII   THE WAR YEARS, 1744-1748

The news that war had broken out between England and France reached Louisbourg on May 3, 1744. The part played by the colonists in the ensuing hostilities was limited. It was nonetheless a period of fear, unrest and discouragement. Communications with Canada became considerably more difficult and the size of the garrison was halved when De Vivier called at Port La Joie to reinforce his contingent en route for Bay Verte. After the fall of Louisbourg, the colonists remained without a garrison, without a priest, and without either a civil or judicial officer. Under these testing conditions Acadian migration to the Island ceased until the restoration of 1749. The English, once the capitulation of Louisbourg was assured, sent a single expedition against the Island. This force divided, one part going to Port La Joie and the other proceeding to De Roma's settlement at Three Rivers. The latter encounter, as already mentioned, was never in question.

At Port La Joie the detachment carried out a plan of destruction similar to that employed at Three Rivers. The garrison, now under the command of Captain de Vivier, retreated up the Northeast River. A counterattack was organized with the assistance of a band of Indians and a handful of Acadians. A total of 9 New Englanders were either killed or taken prisoner in this action, while the remainder retreated to the safety of their ship.[35] In the larger context however, this action was of little importance. The keys of Louisbourg were surrendered to the British on June 17, 1745. Soon afterwards the colonists, in correspondence with the English Governor at Louisbourg, offered their submission if they might be permitted to retain their lands. The agreement stipulated that the colonists would remain unmolested for one year provided six hostages were sent to Louisbourg.

Rumours abounded at this time that the English intended to return all the inhabitants of Ile St. Jean to France in the summer of 1746. These rumours were not unfounded as Rear-Admiral Warren, Governor of Louisbourg, mentioned this possibility in correspondence with the Duke of Newcastle. This suggestion was seriously considered but was not effected as all the available transports were required for an expedition against Canada. Consequently, a declaration of indulgence was issued to the people of Ile St. Jean on June 9, 1746. [36]

The Island remained in the background for the duration of hostilities. The French never made any serious attempt to retake it although De Ramezay did consider using Port La Joie as a staging area in 1746, in his attempt to recover English-held Acadia. However, the English retained possession of both Ile Royale and Ile St. Jean until the treaty of Aix-La-Chapelle.

IX   ILE ST. JEAN RESTORED TO FRANCE

By the terms of the treaty of Aix-La-Chapelle, signed on October 18, 1748, Ile St. Jean and Ile Royale were restored to France. Conditions in the Island at this time were far from satisfactory. The colonists were hard pressed as the crop of 1748 had failed. The French responded promptly. Bigot, the Intendant of New France, sent provisions and supplies to assist the colonists through the winter of 1748-1749. Also, La Galissoniere, Governor of Canada, dispatched a detachment of twenty-five troops, to Port La Joie, under the command of Captain Benoit. Benoit was instructed to provide liberal assistance to those Acadians migrating to the Island with their livestock. These orders were consistent with the French policy of restoration and also reflected the degree to which the livestock resource had been depleted by sale to the English and through local consumption in the absence of official aid.

Acadian migration to Ile St. Jean was provided with an additional stimulus when the British revealed their plans for the settlement of Acadia. Briefly, these entailed the settlement of British colonists in the area and the requirement of an unqualified oath of allegiance from those Acadians who wished to remain. In accordance with this policy, Halifax was founded on Chebucto Bay in the summer of 1749. In the hope of inducing the Acadians to become loyal subjects, the British allowed them freedom of religion and the rights to such lands as they held under cultivation. In return the Acadians were required to take the oath of allegiance within three months from the date of a proclamation to that effect. The final date for receiving the oath was determined as October 26, 1749. Those Acadians who wished to leave Nova Scotia were permitted to do so. However, they were required to obtain permission from the Governor or Commander-in-Chief if they wished to transport any cattle, corn or other provisions.[37]

The French for their part made every effort to encourage Acadian migration to Ile Royale, Ile St. Jean, or to the territory between Bay Verte and the Gaspé. In Ile St. Jean the responsibility for receiving and locating these refugees fell to the new Commandant, Captain de Bonnaventure, and Sieur Degoutin, the sub-delegate of the Intendant. Degoutin, who was appointed to his post in August, 1749, was also held responsible for the King's magazine and the administration of Civil Justice. He was also charged to keep a record of the rations supplied to the garrison, to the habitants in times of famine and to the refugees. De Bonnaventure's primary instructions were to assure the re-establishment of Port La Joie and the provision of accommodations for officers and troops.[38]

As a result of the encouragement provided by French officialdom and the events transpiring in Nova Scotia, a steady stream of immigrants crossed to the Island between 1749 and 1751. In 1748 the total Acadian population on Ile St. Jean was only 735. This figure was increased by 151 in 1749, 860 in 1750, and by a further 326 in 1751.[39]

The problems presented by the onset of this influx were compounded by yet another crop failure in 1749. In response to this crisis, Bigot, who was now supervising the reconstruction of Louisbourg, despatched quantities of flour, salt beef and seed wheat in August and October, 1749. He also placed an order for 6000 quintals of flour from New England. The amounts involved were only sufficient to allow the colonists to subsist through the winter of 1749-1750. The problem of locating the new immigrants was resolved by ceding them the unoccupied or partially occupied lands. Rent was only charged in those cases in which the ancient concessionaires had well-founded titles. The destruction of Beaubassin on April 25, 1750, accounted for the exceptionally large number of immigrants recorded in that year. The scale of this migration perpetuated the problems of the preceding year and did nothing to alleviate conditions on the Island. Bigot was again required to provide provisions and clothing from Louisbourg.

Despite the rapid decline in the number of migrants in 1751 and 1752 a state of confusion persisted at Port La Joie. Certain of the older inhabitants, in particular those who had relied upon a verbal title from the Lieutenant de Roi or sub-delegate of the Intendant, feared for the title to their lands. On the other hand, the new settlers were uncertain as to where they could settle and what they could do. A decree was in effect at this time which prohibited people from engaging concurrently in both fishing and agriculture. De Bonnaventure was consistent throughout this period in his appeals for a more dependable flow of food supplements and additional personnel to handle the administration and distribution of provisions. He also recognized the need for a land surveyor but none was forthcoming.

During this period the new immigrants subsisted mainly on a diet of bread and peas. The provisions sent from Quebec and Ile Royale were insufficient to maintain them in ordinary comfort until they could become self-supporting. The older settlers were not much better off, for despite a succession of crop failures, they were denied supplementary rations. They also resented the manner in which the new immigrants were being settled amongst them on lands that should have been pre-empted for the natural expansion of their own families. French officialdom remained unconcerned at the Acadian level of subsistence. The human suffering in Ile St. Jean was held to be insignificant when placed in the Imperial perspective. The numbers seduced from allegiance to the English were of more importance.

Colonel Franquet, a military engineer in charge of the restoration of Louisbourg, visited Ile St. Jean in August, 1751. In his report he outlined the conditions and prospects of the Island and made certain recommendations for its future development. He inspected Port La Joie and drew up plans for a fort and replacements for its flimsy buildings. He travelled up the Northeast River and noted the small clearings on either bank. He reported a sawmill at Millbrook and made mention of the settlements along the lower Pisquid. He continued to St. Peter's by way of the portage to Savage Harbour. At St. Peters he again drew up plans for permanent fortifications, and on his return to the Northeast River he took the time to roughly survey a new and shorter route for the portage. He also prepared a chart of soundings of the harbour of Port La Joie.[40] After this he sailed to Three Rivers where he correctly concluded that the rights granted to De Roma accounted for the lack of Acadian settlement in the area. He viewed the natural harbour in the most favourable terms and again produced plans for permanent fortifications.[41]

John Caven in his summary[42] of Franquet's report, noted that Franquet was favourably impressed by the Island's physical characteristics. Mention is also made of the plans for fortifications to be constructed at Port La Joie, Point à la Framboise, St. Peter's and Three Rivers. In order to improve overland communications, Franquet proposed that a number of roads should be constructed. The first was to run between Three Rivers and a spot on the Northeast River opposite to Grande Source. A second road was to run from Point Marguerite to East Point and would cross the first at right angles. From this point of intersection a further road was proposed to extend to St. Peter's. Caven closes by noting that the only road under construction in 1752 ran between Point Marguerite and the peninsula at Three Rivers. From this evidence he infers that "Franquet's hints on road-making shared the same fate as his administrative suggestions, and his plans for securing the Island against the aggression of foreign enemies."[43]

Franquet's return to Louisbourg prompted Comte de Raymond to issue further instructions to De Bonnaventure. De Raymond now stipulated that the lack of any clustered settlement was to be rectified by granting, to those colonists already settled, lands of greater depth than width. New colonists were to be located immediately in the resulting clusters. De Bonnaventure was further instructed to make a register of the concessions already granted, and in order to facilitate communications and encourage further settlement, he was to ensure that the existing routes were cleared for use by horsemen. Unfortunately, despite the sagacity of the demands, there is little evidence to suggest that De Bonnaventure extended himself in ensuring their implementation.

X   DE LA ROQUE'S CENSUS OF 1752

This census was conducted by Le Sieur Joseph de la Roque under the direction of the Comte de Raymond in the summer of 1752. A total of 2,223 persons was enumerated in this very detailed account of Ile St. Jean. More than half of those recorded had arrived since the autumn of 1748 when the Island was restored to France. The census recorded the full name of each person, their age and profession, their character and general condition, the time of their arrival on the Island, the amount of improved land held by each family, the number of cattle and livestock and the crops sown.[44]

The main areas of settlement, Port La Joie, St. Peter's and the banks of the Northeast River, continued to reflect not only the communication needs of the community but also the importance attached to the areas of natural pasture. The characteristic linear pattern of French settlement, never in the initial stages more than one farm deep from tidewater, predominated. It should also be noted that the Acadians preferred to expand slowly with the frontier rather than pioneer as isolated individual family groups.

The most extensive new settlement was located in the areas around what are now Pownal, Orwell and Pinette Bays. Three Rivers was notable as the only area to have been abandoned. Settlement had become more dense around Port La Joie and along the Northeast River, and it had also extended up both the North and West Rivers. On the south coast new concentrations of colonists were located at Rivière au Crapauds (now Crapaud) and Rivière des Blonds (now Tryon). On the North Shore, despite small recorded increases at Etang des Berges (Covehead) and Quiquibougat (Rustico), the St. Peter's and Malpeque Bay areas continued as the important settlement centres.

Of the 2,223 persons enumerated, a total of 1,366 moved to the Island between 1748 and 1752. During this same period 93 children were born to the old inhabitants and 14 to the new. The livestock consisted of 98 horses, 2,058 head of cattle, 1,230 sheep, 1,295 hogs, 2,393 ewes, 304 geese, 90 turkeys and 12 ducks. There were also 4 schooners, none larger than 50 tons, 4 batteaux, 15 fishing boats and 11 smaller boats or canoes. A total of 1,490 bushels of wheat, 129 bushels of oats, 181 bushels of peas and smaller quantities of barley, rye, buckwheat and flax seed were sown in 1752.[45]

It seems probable that over 1000 acres had been cleared, but much of this land lay idle as insufficient seed was available. This situation was due in part to administrative neglect and also to localized misfortunes. For instance, in Malpeque, the settlers suffered three successive bad crop years between 1749 and 1751, while the settlers at East Point had their resources destroyed by fire.

A large number of gardens were also recorded and it seems evident that the basic Acadian staples of wheat and peas were supplemented by other vegetables. De la Roque noted that there was no evidence to support the notion that settlers involved in the fisheries tended to neglect the cultivation of the soil. However, despite De la Roque's firsthand knowledge of the Island and the detail contained in the census, his recommendation for additional support from France and Louisbourg were almost totally ignored by official France.

XI THE SECOND ACADIAN MIGRATION

The progress that the English made in establishing both Fort Edward and Fort Lawrence revived Acadian interest in the Island. Prior to 1752 the only organized parish on the Island was that of St. Jean L'Evangeliste at Port La Joie. It was now decided, as a further inducement to the Acadians, that, four additional priests should be stationed and parishes established at Malpeque, St. Peter's, Point Prim and at a suitable point on the Northeast River.

Immigration to the Island in 1752 was limited. During the summer months some seven or eight families arrived. They were joined in the autumn by five German and Swiss families who had deserted from Halifax. The census of 1753 indicated that the total population of the Island increased by 418 in the period 1751-1753. However, the increase recorded in the livestock population was not proportional as the English had become more vigilant in controlling the transhipment of Acadian livestock. Also a shortage of seed still prevented the inhabitants from maximizing their returns. Despite this, the quantities of wheat, peas and oats sown, 2,755, 420, and 435 bushels respectively, were almost double those of 1752. Nonetheless, two-thirds of the land prepared for cultivation was not planted. Conditions were better in the spring of 1754 when, as a result of careful hoarding, almost 8,000 bushels of wheat and 1,000 bushels of peas were sown.[46]

This upswing in agricultural production did not, however, improve the material condition of the Acadian refugees. In a letter dated October 31, 1753, Père Girard described the condition of his parishioners in the vicinity of Pinette and Point Prim in the following words:

Our refugees in general do not lose courage, and hope by working to be able to live; but the nakedness which is almost universal and extreme afflicts them sore; and I can assure you that several will be unable to work this winter for lack of implements. They cannot protect themselves from the cold either by day or by night. . . . All are not reduced to this extremity but almost all are in need.[47]

The census of 1755 was sent by the missionaries to L'Abbé de L'Ile Dieu in Paris. The recorded population totalling 2,969, did not include the large number of Acadians who immigrated to the Island after the fall of Beauséjour and the subsequent expulsion of 1755. This migration commenced in the autumn of 1755 and by the spring of 1756 some 2,000 persons, without resources, had found their way to the Island. Rousseau de Villejouin, who had replaced De Bonnaventure in April 1754, succeeded in moving the aged and infirm to Canada, but he was still left with the problem of providing for the remaining 1,400. Therefore, by 1756 one-third of Ile St. Jean's population of 4,400 was dependent upon the Crown for support.

De Villejouin appealed to Louisbourg for supplies but only a limited quantity arrived in December, 1755. Two additional supply ships arrived in the spring of 1756 and a third was sent from Quebec in the summer. This would have been all but for the fact that a supply vessel, en route to Louisbourg, was pursued by the English and had to discharge its cargo on the Island. Even with this unexpected bonus, De Villejouin reported, in November, 1756, that supplies, at a minimum ration, were sufficient for only two months. The ration per family, per month, consisted of 20 pounds of flour, 10 pounds of vegetables, 12 pounds of beef, 1 pound of butter and 1 pot of molasses. This problem was compounded by a poor harvest which left little seed for the following spring. These pressing conditions were partially alleviated when Prevost, the Intendant at Louisbourg, bought the cargo of a prize taken from the English. These supplies he shipped to the Island and charged De Villejouin to make them last until the spring of the following year.[48] To add to their misery, the colonists in addition to a food shortage, had the threat of invasion imposed upon them when hostilities between England and France resumed in 1756.

The colonists received no respite during 1757. The rumors of English designs on Louisbourg persisted and the crops again failed. Vaudreuil, Governor of Quebec, in correspondence with the Minister in Paris, stated on April 18, 1757, that provisions for the refugees were only sufficient to last six weeks and that the older inhabitants were also in a state of distress. On December 10, 1757, Prevost again wrote to the Minister. He requested supplies of seed wheat, without which there could be no crop in 1758, and other immediate assistance to avert a state of famine. He pointed out that prospects for the winter were bleak, and that the degree of suffering was already extreme.

In both 1756 and 1757 the colonists made efforts to ease their dire circumstances. In the winter of 1756 some 60 young men from the Island were armed and sent to Acadia. They succeeded in surprising the English at Pisquid where they captured a magazine with 300 hogsheads of wheat and 60 of flour. They also assisted some Acadians who were hiding between Cobequid and Tatamagouche in reaching the Island. In the spring of 1757, De Villejouin directed the capture of two boats from the English. However, these exploits, while they may have improved morale, produced few tangible benefits for the halfstarved inhabitants of the Island.

Conditions on the Island at the close of 1757 were deplorable. In the previous five years there had been but one good crop, which itself was limited through a lack of seed. Over 1,400 Acadian refugees, with no viable means of support, were dependent for their survival upon the generosity of the Crown. For the remainder, subsistence levels prevailed. In addition to the very real possibilities of starvation, there continued the constant threat of an English invasion. Indeed, the few good vibrations of this period were totally dependent upon the indomitable Acadian spirit.

XII   LA FIN

The Islanders did what they could to assist in the defense of Louisbourg. A detachment of 200 poorly equipped men was sent under the command of De Villejouin. However, their efforts were to no avail and Louisbourg fell to the English on July 26, 1758. Ile St. Jean, being a dependency of Louisbourg, was included in the articles of capitulation. British occupation and the deportation of the Acadians signalled the end of the French Regime in Ile St. Jean.

For some 35 years, prior to the deportation of 1758, the French settlers had struggled, under conditions of extreme hardship, to provide subsistence for their families and to build the basis of a viable community. However, the good years for the Acadian were few as he was constantly exposed to the pressures applied in a battle of Imperial logistics. There were several well-documented accomplishments as hundreds of acres of woodland were cleared, and several hundred houses and other structures were built. Inevitably, little of this remained for the immigrants of a later era; however, the potentialities were recognized. The importance that the English, in their assessment of Ile St. Jean, attached to the notion that the Island served as a granary for Louisbourg was greater than the facts could ever justify. This requirement was one to which the hard-pressed Acadian could not aspire. The record of the Acadian population on the Island fortunately did not terminate with the deportation of 1758. The statistics do not permit this conclusion as the 300 Acadians located in the Island in 1763 number upwards of 20,000, or nearly one-sixth of the total population of the 1970's. It is fitting indeed that the descendants of the Acadians should still constitute an important and continually increasing segment of the community of Prince Edward Island.

III

Rule Britannia

By DOUGLAS B. BOYLAN

I THE BRITISH OCCUPATION

The resumption of the European Wars in 1755 spelled the end of the French Empire in North America. Though numerous battles were to be fought in the period from 1755 through to the Peace of Paris in 1763, the end of French domination was never seriously in doubt. Hemmed in by the aggressive British colonies to the south and subject to the blockade of the Royal Navy, New France could expect little support from France, even if the mother country had been inclined toward a spirited defence of its North American possessions. Following the collapse of fortress Louisbourg on July 27, 1758, General Amherst issued instructions to Colonel Lord Rollo to proceed against Ile St. Jean; the force of 500 troops plus several naval vessels and French interpreters arrived off Port La Joie on August 17,1758. Despite a certain pretense at preparing for an attack, the French governor was aware of the futility of any resistance against the seasoned British force, and surrendered his small garrison forthwith.

In accord with Amherst's instructions, Rollo immediately commenced to round up the inhabitants and to lay waste to the crops and livestock throughout the countryside. Rollo was impressed, however, by the fertility of the Island soil. Crops and animals were destroyed to prohibit any further sale to the garrison at Quebec, but buildings were left intact in anticipation of future British settlement. Having anticipated the British arrival, a number of the more determined Acadians had departed from the North Shore of the Island in a variety of sailing craft, heading for Northern New Brunswick, along the Bay of Chaleur, and others to Quebec. Of those that remained, about 2,200 were gathered in to Port La Joie with such possessions as they could carry, and then loaded into British transports for a voyage which took them first to Louisbourg and then to France.

33

But not all of the Acadian inhabitants of the Island suffered deportation. Because of the distance from Port La Joie, the settlement at Malpeque, comprising upwards of 300 persons, was left unmolested, and from their descendants came the significant Acadian population of present day Prince Edward Island.

A garrison of 200 troops was left on the Island after the completion of Rollo's mission. Port La Joie, renamed Fort Amherst in honour of the army commander, was refurbished and extended: a redoubt and breastworks were constructed, eighteen cannon were mounted and adequate buildings constructed to house the garrison. With little tumult, but much heartbreak, the French regime had ended. The transition was completed when, after the formal peace treaty between Britain and France, the Island of St. John was annexed to Nova Scotia by a Royal Proclamation dated October 7, 1763.

II   THE HOLLAND SURVEY

The former French possession was no sooner incorporated in the British overseas empire than the Crown was deluged with requests for grants of land on the Island. Some petitioners requested massive land grants (one requested the entire Island!), others more reasonable amounts; some of the settlement proposals made good sense, while others, particularly that of Earl Egmont, amounted to a request for a personal fiefdom. Egmont wished to style himself Lord Paramount of the Island of St. John!

All of the petitions for land grants were directed to the Crown agency concerned with colonies, the Lords Commissioners of Trade and Plantations. Their Lordships were overwhelmed by both the volume and diversity of the claims advanced and faced a quandary as to what advice to present to His Majesty's Privy Council as to the disposition of the Island. In the midst of changing its direction on land grant policy for possibly the third time, the Lords Commissioners of Trade and Plantations received a proposal (in the language of that day, it was termed a "memorial") from a serving army officer, Captain Samuel Holland of the Royal Engineers. Holland's proposal was considered by the Lords Commissioners in early December of 1763 and referred to the Privy Council for its consideration on February 4, 1764.

Samuel Jan Holland has received only passing notice in the chronicle of Canadian history, though he deserves greater attention. Holland was a many-talented man and, in his particular talents, bears a marked similarity to Samuel de Champlain. Both were skilled cartographers; both were trained soldiers and military engineers. Of greater interest, both Champlain and Holland had a passionate interest in the "New World" and wished to see

MAJOR SAMUEL HOLLAND
Surveyor General

permanent settlements established and thrive. Holland had entered the British Army in 1754, and served under Wolfe at the sieges of Louisbourg and Quebec. After the French capitulation in North America, Captain Holland was appointed Surveyor-General of Quebec under the military governor, General James Murray.

In 1763, Holland advanced his scheme to the Lords Commissioners; in it, he proposed a scientific survey to encourage land settlement and the fishery in British North America, particularly in the areas recently ceded by France. Such a survey, as envisoned by Holland, would not only provide accurate maps of the area but would also gather and present detailed descriptions of the land. His proposal met with favour by the Privy Council and was approved by King George III on February 10, 1764. Holland was supplied with a survey party and the necessary supplies and equipment, the whole to be transported to North America in the ship *Canceaux*.

The survey was to commence on the Island of St. John, and general instructions were issued by the Lords Commissioners for the conduct of the survey. The Island was to be divided into three counties of roughly 500,000 acres each, the counties in turn to be subdivided into "parishes" of 100,000 acres. Each parish was to be surveyed into "townships" of 20,000 acres, with each to have, wherever possible, water access, either by sea or by coastal inlet. Three town sites were to be provided for, one in each county, and each parish was to contain a reserve for the construction of a church and a glebe for the support of clergy.

After a stormy passage and a side trip to Quebec, the *Canceaux* arrived at the Island of St. John on October 5, 1764. Holland's survey was hampered at the outset by an altercation with the *Canceaux's* captain as to a division of responsibilities, by a complete lack of adequate accommodation and this early onset of what was to prove a severe winter. His headquarters was established at Observation (now Holland) Cove adjacent to Rocky Point and suitable buildings were hastily constructed in the midst of unseasonably cold weather. In all, four months were consumed with preparations for the survey which, much to Holland's relief, commenced in mid-February of 1765.

Holland deployed four field parties, each assisted by an Acadian guide; by summer the parties travelled by canoe and other small craft, and used dog sleds during the winter months. Little time was lost and, by October 6, 1765, Holland had completed his survey, including the initial mapping, and had compiled a description of the Island. His report met with the complete satisfaction of the Lords Commissioners, and Holland was heartily commended for the excellence of his work. As directed, the Island was divided into three counties (Prince, Queens and Kings), fourteen parishes and a total of sixty-seven townships (popularly referred to as "Lots") each of which had the requisite 20,000 acres more or less. Parish reserves were established and three county towns, Princetown, Charlottetown and Georgetown, were defined and named. Charlottetown, soon to become the colonial and, later, provincial capital, was named in honour of Queen Charlotte of Mecklenburg, consort of George III.

Charlottetown and its attendant Royalty contained a total of 7,300 acres, of which the town proper occupied 270 acres, the common area 565 acres, pasture areas comprised 6,400 acres and roads (none of which existed!) occupied 64 acres. Five "squares" were set aside, one for administrative and church buildings, and the remainder as "green" areas. Along the waterfront, land was reserved for military purposes and for commercial development.

Captain Holland's detailed observations of the Island's features are of particular note: for each township, he compiled detailed notes as to the quality of land for agriculture, the forestry potential, harbours suitable for the fishery, fauna and flora and like information. In all, his survey was conducted in a thoroughly scientific fashion. His manuscript map of the Island is not only technically sound but of great artistic merit. The original, in London, is of immense proportions, measuring approximately eight feet by five feet.

Thanks to Holland's survey, the Lords Commissioners of Trade and Plantations had an excellent idea of what land was available on the Island; how it was to be made available is another story!

Chapter Two

The Beginnings of
Independence, 1767-1787

By F. W. P. BOLGER

The arrival in London of Captain Samuel Holland's survey and accompanying description of St. John's Island resulted in a renewal of interest on the part of those who desired proprietary land grants. Scores of prominent individuals from the military, the mercantile community, the civil service and the gentry had been waiting impatiently since February, 1764, when the British Government had formally approved a plan, whereby the Island was to be surveyed and divided into townships of 20,000 acres, which were to be granted directly and separately to persons deserving the patronage of the Crown.[1] These proprietary claimants eagerly examined Captain Holland's expert findings, and addressed petitions, either to the Privy Council or to the Commissioners of Trade and Plantations, requesting townships on the Island.[2] After a series of meetings, the Commissioners determined the procedure to be followed in the selection of townships. They decided that all applications for grants of land would be considered on June 17, June 24, and July 1, 1767, and that several notices should be published in the *London Gazette,* inviting the applicants or their agents to appear before the Board on those days in support of their respective petitions.[3]

Before proceeding to the distribution of the townships, the Commissioners made three reservations. In the first place, they reserved Township 66, a small lot of 6,000 acres in King's County, as demesne land for the Crown. The second and third reservations were made to the indefatigable petitioners, John Mill, Hutchison Mure, Robert Cathcart and George Spence, who, with their two associates, George Burns and David Higgins, had been carrying on trading and fishing enterprises on the Island since 1764. Township 40 was granted to Spence, Mill and Burns; and Township 59 was assigned to Mure, Cathcart and Higgins.[4] In order to conciliate the Earl of Egmont, and, perhaps, to repay him in part for his herculean efforts in promoting his fantastic feudal scheme designed to give him the whole of

St. John's Island, over which he would have reigned gloriously as Lord High Paramount, the Commissioners requested that he select "one entire parish [100,000 acres] for himself and his family."[5] The Earl was not impressed, and replied caustically that under the new approved arrangements for the Island he "could not now do credit to himself or service to the public by an undertaking there."[6] This curt refusal made it possible for the Board to increase the number of grantees who would share in the callous disposal of the remaining sixty-four of the Island's sixty-seven lots.

Little more than a minimal effort was made to examine the credentials of the applicants as suitable or even interested prospective proprietors. They were merely obliged to make their applications in writing and to state the reasons why they considered themselves worthy candidates for the land grants. They then appeared before the Board personally or by deputy to elaborate orally upon their written presentations and to defend the soundness of their claims. Final decisions on those whose claims seemed preferable were made by the Commissioners on July 8, and the names were then forwarded to the Privy Council for ratification.[7] Personal influence is only too obvious as the names of distinguished military and naval career men, important politicians, merchants and civil servants, appeared with tiresome regularity in the final screened list of grantees. After this screening, the assignment of specific townships was made arbitrarily by lottery. No attention was paid to the relative merits of the townships as rated by Samuel Holland, to the suitability of the individual claimants for particular townships, nor to any preference they might have had. On July 23, the names of the applicants were simply put in a ballot box and drawn in turn, the townships being assigned in order as the names were withdrawn.[8] Thus, on a fateful July afternoon, a whole Island was assigned by lottery to some one hundred fortunate individuals, the vast majority of whom were land speculators, completely disinterested in the real estate they had so effortlessly acquired.

The casual manner in which the board granted away the Island is manifested in the official letter sent to those who received grants. This indifference is revealed, for example, in the letter written on July 24, 1767, the day after the lottery, by John Pownall, the Secretary of the Board, to Viscount George Townshend:

Fate has alloted your Lordship the Township No. 56 on the Island of St. John's. The surveyor describes it in his report to be, in general, of a very fertile soil, has 150 acres cleared and 7 homes, lyes [sic] very convenient for fishing and cultivation and has great advantages from the road, from St. Peter's Bay, and Bay Fortune passing through it.[9]

It is obvious that, so far as the Board was concerned, the disposal of the land on St. John's Island was regarded as nothing more than a cold and indifferent business venture. This approach was more than matched by a substantial portion of the original proprietors. Many of them disposed of their grants as rapidly as they could locate buyers; their interest in their property was as impersonal as the average modern stockholder's in a major corporation. Within the next ten years, the ownership of fully one-fourth of the townships had changed hands.[10] This rapidly changing proprietorship makes the tracing of the ownership of lots a veritable enigma. On only one day in history, namely July 23, 1767, when the original grantees received the following designated townships, can one be absolutely certain of unquestionable rights of ownership:

	Lot
Philip Stevens Esq., Secretary to the Lords of the Admiralty	1
James Hunter, William Hunter, Merchants	2
Chauncy Townshend Esq.	3
Hon. Augustus Keppel Esq.	4
Edward Lewis Esq.	5
William Crowle Esq.	6
James Montgomery Esq., His Majesty's Advocate for Scotland	7
Arnold Nisbett Esq.	8
Hon. James Murray Esq., Governor of Quebec	9
Simon Lutterell Esq.	10
Hunt Walsh Esq., Col. of 28th Regiment of Foot	11
Hutchison Mure and Robert Cathcart, Merchants	12
John Pownall Esq., Secretary to the Lords of Trade	13
John Campbell Esq., Captain in the Royal Navy	14
Guy Carleton Esq., Lieut. Governor of Quebec	15
John Tuttle Esq., David Forbes, John Hayter	16
Bingham Burke, Theobald Burke, Esqrs.	17
Robert Stewart Esq., Lieut. Col.; William Allanby Esq., Captain	18
Walter Patterson Esq., Captain; John Patterson	19
Theodore Holtain, Thomas Basset Esq., Captain	20
Lauchlin MacLeane, Secretary to the Earl of Shelburne; Henry MacLeane, Lieutenant	21
John Gordon, William Ridge Esq., Captain	22
Allan MacLeane, Lauchlin MacLeane	23
Charles Lee Esq., Lieut. Col.; Francis MacLeane	24
Archibald Kennedy, James Campbell	25
Robert (John) Stewart, Lieut.; Peter Gordon Esq., Major	26
James Searle, John Russel Spence, Merchants	27
Samuel Holland Esq., Captain & Surveyor of Lands	28
Rt. Hon. Sir Charles Saunders, Knight of the Bath	29
John Murray Esq., of Philipaugh	30

Several prominent individuals are numbered among these grantees. General James Murray, the Governor of Quebec from 1763 to 1766, drew Lot 9, and his successor, Sir Guy Carleton, received Lot 15. The Lord Advocate of Scotland, Sir James Montgomery, was granted Lot 7, and the Right Honorable Viscount George Townshend, the Lord Lieutenant of Ireland, drew Lot 56. Admiral Sir Charles Saunders, the naval Commanding Officer at the siege of Quebec, was the recipient of Lot 29, Admiral Augustus Keppel of Lot 4, and Admiral Sir George Bridges Rodney of Lot 43. Captain Walter Patterson, the first Governor of the Island, and his brother John Patterson, jointly received Lot 19. Captain Samuel Holland was rewarded, for his arduous labours on the survey of the Island, with Lot 28. The other recipients were less distinguished, although not unimportant. Over forty were army and navy career officers, nine others were members of Parliament, thirteen were merchants, and seven were civil servants. Certain individuals, such as Philip Stevens, Secretary to the Lords of the Admiralty, and John Pownall, Secretary to the Board of Trade and Plantations, were simply fortunate enough to be sufficiently intimate with the establishment to receive Lots 1 and 13. The remainder were largely business adventurers who saw good economic possibilities in the acquisition of property on the Island.

Certain conditions were attached to the land grants which were destined to be bones of contention between the tenants and the proprietors and between both of these and the British Government for more than a century. The first of these stipulated the payment of quit rents to the Crown at the rate of either 2, 4, or 6 shillings per one hundred acres. A quit rent of 2 shillings per one hundred acres was assessed upon Townships 1, 2, 3, 4, 7, 20, 30, 51, 52, 60, 67; a quit rent of 4 shillings on Townships 6, 8, 9, 10, 11, 12, 21, 22, 23, 27, 28, 29, 31, 36, 38, 41, 42, 43, 44, 45, 46, 47, 48, 49, 50, 53, 61, 62, 65; and a quit rent of 6 shillings on Townships 5, 13, 14, 15, 16, 17, 18, 19, 24, 25, 26, 32, 33, 34, 35, 37, 39, 40, 54, 55, 56, 57, 58, 59, 63, and 64. The original grantees also undertook: to settle their lands within ten years in the proportion of one person for every 200 acres, i.e. one hundred persons per township; to introduce as settlers only Protestants, and these were not to come from any of His Majesty's Dominions, unless they were from America and had lived there for at least two years prior to the grants; to reserve on each township one hundred acres for a church and glebe, and thirty acres for a schoolmaster; to reserve, on townships with coastal frontage, five hundred feet from the high water mark to permit the prosecution of the fisheries and the erection of stages and other necessary buildings. Finally, it was specified that if one-third of the land on a township was not settled within four years, the whole township would be forfeited.[12]

From the very outset, the proprietors manifested an almost complete lack of interest in the actual promotion of settlement. The vast majority of them relaxed in England, totally unconcerned with their obligations. Indeed, very few of them even bothered to apply to the Governor of Nova Scotia for the formal deeds of conveyance, giving them legal title to their lots.[13] In one important area, however, they did muster some enthusiasm. After a series of meetings, thirty-two of the more prominent proprietors decided providentially that it would be advantageous to have the Island detached from Nova Scotia and constituted as a separate colony. Accordingly, on May 13, 1768, they addressed a formal petition to the King that stated:

That this Island must, if properly encouraged, become a place of great trade, and of very considerable advantage both to Great Britain and to the Colonies; as well from its convenient situation with regard to the Fisheries, and the fertility of the soil so well adapted to the production of Corn, of Hemp, masts and other Naval Stores, as from the excellence of its Bays and Harbours.

That not withstanding these great material advantages, the settlement of this Island will be very much retarded by its dependence on the Government of Nova Scotia, as no legal decisions can be obtained, nor any matters of property determined without a tedious and expensive voyage to Halifax [where the superior Courts of Judicature are held] which during the winter months is impracticable on account of the ice; this must unavoidably be attended with great detriment both to the Trader and Planter.

That many industrious and able settlers are deterred by these considerations from bringing families and property to a place so circumstanced. That these inconveniences would be effectually remedied and the settlement rendered speedy and certain if it should please Your Majesty to form the Island into a separate Government.[14]

The British Government approved the proposal in principle on the express condition that "the expense attending the execution of the measures recommended, might be defrayed without additional burthen upon this Kingdom;"[15] and the Commissioners for Trade and Plantations and the proprietors were instructed to prepare a detailed plan for the establishment of a separate government and "an estimate of the expense and the ways and means by which it might be defrayed."[16] The British Government, war-weary, and with no settled colonial policy, was prepared, in the interests of frugality and colonial stability, to consider sympathetically any proposal designed to lessen the burden of the Empire. St. John's Island could serve as a remarkable experiment in the method of developing a new colony without drawing on the revenues of the mother country.

After a number of meetings between the proprietors and the Commissioners, an agreement was reached for the defrayal of the costs of the proposed separate government. The proprietors suggested, and the Commissioners concurred, that these costs should be borne exclusively by the quit rent payments for a period of ten years. In order to buttress their proposal, the proprietors suggested that the payment of one half of these quit rents, which, by the original terms of their grants, was not to commence until the end of five years, should be paid from the first of May, 1769, and that, in compensation for this magnanimous sacrifice, the payment of the other half should be deferred for twenty years.[17] The Commissioners gave their blessing to this proposal, but insisted that "the appropriation of the quit rents must not exceed the ten year period, and in the case the amount should fall short, . . . the salaries and allowances to the officers should be diminished in proportion, and no demand whatever brought either upon Parliament, or upon the Treasury to make good such a deficiency."[18] One is naturally led to speculate how often Walter Patterson, the Island's first Governor, and a signator to this agreement, must have sighed as he and his fellow officers of government experienced the bitter effects of this regulation.

The members of the Board, in further concurrence with the instructions from the Privy Council, prepared an estimate of the expenses of the civil establishment and the anticipated revenue from the quit rents. They estimated that the cost of the personnel for the new establishment, which would consist of a Governor, Chief Justice, Secretary and Registrar, Attorney General, Clerk of the Crown and Coroner, Provost Marshal, Agent and Receiver of Quit Rents, and Minister for the Church of England, and contingent expenses would amount to 1,470 pounds. They balanced this expenditure beautifully by calculating the anticipated revenue from the quit rents for the sixty-six townships at precisely the same amount.[19]

The Commissioners, completely satisfied with these arrangements, strongly recommended to the Privy Council the establishment of the Island as a separate colony, and expressed the optimistic view that such a status would "not only facilitate the settlement of the Island, but would also, thereby, promote the interest of the Crown, by more effectually securing the payment of a very considerable quit rent, which would, after a very short period, revert into His Majesty's treasury."[20] The British Cabinet considered these recommendations on June 28, 1769, and endorsed them without hesitation; on the same day, an order-in-council signed by the King authorized the establishment of a separate government for St. John's Island. [21] The British Government was apparently so impressed with the monetary potentialities of the proprietary proposal that it gave instantaneous approval of separate status to the Island. In retrospect, one is led to conclude that this was about the only blessing the Island received from the proprietors, since the iniquitous system of "absentee proprietorship," to which the British Government and the proprietors were party, stifled the social, economic and political development of the Island for over a hundred years.

Although the separation of St. John's Island from Nova Scotia was not authorized until June 28, 1769, certain unauthorized initial steps towards separation had taken place in 1768. On February 26 of that year, the Earl of Hillsborough, the Secretary of State, sent an ambiguous despatch to Michael Francklin, the Lieutenant Governor of Nova Scotia, ordering him to report on the "necessary establishment on St. John's Island . . . taking care in the meantime, to make such temporary Regulations as would provide new settlers with a full and complete participation of those benefits enjoyed by His Majesty's other subjects in the continental parts of Nova Scotia."[22] Francklin seemingly interpreted these orders as an authorization for a separate establishment, and proceeded to the assignment with the characteristic zeal that surrounded all the activities of his colorful career. He expended the entire contingency fund of Nova Scotia in the erection of temporary buildings, in preparing townsites at Charlottetown, Georgetown and Princetown, and in establishing the framework of a sub-government, consisting of a naval officer, a provost marshal, a registrar of deeds, a clerk of council and a magistrate.[23] Francklin's efforts, on behalf of the Island's 271 inhabitants, the 68 English spread over six townships, and the 203 French settled in St. Peter's Bay, Rustico, Tracadie, Malpeque and Bay Fortune, were not appreciated at the Colonial Office, and it was only after a personal defense before the Treasury Board in London that "his reprehensible conduct, the effect of a mistaken zeal for His Majesty's service"[24] was condoned. It seems more than probable that, had not the British Government decided in the interim to establish a separate government on St. John's Island, Michael Francklin would not have been so quickly exonerated for his expenditure of over 2,000 pounds without parliamentary approval.

Shortly after Francklin's absolution, the British authorities began to make definitive plans for the separate establishment on the Island. Captain Walter Patterson, one of the original proprietors, was selected as the first Governor. He was a son of William Patterson of Foxhall, County Donegal,

Governor Walter Patterson, the first governor after the Island became a separate British colony.

Ireland. He had served with the 8th Regiment in America during the Seven Years' War, and was a joint proprietor with his brother, John, of Lot 19. On July 14, 1769, he received his Commission as Governor, and on August 4 of that same year, an order-in-council was passed approving his formal Instructions, and the oath of office was administered to him.[25] The British Government's selection of Walter Patterson as the Island's first Governor was judicious. For the next eighteen years, he devoted himself unstintingly to the difficult assignment of making St. John's Island a viable economic and political community. His faith in, and dedication to the development of the Island under almost impossible circumstances, more than counter-balanced the imprudences that characterized the twilight years of his regime and led eventually to his summary recall and disgrace.

Although Patterson received his appointment in 1769, due to the necessary preparations and the lateness of the season, he did not arrive on the Island until August 30, 1770. On September 10, he convened some of the principal inhabitants, and had his Commission read in their presence.[26] He then appointed John Duport, Phillips Callbeck, John Russel Spence, Thomas Wright, Patrick Fergus, William Allanby and David Higgins as members of his Council.[27] He did not fill the quota of twelve, provided by his Instructions, because he judged there were not enough suitable citizens to serve. On September 19, he took the oath of office as Governor and administered the necessary oaths to the members of the Council who were present on the Island.[28] The summoning of the Supreme Court on September 24, by John Duport, the Chief Justice, meant that the judical and govern-mental machinery of the Island had now commenced. Patterson spent the rest of the autumn "finishing one of the houses built by order of Mr. Franck-lin in such a manner as he hoped would keep out a little of the approaching cold, and in sending to different parts of the continent for provisions to maintain his family during the winter."[29] He also expressed the hope that the Lieutenant Governor [Thomas DesBrisay] would remain in England that year, since there was not "a house to put their heads into, and if they did not bring provisions to serve them until next June, they must absolutely starve, for there was not one loaf of Bread, nor Flower [sic] to make one, to be bought on the Island."[30] Patterson need not have been concerned because his Lieutenant Governor did not grace the Island with his macabre and tiresome presence until 1779.

From the outset, St. John's Island was bedevilled by the failure of the proprietors to honor two of their principal obligations, namely, the promo-tion of the settlement of their lots, and the payment of the quit rents. When Patterson arrived, he estimated that there were approximately one hundred and fifty families on the Island. Most of these were sent to the Island by two proprietors: Lieutenant Colonel Robert Stewart brought approximately sixty families to Lot 18, (fronting on Richmond Bay) from Argyllshire in Scotland, and Sir James Montgomery, the Lord Advocate of Scotland, sponsored a sizeable immigration on the *Falmouth* to Lot 34 (Covehead-Stanhope area).[31] In addition, Samuel Holland, the proprietor of Lot 28, brought some discharged soldiers to his settlement at Tyron. Walter Patterson himself, assisted agriculturally but not numerically by settling some local Acadian French on Lots 17 and 19. But these efforts were not harbingers of a great future immigration.

The only movements of any consequence in the next three years, were those sponsored by the proprietors of Lots 36 and 21. Captain John Mac-Donald, Laird of Glenaladale, and destined to become the Island's most influential and embittered proprietor for some thirty-five years, had purchased Lot 36 in 1770. After mortgaging his estates in Scotland to the Borrodale branch of the MacDonald family, he sent out his brother, Donald MacDonald, in the year 1771, with sixteen families, to prepare for the arrival of the selected immigrants. In 1772, a chartered vessel, the *Alexander,* brought 210 Highlanders to Scotchfort and Tracadie where thriving settlements soon had their beginnings.[32] These Scottish Highlanders were by far the largest group sent out by a single proprietor until the Selkirk movement of the early 1800's. Captain John MacDonald had certainly honored one important proprietary obligation by settling his lot, yet he abrogated one other term of his grant, since the settlers were Catholics rather than Protestants. In 1773 and 1774, Robert Clark and Robert Campbell, the enterprising co-proprietors of Lot 21, settled approximately two hundred people in the New London area.[33] The failure of the other proprietors to match these initiatives led Walter Patterson to report pessimistically in 1774 that the total population of the Island was only 1,215;[34] and five years later, forty-eight of the sixty-seven lots still did not have a single settler.[35] It was becoming only too apparent that the great majority of proprietors had no intention of honoring their obligation to promote the settlement of their estates.

Their attitude was remarkably similar with respect to their quit rent obligations. Their behaviour regarding these payments, with a few exceptions, was one of non-fulfillment. Walter Patterson and his Council were preoccupied with this problem from the moment the Island's separate government became operative. One of the Island's first Ordinances laid down stringent regulations respecting the payment of quit rents. Patterson, in forwarding it to the Secretary of State in September, 1771, informed him that he was obliged to lay down specific regulations for their collection "because of the backwardness in some of the proprietors to pay their quit rent and the very great hardships the officers of government here labor under, on that account for want of their salaries."[36] The poverty, experienced because of the lack of quit rent payments, was graphically described by John Duport, the Chief Justice, in a letter to the Secretary of State, in which he stated that, due to the failure of the quit rent fund, he "had been brought into the greatest distress imaginable, and had stretched his credit to the utmost in procuring Salt Pork and Brown Biscuit to support his family through the winter, and that it would be impossible for him to go on for another year."[37]

The Quit Rent Ordinance, designed to alleviate these sufferings, stipulated that those proprietors who had signed a petition requesting that the Island should be separated from Nova Scotia, should be obliged to pay their quit rents immediately upon the assent of His Majesty to the Ordinance; and in the event of their failure to comply, the Receiver General of quit rents could enter their lots and distrain [seize] for quit rent arrears, and if no sufficient distress could be found, could sell the lots and refund the sale price to the proprietors after the quit rent arrears had been honored.[38] The effects of this Ordinance as well as the others passed by the Governor and Council were largely nugatory since their validity was questionable. Both the Earl of Hillsborough and his successor, the Earl of Dartmouth, informed Patterson that his Ordinances "in the present state of the Island under its present constitution, had no other effect and validity than what they derived from the voluntary consent and adoption of the inhabitants."[39] The next move was clearly up to Patterson.

From the time of his arrival, Patterson had been reluctant, because of the smallness of the population and the lack of adequate road communications, to constitute a House of Assembly. In 1772 and 1773, however, irresistable pressures led him to a change of mind. The British Government, in a series of despatches, insisted that the establishment of an Assembly on the Island "would be the foundation of its future welfare and prosperity."[40] The proprietors also got into the act, and sent a memorial to the Secretary of State, admitting that the Island was suffering distress "owing to the quit rents not being paid, and that a regular payment of them could not be enforced without appointing an Assembly to complete the Legislature."[41] It should be noted that the proprietors were not being completely altruistic, because they admitted that an Assembly could not be convened without the building of adequate roads, and in this memorial they also pleaded for a parliamentary grant for their construction.[42] In addition, the situation of the officers of government became more and more intolerable because of the failure of the quit rent fund. "The Island as a Government," Patterson sadly commented in the spring of 1773, "will shortly come to nothing, for I know of no means the officers have, to maintain themselves any longer, and I am sure it would make any human man unhappy to know in what manner they have hitherto lived. Deprived by their station, of the advantages of a peasant, they are obliged to support the appearances of a gentleman without the means."[43] For these reasons, Patterson was persuaded that he must convene a House of Representatives.

In a despatch of February 17, 1773, he informed Lord Dartmouth that the increase in population during 1772 would enable him to constitute an Assembly in the summer of 1773. He stated, however, that in the election it would be necessary to proceed "by taking the voices of the whole people collectively, as belonging to one county, and waiving all kinds of qualifications, except their being Protestants and residents; it being impossible to have any other terms, owing to the unequal distribution of the inhabitants over the Island, and the small number of freeholders among them."[44] He decided, moreover, to limit the number of members to eighteen, since he wished "to have those who were about to be chosen, as respectable as possible and he knew there were only about that many who would make a very tolerable appearance."[45] The Governor and his Council also decided that the first Assembly should meet in July, 1773.[46] Lord Dartmouth expressed great satisfaction upon learning that Patterson "had at length fallen upon a method of constituting a complete Legislature for the Island;"[47] and he insisted that one of the first responsibilities of the Assembly should be "to adopt such a plan for enforcing the quit rents, as to render that fund effectual to the purpose for which it was allotted, without introducing the disagreeable dilemma, of either, on the one hand, burthening this Kingdom with the Civil Establishment of St. John's, or what otherwise must be the case, of revoking those Establishments that were adopted only upon the condition of the proprietors bearing the expense."[48] Governor Patterson and his Council were certainly prepared to pass legislation to enforce the proprietors' obligations respecting the payment of quit rents. Much more significant, however, would be the degree of support that the Island's Legislature would receive from the British Government when faced with almost unanimous proprietary opposition to such payment.

The elections for the first Assembly were held in Charlottetown on July 4, 1773, and the Assembly met for the despatch of business three days later with the following eighteen members in attendance: Alexander Fletcher, Robert Stewart, John Budd, Graves Aichin, Dugald Stewart, David Lawson, Elisha Coffin, William Craig, John Lawson, John Lord, William Warren, George Burns, Alexander Farquhar, William Lawson, Nathaniel Coffin, James McCallum, Thomas Hopkins and James Hawthorne.[49] This Assembly, which met in the home of James Richardson, and described by

Edward Ryan, the Doorkeeper, as a "damn queer parliament," remained in session for ten days. The most important of the thirteen Acts passed by the Assembly was "An Act for the effectual recovery of certain of His Majesty's Quit Rents on the Island of St. John."[50] This Act, the parliamentary confirmation of the Ordinance on quit rents, did not differ materially from it. It was indeed appropriate that the baneful land question should have made its appearance in the very first session of the Island Legislature since it was destined to occupy center stage in the Island's history for the next hundred years.

On October 1, 1774, Patterson called a second election. He and his Council decided that the present House should be dissolved since the "respectable people who were expected to arrive in the summer of 1774 would give a greater choice of men."[51] The complexion of the new House, which met on October 4, 1774, changed considerably with eight new members in attendance: John White, Robert Watson, Samuel Braddock, Benjamin Chappell, Adrian Van Brankle, James Richardson, John Webster and Cornelius Higgins. The ten returning members were: Robert Stewart, John Budd, George Burns, Alexander Farquhar, Elisha Coffin, David Lawson, William Lawson, John Lord, William Craig and William Warren.[52] Once again, the question of quit rents preoccupied the deliberations of the Assembly. The Quit Rent Act passed in the session of 1773 had been returned by the Colonial Office with minor revisions. These were incorporated and the amended Act was passed on October 17, 1774. This Act, which received Royal Assent in May, 1776, became the statutory nemesis of the proprietors for many generations.

Although legislation was now on the Statute Books to enforce the payment of quit rents, no significant change was apparent in the attitude of the majority of the proprietors. Governor Patterson and the other officers of government were placed in such distressful circumstances during these years that the Governor authorized the payment of part of their salaries from the three thousand pounds granted by the British Parliament for the erection of a church, jail and court house in Charlottetown. But no adequate solution resulted from such a temporary expedient; indeed, the only permanent result was that the colony was deprived of these much-needed buildings for the rest of the century. Since Patterson was of the opinion that the quit rent revenue would never meet the expense of the government, he concluded that some permanent fund must be established. As early as May, 1773, he began to press for a parliamentary grant. He pointed out "that after five years, the whole of the quit rent, yet received, would do little more than pay the establishment [low as it is] for one year."[53] He insisted that the government could not "hold out much longer, and if we are not shortly relieved, and fixed on a more certain footing, I must give up my employment, to some more fortunate man, and content myself with the pleasing reflections of having spent, in His Majesty's service, a fortune which in any ordinary sphere of life would have supported my family with independence."[54]

Governor Patterson increased the pressure in 1774. In forwarding a lengthy report on the affairs of the Island, which had been requested by the British Government, he pointedly suggested that "any inaccuracies should be attributed to the immaturity and unsettled state of the Government, the wheels of which have been hitherto kept in motion only with great difficulty, so that great regularity cannot be expected in the offices, nor have I thought it just, to insist on it, considering the hardships the officers labour under for want of their salaries."[55] Patterson also decided to request a leave of absence, so that he could make a visit to England to pursue the quit rent problem and to encourage the proprietors to promote settlement. In making this request, he expressed the opinion that he "could be of more service to the Island by spending a little time among the proprietors than by remaining at home."[56] The Earl of Dartmouth, who had more soul for the Island's difficulties than most British political figures of the day, readily granted him a twelve-month leave of absence. He also recognized sympathetically "the distress of His Majesty's servants on the Island of St. John from the failure of the Quit Rent fund, and promised to attempt to obtain some allowance in the next Parliamentary Estimate for their relief."[57] It was, therefore, with high hopes that Patterson embarked for England on August 2, 1775.

After his arrival, Governor Patterson arranged a series of meetings with some of the prominent proprietors. As a consequence of these deliberations, a supplicatory memorial, signed by himself and seventeen other proprietors who had paid their quit rents, was forwarded to the Privy Council in February, 1776. The memorial piously emphasized that due to the failure of the other proprietors to honor their commitments "the officers of Government on the Island were reduced to such financial difficulties that they would be unable to hold their employment any longer on the present footing."[58] These proprietors, with no apparent compunction, insisted that no other colony had ever been established on a similar plan, so that "the mode adopted on the Island must have been intended as a public experiment rather than a mere bargain with individuals."[59] They requested that the Island should receive an annual parliamentary grant proportionate to that received by the other British possessions in America, and that the revenue from the quit rents should be applied for ten years as a fund for the construction of public roads."[60] After detailed consideration of this petition and additional memorials submitted by the proprietors and Walter Patterson during the next few months, the Treasury Board and Privy Council adopted a new policy on August 7, 1776. The formal Minute ordered that all quit rent arrears should be enforced by legal proceedings and the sum realized should be devoted to the payment of salary arrears and to the construction of roads. The Minute also approved an annual parliamentary grant for the defrayal of the expenses of the civil establishment of the Island.[61] The 3,000 pound grant approved by the British Government in 1777 represented a veritable coup scored by Patterson and the proprietors on behalf of the Island government, and was one further manifestation of proprietary influence.

While Walter Patterson was absent in England, Phillips Callbeck, the Attorney General, and senior member of Council, served as Administrator.[62] During his incumbency, the government of the Island almost completely disintegrated. Patterson, who was granted a twelve-month leave of absence, extended his sojourn in England to five years. The Chief Justice, John Duport, died of gout and starvation in May, 1774, and his successor, Peter Stewart, did not receive his Commission until July, 1776.[63] William Allanby, the provost marshal and collector of revenue, left the Island in the early spring of 1775, and did not return until 1779.[64] The Lieutenant Governor, Thomas DesBrisay, did not arrive on the Island until October, 1779.[65] George Burns, another member of the Council, was suspended by Callbeck in 1776 for being absent from the Island for over a year without governmental permission.[66] The disorganization of government was further accentuated by the American Revolutionary War. In November, 1775, freebooting American privateersmen conducted a raid on Charlottetown. After plundering some stores and the houses of the principal officers of government, they abducted Phillips Callbeck, Thomas Wright, the Surveyor-General, David Higgins, the naval officer, and proudly presented them to George Washington at his headquarters in Cambridge, Massachusetts. Washington disapproved of this hostile act, and according to Callbeck's account, received them "very politely and allowed them to return to Halifax on a foul-smelling coastal vessel."[67] Until Callbeck's triumphant return to the Island in May, 1776, the only officials available to keep the ship of state in motion were John Budd, the clerk of the crown and coroner, and John Webster, the commissary of stores.

Phillips Callbeck's principal preoccupation during the next three years was with the defenses of the Island. Needless to say, the Island, at the beginning of hostilities, was completely defenseless. There was no militia, ammunition or defense fortifications. The attack on Charlottetown roused the British Government to minimal action. The Newfoundland fleet was consequently augmented and ordered to be especially protective of British possessions in the Gulf of St. Lawrence.[68] Ammunition was sent from Halifax, a seven-gun battery was constructed in Charlottetown, and a few troops were sent from Halifax to defend the town. Callbeck also received instructions from the Secretary of State to enlist an independent force of one hundred men for the defense of the Island. But despite glowing reports to Lord George Germain on his efforts, Callbeck never succeeded in filling the quota. In July, 1778, four provincial companies arrived from New York under the command of Colonel Hierlihy for whom barracks were constructed in Charlottetown.[69] Their military presence made a notable contribution to the defense of the Island, and apart from two plundering raids by privateersmen at St. Peter's and Georgetown, the Island was spared what Callbeck called "wanton depredations"[70] by the Americans for the rest of the American Revolutionary War. Walter Patterson, on his return in 1780, boldly suggested that 215 miles of military roads should be built by the British to facilitate communications across the Island.[71] Lord Germain, at the Colonial Office, however, disapproved of the scheme, and ingeniously insisted that the possession of good military roads would be a menace to the Island, since they would enable the enemy to penetrate into the interior. He also maintained that in the weak state of St. John's Island, "the want of good and open roads might be considered as a great security to the settlement and the inhabitants."[72] Germain's contempt for Roman military precedents meant that the Island would be replete with bridal paths for many more decades.

After his return to the Island in June, 1780, Governor Patterson began immediately to direct attention to the affairs of government. In his first report to the Secretary of State, he opined that "the number of inhabitants had doubled since his departure, that they were comfortable in their situation, had large stocks of cattle, and abound with all the necessaries of life as far as they regard the table."[73] He lavished praise upon Phillips Callbeck, and asserted that the "country was much indebted to him for his unwearied and constant attention to its interests."[74] Patterson did not, however, express the same sentiments regarding Thomas DesBrisay. During Patterson's absence, DesBrisay had disposed of some 116 towns and pasture lots in Charlottetown and Royalty, 58 of which he granted to his own family, in order, as he informed Lord Germain, "to leave independence to his numerous heirs of twelve motherless children, and three grandchildren."[75] Patterson, refusing to condone this untoward act of patronage, requested the Secretary of State to order the return of the lots; and when DesBrisay attempted to rationalize his actions to the Colonial Office, Patterson levelled a written diatribe against him. He apologized for wasting Lord Germain's time on "so worthless a character as that of the Lieutenant Governor;"[76]

and he suggested "that the safest and best way, with regard to Mr. Des-Brisay, was to take it as a general maxim that he never either speaks or writes truth if he has the smallest motive for doing otherwise."[77] The Colonial Office ordered DesBrisay to return most of the lots and this decision contributed further to the personal animosity between Patterson and DesBrisay.

One of Governor Patterson's first official functions upon his arrival on the Island, was to guide the deliberation of the third Assembly. The third general election had been held in Charlottetown in July, 1779, with the following members elected, nine of them for the first time: Thomas Mellish, James Curtis, Walter Berry, David Lawson, Cornelius Higgins, Dugald Stewart, William Craig, David Higgins, James Campbell, John Clark, Benjamin Chappell, William Warren, James Richardson, Thomas Hyde, Alexander Davidson, John Webster, Moses Delesdernier and John Budd.[78] Thomas DesBrisay had convened a session in 1779, and two sessions in 1780, the second of which was scheduled to meet the day that Walter Patterson returned home. Patterson proudly informed the Secretary of State that this session, adjourned for want of a quorum, "met a few days after my return, when the love of novelty prevailed, and brought every member to town, who heard of my return."[79] One of the Acts passed, made provision for the change of the name of the Island from St. John to New Ireland. This appellation, suggested by Patterson in honor of his native land, would have been most appropriate in the light of the Island's "absentee land tenure question." But the Colonial Office replied that this name had already been appropriated, and suggested either New Guernsey or New Anglesea, neither of which was acceptable to the Island Legislature.[80] Thus the Island remained St. John until February 1, 1799, when Prince Edward Island was approved as the future designation of the colony in honor of Prince Edward, the Duke of Kent, who had recognized sympathetically the need for defense works at Charlottetown, but who, unknowingly to the Island authorities, had, at the same time, recommended its re-annexation to Nova Scotia.[81] The only other measure of significance passed in the session, was one that made provision for the establishment of a Militia in Prince Edward Island. Patterson was elated with this Act, and dryly informed Lord Germain that "this measure had been much wished for, but the Assembly would not pass it till now, but my long absence made me appear a new man, and novelty has in these cases often a wonderful effect."[82]

Patterson devoted the remaining seven years of his regime almost exclusively to the land question. He realized that nearly all the proprietors had failed to honor the commitments they had made in 1767, and as a result, most of the townships were liable to confiscation. He and his Council decided in 1780 to attempt to oblige the proprietors to fulfill their primary obligation with respect to the payment of quit rents. It was quite logical for Patterson to challenge the proprietors on this undertaking. The *Treasury Minute* of August 7, 1776, was so specific regarding the immediate collection of quit rents arrears, that Patterson really had no other choice but to act promptly. He realized, moreover, that many of the proprietors, probably the vast majority, would ignore the Council's instructions, and this would mean that thousands of acres of land would be available at nominal prices to interested bidders. Would it not then be possible and perfectly justifiable for Patterson and the other officers of government to acquire sizeable acreages as belated compensation for the arrears in salary they had suffered because of proprietary neglect? It was, therefore, with no misgivings and considerable enthusiasm that the Island government began to focus attention on the quit rent issue.

On September 21, 1780, Patterson rather tactlessly appointed William Nisbett, his brother-in-law, as the Receiver General of quit rents, and James McNutt, his private secretary as deputy Receiver General.[83] The Governor and Council then met on November 26, 1780, and directed the Receiver-General to enforce the law passed in 1774 "for the effectual recovery of certain of His Majesty's Quit Rents in the Island of St. John."[84] This measure stipulated that townships in arrears could be sold at the expiry of six months if the quit rent payments were not made within that period, or if sufficient moveable goods could not be found on the property to satisfy these arrears. An exception was made for the absentee proprietors in Great Britain, who were allowed a full year to honor their quit rent obligations. In order to guarantee the complete effectiveness of his determination to enforce the quit rent arrears, Patterson had an Act passed in the 1781 session of the Legislature which authorized the Receiver General to recover the quit rents payable on those lots not enumerated in the 1774 Act.[85] The issue was now squarely joined between Patterson and the proprietors.

In March, 1781, Governor Patterson directed the Receiver General to commence proceedings in the Supreme Court of the Island against all the townships enumerated in the 1774 Act which were still in arrears. A series of judgements was obtained, and eight whole and six half-townships were authorized to be sold. Lots 24, 31, 32, 33, 35, 49, 57 and 67, and halves of Lots 17, 18, 25, 26, 48 and 65, were then chosen to be disposed of by auction. Patterson contended later in his justification for the sale of these particular lots, that the selection was judicious since "there was not a lot sold on which any money had been expended by way of settlement, nor upon which a single settler had been placed;"[86] and he sarcastically hammered home his point by insisting that the sole exception "was a single and very bad house, built by a proprietor on Lot 18, and, that bad as it was, it was the whole improvement made upon 10,000 acres."[87] He also insisted that "the mode adopted for putting the lots up for sale was such as could not possibly admit of the smallest partiality or collusion since the several lots were balloted for, before the Council, and they were offered for sale by the Provost Marshal, one after another, as they were drawn with the charge of Quit Rents and other expenses upon them."[88]

At the auction of these lots which took place in November, 1781, the officers of government and a few of their friends were the principal bidders. Governor Patterson readily admitted that he "made a few purchases himself, which he certainly would not have made, had it not been the money was owing to me from the quit rents, on account of my former salary; and the same motives induced 1 or 2 more of the officers of Government to make purchases, but all of us would then, much sooner have had the money than the land."[89] Governor Patterson and his officers were later accused of postponing the sales from week to week so as to confuse prospective bidders. Patterson countered with the argument that the sole reason for such postponements "was to give the proprietors additional opportunity to pay the arrears."[90] And to the charge that he and members of his Council had made large purchases, he simply replied that he knew of no principle by which the purchase of lands at a public auction was forbidden to an officer of government, and wondered "who would be an officer of government if by being such he was deprived of his privileges as a citizen; and besides, as they are debarred from trade, if they were also precluded from the fair means of acquiring a little land, it would shut up the only channel they can have of making some provisions for their families."[91] While Patterson and the governing clique were unquestionably on unassailable grounds legally in selling the designated lots at a public auction, yet their purchase of some 230,000 acres of land at nominal prices savored too much of candlestine collusion to withstand the violent reactions of the dispossessed proprietors.

As soon as the proprietors learned of the sale, a chorus of protest emanated from London. Captain John MacDonald, the proprietor of Lots 35 and 36, and on active service with the 84th Regiment in the American Revolutionary War, went to London in 1781, and soon became the leading figure in a spirited proprietary lobby against these sales. He was incensed that Lot 35, which he had recently purchased, had been sold. Sometimes separately, and often in concert with other leading proprietors, he addressed a series of strongly worded petitions to the Colonial Office requesting a remission of the quit rent arrears and the return of the confiscated townships to the dispossessed. The burden of these pleas was that the arrears arose principally from the unsettled state of affairs caused by the absence of so many proprietors on active service in the British Army and Navy during the American Revolution. The Colonial Office was, as usual, quite indulgent with the proprietors. In May, 1783, Lord North, the new Colonial Secretary, informed Patterson that "since several proprietors had represented to His Majesty in Council, the hardships and losses they had sustained by the operation of the Act passed on October 17, 1774, that no further proceedings be had against any lands or allotments of land in the Island for arrears in Quit Rents, and that in cases where proceedings had already commenced, an immediate and effective stop be put thereunto."[92] He also told Patterson that since he had found that "several of the provisions of the 1774 Act were exceptionable,"[93] he would forward, "at the earliest opportunity, the draft of a Bill to be passed by the Legislature for the future regulation of Quit Rents and proceedings in case of arrears."[94]

Lord North honored his promise, and on July 24, 1783, sent the proposed draft of the Bill to Patterson. This Bill disallowed the Act of 1774, rendering all sales under it voidable upon payment by the former proprietors of the purchase money, interest and charges incurred by the present owners, compensation also being made for any improvements.[95] The Bill also provided that in future, the quit rents and all arrears could be paid either on the Island or in London. It was specified, moreover, that the proprietors who paid their arrears until 1783, would be exempt from future payments for six years.[96] Lord North expressed the belief that the proposed arrangements "were so manifestly advantageous to the proprietors that he was persuaded that they would cheerfully comply with His Majesty's wishes in that respect."[97] Captain MacDonald, speaking on behalf of the proprietors, seemed to agree when he stated "that tho we have not got all that we wanted, as we are obliged to pay the arrears of quit rents, yet we have got a great deal in being so eased in the future, and what I value above all things is that the Lots are to be restored again; it is not only a victory but will do us much good."[98]

Governor Patterson was not prepared, however, to comply immediately with the instructions from Lord North. He did not have much room for maneuvering, but he was determined to make the most of the handful of options available for the protection of the interests of the 1781 purchasers. He received the Draft Bill in December of 1783, but did not deign to acknowledge its receipt until April, 1784. Attempting to justify the delay, he informed Lord North that the Bill arrived "so late in the season that it was impossible to have the honor of replying, as the Bill appeared to require very mature consideration, before he could venture to offer an opinion, or take any steps relative thereto."[99] He further contended that he and his Council decided to postpone action on the grounds that the "Bill was so very evidently obtained by misrepresentation and contained also such unjust reflections on His Majesty's Council that I could not, consistent with my duty to His Majesty, or in regard to my own character, do less than beg leave to state facts as they really are, and offer my humble opinion why I apprehend it would be injurious to the country to enact such a law."[100] Captain MacDonald, from his vantage point in London, opined correctly that Patterson and his friends would attempt to thwart Lord North instructions, and predicted prophetically "that a contest would ensue in which the Government of the Island would undoubtedly be overset."[101]

Although Walter Patterson could depend upon the support of the majority of his Council, the attitude of the Assembly was more questionable. He therefore dissolved the House in January, 1784, and issued writs for a general election in March, 1784.[102] Unfortunately for the Governor, the results were not propitious. During the campaign a bitter polarization between Patterson and his rivals began. The father-figure of the opposition was Chief Justice Peter Stewart. The rivalry between Walter Patterson and Peter Stewart, which began with Stewart's claim that Patterson appropriated the lion's share of the lots confiscated in 1781, was intensified by the indignity suffered by the Chief Justice in losing his third wife, at least temporarily, to the blandishments of the Governor.[103] The Governor maintained that he was innocent, "and that it was a vile, false story, contrived by the Chief Justice's children, by a former wife, on purpose to get rid of a stepmother."[104] Available evidence suggests that the Chief Justice had fairly solid grounds for his contentions. At any rate, he dismissed her from his home, and Patterson secured passage for her to Canada. This public scandal must have enlivened conversations in the bucolic Island communities.

The campaign against Patterson was organized by John Stewart, a son of the Chief Justice, who formed what he called grandiloquently the *Country Party*. He was ably assisted by his brother, Charles Stewart, the Clerk of the Executive Council, and his brother-in-law, William Townshend, the Collector of Customs. The Stewart faction, learning during the campaign that the Governor, with the Council's approval, intended to increase revenue by placing a tax on certain imported articles, was able to mobilize strong opposition to the Governor and the proposed tax. Moreover, the Chief Justice supported his family during the campaign, acted as counsel for some of the candidates, and even made appearances at the polling booths on their behalf. John Stewart's *Country Party* won a notable victory, capturing two-thirds of the seats in the Assembly.[105] The Governor had clearly failed in his efforts "to prevent the effects of Mr. John Stewart's artifices and to procure the most respectable Assembly our little community could afford."[106]

The new Assembly, which met on March 6, 1784, chose John Stewart as Speaker. Stewart, a man immortalized in Island history by the sobriquet of Hellfire Jack, and not too unfairly described by Patterson as "a very intemperate young man,"[107] dominated its proceedings. The House spent nineteen days discussing its grievances against Patterson, and then adjourned for fourteen days without the Governor's consent. When the House convened again, after three adjournments for want of a quorum, the Governor, correctly considering its procedures as quite illegal, issued a proclamation on April 13, 1784, declaring that the Assembly had dissolved itself.[108] The members of the Assembly had no alternative but to disperse, but prior to their departure the next day, they hastily posted charges against Patterson on the door of a public building in Charlottetown, censuring him for appropriating monies, lands, and moveable public goods to his own use, granting town lots and other public property to his friends, permitting arbitrary proceedings in the 1781 sales of confiscated lots, and "by conversation and example spreading the principles of infidelity and irreligion thro' the Colony, to the ruin of the most respectable families and the destruction of the peace and harmony of the Colony."[109] Patterson's reply to these charges was the suspension of Chief Justice Stewart and the removal of his cohort, Thomas DesBrisay, from the Council. Patterson charged the Chief Justice "with having abetted his son, Lieutenant John Stewart and others in choosing an Assembly which was a discredit to the Colony, and of divulging a secret of Council at the hustings."[110] The beleagured Governor was still in control, but unfortunately for his future, he was gaining Pyrrhic victories.

A fortuitous set of circumstances afforded Walter Patterson a golden opportunity to strengthen his rapidly waning power base on the Island. The American Revolution was drawing to a close, and thousands of Loyalist refugees were desirous of obtaining land and homes in British territory. Could some of these Loyalists, reasoned Patterson, be encouraged to settle on the Island; and would they not, out of gratitude, support him strongly in his altercations with the British Government and the Stewart-DesBrisay faction at home? Deciding to implement his calculated plan, he despatched his brother, John Patterson, to Great Britain to enlist the support of other proprietors. Some seventeen original proprietors and five other purchasers of lots in 1781 presented a memorial to Lord North in June, 1783, declaring their willingness to grant a fourth part of their property for the benefit of the Loyalists and disbanded soldiers. Among the signators of the memorial were Walter Patterson, his brother John Patterson, John Townson, Isaac Todd and Robert MacKay, all of whom had purchased lots in 1781 and, therefore, were in favor of a plan to make their property more secure. This seemingly generous offer made some 109,000 acres of land available.[111]

Anticipating Colonial Office approval, Patterson issued proclamations and circulated them to various centres on the North American continent giving notice of the quantity of land available; and, in addition, he despatched agents to New York and to the Nova Scotia Loyalist settlement of Shelburne, two centres teeming with refugees, assuring them of the thousands of acres of rich arable land available on the Island. Lord North, in July, 1783, gave his blessing to Patterson's scheme and ordered him to apportion to the Loyalists one-quarter of the proprietory estates and to direct the Attorney General to prepare the deeds of conveyance without expense to the proprietors, who were also to be exonerated from the quit rents on such shares of their land as were actually granted.[112] On paper, the proposition seemed to be commendable, but it proved otherwise in practice. The proprietors, by and large, neglected to give the Attorney General power-of-attorney to issue clear titles, and the result was that many Loyalists refused to settle since they had no desire to become tenant farmers with thousands of acres of land available in other sections of British North America. By the end of 1784, some five to six hundred remained on the Island. Their main settlements were in the Malpeque-Bedeque Isthmus (Lots 16, 17, 19, 25 and 26, with minor concentrations in Lots 32, 35 and 65, and in Lots 49 and 50 along the shores of Orwell Bay).[113] The Loyalists proved to be a valuable and productive class of settlers in spite of the crass failure of the majority of the proprietors to grant them clear titles to the lands on which they had settled.

Although many of the Loyalists were disgruntled because of the broken proprietary agreements, large numbers of those who remained were appreciative of the efforts made by Patterson on their behalf. He settled many of them on the lots sequestered in 1781, gave them clear titles and much more generous provisions than those supplied to their counterparts in Nova Scotia and New Brunswick.[114] As the months passed, they learned with some concern that their titles to the lands, apart from those granted by Patterson, were not absolute. How could they confirm their rights to these lands? Obviously, they must ensure that they exercised some political clout in the Assembly. The elections of March, 1785, gave them a golden opportunity. The campaign, like that of 1784, was a bitter struggle between the Stewart-DesBrisay group and those candidates supported by Patterson. Patterson's candidates, by dint of heavy Loyalist support and the expenditure of a considerable amount of money, swept the Stewarts into political oblivion.[115] Only seven members, and these supporters of Patterson in 1784, managed to win again in 1785. These were: James Campbell, John Throckmorton, William Lawson, James Curtis, James McNutt, John Webster, and Dugald Stewart. Eleven new members, including some Loyalists, won electoral victories. They were: Alexander Fletcher, David Lawson, John Clark, William Craig, John Brecken, George Hardy, Cornelius Higgins,

William Warren, William Douglas, William Schurman and Hugh Fraser.[116] An elated Patterson informed Lord Sydney "that nothwithstanding every opposition which could be made, there was chosen by a great majority the most respectable, and the best intentioned House of Representatives which has ever met on the Island."[117] Walter Patterson now had his pliant Assembly. He would use the Loyalists and their friends in the Assembly to bolster his vulnerable position with respect to the Colonial Office; and the Loyalists would use their political leverage to protect their "special status."

While Patterson was engaged in these political manoeuvres the resident proprietors in England, whose lots had been confiscated, grew impatient. Robert Clark, one of their principal spokesmen, informed the Colonial Office in August, 1784, that the Draft Bill of 1783 had never been presented to the Assembly, and requested remedial action.[118] Lord Sydney, in response to the proprietary complaints, wrote to Patterson expressing great surprise that he "had not shown a greater impatience to justify his proceedings to His Majesty upon a point of so much weight as that of disobeying a positive injunction of His Majesty";[119] and he informed him that he was taking the drastic step "of applying to the Admiralty for a ship of war for the special purpose of carrying this letter to you, upon this important occasion, and to bring back any papers and evidence you and the Council of the Island ought naturally to be anxious to submit to the Lords of the Committee."[120] Patterson and his Council sent their documented defense, with accompanying letters, to John Stuart, the Colony Agent in London, who, in turn, forwarded them to Lord Sydney in February, 1785. The burden of their defense was that the Draft Bill "was grounded upon so many misstated facts that it should not be presented to the Assembly in its present form."[121] After a series of sessions before the Lords of Trade and Plantations, in which both Patterson and the proprietary plaintiffs were represented by counsel, the Commissioners ruled that the Lieutenant Governor "ought to have convened the Assembly and laid before them the draft of the Bill sent from England in 1783, with all convenient speed after it came into his hands, and that the facts and reasons assigned for not having done so, did not justify the neglect."[122] The British Cabinet confirmed this decision, and on May 6, 1785, "peremptorily ordered and required the Lieutenant Governor to lay a slightly revised Draft Bill before the Assembly."[123] A delay in the forwarding of the new Draft Bill to Patterson, gave him an opportunity for additional rearguard action. Having been informed privately of the Privy Council decision, he callously took steps to neutralize its effectiveness. The trump card played by the Lieutenant Governor was destined to constitute too defiant a game and to lead to his recall.

Patterson convened the Assembly in March, 1786, and proceeded immediately to consolidate the purchases made in 1781. A submissive Assembly requested that some action should be taken to confirm these sales since it was feared that the Loyalists and other settlers dwelling on the estates purchased in that year were in danger of the loss of their lands. Patterson was less than honest whèn he later informed Lord Sydney that he "did not directly or indirectly promote this matter";[124] he was certainly more truthful "in candidly confessing that he had not attempted to prevent its taking place."[125] At any rate, in the session a Bill was introduced entitled "An Act to render good and valid in Law all and every of the proceedings in the years 1780 and 1781, which in any respect related to or concerned the suing, seizing, condemning, or selling of the Lots of townships hereinafter mentioned."[126] Patterson also issued a proclamation informing the public of the Bill before the House and inviting representations for or against it. Some thirteen days were spent hearing submissions from proprietary agents against the measure.[127] The "loyal" members of the Island Legislature, however, were not swayed by their arguments and the Bill passed without a dissenting voice in either House. The Act was assented to by Patterson without a suspending clause, on April 22, 1786, and forwarded by the first mail to the startled British authorities.[128]

While Patterson was engaged in these precautionary measures, his eventual fate was being decided in London. The proprietors, believing that Patterson's contumacious behaviour would always thwart their plans, started a lobby with a view to effecting his recall and the dismissal of his Council. In the spring of 1786, they addressed a pointed petition to the British Secretary of State pleading that there could be no redress of their just grievances "as long as Patterson continued to be His Majesty's representative there, and as long as the Chief Justice, Attorney General and the officers of the courts of the Island are in the position to prevent the ends and defeat the attainment of justice."[129] Influenced by this proprietary lobby and thoroughly disillusioned with Patterson's behaviour, the Colonial Secretary decided to grant him a leave of absence which was tantamount to a recall. On June 30, 1786, Lord Sydney wrote to him stating that "so many representations had been made of improper proceedings on your part in the exercise of your power as governor that you must repair to England as soon as possible to give an account of your conduct."[130] He also informed him that Colonel Edmund Fanning, the former Lieutenant Governor of Nova Scotia, was authorized "to take charge of the Island of St. John *during his absence,* and immediately upon his arrival he was to deliver to Fanning the papers and documents necessary to carry on the public service of the Island."[131] Fanning arrived in Charlottetown on November 4, 1786, with his instructions to assume power, but Patterson was not prepared to be dismissed so lightly from office.

Patterson had received the amended version of the 1783 Act and had reluctantly made plans to have the Assembly take legislative action upon it. He used this reason as well as the lateness of the season as justifications for his refusal to return to England. He curtly informed Fanning that he could not deliver to him the seal and official papers, and the reasons would be apparent to him when the legislative session resumed.[132] He was more explicit in his reply to Lord Sydney. He pointed out that the season was much too far advanced to enable him to arrange his personal affairs so as to prevent total personal ruin during his absence.[133] He also argued that if the charges were those he had already answered, then his *ipse dixit* would add little weight; and if there were new charges, then "he would have to remain on the Island to obtain evidence to disprove them, and, therefore, his presence in England would prove a useless trouble to the Colonial Office and to himself."[134] Convinced that he had steered the proper course between *Scylla* and *Charybdis,* Patterson convened the Island Legislature on November 8, 1786.

In the Speech from the Throne, Patterson stated that he had called the members together to "lay before them a Bill for setting aside and annulling the sale of lands which took place in the year 1781."[135] He reminded the Assembly that this Bill should be passed "not because the previous measure was illegal, but rather because it appears very much the desire of His Majesty's Council to have it considered so."[136] The Act received first and second readings, but when it was presented to the Committee of the Whole House, its fate was apparent. The members of the Committee reported that the Bill appeared to them to be highly detrimental to the settlement of the Colony and founded on misinterpretation; and the Chairman of the Committee presented an Address to Patterson stating that the Assembly would not pass this Bill, "which would prove destructive to the prosperity, nay the very existence of the colony."[137] The Address further expressed the hope that the measure passed in March, 1786, confirming the 1781 sales which was based "on equity, humanity, and sound policy would receive the Royal Assent."[138] With this summary treatment of Royal Instructions, the Assembly interred the Act, and with the blessing of the Lieutenant Governor, turned its attention to a private Bill which he had reluctantly introduced as a mild alternative.

The new Bill made provision for the restoration of the lots sold in 1781, with the exception of two and one-half lots. Thomas DesBrisay, Phillips Callbeck and Peter Stewart refused to surrender titles to Lots 31 and 35, and one-half of Lot 18, and their townships were exempted from the Act. The Bill received three readings without debate, and was assented to by the Lieutenant Governor on November 18, 1786.[139] Yet its effectiveness was very considerably lessened by certain clauses which were incorporated into it. In the first place, one clause provided that all purchases made by the Loyalists and others gave them *bona fide* titles to the acquired lands, and these must be confirmed. Secondly, an additional clause obliged the proprietors to make compensation to the 1781 purchasers, and these were so contrived that the heavy payments demanded more than counterbalanced the benefit that would be derived from repossession.[140] The 1781 purchasers were, nevertheless, chagrined, and Patterson, who personally surrendered three whole and four half-lots considered that "his sacrifice was, perhaps, the greatest ever made on such principles by a man in his circumstances."[141]

During the winter of 1787, an anomalous situation prevailed on the Island. Patterson clung tenaciously to office, insisting quite correctly that Fanning's appointment was to obtain only *during his absence*. Meanwhile, Fanning grew impatient, and being convinced that Patterson intended to retain the reins of office indefinitely, issued a proclamation on April 10, 1787, publicizing his appointment, "and ordering all the inhabitants to give their ready obedience accordingly."[142] The next day, Patterson issued a counter proclamation, declaring that Fanning could only govern during his absence, and that every act performed by Fanning "under his present usurped authority must be illegal and of no effect."[143] The altercation continued until spring, with the perplexed inhabitants rallying to support either Patterson or Fanning. The arrival of the first mail from England, in June, settled the question of jurisdiction. Pressed by angry proprietors in London, and completely disgusted with Patterson's disobedience to Colonial Office instructions, the Home Government decided to dismiss him. On April 5, 1787, Lord Sydney curtly informed him that "without entering into the grounds upon which you have proceeded to justify disobedience of His Majesty's orders, I must acquaint you that I have received His Royal command to inform you that His Majesty has no further occasion for your services as Lieutenant Governor of Saint John."[144] On the same day, Sydney wrote to Edmund Fanning acquainting him that "His Majesty from the very extraordinary conduct of Lieutenant Governor Patterson, had thought it advisable to dismiss him at once from office, and has been pleased to fix you in the Government of that Island."[145] For Walter Patterson, eighteen years of devoted, if oftentimes misguided, government in the cause of the Island came peremptorily to an end.

The proprietors in London were not content with the dismissal of Patterson. They also presented a criminating memorial to the Commissioners of Trade and Plantations, containing criminal charges against the superseded Governor and the other officers of government, requesting that the latter be removed from their respective offices. Formal hearings were conducted before the President of the Privy Council in July, 1789, which resulted in the removal of Phillips Callbeck, Thomas Wright, George Burns and John Russel Spence from their seats in the Council, and the dismissal of Callbeck as Attorney General and of Nisbett as Receiver General of Quit Rents.[146] Captain John MacDonald, who served as solicitor at the hearings, was only slightly exaggerating when he noted that "there never was a severer report, nor was there ever such a number of charges so completely proven — as they are found guilty of everything that was alleged against them: they affect to hold it cheap — but the truth is that they are confoundedly galled and they will never get the better of the disgrace."[147]

The Privy Council dealt a final blow to Walter Patterson by disallowing the two Acts he had sponsored in March and November of 1786.[148] Thus, after eighteen years of dedicated service, he stood totally discredited. Did he deserve such harsh treatment? The evidence suggests he certainly did not. He had sufficient authority to dispose of the lands that were sold in 1781; indeed, he had been positively ordered by the British Government to sell the townships of the negligent proprietors. He was certainly guilty of imprudence in selling the townships during the American Revolution, in purchasing too many for himself and in not complying immediately with Imperial instructions to restore them. But he was not guilty of any injustice. He simply suffered personal ruin, and eventual imprisonment for his debts in Newgate, for attempting to force the proprietors to honor their obligations. He would not be the last to pay such a price.

Chapter Three

Land and Politics, 1787-1824

By F. W. P. BOLGER

I EDMUND FANNING AND ESCHEAT, 1787-1805

Edmund Fanning's administration from 1787 until 1805, like those of his successors for the next several decades, was highlighted by the problems created by the proprietary land tenure question. His credentials for coping with these and other issues were not unimpressive. A scion of an established Connecticut family, a New Yorker by birth who had received a good college education at Yale, he became a lawyer and distinguished judge in North Carolina. After devoted and efficient civil and military services to Great Britain in the American Revolutionary War, he was rewarded with the Lieutenant Governorship of Nova Scotia in 1783, followed by that of St. John's Island in 1787. At the age of forty-eight, with a recognized and distinguished career behind him, Edmund Fanning seems to have been content to rest on his laurels. While he governed the Island with shrewdness, cautiousness, dignity and a fair measure of aplomb, he sorely lacked the enthusiasm and initiative so necessary for the settlement of the Island's land problems.[1] Perhaps Fanning's real weakness was that noted by Lord Selkirk, who described him "as a man of no superabundant head, with neither ideas or cleeks in that head to hang inferences upon."[2] At any rate, Edmund Fanning was destined to rule the Island for seventeen years, reacting phlegmatically to every problem while generously indulging his insatiable ruling passion, the acquisition of thousands of acres of landed property on the Island.

The first three years of Fanning's gubernatorial regime were rent with bitter political battles. The adherents of Walter Patterson were determined to maintain the political control they had exercised since 1785, while the opposing faction led by John Stewart, and cradled lovingly in the protective arms of Edmund Fanning, was equally as anxious to assume the mantle of political power. The general election of July, 1787, provided the opposing groups with an opportunity to test their political popularity. During this election, two rival lists of candidates were presented for the first time, "the Richmond Bay list" — the Stewart-DesBrisay faction, and Captain Fletcher's list — the Patterson faction. For this election the whole Island was still one constituency of eighteen seats, with voting taking place on three separate days at St. Peter's, Charlottetown and Princetown.[3]

On July 17, the sheriff reported to Lieutenant Governor Fanning and his Council that the Fletcher list comprising James Curtis, William Lawson, David Lawson, James McNutt, Cornelius Higgins, Thomas Massard, David Irwin, John Throckmorton, William McKie, Ebenezer Nicholson, William Warren, Thomas Hooper, John Robins, John Clark, John Webster, William Douglas, James Campbell and Alexander Fletcher had won the election by a majority of twelve; but he also stated that he could not declare Captain Fletcher's group duly elected because there had been too much disorder, interference and violence in the Charlottetown poll, much of which was due to the officers of the garrison to whom Patterson had granted many favors during his incumbency.[4] The Council decided to set aside the results of this election, and also to change the scheme of representation, by having four members elected from each county and two from the county towns of Georgetown, Princeton and Charlottetown. On August 20, writs for a new election were issued, despite a petition of protest from 113 signators whom Fanning contemptuously described "as of the lowest order and class of inhabitants, more than thirty of whom being either servants, Roman Catholics or minors are not entitled to vote."[5]

The results of this election, while more satisfactory to Edmund Fanning than that of July, were still disappointing. His principal consolation was that both John Stewart and Charles Stewart managed to acquire seats. But Captain Fletcher's group enjoyed a sizeable majority, and when they met in January, 1788, they immediately elected one of their principal spokesmen, Phillips Callbeck, as Speaker.[6] This session, described by Fanning "as filled with the spirit of former party animosity and dissension,"[7] passed only one Bill and that simply an addition to a previous Highway Act. The Lieutenant Governor soon dispensed the members from further attendance, sarcastically reminding them "that not having been furnished by the House after sitting for upwards of four weeks with a sight of a single page of the Journals of their proceedings contrary to what has been the invariable practice in all of His British North American colonies . . . I am unable to bear testimony to that public approbation you very probably might have merited."[8] Fanning did not allow this Assembly to hold another session, but rather prorogued it from time to time, while devoting himself to the reconciliation of the warring factions. In a progress report to a friend at the Colonial Office, Evan Nepean, he confided that "he could have no idea of the rancour and acrimony with which those parties [the Stewart and Patterson groups] have hitherto aspersed and opposed each other."[9] "But thank God," he added, "unanimity is almost wholly restored among all except a *very few* who most probably never will or can be reconciled,"[10] Finally, Fanning dissolved the Assembly in February, 1790, and the newly elected House met in March of the same year.[11]

This new Assembly proved to be so satisfactory to Lieutenant Governor Fanning that he retained it for twelve years, and thus it became the Island's Long Parliament. The year 1790 marks the real assumption of power by the Stewart-DesBrisay-Fanning coterie that ruled the Island in their own interests and those of their immediate friends for over a decade. In the Council, Fanning's appointments assured him of loyal support. He restored Thomas DesBrisay to the Council, and in June, 1789, reinstated Peter Stewart as Chief Justice, both of whom had been suspended by Walter Patterson.[12] He enticed Robert Gray whom he described "as a gentleman of superior merit and worth."[13] a former Captain in his Regiment in the American Revolutionary War, to settle in Charlottetown. He immediately rewarded his protege with two town lots and two twelve-acre pasture lots and also appointed him Assistant Judge of the Supreme Court, Provincial Treasurer, his private secretary, and a member of Council.[14] He cemented the Council's familial bonds by the appointment of William Townshend, the son-in-law of the Chief Justice, as Collector of Customs, Charles Stewart, son of the Chief Justice and son-in-law of Thomas DesBrisay, as Clerk of Council and Registrar of Chancery, and Reverend Theophilus DesBrisay, another son-in-law of the Chief Justice, as Chaplain to both Houses and a member of Council.

In the Assembly, Edmund Fanning also enjoyed excellent support. In 1789, he persuaded Joseph Robinson, a Lieutenant Colonel of the South Carolina Loyalist Regiment, to move to the Island. He was elected to the Assembly in 1790, and became its Speaker for four years until his appointment to the Legislative Council by Fanning. He also named him the Island's second Assistant Judge.[15] When Robinson resigned as Speaker, he was succeeded by John Stewart, the Island's Receiver General of Quit Rents since 1790, who catered to his own and Fanning's whims until his resignation in 1801. With a loyal Assembly, Council and Judiciary, Fanning cautiously and discreetly strengthened his personal position. He purchased 48,000 acres of his predecessor's confiscated lands for £98 [Lots 19 and 67], and was land agent for several influential proprietors, notably Samuel Holland, Lord Townshend, Robert Shuttleworth and Baron Montgomery.

It was, therefore, with mixed feelings that Fanning viewed the movement for escheat that loomed large on the Island's political horizon in the year 1797.

The initial leadership in the escheat agitation came from two men closely associated with the ruling councils of the Island, Lieutenant Colonel Joseph Robinson and Robert Hodgson. When Robinson moved to the Island, he leased one thousand acres of land on Lot 34 from Sir James Montgomery, and in spite of his intimate connection with the establishment, he became sympathetic with the grievances of the tenants. Closely allied with him in giving leadership to escheat was his son-in-law, Robert Hodgson. He had moved to Charlottetown from Shelburne and entered the mercantile business with Ralph Brecken, a leading Island exporter. He was elected to the House of Assembly in 1790, and soon rose to political prominence. By the mid 1790's he was clerk of the Supreme Court, a Justice of the Peace, and one of the leading spokesmen for the tenantry in the Assembly. His championship of the cause of escheat lent considerable prestige to the movement.[16]

Robinson and Hodgson anonymously initiated the campaign for escheat in the spring of 1796. Robinson published a well-documented pamphlet, which Hodgson circulated throughout the Island, setting forth in bold and unmistakable language the case for escheat. It emphatically asserted that "the proprietors had neither settled their lands according to the terms of their grants nor paid their quit rents, and although they would not pay their rents, they were determined that the settlers should pay rent to them."[17] The pamphlet went on to insist that "unless some alteration took place, the people of the Island would drag out their lives in a state of low spirits, much want and misery, and devoid of animation."[18] In order to redress these injustices, the pamphlet stressed that tenants should have "small lots of land granted to them of 100 to 300 acres, having only to pay quit rents to the Crown."[19] It concluded with the strong plea that the tenants "petition the King through the House of Assembly praying that His Majesty would inquire about the non-fulfillment of the conditions of the grants, establish a court of escheat and direct that small grants of land should be laid out to his subjects in proportion to the strength and number of their families."[20]

The circulation of this pamphlet throughout the Colony occasioned a deep-seated interest on the part of the tenantry as to the possibility of the establishment of a Court of Escheat. Meeting after meeting was held culminating in the presentation of numerous petitions to the members of the Legislature demanding a special legislative session. The parliamentary representatives reacted favorably, and on March 23, 1797, fifteen of the eighteen members of the Assembly addressed a petition to Lieutenant Governor Fanning, expressing concern over the agrarian discontent of the citizenry and requesting a special session of the Legislature "to conduct a full legislative enquiry into the present state of the Colony."[21] Lieutenant Governor Fanning was placed in a difficult position by this request. As a large proprietor himself, and agent to several others, he had little sympathy with a movement designed to abolish the proprietary system; and yet, by opposing escheat he could imperil his popularity with the people of the Colony upon whom he depended for local support. He decided that it would not be politic to resist the strident demands of the people, so he drifted with the tide and convened a special session of the Assembly on July 11, 1797.[22]

On July 14, three petitions from inhabitants of the Island were read by James Curtis, William McKie and Ralph Brecken, requesting the Assembly to investigate the land tenure system on the Island.[23] Three days later, a Committee comprised of James Curtis, Charles Stewart and Peter McGowan was appointed to collect all documents "that in any way related to the terms and conditions on which the lands of the Island were originally granted, and all subsequent proceedings relative to the same within the Island, or in England."[24] When the Committee reported a few days later, the record of proprietary failure was so appalling that two more members, Robert Hodgson and Ralph Brecken, were added, and the Committee was further empowered "to consider the actual state of settlement and to report what might be fit and proper to be done thereupon."[25] This additional directive resulted in a most comprehensive and disturbing report of the situation relative to land tenure on the Island.

After a detailed consideration of the Committee's report, the Assembly, with John Stewart presiding as Speaker, passed a series of eleven resolutions which were embodied in a petition to the British Government. The first four, dealing with the number of settlers on the townships, revealed these startling statistics: that on twenty-three townships containing 458,580 acres, there was not a single resident; on twelve townships embracing 423,000 acres, the population consisted of only thirty-six families, which upon an average of six persons to each family, amounted to two hundred and sixteen persons; on six other townships, consisting of 120,000 acres, there were fifty families constituting some three hundred people; and only on the remaining twenty-six townships containing 3,856 inhabitants were the terms of settlement fulfilled.[26] The fifth resolution noted that although Sir James Montgomery, the proprietor of Lots 7, 12, 34 and 51, Edward Lewis and John Hill, the proprietors of Lot 5, and John Cambridge, the proprietor of Lots 63 and 64, had not fulfilled all the conditions of settlement, they deserved special consideration for their herculean efforts in attempting to settle their lots and to make their settlers economically viable.[27] The resolutions further contended that the failure of so many proprietors to implement the terms of their grants was highly injurious to the Island, which, if fully settled, could maintain upwards of half a million inhabitants.[28] In addition, the resolutions drew attention to the prosperity of Nova Scotia and New Brunswick, and attributed this chiefly to "the general escheat and forfeiture of the unsettled grants, and the regranting of such lands in small tracts to settlers which had taken place recently in those colonies."[29] The final and most important resolution implored the British Government to compel the proprietors to settle their townships, and in the event of their failure to comply, to take measures to have their lands escheated and regranted in small tracts to actual settlers.[30]

The Napoleonic Wars precluded the British Government from giving consideration to the domestic problems of her colonies, and it was not until the short interval of peace in 1802-1803 that the new Colonial Secretary, Lord Hobart, gave serious attention to the 1797 resolutions. After carefully weighing a number of proposals, Lord Hobart opted for a compromise heavily weighted in favor of the proprietors. His solution was that a Court of Escheat would be authorized, but only after the proprietors were given a further opportunity to fulfill the terms of their grants with respect to quit rent payments. The arrears of quit rents due to the Crown up to May, 1801, was £59,162, and 17.S.[31] It was decided, "in consideration of the present state of the Colony, and the representations made on behalf of the proprietors, to accept a composition of £18,732, 17.S."[32] In other words, the British authorities decided, principally because of the proprietary lobby of the indefatigable John Hill, Baron Montgomery, John Cambridge and other notables, to reduce the quit rent arrears by £40,430, or by nearly one quarter of a million dollars. In order to differentiate between proprietors who had exerted themselves in settling their lots and those who had not, the composition of the arrears was granted by classifying the lands into five groups, ranging from the fully settled lots on which only four years' payment was to be demanded instead of thirty-two years — 1769-1801 — to the completely unsettled one on which fifteen years' payment was to be levied.[33] This enlightened proposition was strengthened with the provision that "in the event of the failure of the proprietors to make these payments, their lands were to be resumed by the Crown."[34]

Lord Hobart sent special instructions to the unimpressionable Fanning regarding the procedures to be followed to render this new policy operative. He informed him that the Receiver General [John Stewart] had already commenced "to take steps for the settling with the proprietors in England for their payment of their several proportions of the composition which the Government is willing to accept, and would shortly proceed to Prince Edward Island to call in like manner upon the proprietors residing therein."[35] He also stated that provision must be made immediately for "a proper and effectual method of collecting, receiving, and accounting in future for the Quit Rents as they became payable;"[36] and to facilitate proper proceedings, Hobart "enclosed certain clauses in the form of a Bill,"[37] which, he instructed Fanning, "should be passed by the Legislature as soon as possible."[38] With respect to escheat, Lord Hobart startled Fanning by insisting that he must "be prepared to pursue, without loss of time, when circumstances shall render it advisable, the requisite and legal steps for effectually revesting in his Majesty such lands as may be liable to be escheated and forfeited."[39] Hobart advised further, that in the escheat of such lands, "the practice which had prevailed in this respect in Nova Scotia would be a sufficient precedent for the guidance of the Lieutenant Governor of Prince Edward Island."[40] It thus seemed at first glance that the British Government really intended to alleviate the grave evils delineated by the 1797 Assembly resolutions.

Lieutenant Governor Fanning convened the Legislature in November, 1802, and, in the Speech from the Throne, stated that the British Government expected the "Island Legislature to pursue, when circumstances should render it advisable, the requisite and legal steps for effectually revesting in His Majesty such lands as may be liable to be escheated."[41] He also instructed the legislators that they must, with as little delay as possible, pass an Act for the effectual recovery of His Majesty's Quit Rents and for enforcing in the future a due and regular payment of these rents.[42] The members of the Assembly, prior to replying to the Speech from the Throne, sent an Address to the Lieutenant Governor requesting further information regarding their responsibility on escheat legislation, but the very cautious Fanning writhed out of this inquiry by lamely insisting that the initiative on the question of escheat should come from the Lieutenant Governor.[43] The Assembly, on this occasion, did not pursue the matter, but rather addressed itself vigorously to the enactment of the Quit Rent Bill which received three readings and assent within five days.[44] The Lieutenant Governor, deciding that it would be an appropriate time to measure the views of the electorate on the new policies, immediately dissolved the twelve-year old Assembly and issued writs for an election. The people of the Island responded with a tremendous vote of confidence in those who had been in the forefront of the escheat agitation. Robert Hodgson, Ralph Brecken, James Curtis, Peter McGowan and Charles Stewart, the five members of the all-important 1797 Committee, were returned; indeed, Robert Hodgson, the principal escheat spokesman, was probably the most popular individual on Prince Edward Island. He was nominated and elected in three constituencies, winning every vote in Georgetown and carrying Prince and

Queen's counties by 2-1 majorities.[45] The Islanders had certainly given their elected representatives a resounding mandate for escheat.

When the newly elected Assembly met in March, 1803, with James Curtis as Speaker, it immediately came to grips with escheat. Realizing that Lieutenant Governor Fanning still remained indecisive on this question, the Assembly introduced a measure entitled "An Act for effectually revesting in His Majesty, his heirs and successor, all such lands as are or may be liable to forfeiture within this Island."[46] This Bill, passed by both Houses and assented to by Fanning on April 2, 1803, spelled out the procedure to be followed by the Lieutenant Governor and the Courts in the escheat of proprietary lands.[47] Being convinced, moreover, that Fanning would always balk at the prospect of putting his Royal Instructions on escheat into effect, the corresponding Committee of the Legislature wrote to William Knox, the Colony Agent in London, to solicit his support in prodding Fanning to action. The Committee stated "that there were very strong grounds for believing that Governor Fanning would not soon take the necessary steps for revesting in the Crown such lands as were liable to be escheated . . . and although he is a good man and disposed to do what is right, yet from an overcautious mind he would defer taking steps until he received positive and direct orders from the Secretary of State for that purpose."[48] Knox more correctly attributed the Lieutenant Governor's indecision "to be founded on his unwillingness to expose himself to the resentment of the powerful proprietors whose lots are liable to be escheated;[49] and he advised Lord Hobart "to send John Stewart, the Receiver General, to the Island immediately to proceed against the proprietors, and to instruct the Lieutenant Governor to take away discretion and proceed to escheat."[50]

Having completed negotiations with the absentee proprietors on the quit rent composition, John Stewart arrived in Prince Edward Island in October, 1803, and proceeded to deal with their counterparts there. The composition had a very limited effect in bringing in delinquent dues, but it did have the useful effect of changing very considerably the pattern of land tenure on the Island. Many of the proprietors who were either unwilling or unable to pay the quit rent composition willingly sold their lands to other individuals who, it seems, were disposed to engage actively in the settlement of the Island. Nearly one-third of the lands on the Island, eighteen full townships, four half-townships, one-third of two townships along with many smaller tracts were purchased by such individuals.[51] Some of these, like the Earl of Selkirk, who brought eight hundred settlers to his newly acquired townships of Lots 57 and 58, contributed to a relatively rapid increase in the Island population. On the other hand, many proprietors refused to sell their property or to pay the reduced amount of quit rent. They were of the opinion, with some reason, that the payment of the arrears would not be enforced, or that a further diminution might be obtained. The Receiver General, deciding that some of these must be challenged, obtained judgements in the Supreme Court of the Island against the proprietors of ten full townships, five half-townships, and one-third of a township for arrears of quit rents due to the Crown.[52] Once again, as in Patterson's regime, the issue was squarely joined between the proprietors and the Crown. The Island's new Chief Justice, Robert Thorp, pointed up the nub of the issue when he observed that "the higher powers in England are so implicated by holding large tracts of land that nothing beneficial will be done unless Lord Hobart is very peremptory and leaves nothing to discretion."[53] Unfortunately for the Island tenantry, the British authorities were never prepared to be that heroic.

Lieutenant Governor Fanning, approaching the climax of his colorless career, attempted to stymie the honorable efforts of the Receiver General and the Supreme Court. He sent a copy of the Court Order to Lord Hobart in order that he "might be apprized of a measure which in its operation must materially affect and endanger the interests of so many of the proprietors."[54] He informed the Colonial Secretary that had he known of these measures he "would not have given his approbation or concurrence because the Quit Rent Act should not have been enforced until royal confirmation had been received, and because he felt himself bound in tenderness to the interest of the proprietors, several of whom have lately made great exertions and to many others who propose to do the same, to disapprove of such precipitate prosecution by the Receiver General in a time of war unless the same had been authorized."[55] The partial Lieutenant Governor Fanning went one step further and not only urged the Colonial Secretary to disallow the Court Order, but also recommended "a delay in the enforcement of the Quit Rent Act and that the proprietors should be eased in the payment of the arrears due on their lots by extending the payment over three years."[56] In the light of these statements, Lord Selkirk's categorical observation that "the Governor was opposed to escheat"[57] seems valid indeed.

Ordinary common sense should have made it evident to Lieutenant Governor Fanning that even in the most favorable circumstances he need never fear precipitous action on the part of the British Government with respect to the Island's land question. And, in 1804, the circumstances were far from favorable; the resumption of the Napoleonic Wars, an influential proprietary lobby against the Quit Rent and Escheat Acts and a rapid change in Colonial Secretaries, ground the wheels of action on this question to a veritable halt. On July 29, 1804, Fanning received official word of his recall, which he had already learned of in a copy of a newspaper from Greenwich, England.[58] He was informed that in consideration of "his long and faithful service a pension of five hundred pounds per annum"[59] would be provided during his lifetime. Fanning had certainly rendered "long and faithful service," but it was chiefly to the proprietary interests, and in so doing, he contributed to a legacy of disillusionment and agrarian discontent among the citizens of the Island with which his successor attempted to cope during the whole of his incumbency.

II THE DESBARRES INTERLUDE, 1805-1812

Colonel Joseph Frederick Wallet DesBarres, a tireless octogenarian, who had spent the previous sixteen years on the steps of Whitehall attempting to disprove charges of irregularity in his two major public services, the hydrographic surveys leading to the publication of the four volumes of the celebrated *Atlantic Neptune,* and his term as Lieutenant Governor of Cape Breton, was the man chosen to succeed Edmund Fanning. Although the Imperial Government refused to grant him a clear exoneration, his appointment to another Colonial position was a partial vindication of his honor. Thus, in May, 1804, at the age of eighty-three, the cultivated, enthusiastic, amorous, ambitious and only slightly chastened DesBarres was given a second chance by his appointment as Lieutenant Governor of another troubled Island.[60] Colonel DesBarres experienced considerable frustration in reaching his new command. After many abortive attempts to secure passage, he was obliged to remain in England for over a year, and it was not until July, 1805, that he belatedly arrived on the Island. He informed the Secretary of State, the Earl of Camden, that he "was received and escorted by the garrison troops through a numerous concourse of joyful people to the house of Lieutenant Governor Fanning."[61] This was, perhaps, no exaggeration. The Islanders were riding on a wave of expectation that their perennial problems of quit rents and escheat were close to solution; and they looked with enthusiasm to the new Governor to bring these hopes to fruition.

Lieutenant Governor DesBarres did not have to wait long before being officially apprized of the principal political and economic preoccupation of the 6,957 Islanders.[62] A Committee of the House of Assembly, convened by DesBarres in November, 1805, framed an Address to him, requesting any information he was able to afford it on the fate of the Quit Rent and Escheat Acts. His reply that "he had not received any official notification of His Majesty's royal pleasure respecting the measures,"[63] provoked

J. F. W. DesBarres

a spirited remonstrance from the Assembly, which made DesBarres pain-
fully aware of the Islanders' attitude to British Government and to British
officialdom. After stating that the passage of the Quit Rent and Escheat
Acts by the Legislature "was in direct conformity with formal instructions
from the Secretary of State,"[64] an Assembly Address to the British Government asserted that the members of the Legislature "had the strongest
reasons to believe that Royal assent to the Act for revesting the lands
had been graciously afforded by His Majesty, but it appeared to them
that His Majesty's Royal allowance had been withheld and suppressed by
means of unfounded representations of interested individuals in England,
which the Assembly had no opportunity of answering."[65] The Assembly
charged further "that the proceedings which had taken place under the
Quit Rent Act, passed in 1802, by which the Receiver General had
obtained judgements against sixteen lots and shares of lots, had been
suspended through the same injurious means, and thus measures planned
for the settlement and prosperity of the Island were wholly frustrated."[66]
The Address concluded with a plea that "His Majesty be informed of
these obstructions and give orders for their removal."[67]

Lieutenant Governor DesBarres now found himself caught in the vortex
of the land question. On the same day that he received the Assembly petition,
a memorial from some of the resident proprietors on Prince Edward Island
which ran completely counter to the claims of the Assembly, reached his
desk in Charlottetown. It pointed out that John Cambridge, the proprietor
of Lots 63 and 64, Captain John MacDonald, the landlord of Lots 35 and
36, Lord Selkirk, the new proprietor of Lots 57 and 58, Charles and
Edward Worrell, the owners of Lots 39, 40, 41 and 42, and several smaller
proprietors were making tremendous efforts to settle their lots and to
advance the prosperity of the Island.[68] The memorial claimed that the
legislation on escheat and quit rents was prejudicial to the best interests of
the Island and that "the proprietors deserved a far better fate than to be
stigmatized by the members of the House of Assembly who are generally
persons who rent small farms and are possessed of little property."[69] The
memorialists pleaded with the Governor to recommend equal justice for
the proprietors in his submission to the British Government.

It is not surprising that Colonel DesBarres confessed perplexity as to
the posture he should adopt on this controversial issue. "You will obviously
perceive," he wrote to his friend Edward Cooke, "the predicament in
which I stand between the two contending parties."[70] "The one party is
composed," he claimed, "of men of slender property, leaseholders of small
plantations unadorned with education who seem to vie with each other in
their determination by any means to move heaven and earth for obtaining

an universal partitiobonheur of their landlords;"[71] "The other party," he stated, "is composed of proprietors, many of whom have proved themselves [if not positively disinclined] at least unable to settle or improve the tracts of land, originally granted to them respectively, in any manner likely to produce any advantage either to themselves or to the public. The one party contends for a Democratic Institution, the other for an Aristocratical one."[72]

Caught in this dilemma, DesBarres showed a considerable predilection for the proprietary class. He claimed, in a long treatise forwarded to the Colonial Office in 1805, that the 1797 resolutions had come from an Assembly "composed of illiterate country people no better than the cottagers in Great Britain."[73] On the other hand, he accused John Stewart, the former Speaker of the House, "of attempting to form a pro-proprietorial oligarchy, and whose main object in leading the illiterate Assembly and perverting the multitude, was to get all the turning of the roast in their own hands, pack the cards, and play into one another's hands as they might please."[74] He manifested considerable scepticism regarding the establishment of a Court of Escheat because "it tended to infuse too deep a tincture of the levelling sentiments in the people at large — too much cupidity for what belongs to others — too much disrespect for property;"[75] and, yet, on balance, because of the unsettled state of the lands on the Island, he thought "it just to establish a temporary court for the specific purpose of forfeiting the lands of proprietors whose neglect could be considered a dereliction, but this done, the court should be shut up."[76] He did not favor, however, the regranting of the forfeited lands to the tenants in grants of land of one, two or three hundred acres. He suggested, instead, leasehold tenure of 999 years, and maintained such a tenure "was more beneficial to a poor man than a grant of an equal quantity of land in fee simple which he had not the property to set about cultivating."[77] Thus, in the final analysis, the only result of escheat would be to regrant the confiscated property "to some other proprietor more likely to render it productive."[78] This initial stance assumed by DesBarres was not violently partisan and, at this juncture, could have been expected from an encumbered proprietor of some 70,000 acres of land in Nova Scotia and New Brunswick.

The contention of the Assembly that the British authorities had been influenced in their decision on the Quit Rent and Escheat Acts was well founded. The first four decades of the nineteenth century reveal that a tremendous influence was exercised by the proprietors residing in Great Britain. At this particular time, there was a sizeable body of proprietors who were themselves men of considerable political influence, and who at the same time, enjoyed intimate social and political connections with governmental officials. The principal spokesman for this group was John Hill, an obscure merchant from Rotherhithe, England, who had acquired ownership of Lots 5 and 6 in the 1780's. Although his prosperous fishing and lumber business at Cascumpec had been wrecked by the plottings of the equally influential John Cambridge, abetted by some Island officials, he retained ownership of thousands of acres of lands, and his indefatigable efforts in memorializing the British Government reaped handsome dividends.[79] The influence of other important individuals such as Lord James Townshend, the proprietor of Lot 56, the Marquis of Hertford, the owner of Lot 13, Lawrence Sullivan, the proprietor of Lots 9, 22, and 61, the Earl of Westmorland and Viscount Melville, the joint owners of Lots 29 and 53, together with the Earl of Selkirk and the Montgomeries already mentioned, made the proprietary lobby almost irresistible. This is clearly demonstrated by an examination of the fate of the Quit Rent and Escheat Acts.

In 1804 and 1805 these proprietors addressed a number of memorials to the Colonial Office. Once such memorial, signed by most of the proprietors in Great Britain, asserted that the Escheat Act was a veritable act of confiscation, and if carried into execution, "every proprietor without a single exception could be deprived of his estate without remuneration for the money expended in endeavouring to improve his estate."[80] While admitting that the Island had not been settled according to the expectations of the Island government, they, nevertheless, insisted that they could demonstrate that the failure should not be attributed to proprietary neglect but rather "to the dissension which prevailed between the local administration and some of the inhabitants of which the proprietors had been the victims."[81]

Another memorial audaciously asserted that, "since the terms of the grants contained conditions which never could be complied with, the proprietors should be permitted to obtain new patents containing such conditions only which were practicable and meant to be enforced."[82] It would seem that it was the impracticality of one of the original conditions that accounted for the enigmatic failure of Whitehall to endorse the Escheat Court recommended in 1802. In the event of the establishment of such a court, it could be reasonably expected that many Island settlers would move to the escheated townships where they could purchase lands rather than remain victims of a leasehold system which they adhored. Thus, the few proprietors who honored the original commitment in settling their lots could conceivably be denuded of their settlers and, perhaps, subjected to escheat at a future time. The cogency of this argument led the Colonial authorities to pause and to adopt a policy of compromise on escheat. In August, 1808, a *Treasury Minute* authorized the Receiver General to enforce the judgments of 1804 on the sixteen lots and shares of lots on which the composition had not been paid. But the same Minute stipulated "that the operation of the Bill for revesting these lands in the Crown, should in the meantime, be suspended."[83] This recommendation, that the "operation of the Escheat Bill be suspended," became the settled policy of the British Government. The objection of the proprietors, and DesBarres's reservations, were powerful enough to inter escheat in a legislative Limbo.

The disappointment and frustration engendered by the British Government's failure to fulfill the decisions of Lord Hobart resulted in serious and complicated political reverberations in Prince Edward Island. Personal recriminations, the stuff of Island politics, were heightened, and between the years 1806 and 1813, the local *cabal,* which had dominated the Island politically, was challenged, the Assembly was fleetingly controlled by a new political organization the *Loyal Electors,* the Chief Justice was transferred, the Governor was summarily recalled, and his principal advisor, James Bardin Palmer, completely discredited. The control of the *cabal* was first threatened by the results of a general election called by DesBarres in the summer of 1806. During the campaign, a new political society denominated the *Loyal Electors,* exerted considerable influence in the choice of members for the Assembly. Five of the eighteen members elected, James Bardin Palmer, Dr. Angus McAulay, Alexander MacDonnel, Coundouly B. Rankin and James Bagnall were members of this society and attributed their victories to its influence.[84] Their leader and principal spokesman was James B. Palmer, a prominent Irish attorney, who arrived on the Island in 1802, determined to amass a new fortune. As agent to several proprietors and as a competent lawyer, he succeeded financially and soon was a proprietor of some ten thousand acres himself. Colonel DesBarres, distrustful of the Stewart-DesBrisay control and desperately in need of independent legal advice, leaned upon Palmer and gradually took him into his confidence. Within a short time, Palmer was his factotum — Adjutant-General of Militia, Master and Registrar of Chancery, Inspector of Public Accounts, Inspector of Roads, and member of the Council and Assembly alternately.[85]

The membership of the society at first consisted of approximately 40 citizens of Charlottetown and Royalty; but it gradually grew in size and importance including others from surrounding districts. Many of its members were from the Loyalist families who had chafed under the rule of Fanning and considered themselves victimized by the failure of his government to grant clear titles to the land on which they had settled during the

Patterson regime. The society met regularly on the first Tuesday of each month at Bagnall's tavern. Its purpose was "to consider proper legislative measures, to bring about the introduction of upright, independent men, and persons of unimpeached character into the House of Assembly with the view of counteracting a dangerous influence . . . possessed by a set of persons (either personally of by their unprincipled agents) who were engaged in monstrous speculation in land."[86] These objectives, labelled as *Jacobin* and levelling, created panic in the Stewart-DesBrisay faction and eventually aroused fear among the proprietors. Charles Stewart, the solicitor-general and the agent of many proprietors, ably assisted by the Horatius-like Caesar Colclough, the Chief Justice, and Peter McGowan, the Attorney General, made it their personal missions to destroy the society. The activities of the *Loyal Electors* provided a focus for the apparently endemic personal rivalries on the Island. More importantly, the appeal of Colclough and others to the more influential proprietors such as Lord Selkirk added the dimension of proprietary interference to the local politics of the Island.

Affairs in Prince Edward Island reached a crisis in 1810. The vacancy caused by the death of Peter McGowan, the Attorney General, brought the activities of the *Loyal Electors* under investigation. Lieutenant Governor DesBarres recommended that James B. Palmer should receive the appointment. He insisted that Island-educated lawyers, such as Charles Stewart, were largely incompetent, since a colonial education "can afford but little knowledge in theory and still less in practice."[87] "One hundred pounds," he added with Lord MacAulay-like contempt, "would purchase in England, a better selection of Law books than the joint stock of all the lawyers and judges on the Island would exhibit."[88] He expressed the hope that Palmer, "a laborious individual, a man of far more extensive law knowledge, accuracy of judgment and correct practice than any of his colleagues,"[89] would be the next Attorney General. The proprietors in London, however, influenced by Caesar Colclough, concluded that Palmer's association with the *Loyal Electors* made him more than suspect. Lord Selkirk, on their behalf, recommended that Charles Stewart "would be generally agreeable to the most respectable proprietors . . . while Palmer was a person so extremely objectionable in every respect that he trusted there was no possibility of his receiving any countenance from Government."[90] Not only did Stewart receive the appointment, but the exchange of letters resulted in an investigation into the role being played by Palmer and the *Loyal Electors*.

The uncompromising Caeser Colclough, supported by the Stewart faction and a few local proprietors, considered the society as foes of order and fomenters of rebellion. Statements were published that Palmer had "moved for a secret committee to control the affairs of the society."[91] The society published a denial, and asked for an official investigation of its membership, books and activities. While this investigation was proceeding, five members, James Palmer, William Haszard, William Roubel, Elisha LePage and Dr. Angus McAulay presented exculpatory affidavits to the Lieutenant Governor, clarifying the aims of the society and their motives for being members of it. These affidavits were extremely critical of the *Cabal* and, especially of Charles Stewart, the Attorney General, who was designated as leader of the land speculators' *Cabal*.[92] These sworn statements, obtained by Colclough from DesBarres, were treated as libellous documents rather than as evidence for their defense. William Roubel was placed on trial and struck off the Roll of Attorneys for contempt of court by the Chief Justice. This satisfied Colclough and legal action against the others was dropped and the inconclusive investigation came to an end.[93]

The society, although chastened, took an active part in the election of April, 1812, and managed to increase its representation from five to seven. Taking advantage of a small attendance of their rivals at an Assembly session in September, 1812, these seven members sent a formal Address to the Lieutenant Governor, asking for the suspension of the Chief Justice on the grounds that "in filing the affidavits in the Supreme Court he had acted in an arbitrary, disrespectful and illegal manner."[94] DesBarres was now faced with a difficult decision. The investigation into the affairs of the society had led to such mounting antagonisms between Colclough and DesBarres that the Chief Justice no longer attended meetings of the Council. Colclough vividly explained the denouement in a letter to his proprietary friend, Robert Montgomery:

I argued the same way in Council when the Governor, after some very intemperate expressions, threw himself back in his chair, and collecting all the foul breath he could in his mouth, puffed it full in my face. With more temper than I thought I possessed, I cooly got up and said I could not remain to meet such conduct, and as I was retiring, he, in the most contumacious manner continued repeating: "Good morning to you, good Chief Justice, go home and study Law"—to which I only replied that I considered my knowledge of Law was at least equal to His Excellency's of politeness.[95]

This relationship, perhaps, accounted for DesBarres's expeditious decision; at any rate, four days after his reception of the Assembly Address, he suspended the Chief Justice. Although Colclough was briefly reinstated by DesBarres's successor, the British Government decided to exchange him for Chief Justice Thomas Tremlett of Newfoundland who was in similar difficulties. Tremlett arrived in Charlottetown in 1813 on one of his Majesty's ships, and Colclough, still breathing defiance, was transported to St. John's in the same dignified manner.

Meanwhile in London, the turbulent affairs of the Island were receiving serious consideration. The powerful proprietors, influenced by correspondence from Charles Stewart, Caesar Colclough and others, began to exert pressure upon the Colonial Office to have Lieutenant Governor DesBarres removed. After a number of meetings of the proprietors, Lord Selkirk presented to the Colonial Secretary a number of documents prepared by John Hill, which in libellous language, were condemnatory of Colonel DesBarres, James Bardin Palmer, and the *Loyal Electors*. DesBarres was described as a "man sunk into absolute dotage and completely under the guidance of James Bardin Palmer, an adventurer of infamous character, under whose influence all the power of Government are perverted to the worst purpose, who in many instances acted the part of an absolute swindler."[96] The *Loyal Electors* were depicted as a "club composed chiefly of Americans who came to the Island under the specious character of Loyalists who, under the guidance of Palmer, have led the people to hope for a general Escheat of the lands of the proprietors and even to prepare them to welcome an invasion of the Republican Americans."[97] Lord Bathurst, the Colonial Secretary, influenced by these representations, summarily recalled DesBarres in August, 1812, and dismissed Palmer from all the public offices he had held.[98] Not only was DesBarres dismissed, but he also had to suffer the unusual indignity of not being permitted to remain in office until his successor arrived. A touch of comic tragedy enveloped these decisions when DesBarres, the lively nonagenarian, informed the Colonial Secretary that the temporary Administrator, William Townshend, had mustered enough strength to leave his sickbed and repeat the oath of office despite the fact "that he had for several months past, laboured under a complication of afflicting diseases."[99]

Despite his summary recall, the ageless DesBarres, who lived in retirement in Nova Scotia until his death at the age of 102, could well have viewed his gubernatorial regime in Prince Edward Island with pride. He, unlike his predecessor, kept a normal predilection for the proprietary cause in check during most of the period. He attempted valiantly to maintain an impartial stance between the prevailing parties on the Island. He can be criticized for placing too heavy a reliance on James Bardin Palmer; but although he was undoubtedly influenced by him, he was never completely under his dominance. Yet even this reliance was an asset, because in throwing the weight of his support to the activities of the *Loyal Electors*, he had, perhaps unwittingly, encouraged the establishment of the first political party of Prince Edward Island, if not in British North America. Since this party eventually emerged into the Reform Party of Prince Edward Island and made a significant contribution to the eventual solution of the Island's land tenure problem by freeing the people from the incubus of the proprietors, Joseph Federick Wallet DesBarres certainly deserves grateful commendation.

III   THE YEARS OF AUTOCRACY, 1813-1824

Charles Douglas Smith, a brother of Admiral Sir Sydney Smith, the famous naval war hero, through family influence with Lord Bathurst and the Prince Regent, was the man chosen to succeed DesBarres as the Island's fourth Lieutenant Governor. He was a worthy representative of autocracy in the post-Napoleonic era. A man of indomitable courage and integrity, endowed with an arbitrary temperament, Smith was a strong-willed individual, always undiplomatic, often insolent and invariably despotic. He had an innate suspicion of Colonial politicians and Legislatures, and treated them with Cromwellian contempt. Absolutely fearless of superiors, peers and inferiors, he governed — at times misgoverned — the Island, sincerely convinced that at least an all-knowing God was on his and his families' side. Thus, the stage was set on the Island for eleven more years of political and social turbulence.

Smith had been cautioned by Lord Bathurst against "implicitly adopting the suggestions of either of the prevailing parties on the Island, but rather to examine and report to him on the charges and countercharges made by the *Cabal* and the *Loyal Electors.*"[100] After a very cursory study of the situation, he accepted, at face value, the *Cabals'* description of the *Loyal Electors.* He reported to Lord Bathurst that "a Confederacy of a very dangerous description by the name of 'the club' does exist of which Mr. Palmer was and still is the main spring."[101] He opined that "this Club was formed upon the plans and principles of the United Irish and was connected with the Irish in the United States, and therefore all connected with it are disaffected and dangerous subjects."[102] It was with these ingrained prejudices that Smith convened the Assembly in November, 1813. In his Speech from the Throne, he informed the members that he would have called them together sooner, but since he "had heard of the dissensions and strife in the Colony, he was not certain the public good would be served by such a meeting."[103] When the members, quite justifiably, devoted considerable attention to an examination of the expenditures of the public monies, he summarily prorogued the Assembly, self-righteously charging that "he had been actuated by the most sincere desire to pay marked attention to their right to examine the public expenditure, but if this conduct has not been altogether met on their part by a corresponding degree of liberality and confidence, it remained a matter of political regret, and since under present circumstances, further deliberations would be of no benefit, it was expedient to terminate the session."[104]

Smith revealed his contemptuous attitude in a letter of explanation to Lord Bathurst. He stated that "he had hazarded the experiment of convening the General Assembly which soon proved that it was under the domination of the 'Club'."[105] He declared that he "judged it expedient to let them sit for a month in order to give them an opportunity of thoroughly exposing themselves, which they had not failed to do in the estimation of every sensible man in the Colony."[106] "Their having done so little, so lowered them in the opinion of the public," wrote Smith, "that he found it expedient suddenly to surprise them by prorogation to the no small satisfaction of the well-affected part of the inhabitants."[107] Smith's summary dismissal of the Assembly and refusal to convene it for nearly four more years, a procedure not unlike that of the Stuart sovereigns, was the pattern he followed throughout his gubernatorial regime.

The paramount problem and the nemesis of every Governor, was, of course, the resolution of the land question. Smith addressed himself to this question with characteristic self-confidence. In an attempt to solve this contentious issue, he made a number of suggestions to Lord Bathurst who was simultaneously striving to reach a solution. He asserted that there was, in his opinion, "no sufficient reason grounded on strict justice and sound policy, why the quit rents should not be insisted upon by the British Government;"[108] and he expressed the hope that Lord Bathurst "would see the expediency of strictly enforcing their payment on the one hand, and as liberally dispensing them with the other."[109] He contended that if "a landed proprietor was called upon to pay, he would be stimulated, either to settle his lands, or be induced to yield them up to avoid paying Quit Rent for unprofitably territory."[110] This stance, not unlike that of Walter Patterson, was religiously adhered to by Smith until his recall. He recommended that the stipulation requiring the settlers to be foreign Protestants should be discarded. He noted that, in effect, this requirement had always been ignored since the majority of the 15,000 Islanders were "Roman Catholic Highlanders whose want of industry, sobriety and agricultural knowledge was notable."[111] He stated that the Island should be settled in future by Protestants, "but not Protestants from the United States, since Americans made the worst subjects, and nothing but contamination ever came from those regions of rum and rascality."[112] He boldly suggested that "a Court of Escheat should be established on the Island and that the property escheated should be regranted to new settlers."[113] While admitting that the collection of quit rent arrears was a question for the Crown to determine, he stated he "personally favoured the enforcement of Quit Rent arrears and could discern no visible reason why the Quit Rents should not be strictly levied in the future."[114]

In order to arrive at a decision, Lord Bathurst also invited the proprietors in Great Britain to present their views on the question. In a series of submissions they shamelessly exonerated themselves from all blame for the unsettled lands on the Island, and attached the principal responsibility to an unenlightened British Government which had placed impracticable conditions upon the original grantees. They added that three incompetent Governors and a host of avaricious Colonial politicians had magnified the original sin committed by the Imperial authorities.[115] They made three recommendations, the first of which was "that all proprietors should receive an entire remission of all arrears of quit rents up to the present."[116] Their second suggestion was that since the quit rents were not collected in Nova Scotia, "the Island proprietors should be granted a similar indulgence, and if the British Government decided in future to collect the rents in that Colony, they would agree to make payments, provided the rate was reduced to the Nova Scotia levy of two shillings per one hundred acres."[117] Finally, they recommended that "the obsolete stipulation requiring that settlers be foreign Protestants should be relinquished."[118]

In May, 1816, Lord Bathurst, after grappling with the quit rent problem for nearly two years, reached a decision quite favourable to all of the proprietors, but one which was clouded with uncertainties and obscurities. He informed Smith that "after considering the proprietors' memorials, the British Government had reached a determination to relieve them from the penalties they had incurred by the non-performances of the duties required of them under their original grants; and as soon as the order-in-council was prepared, the measure would be communicated."[119] He also ordered Smith to forward a statement of the quit rents collected since 1800, "so that those proprietors might receive the additional advantages which it was in contemplation to afford them."[120] Two months later, Bathurst revealed to Smith that the Colonial Office had decided to relieve the proprietors from the payment of quit rents from 1801 until June 25, 1816, and "to fix a new scale for future payment, which would be prepared forthwith."[121]

Lieutenant Governor Smith immediately set the machinery in motion for the collection of quit rents. He wrote to John Stewart, the Receiver General who was residing in Newfoundland as paymaster of the British troops, and asked him to return to the Island to prepare the quit rent statement requested by the Colonial Office. Stewart completed his statement in November, 1816, and Smith immediately forwarded it to the Colonial Office and pleaded for instructions as to the new scale. It is significant that the total monies collected by John Stewart since 1790 was only £6,392, and out of this amount £2,470 was retained by himself for his salary and contingent expenses. In addition, £400 was paid to his father, the former Chief Justice, for salary arrears, and £1,090 to the DesBrisays for similar arrears.[122] The Stewart-DesBrisay faction, at least, had not laboured unrewarded. For reasons of ill-health, John Stewart resigned as Receiver General, and Smith immediately named his own son-in-law, John Edward Carmichael, Acting Receiver General, and asked the Colonial Office to confirm this appointment.[123] Carmichael fitted perfectly into the Smith scheme of things and obeyed his every wish.

The failure of the Colonial Office to announce immediately the new scale had tragic consequences principally because of Smith's impetuosity. In his eagerness to begin quit rent collections, Smith issued a proclamation in October, 1816, in which he intimated that the "Crown intended to extend to the proprietors immunity to forfeitures to which they were liable under the original grants, to grant them remission of certain arrears, and to fix a scale for their future payment."[124] The proclamation concluded with the instruction that quit rents on the new scale would begin on June 25, and must be paid by December 25, 1816, or measures would be taken to revest the lands to the Crown."[125] Smith later informed Bathurst that failure to "levy the Quit Rents immediately would have led the proprietors to imagine that they were to remain dormant as before."[126] Despite frequent proddings from Smith, the Colonial Office gave no further instruction as to the new scale for nearly two years. Meanwhile, the proprietors completely ignored the demands of the Acting Receiver General throughout the year 1817.

In January, 1818, Carmichael apprized the landowners that "legal measures would be directed against them if they failed to pay the quit rents at the old rate within one month."[127] This directive produced results, and Smith triumphantly reported that "in one month a much larger sum was paid by the small proprietors than was received from them in the previous twenty-six years."[128] The attitude of the larger proprietors was, however, entirely different. Smith informed Bathurst that "the resident proprietors of townships and of half-townships had politically opposed the levying of the quit rents by every means in their power."[129] The Lieutenant Governor decided to challenge them, and in Trinity Term, 1818, his Acting Receiver General commenced proceedings in the Supreme Court for quit rent arrears against the proprietors of six townships, and eighty-four town and pasture lots in Charlottetown. When Lord Bathurst learned of these proceedings from the memorials of dozens of protesting proprietors, he immediately addressed a salty letter of instruction to Lieutenant Governor Smith. Had he and his advisors shown such decisiveness two years earlier, much misunderstanding, misery and embarrassment could have been avoided.

On May 18, 1818, Lord Bathurst sent a despatch to Smith, announcing the details of future Colonial Office policy. He prefaced his instructions with the observations that "he had learned with surprise and regret that Smith had resorted to measures which were likely, from their manner of execution, to become extremely grievous to the Colonists."[130] He charged that Smith "should have realized that there would be no collections until December, 1816, and the delay in assessing the new rate arose from the desire to fully investigate the value of the lands."[131] He informed the Lieutenant Governor that "the new rate was not to exceed two shillings per hundred acres, and in all cases where the payment of a proprietor should exceed £20, or if the proprietor should be resident in Great Britain, he had the option of paying either in London or in Charlottetown."[132] The proprietors were also released from the obligations imposed by their original grants of settling their lands with foreign Protestants, "provided that within ten years from December, 1816, the land should have been settled with other persons in the proportions specified in the original grants."[133] The despatch ordered Smith "to cease all proceedings in the collection of quit rents at the old rate, to return all monies collected above the approved rate of two shillings per hundred acres and to desist from the escheat of lands under judgment in the Supreme Court."[134] Finally, it was intimated that the quit rents must be rigidly enforced in the future, but, unfortunately, no positive instructions were issued, and Smith was merely instructed to forward to the Colonial Office a statement of the quit rents which would become due in future years.[135] The inexplicable contradictions encompassing Colonial Office policy are further indicated in this despatch by the extension of the proprietary quit rent exemption from June to December, 1816. This lack of a settled policy always made the enforcement of quit rents a hopeless task.

Lieutenant Governor Smith's decision to challenge the proprietors not only occasioned the wrath of the Colonial Office, but also destroyed the embryonic popularity he was gaining among the struggling tenants who were benefiting from his escheat policies. Acting upon positive instructions from Lord Bathurst, Smith had escheated Lots 55 and 15 in the name of the Crown in the early months of 1818.[136] He divided the escheated lands among the tenantry who were enabled to purchase one hundred acre farms upon payment of a fee of £5 and an annual quit rent of two shillings per hundred acres. With an appetite now whetted, he was making preparations for the escheat of Lot 52, when Lord Bathurst's famous despatch of May 30, 1818, abruptly ordered him to halt further escheat proceedings. As a result, when he convened the newly elected Assembly in November, 1818, he was no longer hailed as the budding champion of a distressed tenantry, but rather was severely criticized in the Address of Reply to his

Speech from the Throne "for refusing assent to a roads Bill in the last session, and for enforcing the quit rents arrears on the old scale which had produced the most distressing effects, particularly upon the lower classes of the community."[137] Smith, hurt and indignant, refused to receive this Address "on the grounds of its containing unconstitutional animadversions."[138] He held stubbornly to this stance, and the Address of the Assembly was never received, the sole instance of such an occurrence in the proceedings of the Island House of Assembly.

This altercation determined the frigid climate for the remainder of the session. The Assembly immediately framed a series of charges against the Chief Justice for his role in the quit rent proceedings which were described as "oppressive, illegal, and a violent infringement upon the rights of property."[139] Lieutenant Governor Smith was unmoved, and insisted the charges against the Chief Justice were "as unjust as they were intemperate."[140] But when the Assembly moved to proffer charges against the sheriff for his role, the Lieutenant Governor completely lost his cool. He sent his son-in-law, John E. Carmichael, inside the Bar of the House to inform the Speaker that if he "sat in the Chair one minute longer as Speaker, the House would immediately be dissolved," at the same time shaking his fist at the Speaker. "By whose authority?", asked the Speaker. "The Lieutenant Governor's," was the reply. While the Assembly was discussing the order, the Lieutenant Governor arrived, sent for the Speaker, "and holding up his watch to him, said that he would allow the House three minutes to adjourn or he would dissolve it."[141] The House adjourned. Later the same evening, the Lieutenant Governor's son, Henry B. Smith, generously assisted his father by smashing the windows of the Assembly. When the Assembly reconvened, a few weeks later, Smith was ordered to appear before the Bar of the House, where he unabashedly admitted that he "had up with his fist and smashed it through the windows."[142] When the Assembly committed him to jail, the Lieutenant Governor intervened and unceremoniously prorogued the House without the customary Address.

Smith's relations with the Assembly convinced him that he should dissolve it and hold another election. The results of this election, held in June, 1820, were not at all satisfactory to him, as fourteen of the eighteen elected were members of the previous House. Smith attributed their re-election to the *Loyal Electors,* whom he now saw operating under another label. "The *Loyal Electors,*" he informed the Colonial Office, "had recently revived under the mask of Free Masonry, and all the late elections were concerted in the Lodge of this town [Charlottetown]."[143] He added that he could prove "Free Masonry was converted to political purposes in Canada, and that he could trace the chain of connection from thence, hither."[144] Smith had now satisfied himself that he had discovered an international network of political intrigue, and it never seemed to occur to him that an alliance between the Irish in the United States, Freemasons in Canada and on the Island and the *Loyal Electors* made the thread of conspiracy very thin indeed.

The Lieutenant Governor's relations with the new Assembly, convened in July, 1820, were immeasurably worse than with the previous one. The re-elected and highly respected Speaker, Angus McAulay, jealously guarded the rights of the Assembly and would brook no interference from the King's representative. The Assembly unanimously adopted a series of resolutions embodying complaints against the Lieutenant Governor on his handling of the land question and forwarded these to the Governor General for transmission to the British Government. This deliberate by-passing of the Lieutenant Governor by the House revealed the strained relationship that existed between the two. The next day, the Assembly asked for prorogation. Smith was happy to comply with this request. He reported to the British authorities that "only three acts of no importance were passed, and that the Lower House were in their usual state of ill-temper."[145] He added that "holding the Session at all was a necessary evil — that he got it over with as quickly and as quietly as he could, and having succeeded in doing so, there is now no necessity of calling a General Assembly for years."[146] Smith religiously adhered to his decision and did not deign to convene the Assembly during the remainder of his regime.

Charles Douglas Smith's last four years as Governor were unfortunate both for himself and the people of Prince Edward Island; and, as usual, the land question triggered the trouble. The difficulty arose primarily from the failure to implement the Colonial Office decision of 1818 respecting the rigorous collection of the quit rents. Culpability rests primarily with the British Government. It was the responsibility of the British authorities either to confirm the appointment of the acting Receiver General, John E. Carmichael, or to name a new one; and even more importantly, they should have named a Deputy Receiver General in England. Their failure to make these appointments lulled the easily persuaded proprietors into believing that the quit rents would no longer be demanded. On the other hand, perhaps, Smith should have proceeded with their collection, at least on the Island, since J. E. Carmichael had the necessary authority pending either his confirmation or the appointment of a successor. It is, nevertheless, easy to excuse Smith, since his hasty actions on such collections in 1816, and the ensuing trouble must have been deeply imprinted on his mind. At any rate, the years 1819, 1820 and 1821, passed without any public demand for the payment of the quit rents being made, and thus, four more years of arrears

were allowed to accumulate. It was not until June 26, 1822, that J. E.
Carmichael notified the proprietors that his "office would be kept open for
the payment of quit rent arrears for a two-week period in July."[147] This
demand, not being peremptory, and published only in Charlottetown, was
largely ignored by the Island proprietors. In December of the same year,
Carmichael posted a more authoritative notice asserting that "quit rent
payments must be made by the fourteenth of January."[148] A number of
these were placed in Charlottetown, and several others were circulated
throughout the Island. Once again, the proprietors disregarded these orders
and Carmichael, solidly backed by Smith, decided to initiate proceedings
against them.

On January 27, 1823, proceedings were begun on the lands of two of
the principal resident proprietors, Donald MacDonald of Lot 36, and John
Stewart of Lot 37. The choice of Stewart's estate, and indeed, Carmichael's
decision to proceed with the seizures, was based, to a large extent upon
a personal vendetta between Stewart and Carmichael. Carmichael startingly
stated at a later date, "that he would never have proceeded to the strict
letter of the law on the Island respecting quit rent arrears, were it not that a
Mr. John Stewart compelled him by not only personally resisting the payment of the Quit Rent, but also made it his business to dissuade others
from coming forward, telling them they were fools if they did, and loudly
declaring in the public streets of Charlottetown that the demand was made
without any authority whatever."[149] Immediately after prosecuting distress
proceedings upon Lots 36 and 37, the officers moved to the more populous
townships in the Eastern districts of King's County, Lots 43, 45, 46 and
47, and demanded instant payment of arrears or promissory notes redeemable within ten days. The settlers were warned that the refusal to honor
their commitments would result in a sale of their stock and lands. The
inhabitants, largely Gaelic speaking Highlanders with a profound respect
for the law, rushed to Charlottetown and sold their animals and produce
at sacrificial prices to redeem their notes. Those who were either unwilling
or unable to pay were subjected to prosecution, and in February, 1823,
Carmichael obtained judgments in the Supreme Court against the small
proprietors of some 40,000 acres in King's County.[150]

These events created a furor on the Island, and John Stewart of Mount
Stewart promoted a well-organized agitation against Lieutenant Governor
Smith and John Edward Carmichael. A memorial, signed by Stewart and
some forty other leading citizens, was presented to the High Sheriff, John
McGregor, requesting him to convene meetings in Charlottetown, St. Peter's
and Princetown, in order to enable the citizenry to consider their complaints
and grievances against the Lieutenant Governor and the Receiver General

of Quit Rents.[151] When McGregor convened these meetings, contrary to the explicit orders of the Lieutenant Governor, he was summarily dismissed. The meetings were duly held, however, in March, 1823, and serious charges were formulated against Lieutenant Governor Smith. He was charged with depriving the people of their constitutional privileges and of threatening the Island with immediate financial ruin through the levying of quit rent arrears and the accompanying prosecutions.[152] A Committee comprised of John Stewart, Donald MacDonald, Paul Mabey, John McGregor, Thomas Owen, William Dockendorff and Richard Rollings was then appointed to prepare a petition requesting "the immediate removal of Charles Douglas Smith from the Island."[153] The Committee was also instructed to circulate the petition throughout the Island for signatures, and to transmit it to the King of England. The communities of the Island vied with one another in giving written support to this petition.

Lieutenant Governor Smith was placed in an extremely vulnerable position with comparatively little room for maneuvering. He decided to challenge John Stewart, hoping that his downfall would lead to a disintegration of the protest movement. He also attempted to disparage the weight the resolutions would carry at the Colonial Office. He told Lord Bathurst, for example, that the resolutions of the Queen's County meeting were moved by John Stewart and seconded by Donald MacDonald, and approved by "tenants of the two, very few of whom understood English, and were induced to attend from apprehension of being pressed about rent if they did not."[154] He sarcastically informed Bathurst "that John Stewart intended to get himself appointed minister plenipotentiary to be sent to England and he would likely cause His Majesty's Government, both here and there, all the trouble he can since he boasts of having broken [as he calls it] three governors already."[155] In order to restrain Stewart, Lieutenant Governor Smith served writs of attachment against him and the other members of the committee for gross contempt and libel against the Court of Chancery by virtue of their claim that Ambrose Lane, his son-in-law and Master in Chancery, charged exorbitant fees. John Stewart managed, much to the chagrin of Smith, to elude by some two hours, the sergeant-at-arms sent to serve the writ, and escaped to Pictou from where he sailed to England in December, 1823, with the celebrated petition.[156]

Meanwhile, the hearings of the remaining members were conducted before the Chancellor, Charles Douglas Smith. True judgments were delivered by the Chancellor against them, but alarmed by the defiant clamor in the courtroom, and the unmistakable symptoms of rebellion in the countryside, he elected to release them and to defer sentences until they were enforceable. Lieutenant Governor Smith's position gradually worsened.

He appealed to Sir James Kempt, the Lieutenant Governor and Commander of forces in Nova Scotia for military reinforcements. He informed Kempt that "John Stewart, a malignant character of very ancient notoriety in politics, had excited the discontent on the Island."[157] He stated further that the proceedings in Chancery had "stirred up the minds of the country people totally ignorant of the merits of the case and he had not the means of enforcing the law in a population little short of open rebellion."[158] He concluded with an Horatius-like assurance that he would never yield, protected by "a night sentinel posted at my door from dark to daylight."[159]

While the beleaguered Lieutenant Governor was attempting to maintain control of the Island, John Stewart and the proprietors in England were taking steps to decide his destiny. Stewart had arrived in London in January, 1824, and at an interview with Lord Bathurst, pressed the case for Smith's dismissal. He received enthusiastic support from the proprietors under the leadership of John Hill, who was described by a non-admirer "as a man as old in sin as in years."[160] The proprietors literally bombarded the Colonial Office with submissions during the months of March and April requesting that "the Lieutenant Governor and the Chief Justice be immediately dismissed, that the collection of quit rents arrears be suspended, and the sale of lands for such arrears be halted."[161] This irresistible pressure soon paid handsome dividends. In March, 1824, Lord Bathurst instructed Lieutenant Governor Smith "to cease all proceedings for the recovery of quit rents prior to January 1, 1823, and to begin no new collections beyond that date until he had received further instructions from England."[162] This order meant, in effect, that the ever-protected proprietors had been given another five-year reprieve.

Later the same month, Lord Bathurst called Colonel John Ready home from France and offered him the post of Lieutenant Governor of Prince Edward Island. Upon his acceptance, Lord Bathurst forwarded a caustically worded letter of recall to Charles Douglas Smith. He stated that "because of the personal feeling of irritation against him throughout the Island which was not only generally but universally excited, a change in government was an unavoidable measure, and the public tranquility would be compromised by his further continuation in office."[163] Bathurst, therefore, demanded "his immediate resignation" . . . but promised "a retiring allowance of £500 per annum upon his being able to afford a satisfactory vindication of his conduct against the charges preferred, not merely for acts of indiscretion, but also for those of culpable inattention to the public interest, if not of a still more unpleasant nature."[164] The indomitable Charles Douglas Smith was thus abruptly enlisted to join the crowded ranks of the discredited Island Governors.

Lieutenant Governor Smith was only slightly chastened by the turn of events. He accepted his recall with a kind of divine resignation. He assured Lord Bathurst that "in every act up to the present hour, he had no other than the purest motives, and had done nothing but what appeared at the time to be his absolute duty, and that he would not object to have the charges against him posted up at Charing Cross and fully investigated anywhere at Westminister."[165] When the ubiquitous John Stewart returned to the Island in triumph in October, 1824, bearing the new Lieutenant Governor with him, Smith, unrepentant to the last, returned to England.

In May, 1825, he formally answered the charges against him and requested "a complete vindication of his stewardship on the Island."[166] His hopes were almost fully realized. The report of the Under-Secretary, James Stephen, fully accepted by Lord Bathurst, recommended "the confirmation of Mr. Smith's pension since no act of corruption or misgovernment could be charged to him."[167] Stephen's elaboration gave an excellent insight into Smith's weakness:

It seems to me that the charges of corruption, oppression and insolence are satisfactorily repelled, but that he was guilty of indolence and of an implicit and heedless confidence in the various family connections whom he placed in situations of trust. It is manifest also that he was very poor or very penurious, or both, and consequently very unpopular. From his own narrative also, I infer that when he became angry he made use of rude and vulgar language, and that it was not difficult to make him angry.[168]

It would seem that Charles Douglas Smith was fortunate to have received such an exoneration. While it is easy to agree that the charge of corruption was unjustifiable, it is more difficult to erase a very obvious record of oppression and insolence. While he must be respected for his honorable attempts to force the proprietors to honor their obligations, his tyrannical methods leave, unfortunately, a rather blemished memory.

Chapter Four

The Demise of Quit Rents and Escheat, 1824-1842

By F. W. P. BOLGER

I THE END OF QUIT RENTS, 1824-1831

Colonel John Ready, the incumbent Lieutenant Governor of the Island from 1824 until 1831, was the complete antithesis of his predecessor. Gentle and genial in demeanor, with no entrenched views on controversial issues, he always managed to steer an acceptable course among the various contending groups suggesting solutions to the Island's land question. He ingratiated himself with the people of the Island by visiting all parts of it on several occasions; these tours enabled him to understand and appreciate the conditions and needs of the people. He gave a new direction to agriculture, which, he insisted, should be the staple industry of the island. He imported registered stock from Europe, established Agricultural Associations, and gave to agriculture place a priority that it has never lost. He rendered these dedicated services despite a sad personal life occasioned by the death of his wife in Brighton, England, in 1825, and that of his eldest daughter in Charlottetown, in 1827. The British Government made an admirable decision in choosing him to restore some semblance of harmony to an embittered Island.

The new Lieutenant Governor was under no illusions regarding the complexity of the issue that had bedevilled his predecessor. Thus, shortly prior to his departure for the Island he asked the Colonial Office authorities for a positive statement on quit rent policy. He was informed that "the levying of the quit rents must be carried out without oppression, but that they must be enforced, and due notice given that the Receiver General is positively instructed to enforce them."[1] Some credibility seemed to be associated with this instruction, since a few days previous, the Treasury Department had appointed Charles James Briscoe as the new Receiver General. He arrived on Prince Edward Island in early August, 1824, with definitive orders to render the quit rent collection operative. It bespeaks the seriousness with which Briscoe regarded his role, that a few days after being sworn into office by C. D. Smith, he took an additional position as custom's officer at St. Andrew's, New Brunswick, and made his home there.

Shortly after his arrival on the Island, Colonel Ready dissolved the House of Assembly that had not been convened since 1820, and issued writs for a November general election. The membership of the new House which met in January, 1825, was not substantially different from the previous Assembly. The one notable change was the return of John Stewart to the Assembly after an absence of nearly twenty-five years. The respect which he now enjoyed because of the role he had played in securing the dismissal of C. D. Smith was revealed in the Assembly's choice of a Speaker. In the contest for the position, he defeated by a vote of twelve to four Dr. Angus McAulay, the popular and very competent Speaker of the last two Houses. It was evident that the political influence of the *Cabal* was still a dominant force in the political life of the Island. The Assembly, which remained in session for over two months, spent much of its time assessing the land tenure question on Prince Edward Island. A few days prior to prorogation, the Assembly prepared an Address to the Crown which represented a new stance on the part of the elected representatives. This Address requested that "His Majesty direct that the Quit Rents payable on lands on the Island be remitted until the payment of the same was enforced in the neighboring Colonies; and also that His Majesty allow an assessment to be raised on land in lieu thereof, for the purpose of erecting a Government House, other public buildings, and other Colonial improvements within the Island."[2] This request impelled the Colonial Office to review the situation on the Island.

The British authorities were not yet prepared to relinquish the collection of the quit rents. A fresh set of instructions was sent to C. J. Briscoe ordering him to enforce rigorously all quit rents due since January, 1823. He was also instructed either to reside permanently on the Island, "or to appoint a deputy to reside there, and to select a deputy in England to receive rents from proprietors who had the option of paying in that country."[3] It seemed at the moment that the British Government was determined to make the proprietors honor their obligations. The reality, however, was quite different indeed; the simple truth was that the Receiver General could not be found. Some eighteen months later, Lieutenant Governor Ready reported to the Colonial Office that "Briscoe still had not communicated with him and no one had been able to locate him."[4] The Colonial Office fired Briscoe in May, 1828, and authorized Lieutenant Governor Ready to appoint a quit rent collector *pro tempore*.[5] Ready immediately appointed John Stewart who had held the position from 1790 until 1804.

The appointment of John Stewart to the office brought the quit rent question once again to the fore. He presented a position paper to Lieutenant Governor Ready in which he argued that proprietors both large and small would bitterly resent the payment of quit rents unless they were also collected in Nova Scotia. He declared that the five years' arrears to be collected [1823-1828] would amount to some £10,000, and that not even one-third of that amount could be found on the Island. He maintained that such a demand "in the depressed state of the Island would result in a most cruel sacrifice of property."[6] Lieutenant Governor Ready was so impressed with Stewart's arguments that he ordered him to refrain from quit rent collections until he had communicated with the authorities at the Colonial Office. In his submission to the Colonial Office, Ready substantiated John Stewart's contentions and pleaded for the remission that Stewart had requested. Their pleas were substantially buttressed by a petition from the citizenry of the Island which Ready forwarded to the British Government in November, 1828. The burden of their petition was that "the people of Nova Scotia had been granted indulgence after indulgence in the payment of quit rents, and, therefore, the Island people, who were in a state of extreme poverty, should receive similar treatment."[7] The new Colonial Secretary, Sir George Murray, agreed to comply partially with these requests. He decreed that "the quit rents due from the inhabitants of Prince Edward Island and from all other proprietors prior to January 1, 1827, should be remitted."[8] Thus, the proprietors had been given another four-year reprieve. But this concession apparently represented the limits of the indulgence, since Murray also ordered that the quit rents must be rigorously collected in the future.

The 23,266 inhabitants of the Island, through their elected representatives, revealed that they were by no means satisfied with these piecemeal concessions. In the 1830 session of the Legislature, the members decided to challenge the British Government by the passage of a Land Assessment Act. This measure imposed an annual tax of two shillings per one hundred acres of land on the Island for a five-year period. During the duration of the Act, "one thousand pounds was to be appropriated annually for the defrayal of the expenses in erecting a residence for the Lieutenant Governor and the building of a Central Academy in Charlottetown, and the surplus was to be applied to the construction of jails in the three Counties and other public buildings."[9] A proviso was cleverly attached to the Bill suspending its operation until "it was ascertained whether His Majesty's Government would relinquish its claims to the quit rents during the operation of the Act."[10]

The members of the Legislature also forwarded an Address to the King which elaborated upon the motives that had led them reluctantly to pass this measure. "The revenue of the Island, wholly derived from import duties," the Address asserted, "always insufficient for the growing wants of the Colony, was of late decreasing, while objects of the highest import- ance to its welfare were continually demanding the pecuniary aid of the Legislature."[11] "These factors," the Address continued, "compelled the Legislature to devise other means of providing for the numerous calls upon the Treasury of the Island."[12] Among the most imperative of these demands was "the provision of a residence suitable to the high station of Lieutenant Governor, and the building of a Central Academy for the education of the youth."[13] The Address pointed out that "although the Act was necessary and beneficial, the proviso had to be added that assessment would not become operative so long as His Majesty's Government intended to collect the quit rents, because ruinous distress would be entailed upon all classes of the com- munity if both were enforced at the same time."[14] The petition concluded with "an appeal to His Majesty for the relinquishment of the Quit Rents payable from Prince Edward Island."[15]

The appeal of the Island Legislature was sympathetically received by the Colonial Office authorities. A Minute, prepared by James Stephen, the senior Under-Secretary, advocated that the British Government should abandon quit rent collection. "If the government," he logically argued, "for a series of years abstains from enforcing claims of this description, the parties liable to them acquire an equitable right to exemption, and nothing can be more prejudicial to the natural improvement than that it should be overhung by a perpetually increasing charge never enforced, but never remitted."[16] "The best course," he suggested, "would be to give up the quit rents and to obtain in return some grants of money from the Legislature applicable to public purposes."[17] The Colonial Secretary, Viscount Gode- rich, accepted the advice of his senior departmental assistant, and announced on August 1, 1832, that the British Government had confirmed the Land Assessment Act and was prepared to relinquish the collection of quit rents for a period of five years. He wrote to the Island's Lieutenant Governor that "an assessment on all lands, provided it was of a moderate amount, seemed an unobjectionable mode of raising revenue."[18] "For if the rate of assess- ment," he contended, "be such as to fall lightly on the lands under improve- ment, there is no unfairness in the additional weight with which it must fall on uncultivated lands."[19] Goderich escaped from the absentee pro- prietors' wrath on this occasion but his successors were not destined to be so fortunate. The Islanders implemented this legislation immediately, and by 1835, two magnificent structures, Government House and a Central Academy, graced the city of Charlottetown.

It is ironic indeed that on the first occasion when an understanding and sympathetic Colonial Secretary, complemented by an equally competent and discerning Lieutenant Governor, were moving towards the solution of some of the basic problems created by the land tenure question, that the Legislature and the people of the Island were absolutely unresponsive. By 1831 the demise of quit rent collection was not considered an adequate remedy since the whole thrust of the people of the Island was toward escheat. It was fortunate that Lieutenant Governor Ready was spared the ordeal of coping with this question. As it turned out, his period of office terminated just as the people of the Island began to apply pressure for the establishment of a Court of Escheat. As early as June, 1830, Colonel Ready had reminded the Colonial Secretary that he had been "six years on the Island and was prepared to resign."[20] Sir George Murray would not consider his offer of resignation, but rather renewed his Commission. In March, 1831, however, after some additional prodding from Ready, the British Government relieved him of his position and appointed a successor. It must have been a great consolation to Colonel Ready to realize that he had so successfully administered the affairs of the Island that he was the first Governor to avoid either dismissal or recall from office because of the dissatisfaction on the part of either the Islanders or the non-resident proprietors or both.

II   ESCHEAT AT CENTER STAGE, 1831-1837

The Legislative Assembly that sat between the years 1830 and 1834 ushered in a new era in the political and social history of the Island. The first reason that accounted for the new politics was the change in character and complexion of the House occasioned by the enfranchisement of the Roman Catholics in 1830. These citizens, a large portion of whom belonged to the tenant class, cast their ballots almost exclusively for candidates who were sympathetic to tenant demands. In the autumn election of 1830, twelve of eighteen members, five of whom were Catholics, were elected for the first time, and the remaining six were re-elected because they had championed tenant claims in previous sessions and promised to continue this advocacy.[21] The second reason accounting for the change in direction in Island politics was the election of William Cooper in a by-election in July, 1831.[22] Cooper, a resident farmer of some one hundred acres of land in Sailor's Hope, King's County, had formerly been a land agent for Lord James Townshend, the proprietor of Lot 56. After a series of misunderstandings with Lord Townshend, he resigned his position and became the tribune of the struggling tenantry. He was destined to become *Mr. Escheat,* and to be the bane of proprietary interests for the next thirty years. It was, perhaps, more than symbolic that a riot at St. Peter's during the by-election

William Cooper

had forced the Returning Officer to close the poll several hours prior to the termination of the voting, and that the controversial William Cooper should have first been declared an elected member of the House of Assembly by the casting vote of the Speaker after an investigation of several days by a Committee on Privileges and Elections.[23] The stage was now set for the escheat agitation of the 1830's, under the leadership of the imaginative, talented and provocative William Cooper.

The first step in this direction took place in the 1832 session of the Legislature with the appointment of a special Committee of the House of Assembly empowered to investigate the number of townships liable to escheat for the non-fulfillment of the conditions of the original grants. After a thorough enquiry, George R. Dalrymple moved and William Cooper seconded with impassioned speeches, that an Act should be passed regulating the procedure for a Court of Escheat, and that an Address should be presented to the Lieutenant Governor asking him to establish such a Court.[24] The presentation of the Bill with the accompanying Address introduced the new Lieutenant Governor, Aretas William Young, to the burning issue on Prince Edward Island. Lieutenant Governor Young had enjoyed a brilliant military career of some thirty years prior to his appointment on the Island. He retired from the army as a Lieutenant Colonel in 1826, and after five years in a civilian role in the Caribbean, assumed his duties in Charlottetown. He resembled his predecessor in the attitude he adopted on the land question and other issues. He always attempted to be a conciliator, and to play the role of an intermediary between the warring factions. He was, however, much less imaginative than Colonel Ready and really quite timorous. These characteristics made it extremely difficult for him to cope with the demands of an Assembly becoming more and more vocal with each passing day. Thus, when he was presented with the Assembly petition, he waffled. He gave assent to the measure for the establishment of a Court of Escheat, but at the same time informed the Assembly that he would not implement it until he had received precise instructions from the Colonial Office on its attitude to the establishment of such a Court.[25]

Although Viscount Goderich had been quite cooperative on the relinquishment of quit rents, he was not similarly inclined regarding the establishment of a Court of Escheat. In his formal despatch to Lieutenant Governor Young, ruling out the formation of such a Court, he insisted that while the escheat of proprietary lands because they were not settled in the proportion of one person to every two hundred acres might be enough to justify forfeiture under the *letter* of the grants, nevertheless, it was not a fair and equitable ground for proceedings.[26] He said that he "was assured that some proprietors had sent out more than the number of persons required for the settlement of their property in the prescribed proportions, but that these persons had subsequently changed their residences to other lands."[27] "These proprietors would forfeit their grants," he argued, "while other proprietors who made no effort to fulfill their conditions of settlement would escape under the proceedings contemplated by the Assembly."[28] "Since the proposal could not be followed without great injustice," Goderich concluded, "His Majesty's government could not sanction the establishment of a Court of Escheat."[29] The Assembly was not persuaded by the arguments presented by Viscount Goderich, and, in 1833, the members prepared an Address for presentation to the King. The Address asserted "that Viscount Goderich had been misled at the Colonial Office and that with the exception of one or two individuals, none of the proprietors ever brought out settlers who later moved to other lots."[30] The Address concluded with the request that "His Majesty overrule the decision of the Colonial Office and direct that a Court of Escheat, similar to those which have been found so beneficial in the other colonies, be established on Prince Edward Island agreeable to the Act lately passed for that purpose."[31] The Assembly never hesitated to play a broken record over and over again.

The Assembly also formulated plans in addition to escheat to embarrass the proprietary cause. In November, 1832, Viscount Goderich had informed the Legislature "that whenever the financial condition of the colony was such as to enable them to make a moderate but permanent provision for the necessary expenses of Government, he would not hesitate to advise His Majesty to give assent to any act placing the whole revenue of the Island at the disposal of the Legislature."[32] The Assembly, astutely recognizing the potentialities of financial control for the settlement of the land tenure problem, passed a Bill in the 1833 Session which rather deviously implemented the suggestion of Viscount Goderich. This Bill, which was not to become operative until the expiry of the existing Land Assessment Act in 1837, made provision for the civil establishment of the colony by the imposition of a new assessment. It levied an assessment of four shillings and six pence on each one hundred acres of land in the country, two shillings upon each lot in Charlottetown, and one shilling and four pence on lots in Georgetown and Princetown. It also made provision for the forfeiture and sale of the lots if these assessments were not honored.[33]

During the debate that preceded the passage of this Act, many members declared openly that they regarded the measure as an alternative to escheat. Joseph Pope, a prominent merchant and shipbuilder from Bedeque, who was soon to be a leading member of the Assembly, "advocated the imposition of such a land tax since it would amount to a virtual escheat";[34] and Daniel Brenan maintained that the bill should be passed immediately since "at least three-fourths of the cost of the civil establishment would be borne by the absent proprietors."[35] The Attorney General, Robert Hodgson, in forwarding the Act to the Colonial Office, observed that the House of Assembly, "in addition to the desire to have sole control of all revenue, had another motive in imposing the support of the civil Government on the land, namely, to oblige the large proprietors to dispose of their wilderness lands."[36] He also pointed out that "the excitement at present existing and pervading all the farming class of inhabitants in the Colony against the large proprietors rendered the present Act a very popular one, and the small proprietors or freeholders and tenantry will cheerfully pay this tax, as appears by the unanimous declarations of various public meetings held throughout the country to consider the expediency of the Land Assessment Act."[37] Lieutenant Governor Young opined that "since the majority of the proprietors would not be inclined to pay so large a tax on wilderness land, the new bill would encourage them either to sell their lands or render them productive, and thus the settlement of the Island would be greatly facilitated."[38] Despite the high expectation of the Assembly and Lieutenant Governor Young, proprietary interests guaranteed the maintenance of the *status quo*.

Shortly after the arrival of the proposed legislation in England, a heavy proprietary lobby was launched. The influential proprietors of the 1830's, Lord Melville, the Earl of Selkirk, Sir George Seymour, David Stewart and his brother Robert Bruce, and the immortal John Hill addressed strongly worded memorials to the Colonial Secretary. The burden of their presentations was that the projected tax corresponded, in reality, to a thinly veiled escheat. They unblushingly claimed that the vast majority of the Island's 32,392 inhabitants "were taken there at the expense of the proprietors, or induced to settle there in consequence of the encouragement of the resident and absent large proprietors, very many of whom expended large sums, and none of whom have, as yet, received any, or very adequate returns."[39] They insisted that the projected revenue from the taxation "would not produce a revenue adequate to support the present civil establishment since almost one-tenth of the Island could not pay a tax of even two shillings per hundred acres."[40] They also maintained that "many people on the Island were opposed to the measure but were without a legislative voice because the electors there, due to the low qualifications, kept all the proprietors and their agents out of the Legislature."[41] It was, perhaps, this kind of pessimism that led John Hill to declare that "the British constitution in miniature is the damnd'st bore upon earth."[42]

The new Colonial Secretary, E. G. Stanley, indubitably influenced by the proprietary barrage, informed Lieutenant Governor Young in May, 1834, of the disallowance of the Civil Establishment Act. He based his principal objection to the Act on the fact "that there was more than ordinary ground to doubt the productivity of the tax."[43] "Independently of the difficulties and expense of collection," he contended "the avowed intention and expected effect is to bring large masses of land under escheat for non-payment, and although provision is made for selling the land, the effect of pouring so large a portion of land into a market already overstocked would be to reduce the price so far as to render it impossible to find purchasers and in that case, the Civil Government is left unprovided for."[44] Although Stanley did not see fit to recommend this particular Act, he did recognize a principle which was destined to be of far-reaching significance. He stated that he was "of the opinion that a tax [if moderate and reasonable] in the nature of a penal assessment upon non-cultivation, was under the circumstances of Prince Edward Island, a measure at once just and politic."[45] The statutes of Prince Edward Island for the next thirty years provide ample testimony to the implementation of this principle.

The refusal of the British Government either to sanction a Court of Escheat or to grant the Civil List created a chorus of protest in the newly elected House of Assembly and in the country at large. The election of December, 1834, witnessed the return of a number of representatives who had pledged themselves to radical action on the land question. William Cooper, Daniel Brenan, John LeLacheur, Peter McCallum, George Dalrymple, John Ramsay, William Clarke and Charles Binns formed the nucleus of what would eventually be called the "Escheat Party."[46] With William Cooper as its leader, this party dominated Island politics until 1842. An important ingredient of Cooper's plan of action to impress the British authorities with the seriousness of proprietary negligence and oppression was the organization of public protest meetings throughout the Island. The centre of this radical activity was King's County, where Cooper's influence was greatest, but it gradually spread to other parts of the province.

In the 1835 session of the Assembly, Daniel Brenan, one of the four representatives from King's County, presented "a petition with signatures measuring fourteen feet in length, setting forth the injury the country had sustained in consequence of the non-fulfillment of the conditions of the original grants, and requesting the establishment of a court of escheat."[47] The petition was referred to a Select Committee of the House which was authorized to make a study of the whole question of escheat. The ultimate result was another Address from the Assembly which maintained that "only the establishment of a Court of Escheat would solve the land question on the Island."[48] Lieutenant Governor Young, in ill health and embarrassed by still another petition on escheat, neglected to forward the Address to England. His death, in December, 1835, spared him from experiencing the wrath of the Assembly when it learned that the Address had not been transmitted. Sir A. W. Young had been a prudent and able administrator and, in addition, had always shown a deep concern for the plight of the tenantry. In reporting the results of the trial of some tenants who had resisted the payment of rents at Naufrage, it is typical of his sympathy that he should have commented "that under all the circumstances of the unfortunate peoples' situation, they have shown more forbearance and temper than could have been expected."[49] The tenants had a friend in Lieutenant Governor Young and they deeply regretted his death.

His successor, Sir John Harvey, who arrived on the Island in August, 1836, was a complete antithesis in temperament and character. Supremely self-confident, he was determined to govern the Island with the same brilliancy and competency that had characterized his military career. His announced mission was to conduct an active crusade to settle the land question on the Island and then move to some other jurisdiction with larger challenges. Harvey's baptismal fire came with the arrival of Lord Glenelg's answer to the 1835 and 1836 Addresses of the House of Assembly on escheat. Glenelg's views were identical to those adopted by his two predecessors. He stated that "before His Majesty's Government could be party to any forfeiture they would require to be satisfied not only that there were not at the present moment, but that there had not been at any time, the stipulated number of settlers on that estate, and that this circumstance had arisen from the willful neglect of the proprietors."[50] He emphasized that "such an inquiry could scarcely now be undertaken with any success — that it would be tedious and expensive in its process, and that it would tend to alarm the public mind without holding out any prospect of a useful result."[51] He dampened the aspirations of the tenants still further by asserting "that even should there be a forfeiture, the Crown would step exactly into the place of the former proprietor, enforce the observance of the contract, and under no circumstances would gratuitous grants of land be conceded to any persons whatever."[52] Lieutenant Governor Harvey informed Lord Glenelg that he had decided, after consultation with the Speaker of the Assembly, "to publish the despatch in the *Royal Gazette* as this was the quickest and most certain mode of communicating it to the members of the House of Assembly and their constituents with a view to relieving the anxiety so generally felt on the subject."[53] He expressed a high degree of satisfaction with its contents and had no doubts but that it would have the desired effect of putting an end to the excitement which has never ceased to prevail on the subject of escheat. The reaction of the Island tenantry during the next few months revealed the naiveté of Sir John Harvey's premature judgment.

Once again, King's County was the centre of resistance, with William Cooper serving as principal organizer and spokesman. This opposition reached its climax at a meeting on December 20, 1836, at Hay River in the northern part of the county, where a petition to the King embracing some thirty-four resolutions was unanimously adopted. This gathering, attended by over seven hundred tenants, was presided over by three representatives of the Assembly from the county, namely William Cooper, John MacKintosh and John LeLacheur. The provocatively worded petition repeated the demand for a Court of Escheat, and asserted that such a Court had not been sanctioned "because of misrepresentations from a combination of land monopolists in England who have not complied with the original conditions of their grants."[54] The concluding three resolutions, which Sir John Harvey termed treasonable, maintained that the tenants on the Island "were victims of fraud, deceit and oppression on the part of the land monopolists, and this was wickedness in the sight of God, derogatory to the honor of King and the British Nation, subversive to the sacred right of property, and to pay rent longer to landlords was to foster oppression and reward crime."[55] An agrarian movement, advocating the withholding of rents and resistance to the exercise of proprietorial authority, represented the greatest challenge to the proprietary system since its inception in 1767.

Lieutenant Governor Harvey was understandably both disappointed and exercised by the Hay River proceedings. When the House of Assembly met in January, 1837, he tabled the Hay River documents and appealed to the members to concur with him "in reprobating the dangerous, illegal and unconstitutional character of the resolutions wherein the deluded tenantry were encouraged by three elected representatives to forcibly resist the legal measures a landlord might adopt for the recovery of his rights."[56] When Cooper, LeLacheur and MacKintosh refused to make apologies acceptable to the House of Assembly, they were committed to the custody of the Sergeant-at-Arms for the remainder of the session.[57] Lieutenant Governor Harvey was absolutely ecstatic. He informed Lord Glenelg that his despatch ruling out escheat, coupled with the prompt and unequivocal action of the House of Assembly on the Hay River proceedings, extinguished, and forever, the question of escheat by which the minds of so many of the inhabitants of the Island had been so long excited and disturbed.[58]

Colonel Harvey also sent a circular letter to the proprietors in England, informing them that escheat would never again rear its ugly head if they would reciprocate by granting long leases, by agreeing to receive their rent in agricultural produce, and by remitting all arrears of rent from those tenants who were absolutely incapable of paying such arrears.[59] While still in the letter-writing mood, he sent an epistle to James Stephen at the Colonial

Office heaping lavish praise upon himself and his regime. He emphasized that "as a result of his salutary influence, he had been enabled to effect the great object upon which he had set his heart upon his first arrival on the Island, viz., the settlement of escheat forever, the public and unequivocal recognition of the rights of the proprietors and the disabusal of the minds of the deluded peasantry on escheat."[60] He concluded with the request that the British Government recognize his capabilities and "transfer him to a more extensive and important field."[61] Apparently he convinced the British Government that his eminent talents warranted a wider field for their exercise, because he was informed by return mail of his transfer to New Brunswick as Lieutenant Governor of that Colony.[62]

It is unfortunate that Sir John Harvey's transfer was not effective immediately so that he could have remained in his world of fantasy. While awaiting the arrival of his successor, he was shocked back into reality by the reception of an Address presented by a tenant delegation representing different parts of the Island. Their Address to the King demanded " a general escheat of all lands upon which the original conditions of settlement had not been fulfilled;"[63] and the accompanying petition to Lieutenant Governor Harvey requested the dissolution of the Assembly "since it had failed to sponsor escheat in the last Session."[64] Although Harvey refused to comply with the petition, he seemed to realize that, perhaps, escheat was the only viable solution. In May, 1837, he suggested to Lord Glenelg that "a limited Court of Escheat should be established."[65] He claimed that "although only four of five lots were liable to escheat, yet, if the Governor had power to establish such a Court, it would have the effect of at once tranquillizing the minds of the people, and it was, perhaps, the only measure that could have that effect."[66] He concluded with a plea "that the British Government not consider him inconsistent in his sudden advocacy of a Court of Escheat."[67] It must have been galling indeed for Sir John Harvey to admit that he had not after all solved the land tenure question on the Island.

III   *WILLIAM COOPER'S LAST STAND*

Sir Charles Augustus FitzRoy, who assumed the reins of power in June, 1837, became heir to an unenviable legacy on the Island. Shortly after his arrival, he reported to the Colonial Office that "the Escheat Question still continued to cause considerable excitement on various parts of the Island, and that the agitation on the question, instead of having subsided [as Harvey had led us to believe] had latterly gained in strength."[68] At the other extreme of the scale, he stated that he had found the proprietors in a state of ferment, occasioned largely by the passage of another Land Assessment Act in the previous session of the Legislature. This Act had imposed a penal tax of four shillings per one hundred acres on wilderness or unsettled lands, while sustaining the old rate of two shillings per one hundred acres on cultivated or settled lands.[69] The proprietors claimed that this assessment was discriminatory, unwarranted and subversive to the sacred rights of property. FitzRoy, a victim of this polarization during the whole of his incumbency, attempted valiantly to steer a middle course and to find acceptable common ground between the two extremes. On the one hand, he consistently tried to persuade "the deluded tenantry" to cease their agitation for escheat and to withdraw their support from their leader, William Cooper, whom he contemptuously described "as an artful person although very illiterate, possessed of much low cunning and perfectly unscrupulous in making any assertion to serve his purpose."[70] On the other hand, he resolved that he would never "consent to be a mere tool of the proprietors who, from the language they occasionally use, appear to think the Lieutenant Governor is placed here solely to watch over their peculiar interests without any reference to the general welfare of the inhabitants."[71] As in the case of most of the governors, however, the obligation to uphold the rule of law and the rights of public property made FitzRoy more and more the champion of proprietary rights than the protector of the aspirations of the struggling tenantry.

Lieutenant Governor FitzRoy spent his first few months in office visiting the principal areas of settlement on the Island, and as a result of his observations and inquiries, he addressed a strongly worded circular to the proprietors, in which he advocated the granting of important concessions to the tenantry, with a view to allaying the widespread agitation for escheat. He insisted that their failure to grant their tenantry "such terms as they were fully and fairly entitled to, went a long way to account for, if not to palliate the line of conduct pursued by them."[72] "It ought not to be a matter of surprise," FitzRoy pointed out, "that although a tenant may be ready and willing to pay a fair equivalent in rent or otherwise for the land he occupies, that he should feel dismayed at the prospect of being deprived of the hard-earned fruits of the labour of the earliest and best years of his manhood, whether from the accumulation of heavy arrears of rent, which he has been unable to realize from the land, or from the failure of the proprietor to grant him a tenure of sufficient endurance to ensure to his family the profits of his industry."[73]

FitzRoy, like Colonel Harvey, recommended as a solution that the proprietors should give discretionary power to their agents to relieve the tenants of their arrears of rent, in cases where it was impossible that they could ever pay them; that they should grant long leases at the rate customary in the colony, the rent to be payable in the productions of the soil at the market prices; and, in cases where long leases were not acceptable, to allow the tenants to purchase their property, or at least, to grant them a fair evaluation for their improvements at the expiration of their leases.[74] These valid observations by FitzRoy earned him the unbridled wrath of the proprietors. "I deny the right," Lord Selkirk's agent wrote to Glenelg, "and I more doubt the policy or expediency of a Governor of a Colony interfering with the management of private property in the manner adopted by FitzRoy."[75] The proprietors then girded their loins for a determined defense of their threatened stronghold.

For openers, they addressed a memorial to the Colonial Secretary protesting against Royal Assent being given to the 1837 Land Assessment Act, and demanding that they be given an opportunity of presenting their objections before the judicial committee of the Privy Council. The memorial, signed by Robert Bruce Stewart on behalf of the non-resident proprietors, contended that the proposed scheme of taxation "was a flagrant act of partiality and injustice, and an unprovoked attack upon the sacred rights of property, tending to render the lands of the proprietors valueless, and, in short, intended by its framers to penalize the proprietors for not being able to perform impossibilities."[76] The Colonial Secretary forwarded a copy of this memorial to Lieutenant Governor FitzRoy, and requested that he refer it to the Legislature for a reply to the serious allegations made by the proprietors.

A Joint Committee of the Legislative Assembly and Council, consisting among others of T. H. Haviland, Robert Hodgson, Joseph Pope, John Brecken and Edward Palmer, after considering the proprietary remonstrance in the 1838 session of the Legislature, prepared an able and elaborate report in justification of the Land Assessment Act. The Committee emphasized that "the failure of the majority of the proprietors either to sell or lease their lands on acceptable terms, and the opposition they had always given to the public measures connected with the best interests of the resident population by interposing between the local Legislature and the Crown, necessitated the passage of penal legislation."[77] It pointed out that out of a total expenditure of £107,645 during the past twelve years, the non-resident proprietors had contributed less than £5,000, thereby leaving a balance of over £100,000 to be borne by the people resident on the Island.[78] They concluded the report with an appeal that Royal Assent be given to this Act which would have the effect of redressing, to some degree at least, the injustice of the proprietary land tenure system.[79] Lieutenant Governor FitzRoy heartily endorsed the report of the Committee in a private letter to the Colonial Secretary. He maintained that the report "so fully answered the objections of the proprietors to the Land Assessment Act, that the Act should be implemented as a substitute for a Court of Escheat."[80]

The authorities at the Colonial Office continued to temporize on the question. At length, Lord Glenelg decided to forward a copy of the report, along with another document bearing on the question of escheat, to Lord Durham at Quebec for the purpose of obtaining his views on the subject. Lord Durham addressed himself to this question with the despatch and candor that characterized all his investigations in British North America. For his guidance, he arranged a series of interviews with a delegation from the Island consisting of Sir Charles FitzRoy, John W. LeLacheur, Robert Hodgson, George Wright, Thomas H. Haviland, John Lawson and George A. Goodman. All these gentlemen decried the evils of the Island's proprietary land tenure system, which had allowed the proprietors since 1767 to ignore their obligations, and recommended the implementation of the Land Assessment Act as an important first step towards its solution.[81]

Lord Durham's official reply to Lord Glenelg was a severe castigation of the British Government for introducing the proprietary system, and for abetting proprietary influence in its continuation. "The extreme improvidence — I might say the reckless profusion — which dictated these grants is obvious," he wrote, "and the total neglect of the government as to enforcing the conditions of the grants is not less so."[82] "The absent proprietors," he charged, "neither improve the land themselves, nor will let others improve it. They retain the land and keep it in a state of wilderness, and your Lordship can hardly conceive the degree of injury inflicted on a new settlement hemmed in by wilderness land, which has been placed out of control of government, and is entirely neglected by its absent proprietors."[83] "Although the people, their representative Assembly, the Legislative Council, and the Governor have cordially concurred in a remedy," he continued, "some influence — it cannot be that of equity or reason — has steadily counteracted the measures of the Colonial Legislature, and I cannot imagine it is any other influence than that of the absentee proprietors in England."[84] "In order that this influence shall no longer prevail against the deliberate acts of the Colonial Legislature, and the unequivocal complaints of the suffering colonists, my decided opinion is," wrote Lord Durham, "that the royal assent should no longer be withheld from the Act of the Colonial Legislature."[85] These categorical views expressed by Lord Durham led to the immediate confirmation of the Land Assessment Act by the British Privy Council on December 12, 1838.

While heartily recommending the confirmation of the Land Assessment Act as a temporary expedient, Lord Durham doubted whether "this

Act would prove a sufficient remedy for the evil in question."[86] This astute observation was certainly borne out by the course of events in Prince Edward Island in the next four years. In the general election of November, 1838, William Cooper and his Escheat Party reached the apogee of their power, winning eighteen of twenty-four seats;[87] and when the newly elected Assembly convened in January, 1839, William Cooper was elevated to the position of Speaker by a vote of sixteen to six.[88] Leading an overwhelming majority in the Assembly, Cooper arranged the passage of another Escheat Act, providing for the forfeiture of all lands that had not been settled by the proprietors since 1816. When the "establishment", strongly represented in the Legislative Council by proprietors and their agents, rejected this measure, Cooper was promptly appointed as a delegate of the Assembly to proceed to London "to represent to Her Majesty's Government the interests and sentiments of the inhabitants and to support these views before Her Majesty, and, if necessary, before the Imperial Parliament."[89]

William Cooper's mission could scarcely be termed a success. The Colonial Secretary, Lord John Russell, not only declined to grant him the courtesy of an audience repeatedly requested during his three month sojourn in England, but he also communicated his reply to Cooper's proposition directly to the Lieutenant Governor of the Island. Lord John Russell informed FitzRoy that the Colonial Office, in accordance with its settled policy, rejected categorically the Assembly's request for a Court of Escheat.[90] In the same despatch, he spurned two suggestions made by FitzRoy for the settlement of the land question, namely, the resumption by the Crown of the proprietary lands, and a heavier penal tax on wilderness lands. Russell stated that he did not feel at liberty to recommend an advance of £200,000 from the Treasury to purchase the proprietary lands, and he maintained that he could not recommend a heavier penal tax so soon after the imposition of a tax of the same description, and until it could be clearly demonstrated that no adequate remedy was to be expected from that tax.[91] Thus as the year 1839 drew to a close, Cooper and his Escheaters and Lieutenant Governor FitzRoy were all back to square one.

The failure of the Cooper mission to England was such a severe blow to the hopes of the Escheaters that it really sounded the death knell of their party. In the 1840 session of the Assembly, Cooper and his adherents attempted a different approach through the passage of an Act authorizing the Crown to purchase the estates of the proprietors who had not honored the conditions of their grants, and to resell them to the tenants occupying these lands.[92] The promoters of the Bill tried to popularize the measure with British officials by admitting in the preamble "that the Assembly now realized that a Court of Escheat would never be established on the Island."[93]

But the Escheat Party met with nothing but rebuffs in its attempt to accomplish this slightly veiled alternative to escheat. The Legislative Council, while admitting its approval of the principle of the Bill, would not concur in giving assent until the proprietors and the Crown had agreed to such legislation. But it was Lieutenant Governor FitzRoy's attitude that completely frustrated all hopes of sympathetic consideration at the Colonial Office.

By 1840 FitzRoy could no longer abide William Cooper and his Escheaters, and he began to lean more and more to the side of the proprietors and their supporters. He described the Bill to the Colonial Secretary "as an expiring effort on the part of the majority of the House of Assembly to revive their waning popularity with their constituents, and to shift the odium which the abandonment of their escheat principles had occasioned, to the Council."[94] He recommended that the British Government should continue to pursue its firm course and reject this measure "which was an infringement of private rights;"[95] and, he opined, that if his recommendations were complied with "the struggle of the tenantry against the proprietors would altogether cease, and becoming alive to their interests, and the utter incapacity of their representatives, they will before the close of another session become anxious for a dissolution."[96] Sir Charles FitzRoy's prognosis was not too far off the mark, William Cooper's failure to make any appreciable impact at the Colonial Office was a fairly clear signal to the tenantry that the solution of the land question lay with the British Government, and, *a fortiori,* the influential proprietors, rather than with themselves. The Colonial Office's reply to FitzRoy's recommendations on the Assembly's proposed legislation was a further demonstration that the tenantry was at the mercy of the law and their landlords.

In his official despatch, Lord John Russell made absolutely no comments on the Act passed by the Assembly, but simply expressed "regret that the question of the lands on Prince Edward Island still continued to disturb the peace of the Colony."[97] "Altho' this question originates in motives of private interests shared equally by landlords and tenants," he added, "it assumes, in effect, the character of a public question, and as such must be treated."[98] In a further attempt to solve this public question, Russell stated that he intended "to enter into communications with the Resident Proprietors in England to learn whether they had any further propositions to determine the problem which had, for so long a period, agitated the colony."[99] Although Russell had expressed a distinct preference for a proprietary solution, the House of Assembly made capital out of his remark that the land question was "a public question, and as such must be treated."[100]

Thus, in the 1841 session of the Legislature, the Escheat Party once again addressed itself vigorously to the problem. Since the Colonial Secretary had not ruled out the Land Purchase Act passed in the last session, it was introduced again and received the same negative treatment from the Legislative Council. In addition, the members of the Assembly prepared an Address to the Queen embracing eighteen resolutions condemnatory of the policies of the proprietors, the British Government, and especially of the Island's Executive and Legislative Councils which, they maintained, were largely dominated by a few closely related Charlottetown families with proprietary connections.[101] As a final parting shot, the Assembly noted "that since the question of lands is to be henceforth a public question, it is expedient to give publicity to all the leading important facts of the case, and therefore, five hundred copies of the petition should be printed and forwarded to Joseph Hume, M. P., for distribution to such members of the British Parliament, and other influential individuals as he thinks are most likely to advocate the cause of the oppressed cultivators of the Island."[102]

This recalcitrant stand adopted by the Assembly so disgusted Lieutenant Governor FitzRoy that he vigorously championed the proprietary cause during the last few months of his regime. He advised the Colonial Secretary to ignore completely the Assembly of Prince Edward Island since "the members of that body were men of low character and gross ignorance, chosen from the lowest and most ignorant class, men without property and without education."[103] He maintained that since the proprietors seemed to be making some efforts to grant more liberal terms, the sole hope for the resolution of the land question lay in the further encouragement of that process. Finally, he recommended that the Colonial Secretary "should state in the plainest and most equivocal language Her Majesty's determination no longer to entertain any further complaint or representation from the Assembly on the tenure of land in the Colony, and that the Assembly should turn their attention to the development of the great natural resources of the Colony, and to local improvements instead of wasting time in fruitless attempts to infringe upon the private rights of property."[104] Thus, another liberal-minded Lieutenant Governor lost faith in the democratic process as a means of solving the Island's land question. Three months later, at his own request, he was relaxing in the sunny climes of Antigua as its Lieutenant Governor.

James Stephen, the ablest official at the Colonial Office, remarked that "it was barely possible to believe that FitzRoy's plan for allaying the excitement would be effective since men do not usually cease to agitate public questions merely because they are told the Government is resolved to concede nothing beyond a certain point."[105] Despite this reservation, Stephen advised Lord John Russell to endorse FitzRoy's recommendation "since his plan for bringing a close to the great controversy had, at least, the advantage of being exceedingly simple and easy of execution."[106] Russell, in his official reply to FitzRoy, made a positive statement of policy replete with discouragement for the aspirations of the tenantry. He reiterated that "since the original conditions of 1767 were impracticable, any escheat at the present day on the grounds of the failure to fulfill such conditions would be unjust,"[107] and that "the Crown had not at its disposal any funds out of which the lands could be purchased by the Crown to be afterwards sold or granted to the tenants."[108] He also asserted that the British Government intended to maintain the proprietary land tenure system on the Island and was hopeful that the proprietors would offer liberal terms to their tenants.[109] Finally, in FitzRoy's own words, Russell recommended that "the Assembly and Council should turn their attention to the improvement of the resources, and the encouragement of the growing wealth of Prince Edward Island, and leave to the gradual operation of time the settlement of a question which offers no sound footing for direct legislation."[110] Faithful adherence to these guidelines would, he added, lead eventually "to the termination of a fruitless and irritating contest."[111]

The publication of this despatch spelled the end of the Escheat Party as a formidable force in the politics of Prince Edward Island. Disillusioned by the failure of the promises of William Cooper and the other escheat politicians, the tenantry largely abandoned them in the general election of July, 1842. In the election of that year, the number of Escheaters in the House of Assembly dropped from eighteen to seven.[112] Yet all was not lost. The Colonial Secretary ordered FitzRoy's successor, the unpredictable Sir Henry Vere Huntley, to inform the new Assembly that the British Government "must decline to interfere any further in the question in debate between the grantees of lands in Prince Edward Island and their tenantry, experience having sufficiently shown that no beneficial result is to be anticipated from any such interference. The duty of the Government will be limited to enforcing a strict observance of the Law by the contending parties."[113] To the astute George Coles, the future Reform leader, entering the Assembly in 1842, this statement was optimistically interpreted as meaning that the British Government might be prepared to allow the Assembly to settle the land question if a less radical approach were adopted. He gradually persuaded the Escheaters that through the acquisition of Responsible Government they could rid themselves of the incubus of the proprietors. By the intertwining of Responsible Government with the proprietary land tenure question, a new dimension was added to the turbulent political and social history of Prince Edward Island.

Chapter Five

Political Advance and Social Reform, 1842-1861

By W. S. MacNUTT

The 'forties and 'fifties of the nineteenth century were "a harvest time" for Prince Edward Island. Even by 1841 the population amounted to 47,042, a figure that represented a phenomenal growth from the mere five thousand of the turn of the century. By 1848 the number increased to 62,678 and by 1861 to 80,857. These statistics show a curious and surprising contrast to the rather turbulent theme of provincial history, that of the miseries of "an oppressed tenantry," of a struggle for self-government against an obdurate imperial authority, of the sharp rivalries of a multitude of politicians contending for small prizes. As many people arrived and as most remained, it might be fair to infer that the natural attractions of the Island could surmount all human error.

Two great issues, one immediate, the second more remote, dominated politics. The agitation for free land, fanned to high pitch of passion in the election of 1838, was to acquire more sombre and methodical character as William Cooper and the Escheaters failed to produce the spectacular result they had promised. It was only slowly that any precise meaning could be derived from the constitutional provisions of the Durham Report published in London in 1839. Self-government for a small colony was a goal that seemed eminently unrealistic and the watchwords of the Report could readily be perverted to accommodate the material concerns of leading personalities on the scene. It was inevitable that the more abstract of the two issues would be employed for the successful resolution of the more immediate, the freeing of the entire Island from the ownership of absentee proprietors.

The complexity of the situation was deepened in November, 1841, by the arrival of a new lieutenant governor, Sir Henry Vere Huntley, a captain of the Royal Navy whose combative qualities magnified the political intrigues and bitternesses that could obscure the greatest of issues. Like other colonial governors, he had acquired from Lord John Russell's dispatch of

1839 the notion of the increased responsibilities of representatives of the Crown in the appointment and dismissal of public officers. This he was to put to work but not to simplify the constitutional problem or to induce harmony. Fresh from anti-slavery ventures in the Red Sea and from government of the settlements on the River Gambia, he was poorly prepared to preside over a colony where a high degree of self-government was on the horizon.[1] The new Government House at Charlottetown, the provision for an impressive new Colonial Building, the cornerstone of which he was to lay in 1843, were outward and visible signs of the new dignities Prince Edward Islanders were to assert for themselves.

Huntley immediately fell foul of the entire governing group of the colony, the men of property and education who, in the election of 1842 almost completely destroyed the radical movement demanding escheat. In addition to holding all the places in the newly created executive and legislative councils, they were buttressed by an impressive 18 to 6 majority in the House of Assembly. On the escheat question the public humour had become much more conservative for it was generally understood that free land could be won only by gentler methods and by the good graces of the British Government. The party of the landowners and their agents were in control, men who enigmatically represented vested proprietorship yet stood as the champions of a toiling tenantry.

At the head of this group, the Family Compact, as it was to be called from its currency in the political terminology of British North America, was Joseph Pope who early in life had settled at Bedeque and had taken a leading part in the economy of that prosperous region. Putting small capital to judicious purpose as a merchant and shipbuilder, he had become wealthy at an early age and had been able to send his two sons, William Henry and James Colledge, both later distinguished, to England for expensive educations. As Speaker of the new House of Assembly in 1842, he was surrounded by men of established eminence both in politics and trade. All believed that honourable birth and formal education were essential requirements for public service. Virtually all members of the two councils, were bound together by kinship as well as material interest. Foremost among them at this stage was the Colonial Secretary, Thomas Heath Haviland, Sr. who had come to the Island as little more than a boy, and had become a land agent and the holder of several public offices. At his death in 1867 Edward Whelan described him as "the representative man of the old conservative party," distinguished by his dignity, urbanity and courtesy.[2] The Family Compact stood for the gentlemanly ideal, scornful of political upstarts though charitable to the less fortunate who honoured their privileged place in society.[3]

Huntley quickly discovered that he could not guide the ship of state as easily as he had charted his warship through tropic seas. The authority possessed by the Charlottetown oligarchy proved distasteful and, at a time when colonial politics in America were enduring reassessment, he permitted private griefs to influence his conduct of public affairs. The Legislature would not make what he thought was proper provision for Government House where sentries guarded the approaches to his enclave. In petulance he withdrew his patronage from agricultural, educational and other institutions formed to promote the improvement of the province. When the Legislature rejected British overtures for the raising of his salary by £500 he blamed Pope for the discomfiture and his opening address to the session of 1845 contained a rather irrelevant remark upon a certain private debt contracted by Mr. Speaker. The lieutenant governor entered upon open warfare with those who were protagonists for the *status quo,* with those who opposed reform both in the system of landholding and in the administration of government. His contempt for the local politicians is best reflected by his description of what he considered to be their cardinal belief — that only a backwoodsman could legislate for a backwoodsman.[4]

In the House of Assembly Conservatives joined Reformers in demanding the recall of Huntley.[5] The unease of 1845 attained violent overtones when the general election of 1846 completely changed the character of the Assembly and destroyed the ascendancy of the Compact there. Thirteen members new to public life were chosen. From the wreck of the escheat movement in 1842 George Coles had quietly moved to the leadership of its remnant of eight members. He now stood at the head of a majority. Huntley seized upon the opportunity to even scores with the man whom he considered a rival and, in contradiction to the terms of his instructions, dismissed Pope from the executive council.[6] A rebirth of the reform movement apparently had no terrors for him. His objective was to break the influence of the Compact.

The unusual spectacle of a lieutenant governor leaning on a radical party for support now emerged. But the radicalism was of a gentle breed. Chastened by the British repudiation of escheat in 1840 and by the electoral defeat of 1842, the reform party had turned to a philosophy of gradualism and its inspiration was Coles. Born of English West Country stock, a progressive element in pioneer farming, in the environs of Charlottetown, he had in his youth leisure for travel. At the age of nineteen he commenced a term of four years' residence in Somerset, the homeland of his parents, and in 1833 returned to the Island as a brewer and distiller. A capacity for management led him into other activities so that T. H. Haviland could harshly describe him as "a working butcher" who laboured with his hands and as "ignorant and uneducated."[7] But, educated or not, Coles had a ruminative quality and a willingness to plan for the long haul. He had come to the opinion that escheat, the great goal of the rural public, could be achieved only by a more educated people and that a superior system of schools could come only with Responsible Government. This conviction gained strength from visits to the United States where free, public education was commonplace.

The recommendation of the Durham Report that governments should change in accordance with changes in the composition of popular Houses of Assembly had met with mixed reception in British North America. Much complaint had been removed by Lord John Russell's dispatch that public office could be held only by reason of public confidence. The establishment of two separate councils, legislative and executive, had in theory distributed power more widely but on Prince Edward Island, the Reformers declared, the ascendancy of the Compact had been strengthened. The probability of a complete turnover of all leading offices following a general election seemed unnatural and alien. The Legislatures of Nova Scotia and New Brunswick were dominated by men who believed that this kind of innovation was undesirable and impractical. Prince Edward Island, where fewer educated and experienced men were available and where public charges were still paid in part by the British Parliament, could move, but with greater caution.

Yet following their electoral victory the Reformers immediately raised the banner of Responsible Government and Huntley gave them cheer by appointing Coles to a seat in the executive council. The place was first offered to Alexander Rae, contemptuously described by his opponents as an itinerant schoolmaster, who had been prominent with Cooper in the earlier agitation for escheat but who now deferred to Coles whose debating skill in the legislature had established a sure leadership of the party. In the session of 1847 Coles succeeded in securing the passage of resolutions favouring Responsible Government. Amid scenes described by Huntley as theatrical he was accused of addressing the gallery rather than Mr. Speaker.[8] But the principle was now firmly established; and the governing group had to face the unwonted spectacle of a man not of their own ilk in complete command of the popular assembly and raised to the dignity of executive councillor. Responsible Government, they threatened, was merely a curtain behind which the escheat agitation would once again raise its head and challenge the rights of property. While he faced enraged opposition in the legislative halls of Charlottetown Coles was blamed for another kind of conflict across the water. In an election riot at the Pinette poll in the Belfast district Scots and Irish attempted to solve their clannish differences with clubs and stones. Several lives were lost and scores injured.

Responsible Government was a good slogan but it had a variety of meanings and, amid the constitutional disarray of British North America, no colony could offer a more remarkable distortion of British practice. Huntley was the first colonial governor to accept Responsible Government in principle but he created a constitutional absurdity. When George Coles faced the electors of First Queen's in a by-election he was shocked to discover that his colleagues in the executive council, led by Haviland, supported his opponent. The British principle of cabinet solidarity was sublimely ignored as "libelous placards" were passed about the electorate. Coles urged Huntley to dismiss his hostile fellow-councillors, an expedient Huntley doubtless would have enjoyed but which he did not dare put to use. Yet when Coles won a brilliant victory in the election, Government House was extraordinarily illuminated as his supporters made their way there by torchlight and the winner received unusually hearty congratulations. The representative of the Crown was incontrovertibly identified with a party. On that night there were windows broken in the homes of leading members of the Compact and party spirit attained its crescendo. A bill of indictment for damage against Coles was brought by the Grand Jury at the next session of the Supreme Court. "Mr. Coles has sold himself to Sir Henry V. Huntley for self-aggrandizement" was the cry of the Compact.[9]

Locally the question became one of the duration of Huntley's stay on Prince Edward Island. Enjoying the pursuit of literature as well as the alarms of politics, he hoped for an extension of his term of office and the power to remove from the executive council all who opposed his politics. In this aspiration he was strongly sustained by the Reformers when a petition was sent to London headed by the names of Coles and Edward Whelan, the brilliant young journalist who had come from Joseph Howe's printing establishment in Halifax in 1843 and who, in *The Examiner,* was directing massive broadsides against the Compact. At St. Peter's Bay, a stronghold of reform where escheat was the ultimate objective, a meeting of four hundred persons strongly endorsed the lieutenant governor.[10]

Time and circumstances favoured Responsible Government. But Huntley and the Reformers were premature in their expectations. Huntley had been rebuked by Gladstone, Colonial Secretary to the Conservative Government of Britain, for his dismissal of Pope from the executive council. The new Liberal Government of 1846 found him an equally unsatisfactory instrument for curbing the turbulent rivalries of the colony. Responsible

George Coles

Edward Whelan

Government was about to be inaugurated in the larger colonies but Earl Grey, the new Colonial Secretary, was highly dubious about Prince Edward Island owing to "the smallness of the society." Huntley's motives were questionable but his bland and surprising pronouncement in favour of Responsible Government brought him to the van of reforming opinion at the time. When a delegation from the Compact, Joseph Pope, Edward B. Palmer, a rising young lawyer, and Andrew Duncan, a prominent shipbuilder, went to London to ensure his removal they nevertheless achieved their aim without difficulty. Huntley was in something like disgrace and his term of office was not prolonged.

For the Compact this was a fleeting and insignificant victory. Earl Grey had resolved to put the Durham recommendations on Responsible Government into effect for the larger colonies and in 1847 there was no doubt that winds of change were strongly blowing. The Compact could hope only for delay in the discarding of the system that maintained their control over colonial administration. Hope was strengthened by the honest doubts of the Colonial Secretary that Prince Edward Island was really prepared for the transfer of power to a government whose mandate rested on the majority of the Assembly. Hope was still further encouraged by hesitations, publicly shown, even among the Reformers, as to whether or not the highly centralized system of British cabinet government, which imparted immense power to a prime minister, was really desirable for the colony.

The feeling against the more literal features of the change contemplated in the Durham Report was not exclusive to Prince Edward Island. It was strongly shared by J. W. Johnston and the Conservatives of Nova Scotia and by prevailing strands of opinion in New Brunswick. The debates in the Assembly of 1847 revealed the doubts of men steeped in the colonial tradition and habits of mind. Coles had an overpowering majority behind him but he asked for only four of nine places in a new executive council to be formed on the Responsible formula. Nine Reformers accepted an amendment to the resolution favouring Responsible Government proposed by Francis Longworth, Conservative leader in the Assembly. It asked that public offices should not change hands with a change of government, that unsalaried executive councillors should govern by means of salaried, permanent officers who should be mere instruments of policy.[11] Under such a proposal even the most important office-holders such as the attorney general and provincial secretary would come into the category of civil servants.

It was highly novel to all shades of opinion that the provincial secretary should become a bird of passage, appearing and disappearing because of change of membership in the House of Assembly. Were there sufficient capable men in the province to take the place on such limited tenure? How much compensation should be given to existing office-holders who would be compelled to retire with the introduction of the British system? Payment of pensions was an unpopular expedient. Only within the century had the British party system acquired the rigidity that divided members of the House of Commons into disciplined supporters and opponents of the government. In neighbouring Nova Scotia party warfare, behind the inspiration of Joseph Howe, was acquiring a savagery that awed the conventionally minded. Responsible Government implied party unity and discipline, hitherto unknown in any colony, that deprived the assemblyman of his independence, his freedom to vote as he pleased. And it was rather terrifying to contemplate the head of a government, with a compliant executive council and an obedient majority of the House of Assembly at his command, in control of all revenues and patronage. Such centralization of power was alien to colonial experience.

Just as in New Brunswick and Nova Scotia the complete British form of government was not acceptable at one quick stroke. But its central feature, an administration based on the consent of the people expressed through their representatives, was now an aspiration that not even the Compact would deny. The aspiration acquired the greater ardour as Earl Grey and Lord Elgin, the Governor General, introduced Responsible Government to Canada, New Brunswick, and Nova Scotia, early in 1848.

To sophisticated outsiders it seemed that Prince Edward Island, like Newfoundland, held an anomalous place in the North American empire that was embarking on internal self-government work in a harmonious way. This scruple had been applied even to New Brunswick and Nova Scotia but in Prince Edward Island there was the additional consideration that political life was a war of social classes, a conflict between landlords and tenants, an oversimplified interpretation that still possessed some validity. Grey was sustained in his hesitations by the opinions of the new lieutenant governor, Sir Donald Campbell, who was required to report on whether or not the Island was prepared for self-government. Four-fifths of the tenantry, said Sir Donald, were ignorant, sprung from the pauper classes of the British Isles. From West Point to East Point there were not twenty men capable of participation in government. Only in Charlottetown were there individuals of property and intelligence fitted for public service.[12] The considered upper-middle-class opinion, fashionable in Britain, was that leisure was a necessary qualification for legislators and administrators.

Another reason advanced by Campbell for the denial of Responsible Government to the Island was that it would lead to a renewed agitation for escheat. He insisted that many of those who were in the vanguard of the movement for Responsible Government had precisely that objective in mind. Responsible Government, he contended, should not be given to the Island because it would generate a feeling of hostility to the proprietors, endanger private property on the Island and lead to the election of unscrupulous politicians pledged to bring about an unwarranted escheat of proprietary lands. In Prince Edward Island, the land tenure problem added a complex dimension to the struggle for Responsible Government.

A spell of grace was therefore given to "the old system" though it would be a short spell. The British Government, eager to speed colonial self-government in a general way, was in no humour to endure particular griefs, even from a small society. Trouble came quickly as Coles resigned his seat in the Conservative-dominated executive council, the more effectively to lead his ebullient Liberal majority in the Assembly. Party ranks closed as the issue of principle became more poignant. Yet the session of 1849 enabled the Conservatives, trying desperately to evade the implementation of Responsible Government in its literal purity and to enforce compromise, to revive the confusions of 1847. It seemed eminently unreasonable that office-holders of established experience and worth should be compelled to resign. According to the Liberals, Sir Donald Campbell was completely under their influence. With something like religious conviction the lieutenant-governor was attempting to persuade Earl Grey that Responsible Government should be implemented only if the franchise were narrowed and the electorate reduced to men of substantial property.

Yet Coles and the Liberals, by 1849 more knowledgeable and confident, held hard to the doctrine that Responsible Government must come to Prince Edward Island just as completely as to the adjacent provinces. Their spirit was sharpened by the order from Whitehall that the £3,000 grant for the civil establishment, provided by Parliament since 1776, would be reduced to £1,500 to pay for the salary of the lieutenant governor only.[13] The Assembly's power of the purse was notably increased and threats were made to reduce supply so that salaries of office-holders could not fully be paid. Rather desperately Campbell attempted to reverse the trend by dissolving the Assembly in January, 1850. It was a forlorn hope. When the new Assembly met in March, Alexander Rae, the veteran Reformer, was elected Speaker by 19 to 5. Public opinion, to Campbell and the Conservatives a victim of demagoguery, was overwhelmingly on the Liberal side. Personal vendettas came to the force as Conservative office-holders were accused of fraud and corruption, as the champions of Responsible Government were charged with an unscrupulous greed for office and patronage. High principle may have been at stake but to cynics the parties were known as Snarlers and Snatchers, each prepared to promise the tenantry as much as it dared.[14]

Political acrobacy was in vogue as Joseph Pope turned his back on the Compact and joined the Liberals.

Responsible Government did not come in 1850 but the legislative session of this year was the critical phase in which the battle was virtually won. Alleging that "the masses" of Prince Edward Island were superior in intelligence to those of the Mother Country and the neighbouring provinces, Coles and his party firmly rejected bargaining and compromise.[15] Campbell offered to include three Liberals in a new executive council of nine, a proposal Coles, from his position of strength, could afford to scorn. He won a vote of want of confidence in the government by 17 to 3. When Campbell was unshaken the ultimate weapon of an embattled House of Assembly had to be employed — refusal of supply. Prince Edward Island faced a year in which no financial provision was made for public services. When it was prorogued in March the House of Assembly had presented the British Government with an ultimatum for final decision.

Until his death in October, Sir Donald Campbell presented objections to the full implementation of Responsible Government but they reached a British Government no longer disposed to continue the debate. Grey did not really need to be reminded of his oft-quoted dispatch to Sir John Harvey of 1846, declaring that the British Government would not rule the province "in opposition to the opinion of the inhabitants." A new form of pressure on official London, originated by Coles through the Society for Colonial Reform, was really unnecessary. The people had displayed their confidence in self-government in the election of 1850. Supported by the opinion of Lord Elgin at Toronto, Grey would now defer to the wishes of "a small society."

It was probably fortunate that a new lieutenant governor was available to introduce the Responsible system. Carrying a dispatch that had been prepared in May, 1850, Sir Alexander Bannerman arrived early in 1851 with instructions to select an executive council in accordance with the wishes of the majority of the Assembly.[16] Conditions imposed were that the Legislature should not interfere with the rights of private property except by measures considered equitable, that the Assembly should provide for an appropriate civil list to ensure remuneration for public officers, that pensions be provided for public officers about to be displaced. Privately, Bannerman was instructed that the subsisting rights of both proprietors and tenants must be protected; and he was further advised that he must uphold the law and could use military force if necessary, so that there would be no infringement upon the rights of private property. High tension prevailed when the Legislature met on March 25. Six days later, when Bannerman announced the terms, the Liberals were elated. The conditions were generally satisfactory except for the distasteful stipulation that pensions be provided for their office-holding opponents. Delay followed when Coles proposed a tax on the great estates to meet anticipated charges. Technicalities were overcome and an assessment of one farthing per acre on all landholders of more than five hundred acres answered the problem.[17]

On April 23 the executive council resigned and Bannerman called on Coles to form a new administration.[18] Music and merry-making, illumination of the homes of the Reformers, a series of joyful visitations, featured the evening life of Charlottetown. It is dubious that the population at large understood all the implications of the constitutional change that had taken place. They hoped it would lead at least, to the settlement of the iniquitous land tenure system. But the cry for Responsible Government had acquired a wider connotation, a feeling that the Island could move to the same plane as the large colonies, a hope that the privileges of adulthood would be conferred by the parent state. Realization of an emotional ideal as well as constitutional advance came on April 23.

The new era quickly lost its lustre as Coles took a grip on office and as Edward Palmer, dispossessed of the solicitor generalship, enlarged the rump of the Compact into a loosely organized party recognized by the Conservative label. Patronage was now removed from Downing Street and Government House so that the prizes of electoral victory became the greater. Those accustomed to the more refined methods of acquiring political reward of former days said that the new and fierce breed of party warfare represented a decline in civilized virtues, a plaint now familiar in New Brunswick and Nova Scotia. Contrary to the fears of landholders and their agents, Coles took no violent measures against absentee proprietorship. His first reform was the so-called Free Education Act.

This legislation, which strengthened and elaborated upon an earlier Act of 1847, enforced assessment on all householders in districts where schools had been established. Governing the licensing of teachers who required certification from the headmaster of the Central Academy, it classified them in two groups. If one of the second, or higher, class were competent to teach "Latin and the higher branches" he was entitled to an additional ten shillings a year for each scholar he instructed. The Board of Education, consisting of seven members, was given control over all schools receiving financial aid from the government, and was enjoined to establish not more than a total of two hundred schools which should be three miles apart from one another. Each district was responsible for the construction of its own school. In the event of need, the Board, on recommendation of the School Visitor, an official instructed to visit each school twice a year, could grant the sum of five pounds.

The element of compulsory attendance was lacking but the Act of 1852 achieved quick results. Its principal feature was the willingness of the government to pay the salaries of teachers and give direction to the inhabitants of school districts where zealous majorities frequently encountered opposition from indifferent minorities. John M. Stark, who came from Glasgow as Inspector of Schools, was exuberant on the progress gained as early as 1854. Prince Edward Island was far ahead of Great Britain in the facilities offered for public and free education. All that the people of a community were expected to do was to build a schoolhouse and supplement the teacher's salary. Schools opened numbered 169 of which 30 were in Prince County, 94 in Queen's County and 45 in King's. In addition, the Acadians of Prince and Queen's Counties had opened 13. They were miserably appointed and books were scarce. But in 1855 Stark could reckon that one in five of the school-age population was receiving formal instruction.[19]

Proceeding on a programme of reform, Coles modified the Franchise Act in 1853. Occupancy of land was no longer the sole qualification for the vote so that the change offered virtually universal manhood suffrage. But owing to the necessity of procuring the approval of the Colonial Office it could not take immediate effect and during the interval of waiting Coles suffered a setback. Making Responsible Government work was not so easy as polemicizing upon its virtues. Politicians were capable of frailties under any form of government, responsible or not, and in April the Reform cabinet was split asunder when Coles attempted to regulate the salaries of the attorney general and the registrar of deeds. The unity of party was lost and when Coles, in an attempt to re-establish a majority, appealed to the people in a summer election, he was defeated by a rejuvenated Conservative party headed by John Holl and Edward Palmer. Their ultra-democratic cry, reminiscent of political tension in the lost thirteen colonies, was that salaried officers should hold seats neither in the Assembly nor the executive council, that paid officials, the placemen, should be the servants, not the masters, of the public.

Sir Alexander Bannerman had no liking for this Conservative deviation from the British practice of government and refused the plea that the Legislature should immediately be called to exclude by legal enactment the holding of departmental offices by its members. Rather undemocratically, Coles remained in office. It was not until March of 1854, when he faced a hostile majority in the Assembly, that he resigned. Taking office, the Conservatives immediately encountered obstacles. In the appointed Legislative Council sat an overwhelming Liberal majority and it quickly became apparent they could introduce no important legislation with confidence of its complete passage. Not surprisingly Holl and Palmer commenced to agitate for an elected second chamber, the echo of an appeal familiar in the neighbouring province. The Liberals retorted that the cry was Yankeefied and populist, a version of democracy contrary to British practice and tradition. Rather suddenly the Liberals became conservative and leaned heavily upon the traditional wisdom of the British constitution. Now in opposition, Coles and his colleagues, especially Edward Whelan, argued that an appointed second chamber was a safeguard for the rights of property and a protection against rash and improvident legislation.

Bannerman balked at these unConservative proclivities of the Conservatives and when he appealed to the Colonial Office for instructions was told to use his own discretion. Suddenly, against the wishes of his constitutional advisers, he invoked the royal prerogative of dissolution of the House of Assembly. This drastic expedient, which glaringly exposed him to charges of favouritism and violation of British usage, placed him under a cloud of disapproval when he left for the Bahamas a few days before the election. He justified himself by the British approval of the Franchise Act of 1853 which arrived in time to argue that the electorate should be given a fresh opportunity to declare itself under its terms.

Among theorists of the constitution Bannerman's summary initiative was open to fierce dispute but the considered opinion must be that it was justified by results. Public opinion endorsed the dissolution when Coles and his party were returned in the July election with 17 of 24 seats. The Conservative administration had lasted but four months.

It was an auspicious time for a well-established government as the prosperity of the 1850's came to Prince Edward Island. The strident political agitation of the 'forties had sprung from a bedrock of economic adversity and painful uplift as new population broke the soil. Most of the newcomers of this decade were Irish who generally mingled with the rural population though they were to be found more thickly along the border lines of the counties and in the extreme West.[20] Many of them squatted on proprietorial lands and their enigmatic position before the law made an additional corollary to the complex problem of land tenure. Locally they acquired sympathy but an Act of the Legislature of 1843 requiring proprietors to compensate them for improvements before eviction was disallowed by the British Government.[21] Calamity had come in 1845 when the potato crop rotted away and in 1846 the Legislature prohibited export in order to conserve seed. As a cash crop timber was failing for supplies were dwindling. Much of it was cut on lands of absentee proprietors and purchased by local merchants who turned the blind eye to its origin. Trespass and disorder of all kinds were general. H. D. Morpeth, Lord Melville's agent on the Island, reported that the Belfast riots caused dismay for the whole future of the Island among "the loyal and respectable," that in a few years it would resemble a convict settlement, that the affair arose from a determination of the Irish to show that they were as strong as the Scots. There was the morbid reflection that religious troubles are never healed.[22]

Yet in 1849 Morpeth could entertain more hopes for the Island than ever before. Crops were excellent and the tenants of Melville Road, given the boon of six years of tenure without payment of rent, would be able to pay following the harvest. They were considerably better off than the majority of tenants who, he felt, were honestly unable to pay cash to other landlords.[23] This improvement, though necessarily uneven, merely heralded much better times. Between 1850 and 1854 the public debt was reduced from £28,000 to £3,000 and the annual revenue increased from £22,000 to £35,000. The economy of the Island was immeasurably helped by a thriving shipbuilding industry. Between 1830 and 1864, 2,362 vessels were built on the Island, an average of 70 per year.

The diversified economy of the Island, its self-sufficiency in food supply, the large number of small sales of oats, fish, cattle and timber, transported in little ships to Great Britain, the United States and Newfoundland, made it relatively indifferent to the revolution in terms of trade at the mid-century. Yet it was not immune to the flood of commercial speculation as British North America contemplated the loss of tariff preference in Britain and the widening markets of the United States. Nowhere did the cry for Reciprocity gain favour more quickly and with such unanimity. As Nova Scotia refused and as New Brunswick offered to bargain, the Islanders were willing to surrender their inshore fisheries to the Americans who were legally excluded by the Convention of 1818—and without compensation.[24] Moralists had always accused them, except for the Acadians of Rustico and a few other areas, of failing to take advantage of proximity to one of the greatest fisheries in the world. But the plain fact was that the people of almost every shore had always made the Americans welcome, had found their illegal visitations more lucrative than taking to the sea on their own. This was in spite of the building of little ships and, in the 1850's, the attraction of fish-canning as a profitable enterprise. Those inclined to the sea found Yankee wages higher than local promoters would pay. The supply of bait and fresh provisions to the fishermen of Gloucester and Cape Cod, the servicing of their vessels, brought quick cash. In October, 1851, following a severe storm, seventy-two American vessels were driven ashore or sought refuge in Island harbours, a measure of the immensity of this commercial intercourse which is unrecorded by statistics. "There is no colony in North America," wrote Sir Alexander Bannerman in 1853, "where a stronger disposition has prevailed in the government and people . . . for promoting free and friendly intercourse with the United States."[25]

At the opening of his second administration Coles was privileged to call the Legislature to ratify the Reciprocity Treaty on behalf of the province. There was no violent derangement of trade. The demand for oats in the United Kingdom never diminished and the old pattern of commerce remained intact. But there was the most significant addition of a steady growth of exports to the United States until in 1858 this market received forty percent of the total volume. Green's Shore became the port of Summerside, centre for the rich farming district of eastern Prince, stimulated not only by increased American demand but also by the construction of the European and North American Railway in New Brunswick, the eastern terminus of which was nearby Shediac. As potatoes took a strong second place to oats, Charlottetown still shipped half the total exports but there was lusty development at Georgetown, Souris, New London, Crapaud, Murray Harbour and Cascumpec (about to become Alberton following the visit of the Prince of Wales in 1860).

Prosperity brought competence to deal with the remaining absentee land proprietors. The method was the eminently sensible one of buying out proprietors as opportunity arose and the Land Purchase Act of 1853 had empowered the government to do so. Forceful methods had yielded no returns. Since the advent of Coles to political prominence the question had been kept in the background of controversy though proprietorial nerves had been on edge because of evasive and unsure pronouncements of the British Government. Vote-seeking politicians sustained the hopes of tenants for action, "blowing into the flame the never altogether extinguished embers of the escheat question."[26] From exchanges within the Colonial Office it is fair to surmise that its officials believed in the necessity of drastic decision to undo the mischief of 1767. Yet, in the morality of the age, the rights of property were a leading article of faith. Since the date of original grant virtually all of the land had changed hands many times. "Too late" was a good excuse for ignoring the problem and no Colonial Secretary cared to face up to the dilemma. Contrary to opinion frequently and violently affirmed on the Island, it was not only proprietary influence that forestalled action. To the philosophical mid-century British Liberals it was the moral scruple that counted. The situation was slowly easing as the number of freeholders more than doubled between 1841 and 1861.[27]

But all depended on the goodwill of individual proprietors. The Countess of Westmorland earned the gratitude of tenants on Lot 28. Leases were notably generous on the Selkirk lands where freehold was encouraged by easy terms of purchase. Yet on the Worrell estate, comprising a huge section of northern King's County, leases were given for but forty years' duration. Robert Bruce Stewart, a proprietor of over 60,000 acres, was also niggardly with his leases. Most infuriating of all was the possibility of eviction or the raising of rental rates following years of toil on wilderness land. Nasty incidents were frequent. Embattled champions of the poor told of people burning their houses, destroying their crops and abandoning the province rather than pay increased rates. In 1843 the tenants of Lot 45 resorted to violence when one of their number was legally evicted. The sheriff was chased from the scene, the home of the proprietorial forest ranger was burnt, and a letter was sent to the lieutenant governor warning that if constables were sent to Hay River they would meet with violence. The threat had to be faced and forty soldiers of the Charlottetown garrison were sent to East Point. They remained a fortnight and all was, superficially at least, calm.[28]

The first great stroke to resolve the problem was the government's purchase, late in 1854, of the Worrell estate of 81,303 acres at a price of £24,000. Yet there remained the great holdings of Sir Samuel Cunard of something like 225,000 acres, comprising a huge area east of Charlottetown and south of the Hillsborough River, most of the lots to the west of the bays of Egmont and Cascumpec, the entire Murray Harbour area, most of the Island's northeastern tip, and fragments elsewhere. Excluding the Selkirk estate, the unsold remainder of which was bought in 1859, there were a dozen other major holdings, ranging from 1,500 acres to 66,000.

Coles had an impressive record of success. He had made free education available to the entire population. He had enlarged the franchise and substantially reduced the severity of the land question. But reform and innovation took second place as age-old religious rivalries scarred the general prospect of social and economic progress and dissolved the large Liberal majority of 1854.

As church buildings arose in every hamlet as well as on the streets of the rapidly growing towns, it was an age of self-righteousness as well as of reform. There was the elemental animosity between Protestant and Catholic in a population roughly divided on a 55-45 ratio. The early rivalry among Protestant denominations was rapidly subsiding as the Church of England lost its dubious privilege of establishment and as numerous church groups, some new and some old, found unity in evangelical zeal. Their energies encroached on civil affairs, especially in advocating prohibition of the sale of spirituous liquors. A branch of the Sons of Temperance, founded in 1848, saw favour in politicians who would enforce their views by legislation. They severely harassed Coles but he was able to resist the ill-fated expedient of complete prohibition accepted in New Brunswick.[29]

Much more ominous to the government was the so-called Bible question, the demand by militant Protestants for religious teaching in the schools. There had been a flurry of agitation in 1845 for a daily Bible lesson in the Central Academy. Notwithstanding the stricture of the law that there should be no religious test, many Protestants could not approve of "a godless, secular education." When eighteen petitions favouring religious teaching reached the Legislature, a large majority of the Assembly, after heavy but dispassionate debate, refused to contemplate amendment of the Act governing the Central Academy.[30] The feeling that in a mixed society no religious instruction should be offered within the school system prevailed at the passing of the Free Education Act of 1852. Bible reading was tolerated but explanation was forbidden. This formula for consent was satisfactory until late in 1856 when John M. Stark realized his grand ambition for the opening of a provincial normal school. In his speech he made the announcement that prayer would be given at the beginning and end of each day's lesson and that a daily Bible reading would include "illustrations and picturing out".

Under the administration of Right Reverend Bernard Macdonald, the Catholic Church had become a zealous and highly organized instrument for its faith. Wherever there was a sizeable Catholic community there were a priest and a church building. The diocese of Charlottetown now had its cathedral and in 1855 Bishop Macdonald had opened St. Dunstan's College which continued the work of St. Andrew's, closed ten years before, in offering a higher education to those enrolled. When Stark made his pronouncement it seemed a challenge to Catholics. The Bishop's letter of protest to Coles declared that Catholic children should not kneel in prayer under a master not of their own creed. He was satisfied with the *status quo* in the schools by which "nothing favourable or unfavourable to any religious denomination must be inculcated."[31] Coles had little choice but to repudiate Stark's pronouncement which was unauthorized by the Board of Education. Amid the tensions of the months ahead Stark was compelled to resign his inspectorate.

The winter of 1856-57 saw the acceleration of emotional fervour as Protestant denominations appealed for religious instruction in the schools, as the press took up the controversy with gusto, and as Stark appeared a martyr to the cause of compulsory Bible reading. When the Legislature met in February, the politicians were compelled to take a stand. The issue became a party one when Coles moved to renew the laws governing education without making provision for compulsory Bible reading. As the Conservatives perceived an election-winning issue, he was accused of attempting to outlaw the Bible. The fury of religious passion became a vehicle for political rivalry and spread to the neighbouring provinces. Coupled with the anti-Catholic, anti-Irish campaign waged by Joseph Howe in Nova Scotia, it aroused fears that society would be permanently divided on religious lines.[32]

Liberal discipline vanished before the onset of this assault. In the session of 1858, Coles's educational programme was saved only by the casting vote of the Speaker. The controversy was sustained at a high pitch by the *Protestant Protector* and by Edward Whelan in *The Examiner*. By this time the government was in such sad array that, having lost five by-elections in seeking seats for salaried officers, Coles was compelled to place some of them in the appointed Legislative Council. He was accordingly accused of betraying Responsible Government.[33] But in the general election of 1858 he won 16 of 30 seats. When one of his supporters was declared unqualified for a seat in the Assembly he found it impossible to form a cabinet and a new dissolution was necessary. In 1859 the Conservatives, under Edward Palmer, won by 19 to 11.

In spite of the displeasure of the Colonial Office, the Conservatives put into effect their long-standing contention that members of the executive council should not be salaried and that departmental heads should not hold seats in the Assembly. Liberal scorn of unBritish practice availed nothing but the experiment was soon abandoned when Palmer found that he could not serve without remuneration. Likewise, the Conservatives had to retreat from their premise that executive councillors should not sit in the Legislative Council. Representation there became imperative and, because of the Liberal majority, they once again advocated an elected second chamber.[34] The Colonial Office delayed the implementation of this unBritish departure by instructing the lieutenant governor to add five members, thereby ensuring a Conservative majority and preventing obstruction to the will of the popularly elected Assembly.

Blithely the government ignored the Bible question which, according to its adversaries, had brought it to power. Yet for many years it remained prominent in the public mind as William H. Pope, allegedly having no religion of his own but learned in theology, fought a war of propaganda with members of the Catholic clergy and with Edward Whelan in the columns of *The Examiner*. It is commemorated by heroic couplet:

> I must not, by the way, forget
> How thy brave Parsons all
> Their faces like a flint have set
> To bring about the fall
> Of that Poor Pius, friendless soul,
> The aged Pope of Rome,
> While to deprive him of control
> They arm their Pope at home.[35]

It was much more profitable for the Conservatives to turn to a problem on which there was infinitely less division of opinion. Still abused as the party of the rent-roll and the Family Compact, they had learned the techniques of Responsible Government and had outshone their opponents in the art of popular appeal. In turning to the land question, they were strengthened by the advent of John Hamilton Gray, a native son who had spent a lifetime in the British Army, and had returned to finish his career in politics. In 1859 his resolution in the House of Assembly proposed Her Majesty's appointment of "a discreet and responsible person" to negotiate with remaining proprietors on the reduction of existing liabilities and on measures that would enable tenantry to convert leasehold into freehold. When the Duke of Newcastle, the Colonial Secretary, consulted Sir Samuel Cunard, easily the outstanding proprietor, there came the counter-proposal that a commission of three members, representing the Queen, the proprietors and the House of Assembly, should be constituted and that their recommendations should be binding.[36] In April, 1860, the House of Assembly accepted this suggestion and offered Joseph Howe of Nova Scotia as its nominee. John Hamilton Gray of New Brunswick was named by the Queen and J. W. Ritchie of Halifax, "small man but bigger lawyer," by the proprietors.[37]

The enquiry commenced in September and sessions were held in the three county towns. Proprietors and tenantry were represented by counsel and individuals had full opportunity for stating their complaints. The report, tabled in July, 1861, took the Imperial Government to task for past error but would not contemplate escheat which could call in question every title to land on the Island. Instead, it recommended a loan of £100,000, guaranteed by the British Government, to buy up the properties of landlords on the terms of the Land Purchase Act. Optimistically, it prophesied that the revenues of the Island would rapidly increase so that interest payments, low because of the guarantee, could easily be met. An elaborate plan to enable tenants to become freeholders on easy terms was included, involving a discount to those who paid rent in cash for twenty years, instalment buying with concurrent reduction of rent, arbitration where landlord and tenant could not agree on a just price. Free grants were asked for the descendants of the Loyalists, allegedly cheated by unfulfilled promise after the American Revolution, and the Indians.[38]

The proprietors and the Assembly, representing the tenantry, were bound by the Award, but not the Crown. When the Legislature quickly passed two Acts to bring the recommendations to fruition, the Duke of Newcastle at once disallowed them. Specifically, the British objection was based on the refusal of the proprietors to accept arbitration from tribunals established by the Island Government. The Commissioners, it was reasoned, had exceeded their powers. They had been entitled to make awards themselves but not to pass the duty to others.

The refusal, completely unequivocal, aroused disappointment and anger to such a degree that the early 'sixties were to bring riot and violence. As John Lepage, the Island Minstrel, wrote, nothing ever promised so much and performed so little.[39] Deeply conscious of error and procrastination in the past, the British Government referred the unpleasantness to a later generation of administrators. The right of property, sanctimoniously upheld, still prevailed. Proprietorial backstairs influence was denounced for the defeat and both political parties were happy to pass the blame over the water:

> "Some say thou'rt governed by the Queen,
> And this doth please the Bard,
> Some 'praps' who say not what they mean —
> Say — by Sir Sam Cunard."[40]

Discontent and revulsion came from the urge for self-respect as well as from the feeling of being exploited by alien landlords. All through North America the ownership of land was a mark of competence while tenantry was a badge of inferiority. Poverty there still was but the Island was enjoying a continuing and growing prosperity in 1861. It was benefiting from the Reciprocity Treaty to a greater degree than either New Brunswick or Nova Scotia and the outbreak of the American Civil War was to increase the beneficent results. It had acquired a reputation for its high volume of agricultural exports. The proportion of native born to immigrants was steadily rising and, in the literary productions of John Lepage and others, it is possible to perceive what could almost be described as an incipient nationalism, a devil-may-care attitude to the rest of the world that was nourished by a complacent insularity. Implementation of the 1861 report would simply have meant that, instead of paying rent to landlords, farmers would pay interest to the government as mortgagee. Perhaps the impact of the blow was more important psychologically than materially.

The sense of shock was the more acute because of the commercial and social progress of which the Islanders were now freely boasting. In 1855 Charlottetown had been incorporated as a city and the Bank of Prince Edward Island had been formed. The Central Academy had become Prince of Wales College in 1860. Numerous churches filled a social as well as a spiritual need. Amidst the general satisfaction, the Canadian overture of 1858 for political union had encountered little more than silence. There was nothing to indicate that the years would bring to a conclusion the high degree of local autonomy Prince Edward Islanders now enjoyed.

Chapter Six

Nation Building at Charlottetown, 1864

By F. W. P. BOLGER

In the Legislative Council Chamber of Province House in Charlottetown late in the evening of September 8, 1864, Thomas Heath Haviland, at a banquet in honor of the delegates to the Charlottetown Conference, concluded his remarks with these prophetic words:

I believe, from all that I can learn that the Provinces will, ere long, be one country or nation, from the Pacific to the Atlantic. Never before was there such an important meeting as this held in the history of British America; and it may yet be said that here, in little Prince Edward Island, was that Union formed which has produced one of the greatest nations on the face of God's earth.[1]

Fifty years later, in the same room, a bronze tablet was unveiled in commemoration of this Conference on which the following inscription was engraved:

Unity is strength. In the hearts and minds of the delegates who assembled in this room on September 1, 1864, was born the Dominion of Canada. Providence being their guide, they builded better than they knew. This tablet erected on the occasion of the fiftieth anniversary of the event.[2]

Thus the prognosis of T. H. Haviland was fulfilled. Prince Edward Island by virtue of the Charlottetown Conference has since been recognized as the Cradle of Confederation. While the provision of the cradle unquestionably merits for Prince Edward Island a very important share in the birth of the Canadian nation, her maternity should not be unduly exaggerated. Rather, her attitude to Confederation provides a unique picture of consistent opposition and obstruction until economic and political necessity forced her into union with Canada. This attitude might best be described as one of aloofness. The story of Confederation in Prince Edward Island between 1864 and 1873 is largely one of vehement resistance to British, Canadian and Maritime pressures upon this isolationist position.

The aloofness of Prince Edward Island resulted, in the first place, from a deep-seated provincialism and insularity. Situated in the Gulf of St. Lawrence and practically isolated from the mainland for five months of the year, Prince Edward Island had very limited contact with the other British North American provinces. This geographic isolation made the outlook of the people extremely insular and parochial and partially accounted for their lack of interest in broader movements such as Confederation. Moreover, the people of the Island were deeply preoccupied with land and religious controversies. These unsolved problems assumed a place of such supreme importance that the broader forces encouraging Confederation in other parts of Canada were not strong enough to distract the Islanders from questions intimately affecting their material and spiritual lives.

Political reasons were also responsible for Prince Edward Island's lack of interest in Confederation. The Islanders cherished the political independence they had enjoyed since 1769, and when they attained Responsible Government in 1851 they had even a profounder attachment to their independence. Furthermore, their failure to persuade the British Government to resolve their proprietary land tenure question left them with an innate suspicion of distant administrations. And, finally, the realization that they would have an insignificant voice in a centralized legislature, led them to fear that their local needs would be disregarded. Edward Whelan, the editor of the *Examiner,* expressed the views of most Islanders when he wrote just prior to the Charlottetown Conference "that the people think, and especially those in remote sections, perhaps justly enough, that under one large Parliament, legislating hundreds of miles away, their wants would not be as well cared for as they would be by a Parliament sitting within a day's drive of all of them, and directly under the control of all."[3] It was such parochial reasoning that convinced the Islanders that Confederation was tantamount to political suicide.

Economic reasons also accounted for Prince Edward Island's aloofness to Confederation. The Island in the 1850's and 1860's enjoyed a high degree of economic self-sufficiency. The finances of the province were satisfactory, since revenue usually exceeded expenditure, and the public debt was little more than the revenue for a single year.[4] Shipbuilding was an important and lucrative business. The products of the Island's staple industries, agriculture and fishing, were readily sold in Europe, the West Indies, and especially in the United States where the Reciprocity Treaty of 1854 had opened up a steady market. Since Canada was essentially agricultural and also possessed extensive fisheries, it did not provide, and could not be expected to provide, a market for the staple commodities of the Island. Since the Island, because of the complete absence of minerals, could hardly hope to become a manufacturing province, the people concluded that Confederation would mean economic extinction. And to complete the dreary economic outlook, the people feared the effects of a Canadian tariff and an oppressive federal taxation from which they would derive little financial benefit. In fine, Islanders maintained that Confederation would decrease revenue and increase taxation, and as a result prove financially disastrous.

Until 1864 Prince Edward Island was able to treat quite cavalierly all suggestions for a closer political and economic union of the Colonies. Confederation was always considered as little more than an abstraction. In 1859, when the Governor General of Canada, Sir Edmund Head, sent to Prince Edward Island, a Canadian Minute of Council suggesting a meeting of all the Colonies to consider federal union, the Island's House of Assembly replied frigidly and evasively that such a union was one involving interests of too extensive a character to admit of a discussion in the session of the Legislature then in progress. Later in the same year, Governor General Head's recommendation for consultation among the Colonies on reciprocal free trade was summarily rejected because the Island government considered it would be "extremely difficult, if not impossible to draw a line whereby the manufactures of the North American Colonies would be admitted free into Prince Edward Island, and the same articles produced or manufactured elsewhere be subjected to duty."[5]

Three years later the Island's Assembly shelved a similar suggestion from Lord Monck by simply replying that "it would be inexpedient to entertain the question of free trade with Canada until the matter had been submitted to the people at the next general election."[6] A further proposal for discussion among delegates to be chosen by the provinces to consider federal [or Maritime] union forwarded by the Nova Scotia government and the British Colonial Office in 1863, received the same cautious consideration. In the debates on this proposal in the Assembly, the Speaker, T. H. Haviland, set the tone by proclaiming that he would never consent to sell his "birthright for a mess of pottage;"[7] and it was only after the Conservative and Liberal leaders, John Hamilton Gray and George Coles, assured the House "that a consultation of delegates could be of no disadvantage to Prince Edward Island,"[8] that it was agreed "to consider attentively"[9] such a proposal. The *Islander* succinctly captured the tenor of the debate with its observation that "a considerable discussion was held upon the question of Annexation of Prince Edward Island to the neighboring Colonies, but the general impression seemed to be that 'our tight little Island' should retain its independence."[10]

The proposal for a constitutional rearrangement of the Colonies in British North America became more than academic in the year 1864. At the outset, this proposition was restricted to the three Maritime Provinces. Once again, the initiative came from Nova Scotia, which was, perhaps, yearning for a restoration of the ancient boundaries she had enjoyed until Great Britain detached Prince Edward Island in 1769, and New Brunswick in 1784. At any rate, her Administrator, General Hastings Doyle, wrote to the Governors of Prince Edward Island and New Brunswick that his government intended to submit a resolution to the Legislature authorizing the appointment "of delegates [not to exceed five] to attend a conference on the union of the three Provinces,"[11] and he suggested that the Prince Edward Island and New Brunswick governments present resolutions "as nearly identical as possible"[12] to their Legislatures. In Nova Scotia, Dr. Charles Tupper's resolution for the appointment of delegates passed without a dissentient voice on the day it was introduced; and in New Brunswick, pressed by exhorations from the only consistent advocate of Maritime Union in the three Provinces, Lieutenant Governor A. H. Gordon, a similar resolution was passed without a division. But in Prince Edward Island there was vehement resistance both to the principle of Maritime Union and to the sending of delegates to a Conference on the subject. Prince Edward Island was already serving notice that Maritime Union was unlikely to become a reality.

The leader of the Conservative government, Colonel John Hamilton Gray, who was much more sympathetic to a general intercolonial union, introduced the discussion on Maritime Union by proposing a resolution for the appointment of delegates, not "for the purpose of arranging a preliminary plan,"[13] not "for the purpose of considering the subject of union,"[14] but only "for the purpose of considering the expediency of a union of the three provinces."[15] Colonel Gray spoke disparagingly of his own resolution. "If," he said, "the Provinces of Nova Scotia and New Brunswick were to be annexed to Prince Edward Island, great benefits might result to our people; but if this Colony were to be annexed to these Provinces, the opposite might be the effect."[16] He wondered whether "Charlottetown or Summerside would be the capital of Cabotia or Acadia, or whatever the country may be called; and are we to be the Ottawa of the United Provinces, and are buildings to be erected here, costing as in Canada, millions of dollars?"[17] And if not, he pondered, "are we to be required to keep our Representatives at some capital in one of the sister provinces from winter to spring — or are they expected to take pole in hand and leap from iceberg to iceberg across the Straits in the dead of winter?"[18] Because there were so many imponderables, he advised the House that the only prudent course "was to authorize the appointment of delegates, in the first place, simply to discuss the expediency of union."[19]

The most effective speeches delivered in the debate for and against the proposed union were those of the Provincial Secretary, William Henry Pope, and of the Speaker, Thomas Heath Haviland. Pope was the only member of the Assembly who warmly advocated Maritime Union, and even his arguments were far from convincing. After pointing out that the 35,000 Roman Catholics and 45,000 Protestants were arrayed in bitter antagonism, he argued, "that if the Island were united with the neighboring Provinces, our Protestant population would have less cause to dread Papist supremacy than they have at present, religious animosities would be weakened, and great good would be the consequence. If we are left to ourselves we shall share the fate of the Kilkenny cats."[20] "We have," he continued, "no mines, no minerals, no quarries of limestone, no extensive forests. I desire that my native land share the greatness of Nova Scotia and New Brunswick, and not remain as at present, the scene of unseemly contests which prevent all useful legislation."[21] Haviland countered that if they "sold their birthright, they may expect their country to retrograde as Cape Breton has since her annexation to Nova Scotia;"[22] and he asserted it was more prudent "to bear the ills we have, than fly to others we know not of."[23] With a dash of local pride and sentiment, he reminded the House that "the Tilleys and the Tuppers would fain have a wider field for the exercise of their talents and the extension of their sway, but it is our duty here to protect the rights of those whose representatives we are, and what public man will not hesitate, ere he votes that our institutions shall become non-entities?"[24]

As the debate progressed it became evident that Colonel Gray's resolution was in danger of being rejected. The members of the Assembly were greatly influenced by Haviland's speech. Francis Kelly, for example, said he was so impressed "that if I had a thousand votes, I would give them all in opposition to the resolution."[25] At length, George Howlan, a leading member of the Liberal Opposition, moved an amendment that it was "inexpedient under the present circumstances to appoint delegates."[26] George Coles, leader of the Liberal Party, heartily supported his leading backbencher, maintaining that "to authorize the appointment of delegates would be a bogus affair, as it appears that not more than one Hon. Member or two are at all in favor of union."[27] He ridiculed W. H. Pope's advocacy of Maritime Union for religious motives, and said this argument was "a piece of political claptrap."[28] He maintained that it would be an insult "to send delegates as a matter of courtesy since this was too serious a question for mere forms."[29] His astute lieutenant, Edward Whelan, argued that "the sending of a delegation to the proposed Conference was nothing but a farce."[30] He insisted moreover, that any form of union whether federal or Maritime was absurd while the "Island remained tied to the apron-strings of our venerable mother, Great Britain."[31]

Colonel Gray now realized that his derogatory remarks, and those of the Speaker, T. H. Haviland, had been taken very seriously. Moreover, the Opposition amendment threatened the life of his Government, since a defeat on his resolution could have resulted in a vote of non-confidence. For this reason he decided to change his tactics. He informed the Assembly that he would heartily approve the proposed union, "if the other Colonies would agree to build the Provincial Buildings here, and engage to aid us in abolishing our landlord system."[32] He then stated that his original resolution was a party question. Consequently, the Conservatives rallied their forces, defeated the amendment, and upheld the resolution on a straight party vote of eighteen to nine.[33] But the debates clearly revealed that the Assembly was almost unanimously opposed to Maritime Union. An innocuous and watered-down resolution authorizing the appointment of delegates to discuss not union but only "the expediency of union" was passed only after the Government had made it a party question because it considered it would be discourteous to refuse to attend the Conference.

In the Legislative Council there was even less enthusiasm for a Maritime Union Conference. "Now in sending delegates," A. A. MacDonald argued, "we make an admission that there are grounds on which we can be united under one Legislature."[34] "I believe," he continued, "that nineteen-twentieths of the population feel our position would not be improved by a change of Government such as that despatch contemplates, by a Legislative Union of the neighbouring Colonies; and therefore, as I entertain these views, I cannot support the resolution."[35] Edward Palmer, the Attorney General, asserted that he "was at a loss to conceive what advantages to Prince Edward Island would accrue from the union since we would submit our rights and property, in a measure, into the hands of the General Government, and our voice in the United Parliament would be insignificant."[36] "We had better," he cautioned the Council, "let well enough alone and remain as we are."[37] George Beer, who sponsored the resolution, thought "that so much would be lost by union that it was better to rub along as we are."[38] Since the eleven members who participated in the debate all opposed Maritime Union, it seemed that the resolution to appoint delegates to confer on the subject would be defeated. But Edward Palmer saved the situation. He suggested that an Island delegation should attend the Conference as watchdogs in case Nova Scotia and New Brunswick discussed questions that affected Prince Edward Island.[39] This tactic enabled the resolution to pass on a narrow party vote of six to four.[40] The delegates, who would be appointed, certainly did not have a mandate for Maritime Union.

But the mere approval of a Conference did not mean that Maritime Union was close to fruition. Indeed, in the atmosphere of distrust, lethargy and unreality surrounding the movement, it seemed unlikely that the projected Conference would ever be held. A. H. Gordon, the only consistent advocate of Union, had hopefully suggested to George Dundas that the Conference could be held late in July or early in August.[41] But Dundas, after consulting his Executive Council, replied that "while there did not appear to be any objection to the time of the Conference, this would, however, in a measure, depend upon the place decided upon for the meeting of the Delegates."[42] His answer almost seemed to imply that the Conference must be held at Charlottetown. In addition, there was absolutely no public enthusiasm for Maritime Union. "The subject of a union of the Maritime Provinces," the *Islander* sadly commented on June 24, 1864, "appears to be attracting but little attention among our neighbors. Their press scarcely ever alludes to it. In this Island, however, the newspapers generally have declared against it, and it is seldom that one meets among our agriculturists a man who will listen to anything in favor of a proposition which will deprive the Island of its existence as a separate Government."[43] These observations were an accurate appraisal of the situation. Maritime Union never really got on the rails, — or, perhaps, more accurately, — was always off the rails. Week after week passed without anyone showing the least interest in arranging a time and place for the Conference. In short, by the early summer of 1864, Maritime Union had all but vanished. Undoubtedly, the resolutions on union would never have been implemented had not ouside forces impelled the Maritimes to arrange a Conference. Maritime Union would never have generated enough energy to reach the conference table on its own.

It was Canadian initiative, or perhaps, Canadian interference that occasioned the arrangement of the Conference on Maritime Union. The new Canadian Coalition formed in June, 1864, was committed to a general federation of all the British North American colonies. Since the projected Conference on Maritime Union seemed to supply an excellent occasion for the presentation of the new scheme, the Canadians decided to ask for an invitation. On June 30, 1864, therefore, Lord Monck addressed official despatches to the three Maritime Governors asking whether a Canadian delegation might be permitted to attend the Maritime Union Conference "to ascertain whether the proposed Union might be made to embrace the whole of the British North American Provinces."[44] The Nova Scotia and New Brunswick governments replied immediately that, of course, the Canadians would be welcome. But the cautious and lethargic George Dundas needed an additional two weeks to muster sufficient energy to make an affirmative reply. However, if the Canadians were going to attend the Maritime Union

Conference, it seemed logical that the dilatory Maritimers should attempt to determine a place and time.

Once again, the initiative came from Nova Scotia. Since Charles Tupper realized that Prince Edward Island was the reluctant partner, he obtained Leonard Tilley's permission to suggest Charlottetown as the most suitable place for the Conference. Fortified by this informal agreement, Lieutenant Governor MacDonnell of Nova Scotia wrote to the Governors of New Brunswick and Prince Edward Island requesting them to select a time and place for the Conference "most appropriate and most agreeable to themselves,"[45] while adding that he "could see some advantages in the selection of Charlottetown for that purpose."[46] Two more weeks elapsed before there was further action. Since neither Colonel Cole, the Administrator of New Brunswick, nor George Dundas had deigned to acknowledge his despatches, he decided to pay a visit to Charlottetown.

MacDonnell arrived in Charlottetown on a schooner, fittingly named the *Daring,* on Sunday, July 24, and left on Monday, July 25. The *Protestant,* commenting on his visit, remarked that the "Governor had arrived unexpectedly."[47] It was, perhaps, the shock of the visit that propelled the phlegmatic Dundas into a spate of activities. Shortly after MacDonnell's departure from the Island, he wired Colonel Cole, and asked him "to telegraph, if your Ministers approve Charlottetown, and the first of September for the Conference."[48] Cole immediately replied that his government was "willing to accede to His Excellency's suggestion that the Conference should be held in Charlottetown on September 1st."[49] On the evening of July 25, Dundas called a meeting of his Executive Council, and on its advice, appointed the Prince Edward Island delegation.[50] Three days later he informed Lord Monck of the time and place of the Conference, and assured him that he would "rejoice to receive in Prince Edward Island those gentlemen who may be delegated to attend the Conference."[51] Thus, ironically, the final arrangements for a Conference on Maritime Union were made largely as a result of Canadian goading. Yet, it was fitting that the initiative should come from Canada, since the Conference was destined to be devoted mainly to a consideration of federal rather than Maritime Union.

The announcement of the names of the delegates, and of the time and place of the Conference, resulted in a mild flurry of comment on union in the newspapers in Prince Edward Island. But it was federal union, not Maritime Union, that they discussed. Throughout the month of August, the *Monitor* featured editorials on Confederation, based mainly upon materials drawn from the mainland and Toronto papers. By the end of the month it was viewing "the forthcoming Conference in Charlottetown as, perhaps, the most important event — as far at least as the future destiny of these

Colonies is concerned — that has occurred during the present century."[52] It went so far as to express the hope that the deliberations of the delegates "would culminate in the creation of a great nation in this Western hemisphere of which neither we nor our remotest posterity will ever have cause to be ashamed."[53] George Coles, writing in the *Examiner,* comforted his readers with the naive observation that "Charlottetown, no doubt, would become the place for the meeting of the United Legislature, for no part of North America enjoys such an invigorating climate as that part of P.E. Island in the summer months; and our Canadian friends will be glad, I am sure, to spend a month or two in public business here, if only to escape the fever and ague of their own Province."[54]

Edward Whelan, the brilliant editor of the *Examiner,* although sceptical at the outset, gradually grew enthusiastic for federal union. "We discern the necessity for union," he wrote, "in a thousand forms. We see it in the want of uniformity in our tariffs, in our customs' regulations, in our currency. Above and before all [and this should be the first consideration with the inhabitants of this Island] a union will relieve us from the provoking intermeddling of the Colonial Office in our local legislation."[55] The Island's two religious organs expressed serious reservations, and in so doing, were better mirrors of public opinion. "We are opposed at present," the *Protestant* commented, "to even a federal union unless some advantage is pointed out of which we have not heard."[56] And the Catholic *Vindicator* said it would be foolhardy to become part "of an expensive and complicated Federal Union, the results of which may be witnessed in the neighbouring Republic in the unnatural and fratricidal war being waged there."[57]

But the fourth estate left no doubt that it was federal and not Maritime Union that they had in mind. "Our little Parliament," the *Examiner* wrote, "is a poor concern, the Lord knows — and we are not overwhelmed with respect for it, — but bad as it is, we are disposed to keep it, and we will try to make it better at the next election."[58] On the very day that the Charlottetown Conference opened, the *Monitor* favored the delegates with a frank exposition of Prince Edward Island's repugnance to Maritime Union. "We have no hesitation in saying," he asserted, "that all attempts to bring about a 'legislative union' of the Provinces will be stoutly resisted both by the people and legislature of this Island."[59] He went on to maintain that if the Conference was "to be productive of any very beneficial results, ' a wider range' will have to be given to its deliberations than appears to have been originally intended."[60] He even went so far as to agree with Tilley's mouthpiece, the Saint John *Morning News,* in warning the delegates that it was "their bounden duty to discuss the question of federation, so far as it affects the North American Provinces."[61] These views were certainly consonant with the Island's sentiments on union. Maritime Union was absolutely unacceptable. But federal union, since it had the advantage of preserving the Island's cherished Legislature, could, at least, be discussed. At this stage the Islanders were not prepared to make any further commitment.

The reception accorded to the delegates to the Charlottetown Conference was a perfect reflection of the Islanders' lack of interest in union. The Nova Scotian delegation arrived on the *Heather Belle* from Brule, Nova Scotia, late in the afternoon of August 31. The Island government did not meet them on arrival, and they were obliged to find their own accommodations at the *Pavilion,* one of the Island's twenty modest and overcrowded hotels. "Not a soul belonging to the Government," the *Examiner* sarcastically commented, " was on the wharf to receive them — there was not a carriage of any kind, — not even a truck to take their luggage to the hotels or boarding house; and they were suffered to find out, by rule of thumb, where they could get something to eat and a bed to lie upon."[62] The New Brunswick delegates arrived a little before midnight on the same day, on the *Prince of Wales* from Shediac. The *Examiner* again commented "that neglect and impartiality was measured out to them . . . with beautiful impartiality."[63] This was a slight exaggeration, since W. H. Pope, the Provincial Secretary, was on hand to meet them, and directed them to the *Mansion House,* where they managed to find accommodations.

On the morning of September 1, the Canadian Government steamer, the *Queen Victoria,* bearing the unofficial Canadian delegation, reached Prince Edward Island, which George Brown thought was "as pretty a country as you ever put your eye upon."[64] W. H. Pope once again represented the Island. He manfully embarked at Pope's wharf, and was rowed out to the *Queen Victoria* anchored just inside Charlottetown Harbor, "in a canoe or flatbottomed boat, with a barrel of flour on the bow, and two jars of molasses in the stern, and with a lusty fisherman as his only companion to meet the Hon. T. D. McGee and the other distinguished visitors from Canada."[65] After an official exchange of greetings, the Canadians came ashore with some pomposity, according to George Brown's lively account:

Our steamer dropped anchor magnificently in the stream and its man-of-war cut evidently impressed the natives with huge respect for their big brothers from Canada. I flatter myself we did that well. Having dressed ourselves in correct style, our two boats were lowered man-of-war fashion, and being each duly manned with four oarsmen and a boatman, dressed in blue uniforms, hats, belts, etc., in regular style, we pulled away for shore and landed like Mr. Christopher Columbus who had the precedence of us in taking possession of portions of the American continent.[66]

George Brown was not quite correct in saying that the Canadians "took possession." There was not even sufficient hotel accommodations for the delegation. Some of them got space at the *Franklin* and in the private homes of the Island delegates; but the majority was obliged to remain aboard the *Queen Victoria*.

The Prince Edward Island government received several severe strictures from the various journals for the discourteous reception offered the different delegations, and for its failure to provide sufficient hotel accommodations. "Surely some of our delegates at least," wrote the *Protestant* bitterly, "might have made an effort to meet their brother Delegates at the landing place. But our people are slow, and the Government slower; the former do, indeed, sometimes wake up to such trifles as a monkey-show or a house-dance, and allow themselves to be fleeced in a few days of 700 to 1,000 pounds; but the latter very seldom show any activity except on the eve of a general election."[67] The government felt compelled to justify itself by claiming that the Nova Scotia delegation had arrived early and the New Brunswick delegation late. But the truth seemed to be that the Slaymaker and Nichols' Olympic circus, the first circus that had visited Charlottetown in some twenty-one years, had distracted the members of the Island government. "What is the cause of this wonderous migration?" a correspondent from the Saint John *Morning Telegraph* asked in Summerside: "the circus, sir, the circus, came the reply from one to the other as the surging throug moved on to board the ship for Charlottetown."[68]

Moreover, many of the papers were not too impressed with W. H. Pope's official welcome to the Canadians. "The Secretary," *Ross's Weekly* commented sarcastically, "made a respectful visit alongside the Canadian steamer 'Queen Victoira' [sic] seated on an unclean barrel, and in full command of an imbibing oyster boat propelled by a paddle and an oar. The Stewart [sic] of the steamer, taking the Secretary for a *Bumboater,* said: 'I say, skipper, what's the price of shell-fish?' But William the Secretary opened not his shell."[69] The government explained that its failure to provide sufficient hotel accommodations for the Canadians was due to the fact that their delegation was much larger than had been anticipated. The truth was that the hotels were overflowing with people who had poured into Charlottetown to see, not the Conference, but the circus. "The large influx of people," the Saint John *Morning Telegraph* commented humorously, but truthfully, "was not because the whole Island population clamorous for a union were flocking to Charlottetown to enforce their views . . . but because the inhabitants were travelling, many of them a distance of some sixty miles to see the circus."[70]

The historic Charlottetown Conference opened officially on Thursday, September 1, at two in the afternoon. Nova Scotia was represented by Charles Tupper, William A. Henry, Robert B. Dickey, Jonathan McCully and Adams G. Archibald; New Brunswick by S. L. Tilley, J. M. Johnson,

J. H. Gray, Edward B. Chandler and W. H. Steeves; and Prince Edward Island by John Hamilton Gray, Edward Palmer, W. H. Pope, George Coles and A. A. MacDonald.[71] John Hamilton Gray, the Premier of the Island, was selected as chairman; and Charles Tupper and Samuel Leonard Tilley, the Premiers of Nova Scotia and New Brunswick, were named as joint secretaries.[72] This decision was just made when it was announced that the Canadians had arrived. After a short discussion, the delegates agreed to postpone their discussions on Maritime Union until after the Canadians, as visitors to the Conference, had expressed their views on federal union. The alacrity with which the Maritime delegates reached this decision suggested that they were delighted to shelve their discussions on Maritime Union. The Canadians were then invited into the Legislative Council Chamber to meet the Maritimers. The eight-man Canadian delegation consisted of John A. Macdonald, George E. Cartier, Alexander T. Galt, George Brown, William McDougall, Hector Langevin, Thomas D'Arcy McGee and Alexander Campbell.[73] The rest of the afternoon was spent in the exchange of greetings. George Brown noted that "the Canadians were presented in great style to the Conference, and having gone through the shake elbow and the how-d'ye-do and the fine weather — the Conference adjourned to the next morning at ten, then to meet for the serious despatch of business."[74] That evening all the delegates went to Government House for the opening dinner of the Conference.[75]

On Friday morning, September 2, the delegates assembled in the Council Chamber at ten o'clock, "and Canada opened up her batteries."[76] George E. Cartier began the case for the Canadians, exposing the general arguments for Confederation.[77] The Canadian choice was prudent, because Cartier was well known in the Maritimes as a strong proponent of provincial autonomy and so would allay some of the Maritimers' fears on that issue. He was followed by John A. Macdonald who spoke on British constitutional practices, the precedents for union in the other British Colonies, the need for a strong federal government, and the dangers that must be avoided in a Canadian federal system.[78] The speeches of these two gentlemen and the questions that ensued occupied the Conference until adjournment at three o'clock in the afternoon. At four o'clock the delegates continued the formal series of social engagements that were an important part of each day's activities. W. H. Pope was the host, and he provided "a grand *déjeuner à la fourchette,* oysters, lobsters and champagne and other Island luxuries."[79] The evening was free and the delegates spent it, Brown recounted, "walking, driving or boating as the mood was on us."[80] Brown himself, who stayed with W. H. Pope during the Conference, spent a delightful evening, sitting peacefully on the balcony of Pope's commodious residence on the

The Delegates to the Charlottetown Conference

1. Col, the Hon. John Hamilton Gray, M. P. P., Prince Edward Island—Chairman of Convention.
2. The Hon. John A. Macdonald, M. P. P., Attorney General, Canada West.
3. The Hon. George E. Cartier, M. P. P., Attorney General, Canada East.
4. The Hon. Thomas D'Arcy McGee, M. P. P., Minister of Agriculture, Canada.
5. The Hon. Wm. A. Henry, M. P. P., Attorney General, Nova Scotia.
6. The Hon. Wm. H. Steeves, M. E. C., New Brunswick.
7. The Hon. John M. Johnson, M. P. P. Attorney General, New Brunswick.
8. The Hon. Samuel Leonard Tilley, M. P. P., Provincial Secretary, New Brunswick.
9. The Hon. Robert Dickey, M. L. C., Nova Scotia.
10. Lt. Col., The Hon. John Hamilton Gray, M. P. P., New Brunswick.
11. The Hon. Edward Palmer, M. L. C., Attorney General, Prince Edward Island.
12. The Hon. Edward Botsford Chandler, M. L. C., New Brunswick.
13. The Hon. H. L. Langevin, M. P. P., Solicitor General, Canada East.
14. The Hon. Charles Tupper, M. P. P., Provincial Secretary, Nova Scotia.
15. The Hon. A. T. Galt, M. P. P., Finance Minister, Canada.
16. The Hon. Adams G. Archibald, M. P. P., Nova Scotia.
17. The Hon. Andrew A. MacDonald, M. L. C., Prince Edward Island.
18. The Hon. A. Campbell, M. L. C., Commissioner of Crown Land, Canada.
19. The Hon. Wm. McDougall, M. P. P., Provincial Secretary, Canada.
20. The Hon. W. H. Pope, M. P. P., Colonial Secretary, Prince Edward Island.
21. The Hon. Jonathan McCully, M. L. C., Nova Scotia.
22. The Hon. George Coles, M. P. P., Prince Edward Island.
23. The Hon. George Brown, M. P. P., President Executive Council, Canada.
24. Major Bernard, Secretary to the Attorney General, Canada West.
25. Mr. Charles Drinkwater, Private Secretary to the Attorney General, Canada West.
26. William H. Lee, Clerk Ex. Council, Canada.

Mount Edward Road, "looking out on the sea in all its glory."[81] Thomas D'Arcy McGee, the orator of Confederation, gave a lecture on Irish history to a large crowd at the auditorium of St. Joseph's school.

On Saturday, September 3, the Conference resumed at ten in the morning. Alexander T. Galt, the principal speaker for the day, occupied much of the session with a detailed consideration of "the financial aspects of the Federation and the manner in which the financial disparities and requirements of the several Provinces might be arranged."[82] The Maritimers, introduced for the first time to the concepts of regional disparity and equalization payments, peppered the omniscient Galt with questions for the rest of the session. At three o'clock, the Conference adjourned to the luxurious *Queen Victoria,* where the Maritime delegates were hosted by the Canadians at a sumptuous luncheon. Canadian hospitality was so lavish that the delegates were on board eating and drinking until late in the evening. Sufficient unity pervaded the gathering to permit the unofficial proclamation of the new nation. George Brown vividly related that he and Cartier "made eloquent speeches — of course — and whether, as a result of our eloquence, or the goodness of our champagne, the ice became completely broken, the tongues of the delegates wagged merrily, and the banns of matrimony between all the provinces of B. N. A. having been formally proclaimed and all manner of persons duly warned then and there to speak or forever after to hold their tongues — no man appeared to forbid the banns and the union was thereupon formally completed and proclaimed!"[83] The luncheon on board the *Queen Victoria,* despite the relaxed atmosphere, or perhaps, because of it, marked in a very significant way, the first stage in the beginning of Confederation.[84] Later in the evening, "Colonel Gray gave a grand dinner at his beautiful mansion at Inkerman,"[85] to the weary delegates.

After a respite on Sunday, the Conference met again on Monday, September 5, at ten in the morning. George Brown spoke on the constitutional aspects of the proposed union, the manner in which the several governments, local and general, would be constructed, the powers that would be ascribed to each, and how the judiciary would be constituted.[86] His speech and the questions that followed occupied the delegates until adjournment at three. At four o'clock, the delegates were entertained at George Coles's farm residence on the outskirts of the city. As Coles was a farmer, brewer and distiller, he was able to keep pace with the high culinary standards already established. George Brown reported that he gave them "a handsome setout" assisted by "a number of handsome daughters, well educated, well informed, and sharp as needles."[87]

On Tuesday, September 6, the delegates started earlier. They went to Government House for a group picture on the verandah at nine-thirty.[88] They then met in session at the Council Chamber at eleven, discussing the several details of the Confederation scheme. The Canadians completed their proposals at this session, leaving to the Maritime delegates the decision about what should be done. At four o'clock in the afternoon, Edward Palmer gave the delegates a luncheon at his home on Queen Street, and in the evening, Mrs. Dundas entertained at a formal ball at Government House, which Brown described "as a very nice affair, but a great bore for old fellows like me."[89]

On Wednesday morning, September 7, the Maritime delegates at last got down to their first serious consideration of the subject that had occasioned the Conference. For purposes of discussion, Dr. Charles Tupper moved and Robert B. Dickey seconded a resolution stating that "[whereas in the opinion of this Conference, a Union of Nova Scotia, New Brunswick and Prince Edward Island under one Government and Legislature, would elevate the status — enhance the credit — enlarge the influence — improve the social, commercial and political conditions — increase the development and promote the interest generally of all these Provinces — Resolved that the time has arrived when such union should be effected]."[90] After a desultory discussion, the delegates decided to postpone further consideration of Maritime Union and to promote federal union. The Canadians were then invited into the Council Chamber and the Maritime delegates informed them that they "were unanimous in regarding Federation of all the Provinces to be highly desirable — *if the terms of union could be made satisfactory* — and they were prepared to waive their own more limited question until the details of our scheme could be more fully considered and matured."[91] It was then agreed that the Conference should adjourn until Saturday, September 10, when it would meet again in Halifax. That same afternoon, the Canadian delegates hosted Governor and Mrs. Dundas and a large number of ladies on the *Queen Victoria*. George Brown regretted that he could not be present, "having been laid up with a bilious attack, the natural result of such a round of dissipation."[92]

Thursday, September 8, was excursion day, with the delegates driving out to Stanhope on the North Shore of the Island for sea bathing, a picnic on the sandhills and some plover shooting in the marshes.[93] That night the *pièce de resistance* of the whole Conference was an elaborate banquet and ball, at which the City of Charlottetown was host. Province House, where the Conference had taken place, was prepared for the festivities while the delegates were on tour. The Legislative Council Chamber served as the drawing room and banquet hall. The Legislative Library was fitted up into a reception room, where abundant quantities of tea, coffee, sherry and champagne were available. The Legislative Assembly, where the guests did their dancing, was decorated with flags, evergreens and flowers, and with the most brilliant illuminations that Mr. Murphy, the local manager of the gas works, could supply.[94] The gallery of the Assembly was "occupied by two Bands of the City, Violinists, etc., who discoursed appropriate music."[95] "One would almost have imagined," wrote the *Protestant,* "from the profusion of evergreen and flowers, that the nuptials of the Provinces were about to take place; but after a little we discovered that it was only the wooing under the mistletoe."[96]

The editor of the *Monitor,* with an eye for detail, described the reception and dance in glowing terms:

The guests began to arrive a little after eight o'clock. At nine, His Excellency the Lieutenant Governor and Mrs. Dundas were announced and were received by His Worship the Mayor and three other members of the Managing Committee who conducted them to the robing room. The delegates from Canada, Nova Scotia, and New Brunswick arrived shortly afterwards, and were escorted by the Mayor to the Council Chamber, which was fitted up as a Drawing Room, and where they were received by the Lieutenant Governor and Mrs. Dundas. At ten o'clock the party repaired to the Ball Room, the Hon. J. A. Macdonald, Attorney General of Upper Canada, having Mrs. Dundas on his arm, and the Lieutenant Governor having Mrs. T. H. Haviland on his arm. The Band played the National Anthem as they entered — after which the first set of quadrilles was opened, the delegates and the partners with whom they entered joining in the dance.[97]

The dancing continued until twelve o'clock, when the party withdrew to the Council Chamber where it found the table "literally groaning under the choicest viands prepared in Mr. Murphy's choicest style."[98] It was providential indeed, that the guests were conducted to the banquet hall, if the slightest credence is put on John Ross's description of the dance: He related that at the Ball, where revelry presided, "pleasure panoplied in lustful smiles meets and embraces exuberant Joy. . . . The fascinating dance goes merrily and the libidi[n]ous waltz with its lascivious entwinements whiles in growing excitement; the swelling bosom and the voluptuous eye tell the story of intemperate revel."[99] At any rate, after ample justice had been done to the various foods on the banquet table, the proposal and response to toasts continued until after three in the morning of September 9. George Brown told his wife that he was delighted "that he had escaped about twelve just as supper was approaching, because the Goths commenced speech-making, and actually kept at it for 2 hours and three-quarters, the poor girls being condemned to listen to it all!"[100] It was nearly five o'clock in the morning when a relaxed but tired group of delegates went aboard the *Queen Victoria* for the voyage to Nova Scotia.

The *Queen Victoria,* like the delegates, was unable to stir for a few hours. A dense fog, which the Islanders assured the Canadians, "had come over from Nova Scotia and New Brunswick to do honor to the delegates from those Provinces," delayed the departure until eight o'clock.[101] At a little after midday they reached Pictou, where most of the delegates disembarked and started an overland journey to Halifax. At four o'clock on Saturday, September 10, the Conference reconvened, the Canadians again sitting as visitors but dominating the discussions. On Monday, September 12, the Maritime delegates held a private session on Maritime Union. Since they could not reach any agreement, the Canadians were admitted once again. At this joint session lasting some three hours, the delegates unanimously endorsed John A. Macdonald's proposal to "advise the Governor General of Canada to invite the Lieutenant Governors of Nova Scotia, New Brunswick, Newfoundland and Prince Edward Island to appoint delegates to attend a Conference at Quebec, to take formally into consideration the subject of a Union of all the British North American Colonies."[102] That evening the Nova Scotia Government tendered a "sumptuous" dinner at the Halifax Hotel to the delegates, where numerous speeches in favor of federal union were delivered. The agreement on the holding of a formal conference on federal union seemed to have added an atmosphere of exuberent optimism. John A. Macdonald, fittingly enough, expressed the new spirit. "Everyone admits," he said, "that Union must take place sometime. I say now is the time."[103] "For twenty long years I have been dragging through the dreary waste of Colonial politics. I thought there was no end, nothing worthy of ambition, but now I see something which is well worthy of all I have suffered."[104]

The Conference was, in effect, over. But since Charlottetown and Halifax had been honored, courtesy visits had to be made to Saint John and Fredericton. On Wednesday, September 14, the Conference was on the move again. The delegates visited Saint John, and that evening the New Brunswick delegates entertained at a public dinner in Stubbs's Hotel where more oratory in praise of federal union was heard. The only discordant note was sounded by George Coles. In a playful speech he spoke of the wooing of Prince Edward Island by Canada, and maintained that "the blandishments of the wooer had not altogether prevailed."[105] He added prophetically that "before he would consent to the wedlock, he must understand fully whether Canada, with her expansive territory and great debt, was able to maintain her in the connection as well as she was in her present condition."[106]

On Thursday, September 15, the delegates set out by steamer for Fredericton. They paid a courtesy call on Lieutenant Governor Gordon. Cartier, Galt and Brown spent the night with the Governor, who plied them with questions and offered tons of gratuitous advice.[107] By late afternoon, September 16, the delegates were once again back in Saint John, and there they parted. The Canadians left by special train for Shediac, where they embarked upon the *Queen Victoria* for the voyage back to Quebec. After their departure, the Maritime delegates met at Stubbs's Hotel to discuss the subject for which the Conference had been convened. Once again, no agreement could be reached, so it was unanimously decided "to adjourn until after the Conference to be called at Quebec, had formally discussed the larger question in all its bearings."[108] Maritime Union, which never had any real support, was gradually but inexorably fading into oblivion.

The demonstration that Maritime Union was an impracticable plan was the first definitive result of the Charlottetown Conference. The attraction of the larger union, together with Prince Edward Island's hostility to the smaller union, soundly defeated the Maritime Union project. Lieutenant Governor A. H. Gordon, who accompanied the New Brunswick delegation to the Charlottetown Conference and remained for two days with George Dundas, summarized the attitude of the Island delegates to Maritime Union. "Those from Prince Edward Island," he bitterly commented, "were, almost without exception, hostile to the original proposal of a Legislative Union which the Conference was assembled to consider, but appeared not disinclined to the adoption of a Federal Union with Canada, provided their separate Legislature was maintained as now existing, and pledges were given that the whole revenue from the Island should be expended within its limits!"[109] Prince Edward Island's further insistence that the capital should be located in Charlottetown brought the proceedings to a complete impasse.[110] This demand was tantamount to a refusal to unite with the mainland provinces, because the Island was practically isolated during the winter months, the very time when the Legislature would normally meet. As a consequence of these stances adopted by the Prince Edward Island delegates, Maritime Union, as Gordon related, gradually drifted out of sight.

But it would be inaccurate to saddle Prince Edward Island with the whole responsibility for the failure of the Maritime Provinces to reach agreement on Maritime Union. Prince Edward Island has often been called the "reluctant province" because of its opposition to such a union. But there is really only a difference in degree in the attitude of the three Provinces. As Murray Beck, the distinguished Canadian political scientist, observes: "Prince Edward Island has been somewhat more reluctant than reluctant Nova Scotia and reluctant New Brunswick."[111] In the brief debate at the Charlottetown Conference on Tupper's resolution, there were only minimal differences in the distaste of the three Provinces for Maritime Union.

Charles Tupper was content with his proposal of the resolution and advanced no arguments in its support. Leonard Tilley maintained that the agitation of a Legislative Union would delay Confederation, and, moreover, it was better for New Brunswick not to enter Maritime Union, "because it would have to divide its crown lands with Nova Scotia and P.E.I."[112] John Hamilton Gray of Prince Edward Island insisted that it was preferable for the Island to remain separate from the mainland provinces, because in a legislative union, "P. E. I. would not get the consideration we now expect from Canada, and if we were united, we could not avoid going into the Confederation."[113] Thus, Maritime Union was definitively waived at the Charlottetown Conference, and the three Provinces henceforth gave wholehearted and undivided attention to Confederation.

A second important result of the Conference was that the deliberations at Charlottetown had revealed that there was sufficient agreement on the principle of a federal union to justify the continuation of the discussions in a subsequent formal Conference at Quebec. Moreover, the broad agreements reached at Charlottetown greatly facilitated the completion of a federal plan at Quebec. John A. Macdonald, who may be regarded as the architect of Canadian federal union, emphasized the accomplishments at Charlottetown during the Canadian Confederation debates. "So satisfactory to them [the Maritime delegates] were the reasons we gave at Charlottetown," said Macdonald, "so clearly, in their opinion, did we show the advantages of the greater union over the lesser, that they at once set aside their own project, and joined heart and hand with us in entering into the larger scheme, in trying to form, as far as they and we could, a great nation and strong government."[114] He went on to assert that "because of the full and free discussions at Charlottetown," the delegates to Quebec, on the very first day of the Conference, were able to pass unanimously a resolution "that the best interests and present and future prosperity of British North America would be promoted by a Federal Union under the Crown of Great Britain, provided such a union can be effected on principles just to the several Provinces."[115] Later in the same debate, he contended, "that if the Charlottetown Conference had not been held, never, perhaps for a long series of years would we have been able to bring the scheme to a practical conclusion."[116] These tributes to the Charlottetown Conference prove beyond question its importance as a prerequisite to Confederation.

A third, and in many ways, the most important, consequence of the Conference, was the agreement on some basic principles that should be embodied in the federal plan. These proposals were not definitively settled, but the general outline of a constitution appeared from the deliberations at Charlottetown. The Confederation was to consist of three sections, Upper

Canada, Lower Canada, and the Maritime Provinces, the latter to join either collectively or separately; and provision was made for the later admission on equitable terms of the North West Territory, British Columbia and Vancouver.[117] Each of the Provinces was to have a local Legislature and Executive, charged with the control of all local matters; and there was to be a general Legislature and Executive, vested with control of affairs common to the whole country.[118] The Federal Legislature was to be bicameral, consisting of an Upper and Lower House. The principle of sectional equality for membership in the Upper House was approved and its numerical composition tentatively determined. A. H. Gordon informed Cardwell that "it was agreed that the Council should consist of 60 members, 20 from Upper Canada, 20 from Lower Canada, and 20 from the Maritime Provinces,"[119] The appearance of Newfoundland at Quebec, and Prince Edward Island's change of heart, however, led to protracted debates on this question at Quebec. It was also generally agreed that representation in the Lower House should be based upon population. Indeed, Edward Palmer proudly said later that he was "the only one who objected to this principle in Charlottetown."[120]

There was also general agreement on the division of powers between the federal and local Legislatures. On the all-important decision on residual powers, there was considerable controversy as to whether or not there was agreement. At Quebec, Charles Tupper insisted that "at Charlottetown, it was specified that residual powers should be reserved to the general government."[121] But George Coles disagreed and said that "this was not laid down as a basis at Charlottetown."[122] On the question of the financial arrangements, there seemed to have been considerable agreement on the principle that the Federal Government should assume the debts and assets of the several provinces and, in turn, compensate them for the loss in revenue by distributing the public revenue according to population.[123] George Coles later maintained that the delegates to the Charlottetown Conference agreed to give £200,000 to Prince Edward Island to purchase the proprietary estates, and thereby, enable it to settle the proprietary land question.[124] Although this proposition, much to Coles's disgust, was not implemented at Quebec, the delegates never denied they had made this promise in Charlottetown. The admission that a federal union was feasible, and tentative agreement on a proposed constitution, were major accomplishments indeed.

A final result of the Charlottetown Conference was that it made Confederation a practicable objective. At Charlottetown, twenty-three of Canada's leading statesmen dedicated themselves to the building of a new nation. At discussion tables and at banquets their enthusiasm increased for this common goal. Not all of them were destined to persevere, but enough of them retained their zeal to see their objective accomplished. Colonel J. H. Gray was prophetic when he expressed the view that the Charlottetown Conference "would serve as the harbinger of such a union of sentiments and interests among the three and a half millions of freemen who now inhabit British America, as neither time nor change can forever destroy."[125] As a distinguished Canadian historian, Peter Waite, correctly notes, the Charlottetown Conference "was more than a Canadian triumph; it was the first appearance of an authentic national spirit."[126]

The Charlottetown Conference was, of course, preliminary to the more famous Quebec Conference; but in many ways, Quebec was merely the natural and logical conclusion to Charlottetown. Because the Charlottetown Conference could only "officially" discuss Maritime Union, there could be no formal resolutions on federal union. But this does not alter the fact that the Conference was, in effect, a Conference on Confederation. Indeed, the Quebec Conference largely formalized, refined and systematized constitutional principles agreed upon at Charlottetown. The Charlottetown Conference was the all-important first step in the building of a new Canadian edifice. Canada's nation building unquestionably began in Charlottetown, thereby, meriting for Canada's smallest Province the title — Cradle of Confederation.

The enthusiasm generated by the Charlottetown Conference was so overwhelming that, for the nonce, Prince Edward Island seemed to be partially captivated. The Conference had virtually shelved Maritime Union and this delighted nearly every Islander. The plan of union advanced at Charlottetown assured the Island of the maintenance of its cherished institutions. Moreover, high hopes were entertained that a federal union would lead to the settlement of the contentious land question. But the Island still had serious reservations. "As to little Prince Edward Island," the *Protestant* wrote on October 1, "we believe her purchase price is nearly fixed; only let any government, legislative, federal, or mongrel, but offer 200,000 pounds sterling, to buy out the proprietors' claims, and give them free lands, and we believe the Islanders almost to a man would hold up their hands for the union."[127] The *Vindicator* insisted that "the delegates to Quebec must insist upon Mr. Coles's proposition for a free grant of £200,000 sterling, wherewith to buy up the proprietary lands as a *sine qua non* of our acceptance of a Confederation.[128] It was clear that Prince Edward Island's principal objective was to extricate itself from the incubus of the proprietors. But at what price? She was certainly not prepared to acquire a new Lord and master in a powerful government at Ottawa. Confederation, it seemed, demanded a price the Islanders were not prepared to pay.

Chapter Seven

Prince Edward Island Rejects Confederation, 1864-1867

By F. W. P. Bolger

I OPPOSITION AT QUEBEC

The Maritime delegates had a respite of less than three weeks before their departure for the second Canadian Confederation Conference. The Canadian Government, wanting the Maritimes to travel with appropriate panoply, sent the "Confederate" steamship, *Queen Victoria,* to bring them to Quebec. She arrived at Pictou, Nova Scotia, on October 5, where the Nova Scotia delegation, accompanied by Lieutenant Governor MacDonnell and his wife, came on board. The ship reached Charlottetown at about noon on October 6. The party disembarked and was escorted by the Island delegates on a brief visit to Government House, and then to a luncheon at Col. J. H. Gray's commodious residence at Inkerman. Later that afternoon, the party, now including five of the seven Island delegates, boarded the steamer for Shediac, where it met the New Brunswick delegation. After a pleasant voyage of three days, the delegation reached Quebec at an early hour on Sunday evening. Comfortable apartments had been provided for the delegates at the St. Louis Hotel. Later that evening, Governor General Monck and his Executive Council entertained the visiting delegates and their ladies at an elaborate dinner at Government House. It appeared to the delegates that Quebec would be Charlottetown 'writ large'.

On Monday morning, October 10, in the elegant reading room of the Legislative Chamber overlooking the majestic St. Lawrence, the Quebec Conference assembled for its first session. The membership was larger and the atmosphere more formal than it had been at the 'unofficial' Charlottetown Conference.[1] Robert Harris's immortal portrait of rows of earnest and sombre faces has captured the mood of the Conference. At the very first session, the delegates, fully realizing that they were playing for keeps, introduced the aura of seriousness that prevailed for the next nineteen days.

The Delegates to the Quebec Conference

27 29

8   6

24 4

5

17

2

14 23

20

10

9

1   15

7   11

13 3

26 12

25

18

22 16

21

30 19

28

CANADA

1. Hon. Sir. E. P. Taché, M. L. C., *Receiver General and Minister of Militia.*
2. Hon. J. A. Macdonald, M. P. P., *Attorney General, Canada West.*
3. Hon. George E. Cartier, M. P. P., *Attorney General, Canada East.*
4. Hon. George Brown, M. P. P., *President of Executive Council.*
5. Hon. O. Mowatt, M. P. P., *Postmaster General.*
6. Hon. A. T. Galt, M. P. P., *Minister of Finance.*
7. Hon. J. C. Chapais, M. P. P., *Commissioner of Public Works.*
8. Hon. H. L. Langevin, M. P. P., *Solicitor General, Canada East.*
9. Hon. J. Cockburn, M. P. P., *Solicitor General, Canada West.*
*Hon. Wm. McDougall.
*Hon. T. D'Arcy McGee.
*Hon. A. Campbell.

NOVA SCOTIA

10. Hon. C. Tupper, *Provincial Secretary.*
11. Hon. W. A. Henry, *Attorney General.*
12. Hon. J. McCully, M. L. C., *Leader of the Opposition.*
13. Hon. R. B. Dickey, M. P. P.
14. Hon. A. G. Archibald, M. P. P.

NEW BRUNSWICK

15. Hon. S. L. Tilley, *Provincial and Financial Secretary.*
16. Hon. W. H. Steeves, M. L. C., *Member of the Executive Council.*
17. Hon. J. M. Johnson, *Attorney General.*
18. Hon. E. B. Chandler, M. L. C.
19. Lt. Col. Hon. J. H. Gray, M. P. P.
20. Hon. C. Fisher, M. P. P.
*Hon. P. Mitchell.

NEWFOUNDLAND

21. Hon. F. B. T. Carter, *Speaker of the Legislative Assembly.*
22. Hon. J. A. Shea, *Leader of the Opposition.*

PRINCE EDWARD ISLAND

23. Col. the Hon. J. H. Gray, *Leader of the Government.*
24. Hon. E. Palmer, *Attorney General.*
25. Hon. H. Pope, *Provincial Secretary.*
26. Hon. A. A. MacDonald, M. L. C.
27. Hon. G. Coles, M. P. P., *Leader of the Opposition.*
28. Hon. T. H. Haviland, M. P. P.
29. Hon. E. Whelan, M. P. P.
30. H. Bernard, *Secretary.*

*Absent from Photograph.

Because the Charlottetown Conference had not been formal, the problem of voting had not been introduced. Were the delegates to vote individually? Were they to vote by provinces? Should each province have the same number of votes? After a spirited discussion, Edward Palmer, soon to become the chief malcontent of the Conference, moved that in all questions except those of order each delegation should have one vote.[2] The motion placed the Canadians in an embarrassing position. Through the passage of Palmer's motion they would have only one vote, while the Eastern provinces would have four; and yet, to defeat the motion, they had to argue that their province was individually of more significance than the others. At length, John A. Macdonald saved the situation by suggesting that Canada should have two votes by virtue of its historic duality. Since the four Atlantic provinces would still have four votes to Canada's two, even Palmer supported Macdonald's amendment, which then passed unanimously.[3] But Prince Edward Island had served notice that it was going to be an obstructive force at the Quebec Conference.

The composition of the Prince Edward Island delegation made it extremely difficult for it to present a united front. Four members of the incumbent Conservative Government, John Hamilton Gray, the Premier, Edward Palmer, Attorney General, W. H. Pope, Provincial Secretary, and T. H. Haviland, Solicitor General and Speaker, were associated with A. A. MacDonald, Edward Whelan and George Coles, the three chief spokesmen of the Liberal Party. Personal recriminations, an important ingredient of Island politics, were by no means left behind on Prince Edward Island. Moreover, a further note of bitterness was added when divisions began to cut across party lines. Edward Whelan, the most articulate delegate, joined John Hamilton Gray, William Henry Pope and Thomas Heath Haviland in giving low-key support to the scheme as it unfolded in Quebec, while Edward Palmer, the sombre and astute Attorney General, lined up with George Coles and Andrew Archibald MacDonald in forthright opposition. But despite these sharp divisions, all the delegates managed to close ranks when Prince Edward Island's interests seemed threatened by the federal scheme. The Prince Edward Island delegation was in the vanguard during the bitter controversies the Conference encountered in reaching a *modus vivendi* on the composition of the Senate, representation in the House of Commons, the division of powers and the financial settlement.

When the delegates proceeded to a consideration of the composition of the Upper House, an intense controversy erupted which nearly ended the Conference. On Thursday, October 13, John A. Macdonald moved that the three sections, Upper Canada, Lower Canada, and the four Maritime provinces should each be represented in the Senate by twenty-four members.[4] Leonard Tilley immediately countered with a motion that Canada East and Canada West should each have twenty-four members, and the four Eastern provinces thirty-two.[5] Tilley's proposition seemed perfectly reasonable to the Maritimers, since Newfoundland had not been considered as belonging to the Maritime division in Charlottetown, and, therefore, its inclusion at Quebec seemed to warrant the suggested adjustment. The Maritime delegates spent the next five days in a determined bid to achieve a larger membership, while the Canadians argued just as vociferously for the retention of their sacred principle of sectional equality. By Friday afternoon, October 14, the situation was so tense that Edward Whelan wrote pessimistically "that with so much diversity of opinion, it is very difficult to say whether this convention will be compelled to break up prematurely. Matters do not certainly look very promising for a completion of the deliberations. I hope there may be concession and reconciliation, but I have grave doubts respecting a satisfactory result."[6]

The Maritime delegates presented resolution after resolution aimed at giving them a larger membership, but their arguments were weakened by their failure to base them on principle rather than upon expediency. Why did they not assert their demand for larger representation as a right based on provincial sovereignty? A. A. MacDonald of Prince Edward Island made the strongest bid for provincial equality. He stated that he "considered each province should have equal representation in the Federal Upper House, and he instanced the different states of the Union, which, however diversified in area, were each represented by two Senators in the General Government."[7] But he failed to follow his argument through to its logical conclusion. Instead, he suggested that "since each province now possesses a constitution of its own, similar in the case of the smallest to that in the largest province, with equal rights and privileges, the smaller provinces should claim better representation that the resolution provided . . . and, therefore, we should take the number in our own present councils as our basis, and allow each Province half of that number in the Federal Legislative Council."[8] But he was afraid to lay down an unqualified doctrine on provincial rights. All the delegates fancied that the sovereignty guaranteed to the several States by the American Constitution had caused the disastrous Civil War. Such a fateful error must be avoided in British North America. MacDonald, therefore, did not insist upon this unpopular principle, and ended his argument on sheer expediency. His proposal was not seriously entertained.

But the debate dragged on interminably, and the exasperation of the delegates heightened. At length, on Monday, October 17, a week after the Conference opened, John A. Macdonald broke the deadlock by accepting a previous motion by Charles Tupper that removed Newfoundland from the Maritime division and allotted her four additional Senators in her own right.[9] The principle of sectional equality had been approved but by the dint of a small concession. The Prince Edward Island delegation remained adamant. George Coles and A. A. MacDonald proposed amendments which gained no support. After an Island caucus, they voted against the compromise which was unanimously supported by the other provinces. Prince Edward Island was almost ready to settle down into a state of sullen opposition.

But other questions related to the Senate prolonged the debate, notably, the method of selection and qualifications of members. Shortly after the approval of the principle of sectional equality, John A. Macdonald moved that the Senators should be appointed for life by the Crown under the great seal of the general government.[10] To Prince Edward Island, appointment by the general government meant that the Upper House would not serve as a defender of provincial rights. George Coles and A. A. MacDonald immediately opposed Macdonald's resolution. Coles demanded instead that the members of the Upper House should be chosen by a majority of both branches of the provincial Legislatures. A. A. MacDonald supported Coles's motion, and maintained that only by provincial appointment would the popular opinion of the provinces be expressed in the Upper House.[11] Although Coles and MacDonald could not muster support for their resolutions, the debate dragged on for two days until John A. Macdonald's resolution was finally accepted. On the question of property qualifications for membership in the Upper House, Prince Edward Island took the lead, supported by Newfoundland, in demanding lower qualifications than those proposed by John A. Macdonald. On this point, their arguments prevailed, and agreement was reached when the other provinces agreed to lower the property qualifications. "At the Quebec Conference," John A. Macdonald later explained, "we were all in favour of a higher qualification, but it was reduced to suit Prince Edward Island and Newfoundland."[12]

Additional problems were encountered when the Conference attempted to reach agreement on the appointment of the first Senators. The majority of the delegates preferred that they should be selected from the existing Legislative Councils. But George Coles eventually led the Conference to accept the proposition that the first Legislative Councillors would be chosen at large "by the general government on the recommendation of the local governments, due regard being given to the claims of the members of the Opposition in each province so that all parties be as nearly as possible fairly represented."[13] "That favored place, [Prince Edward Island]," Whelan commented, "was to have the whole Island as a choice. Whether this may be deemed complimentary to the Island, or whether it was supposed the present Legislative Council there does not or is not likely to afford suitable materials for a selection, are points which I am not prepared to discuss."[14] The debate on the composition of the Senate was now finally over. But it had lasted for seven long days, and, up to this point the settlement of problems relating to the Senate was the only solid achievement of the Conference. Nation-building at Quebec seemed to be grinding to a halt.

In the evening of October 19, Prince Edward Island embroiled the Conference in another altercation. This was over the question of representation in the House of Commons. George Brown introduced a series of resolutions on the composition of the House of Assembly whereby Canada West would have eighty-nine members, Canada East, sixty-five, New Brunswick, fifteen, Nova Scotia, nineteen, Newfoundland, seven, and Prince Edward Island, five.[15] At the mention of the contemptible number of five seats, the disgust of some of the members of the Island delegation became complete. T. H. Haviland began the opposition to the principle of representation by population. "Prince Edward Island," he said, "would rather be out of Confederation than consent to this motion. We should have no status. Only five members out of 194 would give the Island no position."[16] Ambrose Shea of Newfoundland boldly suggested that the principle of representation by population had been settled in Charlottetown, and Prince Edward Island should be satisfied with the five members to which her population entitled her. This remark aroused the ire of Edward Palmer who maintained that he "never understood that any proposition at Charlottetown was to be binding as to representation by population."[17] "It was there made by those from Canada," he added, "and I did not think it necessary to remark on it, as it was a mere suggestion then thrown out by Canada for consideration."[18] Besides, he continued, what did Shea know about the subject? He had not even been at Charlottetown! He concluded his remarks with the assertion that "not even two or three more members would induce him to give his assent to the scheme."[19]

But the Island delegates were not united in their interpretation of the agreement at Charlottetown. George Coles contended that he fully understood that membership in the Lower House was to be settled on the basis of representation by population.[20] "I think that we came here prepared for representation by population," he added, "and I regret that the Attorney General of Prince Edward Island [Edward Palmer] had not previously stated that he could not accede to the principle and withdrawn from the Conference."[21] Colonel Gray stated that Palmer's remarks placed the Island delegation in a humiliating position, and agreed with Coles that they had expected "to treat on the basis of representation by population."[22] Edward Whelan, however, kept the issue alive by insisting that he was not "satisfied with the representation of five in the Federal House of Commons."[23] "Our resources are large," he argued, "and our people would not be content to give up their present benefits for the representation of five members. It may be said that the Confederation will go on without Prince Edward Island, and that we will eventually be forced in. Better however, that, than we should willingly go into Confederation with that representation."[24] This open quarreling among the Island delegates presented an interesting spectacle for the other delegates. But they had had enough, and A. T. Galt suggested that the Conference should adjourn until the following morning to give the Island delegates an opportunity to consider the question in private.

On the following morning, before the Conference began, Colonel Gray called a meeting of the Island delegates. At this caucus all the delegates agreed to contend for an additional member.[25] Colonel Gray initiated the Island's novel approach. "I am instructed by my co-delegates to say," he argued weakly, "that the promise of five members is unsatisfactory. Prince Edward Island is divided longitudinally into three counties, each returning ten members. But they are always opposed to change of representation. We cannot divide the three counties into the five members."[26] George Coles stated that he agreed with this proposition rather than with "Mr. Brown's motion, because it allows us to give our three counties two members each".[27] W. H. Pope asserted that "the circumstances of Prince Edward Island were such that he hoped the Conference will agree to give us such a number as we can divide among our three constituencies."[28] "Nature as well as the original settlement of the Island has made the three counties," he insisted, "and it would give rise to much difficulty if we had to adjust five members to the three counties. I cannot ask it as a matter of right, but one of expediency, as one without which it is impossible to carry the measure in Prince Edward Island. I, therefore, ask for six members."[29]

The appeal of the Island delegation, based upon the weak and rather ridiculous argument that it was difficult to adjust five members to three counties, did not carry much weight. Brown and Galt maintained that the Conference could not depart from the principle of representation by population. The Island's sister provinces in the Maritimes, from whom the Island might have expected some fraternal support, listened in respectful and embarrassed silence. The Islanders realized that it was useless for them to continue their case at the Conference. At length, George Coles advised them to submit and "let Prince Edward Island settle the problem when the question came before them."[30] The intimation certainly was that Prince Edward Island would not enter Confederation. Two days later Edward Palmer wrote to David Laird, the editor of the *Protestant,* that he was so "thoroughly disgusted at the course events had taken here that he would be disposed to 'sit by the waters of Babylon and weep for years', if I thought our Island people would be taken in by the scheme."[31] As far as Palmer was concerned, the Island's support for union "would almost entirely depend on what *number of representatives* would be allowed [her]."[32] The arguments of the Islanders had not prevailed, and for the rest of the Conference they assumed an attitude of either indifference or outright opposition.

George Coles, one of the Island's leading opponents of the Quebec scheme, caused another spirited controversy on Monday, October 24, on the question of the division of powers between the federal and the local Legislatures. He immediately made an effort to strengthen the local governments by moving that "the local Legislatures shall have power to make all laws not given by the Conference to the General Legislature expressly."[33] This resolution was diametrically opposed to John A. Macdonald's sacred principle that he had enunciated in Charlottetown whereby residuary power must be granted to the central government. Prince Edward Island had caused trouble again. Coles, moreover, had the strong support of E. B. Chandler of New Brunswick who argued that the subjects assigned to the local governments were so insignificant that the union would really be legislative rather than federal. Charles Tupper answered Coles and Chandler. He maintained that "those who were at Charlottetown should remember that it was fully specified there that all powers not given to local governments should be reserved to the Federal Government."[34] But Coles was not ready to submit. "I did not understand," he insisted, "that this was laid down as a basis at Charlottetown. I thought the only thing specified was representation by population."[35] At this point, John A. Macdonald arose in support of his principle. He maintained that to adopt Coles's resolution would be to adopt the worst features of the American Constitution. He told the Conference that to grant residual powers to the local governments would be a source of radical weakness, and "would ruin us in the eyes of the civilized world."[36] Macdonald's speech won the Conference, and, in the end, all the delegates voted for the principle. Prince Edward Island had once again demonstrated its opposition to a key proposal, but as on other occasions the delegates were obliged sullenly to submit.

Two days later, on Wednesday, October 26, when the Conference began a detailed discussion of the financial arrangements, Prince Edward Island resumed its customary role of opposition. Nearly all the Island delegates argued that it was impossible for them to accept A. T. Galt's financial proposals. W. H. Pope, the Island's financial spokesman, maintained that the Island was not receiving adequate compensation for the transfer of her custom duties to the Federal Government. The loss of this income, and the absence of Crown lands, mines and industry necessitated, he insisted, more preferential consideration than that guaranteed by Galt's proposals.[37] But it was Galt's failure to provide the £200,000 [or possibly the interest on it yearly] for the purchase of the proprietary lands that motivated the deepest resentment. The Islanders maintained that it had been agreed in Charlottetown that this amount should be made available. "I was struck with amazement" George Coles said later, "when this provision was omitted."[38] Coles promptly made a motion that "a sum equal to the interest of the amount necessary to purchase the proprietary lands be paid annually to Prince Edward Island."[39] A. A. MacDonald spoke at some length in support of Coles's resolution and maintained "that the only advantage he could see that would accrue to the people of his province under the proposed Confederation would be to have the lands purchased by the Government."[40] The members of the Conference gave no support to Coles's motion. George Brown nobly insisted that Prince Edward Island in Confederation would have more money than she would know what to do with. George Coles continued to protest and told the Conference that since it refused his proposition, "they might as well strike Prince Edward Island out of the constitution altogether."[41] Further verbal protestations seemed fruitless, so the Island delegates merely registered their disapproval by voting in solitary opposition to A. T. Galt's proposals. Their disgust was now complete. On October 27, the final day of the Conference, A. A. MacDonald was the only Islander in attendance. It was apparent to all that Prince Edward Island would not likely accept the federal plan drafted at Quebec.

Immediately after the session at Quebec, the delegates began a triumphal tour of the principal Canadian cities. Elaborate banquets were tendered the delegates during the perambulations and many orations were delivered in praise of federal union. The delegates discreetly revealed their sentiments on the main provisions of the "Quebec Plan." These receptions seemed to elevate the spirits of the disappointed Islanders, and they showed no disposition to depart from the laudatory sentiments expressed by most of the delegates. In Montreal, Edward Whelan, in the course of an enthusiastic speech on the advantages of union, maintained that "nothing now could possibly prevent us from becoming a powerful confederacy;"[42] and he promised that "while deferring reverently to the public opinion of his own province, he would cheerfully go amongst his people, and explaining it as well as he could, he would ask them to support a measure that would enhance their prosperity."[43] T. H. Haviland, at the same banquet, promised that "Prince Edward Island was honorably prepared to do something — all in its power — to organize in America a constitutional monarchy which should be able to spread these institutions in which there was the soul of liberty."[44] He expressed the hope that by virtue of the deliberations at Charlottetown and Quebec, "ere long we should be a nation of interests no longer distinct, but one people under the same old time-honored flag which now floated over us."[45] Colonel Gray spoke in favor of Confederation on many occasions during the tour. At Ottawa, for example, he concluded a glowing tribute to the proposed union with the hope that all the people "would soon have their territory washed by the Atlantic at Halifax and by the Pacific at Vancouver Island."[46] W. H. Pope assured his audience at St. Catharine's that "Prince Edward Island would be a member of the new Confederation because it desired those advantages which would result from union."[47]

Even the two chief malcontents of the Conference, Edward Palmer and George Coles, expressed reserved enthusiasm for the scheme. At the *dejeuner* in Ottawa, Coles stated "that for the past two months — first at Charlottetown and then at Quebec — they had been trying to draw up the marriage settlement — and he had to announce to them that they had succeeded in framing a marriage settlement, which though in some respects not what some of them might have wished, he hoped would, taken as a whole, give satisfaction to the entire family."[48] Edward Palmer, in a speech which later caused him much embarrassment, waxed eloquently at Toronto in favor of the federal scheme. "Yes, I hesitate not to say," he stated, "that from all that has been witnessed by the delegates representing the Island, that they will not hesitate to recommend to their people the great union which I hope to soon see accomplished."[49] "We desire to come into the Union," he asserted in his peroration, "to form part of the great Empire which is to be constructed out of these provinces of British North America, sharing the glories of the Mother Country, which we all desire to see perpetuated and increased."[50] Palmer said, on his return to Charlottetown, that neither he nor Coles should have been expected to criticize Confederation at a public dinner in their honor, because the criticism would have dampened the enthusiasm of post-prandial cordiality. He asserted, moreover, that he was expressing, not his own sentiments, "but rather the sentiments of what I knew too well were those of a majority and a large majority, of my fellow delegates."[51] Whatever their motives on these occasions, these were the last utterances in favor of federal union that flowed from the lips of Edward Palmer and George Coles.

The historic Quebec Conference was now over. Would the Island delegates recommend the plan engrossed there? Their attitude was all-important because the Conference was only the first step towards the accomplishment of Confederation. The Provincial Legislatures would have to endorse the "Quebec Plan" and this acceptance would, in a large measure, depend upon the willingness of the delegates to convince the people and their legislative representatives of its benefits. The record of hostility and opposition at Quebec by the Island delegation in general, and by Palmer, Coles and MacDonald in particular, did not augur well for the Island's acceptance of the Quebec scheme.

II   AWAY WITH CONFEDERATION

On December 30, 1864, W. H. Pope wrote in the *Islander* "that Prince Edward Island would not accept the offer of Confederation with her great and flourishing neighbors."[52] "We have done our duty," he added, "we have urged Confederation — the people have declared against it, and by-and-by, when in Prince Edward Island the desire for Confederation will be as loudly expressed as today is expressed the desire to avoid it — and that hour we predict will come — we shall have our reward."[53] This statement was a precise analysis of the situation on Prince Edward Island. The vast majority of the Island population, influenced by the arguments of those delegates opposed to Confederation, adopted an attitude of positive hostility towards the Quebec Resolutions. The moulding of public opinion against Confederation was largely the result of the efforts of three of the Island delegates. George Coles, Edward Palmer and A. A. MacDonald opposed the federal plan while W. H. Pope, J. H. Gray, T. H. Haviland and Edward Whelan espoused it. Shortly after the return of the delegates the controversy began. Verbal and newspaper battles were waged on the merits and demerits of the scheme. The controversy was carried to the public platforms of nearly every hamlet on the Island. Party lines were split and the life of the Conservative government was seriously endangered. There were resignations from the Executive Council and even the cautious Lieutenant Governor was drawn into the dispute. Confederation proved to be one of the most acrimonious issues ever introduced into the political life of the Island.

The controversy began on November 10, 1864, when the Charlottetown *Monitor* published with substantial exactness, the seventy-two Quebec Resolutions.[54] It would appear that Edward Palmer furnished the *Monitor* with these. He arrived in Charlottetown on November 9, and since he was a frequent contributor to the *Monitor* before and during the Quebec Conference, it appears likely that his return was connected with their publication. The next day Palmer came out publicly against Confederation, addressing a large crowd in Market Square on the great evils of the scheme.[55] W. H. Pope and Col. J. H. Gray returned the following day and immediately began a defense of the Quebec Resolutions. On November 18, 1864, Colonel Gray addressed an appeal to the people of the Island that was published in all the newspapers. His request for support of Confederation was based upon the premise that it would lead to the settlement of the contentious land question. "Shall we refuse," he asked, "to now enter a Confederation which secures to us the most liberal terms under which the proprietors' lands can be purchased, and our tenantry made happy and free?"[56] He maintained that in Confederation "the local Legislature would no longer be slighted and thwarted, and its most solemn enactments trampled underfoot."[57] On the contrary, its legislation on the land question would become effective by virtue of "the protection of a strong government under whose shield we shall command the respect of Downing Street."[58] "Confederation," he concluded, "is a question of life or death to Prince Edward Island. I pray to the most high God to direct your decision."[59]

William Henry Pope immediately rushed to the assistance of Colonel J. H. Gray. His first move was an attempt to undermine Edward Palmer's stand by accusing him of blatant inconsistency. He published Palmer's Toronto speech in the *Islander* and maintained that "he was astounded when he was informed on his return to the Island that Palmer had declared himself decidedly opposed to the union."[60] When Palmer pointed out that he had vehemently opposed the proposed union at the Quebec Conference, Pope simply replied that his speeches at Quebec were not sufficiently explicit to enable him "to learn what was Mr. Palmer's opinion of the union, — whether he desired to see it accomplished or not."[61] It would seem that Pope was hardly being fair to Palmer. Palmer's actions after his return to the Island followed logically from his performance at Quebec. Ambrose Shea of Newfoundland wrote to A. T. Galt that "old Palmer has not disappointed any of us."[62] He mentioned that there were "some small mercenary motives at work in dictating Palmer's course."[63] Mercenary motives may have had some minimal influence in Palmer's decision; stability in office, perhaps, even Gray's position as Premier could be his reward for leading the people in an anti-Confederate stance they were likely to adopt. But none of these interpretations do Palmer justice. He was the chief malcontent at Quebec, and no person familiar with his role there should have been "astounded" when he announced his opposition to the scheme on his return to Charlottetown.

Edward Palmer, who was described by Whelan as "the steadfast apostle of *the stand-still, the do-nothing, the Sleepy Hollow school*,"[64] was highly incensed by the publication of his Toronto speech. "I did not deem my consistency called into question," he retorted, "by what may have fallen from me during an unstudied complimentary speech at a *dejeuner* where controversy was neither invited nor expected, and would have been deemed out of place if introduced, and where it was invariably the good fashion

during the whole tour, for everyone who was called on to return thanks
for the princely hospitality shown us, to reciprocate, as far as possible,
what was most pleasant and agreeable to their kind hosts."[65] He invited
Pope and Whelan to study his performance at Quebec. What about his letter to the *Monitor,* at the height of the Quebec Conference, soundly condemning the scheme and expressing "the earnest hope that our own
Legislature would discard it because the paltry proportion of representation we are to have in both branches of the Legislature, is little more than
nominal, and leaves us at the mercy of the other provinces."[66] He repeated
his admonition to the people of the Island, and cautioned them "not to
suffer their interests and those of their posterity, to be irredeemably sacrificed for the sake of the aggrandizement of a very few individuals of the
present day."[67]

The Conservative government was in disarray. The Premier, J. H.
Gray, and his Provincial Secretary, W. H. Pope, were at loggerheads with
the Attorney General, Edward Palmer. The Premier decided that he could
no longer lead the Conservative Party. Public opposition to Confederation
was on the increase. His appeal to the Island people to support Confederation had received a hostile response. At length, on December 16, 1864, he
resigned. He informed Lieutenant Governor Dundas that he considered
Edward Palmer's attempt to justify his speech at Toronto "an insult not only
to the gentlemen of Toronto, but particularly so to the delegates from the
other Provinces, and calculated to bring into contempt the people and
government of the Island."[68] "Were I to continue in a government of which
Mr. Palmer is a member," he concluded, "I might be supposed to countenance conduct so highly reprehensible — the duty I owe to myself and the
people of this Island obliges me to withdraw from the Executive."[69] Gray
was undoubtedly a man of great honor and could not condone Palmer's
conduct. Such was the resentment between the two men that they could
not remain in the same Cabinet. In the anti-Confederate atmosphere of
Prince Edward Island, Gray, not Palmer, had to go. Gray told Charles
Tupper that had he "brought his [Palmer's] conduct before the Council,
and insisted on his resigning, or that I would have done so, such was the
storm, that I wd. have been told that I sacrificed and persecuted him on
account of his exposure of my treason. I am not afraid that ere long calmer
councils will prevail and that justice will be done me."[70]

Calmer councils did not prevail. Shortly after the acceptance of Col.
J. H. Gray's resignation, the Executive Council, prodded by W. H. Pope,
demanded a reply from Edward Palmer to the charges made against him
by Colonel Gray. Edward Palmer replied immediately, but in so doing, he
undermined his position. He maintained that he had received no support

from Gray at the Quebec Conference when he attempted to show the in-justice of the Island's receiving only five members. He asserted that Gray had stated he was humiliated by Palmer's demand for additional members.[71] He claimed further that W. H. Pope spoke immediately after Gray, "and repeated nearly in the same terms, but in a still more emphatic tone, the statements of Gray."[72] He concluded that both Gray and Pope by their behaviour at Quebec had acted "in direct opposition to their duty and the vital interests of the Island."[73] As soon as Palmer's letter was read in Coun-cil, James College Pope resigned. He was William Henry's brother, and a close colleague of J. H. Gray. Although an anti-Confederate himself, it would seem that he was so annoyed with Edward Palmer that he, like Gray, could not remain in the same Cabinet. The Cabinet obviously had to be reshuffled. It appeared that Palmer was about to get the nod from Dundas to become Premier when William Henry Pope dropped a veritable bomb-shell.

W. H. Pope's reply to Palmer's charges was irrefutable. He informed Dundas and his Council that he "did not repeat nearly in the same terms, but in a still more emphatic tone, the statements of Colonel Gray."[74] "I am prepared to prove to your Excellency," he sarcastically continued, "that I was several miles away from the Conference at the time Mr. Palmer stood forth as the champion of the 'vital interests of Prince Edward Island', and that I did not enter the Conference until the next day . . . when I to the best of my ability, argued that Prince Edward Island, for reasons which I then stated, be allowed six members."[75] Edward Palmer had overreached him-self. Pope's letter clearly indicated that he was guilty of mendacity. The next day, Palmer resigned without comment. Edward Whelan's analysis was that "Palmer's resignation was not a voluntary one. If Mr. Palmer con-tinued in the Council, it would have been irretrievably broken, because he had not the power and influence requisite to reconstruct it after Col. Gray and J. C. Pope retired. He was forced to go."[76] These observations were not far off the mark.

The Conservatives then made a number of unbelievable moves in order to cling to office. The Executive Council first asked Gray to "again occupy the position from which he had retired."[77] Gray declined the dubious honor. He felt that the Council, with the exception of W. H. Pope, had too readily sacrificed him when he offered his resignation, and he would not accept its show of belated friendship. He was, perhaps, comforted by John A. Macdonald's assurance that "his course in the crisis in Prince Edward Island was only what we expected from a soldier and a gentleman, and long after the present events have lost their interest it will dwell in the memories of your family and friends."[78] In an amazing move, J. C. Pope withdrew his resignation and accepted the office of Premier. Perhaps like Sir John A. Macdonald's successor, Sir John Abbott, he received the post "because he was not particularly obnoxious to anybody." Edward Palmer, although no longer a member of the Executive Council, astonishingly enough, remained as Attorney General; and to fill the vacancies in the Council, the Conservatives secured the services of T. H. Haviland and Kenneth Henderson. Dundas described Haviland as "a prominent advocate of the project of the Quebec Conference, and Henderson as a decided opponent of the scheme."[79] By these appointments, the Conservatives maintained a precarious balance on the Confederation question. They managed to survive the first crisis occasioned by the Confederation drama, but there were many shoals ahead for this loosely united group.

But it was in the country at large rather than in the narrow confines of the Executive Council that the Confederation question was being decided. And in the country, the proponents of the Confederation scheme, notably W. H. Pope and Edward Whelan, were meeting with little support. The *Monitor,* commenting upon Palmer's resignation, noted "that Mr. Palmer had more friends at the present time than he ever had since he entered the political arena, and the more he is denounced and condemned, by the Colonial Secretary [W. H. Pope] the more closely will those friends rally to his support."[80] Edward Whelan devoted column after column in his newspaper to the advocacy of Confederation. But he had to admit to A. T. Galt in mid-December that Prince Edward Island "was dead set against Union in all shapes and forms."[81] "Pope and myself," he added, "have nearly all the fighting to do on the other side, and we are not in the least dismayed by the odds against us."[82] But the odds proved insuperable. By the end of December, Edward Whelan had to content himself with articles that endeavoured to prove the inevitability of Confederation and the Island's eventual entrance into it, regardless of her present attitude. On December 26, he wrote sarcastically in the *Examiner:*

The cause of Confederation happily does not depend on the will of the small politicians of the small Island of Prince Edward. If the cause be fought with success on the mainland, its consummation cannot be delayed through the petulance of this little place. . . . But we cannot resist smiling at the exceeding simplicity of those who think that the other Provinces will be confederated, while the British Government must go to the expense of keeping up a protectorate over this patch of sand bank in the Gulf of St. Lawrence where the inhabitants think they have such a paradise as would be contaminated by alliance with their powerful, prosperous, and wealthy fellow subjects on the mainland.[83]

In the same month, William Henry Pope sadly admitted that "in this little Island, the proposition for Confederation has so far been anything but favourably received."[84] Some weeks later he opined that "Confederation in the coming session will be almost unanimously rejected in both Houses of Legislature of this Island."[85]

Edward Whelan and W. H. Pope were being realists. During the months of December, 1864, and of January and February of 1865, scores of public meetings were held in various places on the Island to discuss the Quebec Resolutions. One or more of the delegates to the Quebec Conference, along with the local members of the Legislature, usually addressed these gatherings. At the conclusion a series of resolutions expressive of the sentiments of the meetings was tabled and voted upon. An examination of these resolutions reveals an endless litany of reasons why Prince Edward Island should remain out of Confederation. In Charlottetown, for example, the Quebec Resolutions received a most comprehensive discussion. The debate in the Mechanics Institute lasted three evenings. W. H. Pope, T. H. Haviland, Edward Palmer, George Coles, Edward Whelan and a large number of local political figures spoke at great length. In the early hours of February 13, 1865, a large majority carried a resolution stating that "the details of the scheme agreed upon by the Quebec Conference, especially in reference to finance and representation are most injurious, unjust, and illiberal and confidently relies that the said details will by no means receive the sanction of the Legislature or government of this Island."[86] W. H. Pope was certainly correct when he wrote "that the great majority of the people appear to be wholly averse to Confederation."[87]

By February of 1865, it was generally admitted that Prince Edward Island would refuse to accept the Report of the Quebec Conference. One is naturally led to inquire why the Islanders had become so quickly and so unreservedly prejudiced against the Quebec Resolutions. Three of the delegates, Colonel Gray, W. H. Pope and Edward Whelan maintained that Edward Palmer and George Coles were primarily responsible for the Island's hostile reaction.[88] "When I returned from Canada after our happy intercourse," Gray wrote to Tupper, "I found the whole community poisoned by Mr. Palmer — "we were sacrificed ['] taxation of millions for defence" "our Militia to be drafted for slaughter to the confines of Canada" — "I *had sold* the country."[89] W. H. Pope blamed both Palmer and Coles, but especially Palmer, for the Island's attitude. "Mr. Palmer," Pope said, "was a delegate too from this Island at the Conference at Quebec and is thoroughly acquainted with the proposed scheme; and when he, a gentleman of education and high position in the Colony expresses his opinion of the union in such terms, it cannot be a matter of astonishment to any that the people should refuse even to consider a proposition which the Chief Crown Law Officer of the Colony has publicly warned them against, as calculated irredeemably to sacrifice their interests and those of their posterity."[90] "The Honorable George Coles," Pope added, "has also done all that he could to incite the popular indignation against the Canadians. The exertions of the Hon. Messrs. Palmer and Coles have produced an impression upon the public mind hostile to Confederation, which it will take some time to remove."[91] Edward Whelan petulantly wrote to A. T. Galt that "two of our delegates, Palmer and Coles, are out against it [Confederation] most vigorously and the asses of country people who can't see an inch beyond their noses, and who are afraid they are going to be tremendously taxed, sympathize with Palmer and Coles."[92] These impressions were apparently shared by John A. Macdonald, since he concluded a letter to J. H. Gray with the request that he "present his best regards to those of the Prince Edward Island delegation whom you may meet, always excepting Messrs. Palmer and Coles."[93]

The exercise in public relations came to an end late in February, 1865, when Lieutenant Governor Dundas called the Legislature into session, and asked the members "to give their earnest consideration to the question of Confederation, the most momentous subject ever committed to them."[94] The members of the Legislature were quite cognizant of the attitudes of their constituents. As the *Islander* remarked, "the people of Prince Edward Island were, with very few exceptions, unanimous in their cry, away with Confederation. We will have nothing to do with it."[95] The Legislature spent the next few weeks giving legislative expression to these sentiments.

III   CONFEDERATION DEBATES, 1865

The official consideration of the Quebec Resolutions began on March 24, 1865, with a heated dispute between J. C. Pope, the Premier, and W. H. Pope, the Provincial Secretary. When J. C. Pope prepared to move the House into Committee to consider the Quebec Resolutions, his brother promptly took the floor and moved eight resolutions in favor of Confederation.[96] J. C. Pope, not unnaturally, was quite vexed with his brother's tactical maneuver. He accused him of having manifested a great lack of courtesy toward the leader of the government, and he also charged him with placing the government in a false position, since only two of the members, W. H. Pope and T. H. Haviland, were in favor of union. He then returned the compliment by moving that all the resolutions submitted by his brother should be struck out and five anti-union resolutions substituted for them.[97] This fraternal conflict was a fitting prelude to the bitter debate that ensued.

W. H. Pope's adroit move did have one tactical advantage. It enabled him, as mover of the resolutions, and J. H. Gray, as the seconder, to present the case for Confederation before the anti-Confederates had a chance to speak. Although W. H. Pope admitted that not more than four or five members would vote for his resolutions, he bravely defended the "Quebec Plan." The central argument he advanced was that Confederation was an absolute necessity for defense against the United States. "To my mind," W. H. Pope argued, "it is very evident that we must choose between consolidation of the different provinces, and absorption into the American Republic. Consolidation — the placing of the revenues and men of the several provinces under the control of a central power would, in the event of war, be absolutely necessary for the efficient organization of our Colonial resources."[98] Colonel Gray, the military expert, used arguments of similar purport. "We have little prospect for the future," he emphasized, "beyond a dwarfed existence and ultimate absorption into the neighboring Republic. One of these must be chosen, the other rejected — there is no other alternative. Yes, Mr. Speaker, federation or annexation is what we must regard as our future."[99] T. H. Haviland used the same approach. "But, Mr. Speaker," he pleaded, "in whatever motives the idea of this Confederation may have had in its origin, the result of the defeat of the project will be, I have no hesitation in saying, our absorption into the United States. Already the handwriting is on the wall, and it needs no prophet to expound its meaning that Union or Republicanism awaits us."[100] Their arguments made the case for Confederation considerably stronger, since not even the most dedicated anti-Confederate wanted annexation. Therefore, most of them felt obligated to refer to the defense question. But they refused to admit that Confederation was the only alternative and tended to dispose of the question in a facile manner.

The anti-Confederate case was presented without any reservations. Sixteen speakers dwelt at considerable length on the political and economic reasons why the Island should not endorse the Quebec Resolutions. Representation by population, inadequate representation in the Upper House, fear of Canadian political influence, and the expected reduction in the significance of the Island's local institutions were the main political objections to Confederation. All the anti-Confederate speakers contended that the allotment of five representatives to the Island was a grave injustice. J. C. Pope, the Premier, asserted "that statistics warranted the belief that in a few years the Canadian population will be so increased by immigration that the Island would lose in the halls of Legislation even the small voice which she might raise at her entrance into union."[101] George W. Howlan commented pessimistically that "since representation was to be arranged every ten years according to population the Island's representation would decrease, and we would be left without a member at all."[102] If there were still doubts,

Nicholas Conroy sealed the argument with the assertion that in "having but five representatives in a parliament composed of one hundred and ninety-four members, we might as well have none at all."[103] The principle of sectional equality in the Senate was not popular. Frederick Brecken stated "he could see no reason why the constitution of the Upper House should not have been assimilated to that of the Senate of the United States."[104] George W. Howlan argued for provincial equality. "Rhode Island," he reminded the Assembly, "had the same number of representatives in the Senate as New York. The difference between the population of these states was twenty to one, greater fully than it is between that of Upper Canada and this Island; yet while this Report allows Upper Canada twenty-four members in the Legislative Council of the Confederation, this Colony is only allotted four."[105] The Assembly was obviously playing over again the record the Island delegates had cut at Quebec.

Most of the anti-Confederates expressed a deep-seated fear of Canadian political influence. James Warburton typified this dismay by referring to the union of Canada and Prince Edward Island as "a union of the Lion with the Lamb because we would be devoured by the Canadians."[106] All the members were convinced that their local Legislature would become insignificant. "In this House," said George Coles, "scarcely anything would be left us to do, but to legislate about dog taxes, and the running at large of swine. We would be the laughing stock of the world."[107] Frederick Brecken flippantly remarked that after Confederation there might be a party "to bring in a measure that all pigs should wear rings in their noses, but on such a question it would be difficult to keep together either a Government or an Opposition, unless they were to differ as to the description of the metal the rings should be made of."[108] Peter Sinclair sentimentally reminded the Assembly that by this scheme they would be practically required to give up their political independence. "What," he asked, "is dearer to a man than his country and its institutions? By accepting Confederation, we would be surrendering everything which we hold politically dear."[109] The diminution of the power of the local Legislature was the weighty argument with the people of Prince Edward Island.

The economic objections to the Quebec Report were many and varied. George Howlan insisted that in Confederation "Prince Edward Island would be required to give up a large and increasing revenue to the politicians of Canada, who have never been able to govern their own country, for a very small return."[110] Most of the anti-Confederates, like John Longworth, pointed out that the Island's trade position would be adversely affected by Confederation. "Our exports would not go to Canada," he realistically argued, "because she does not need our agricultural produce, still we would be compelled to purchase many manufactured articles there, for if we shut out the Americans by hostile tariffs they will not trade with us, and British goods will be excluded in the same way."[111] All the speakers maintained that they would be subjected to a heavy federal tax from which they could expect little return since the financial outlays would be on expensive federal projects in the other provinces rather than on the Island where their needs were minimal. In short, all agreed with Joseph Hensley "that their taxation would be greatly increased without corresponding advantages."[112]

Some of the anti-Confederate speakers drew the attention of the Assembly to the fact that the land question, the only substantial grievance of the Colony, was not to be settled in Confederation. "The delegates would have some show of argument in favor of this Colony entering the Union," George Howlan argued, "if they could come to this House and tell us that the long-vexed Land Question was at last to be set at rest."[113] George Coles was most emphatic in denouncing the Quebec Resolutions because of the absence of a provision for the settlement of the land tenure problem. "At the Quebec Conference," he proudly informed the Assembly, "I said that if the grant for the purchase of the lands of this Colony was not conceded, they might as well strike Prince Edward Island out of the constitution altogether."[114] The majority of the Assembly certainly seemed to agree with him that the Island should be struck out of the constitution. Some financial concession, such as the £200,000 grant, could conceivably have reconciled a few members to the Quebec Resolutions. But it is incontestable that even this concession would not have substantially altered the almost unanimous expression of opposition to Confederation.

Many of the anti-Confederate proponents took cognizance of the arguments advanced by W. H. Pope, Colonel Gray and T. H. Haviland that Confederation was the only alternative to absorption by the United States. But they would not admit that the Island was really faced with this choice. They contended that the Mother Country held the key to their future. "It will be many years hence," Frederick Brecken maintained, "before these colonies will be able, unaided by the British arm, to defend themselves against an invading foe. Separate or united, without that we shall be powerless to defend ourselves."[115] Joseph Hensley likewise asserted that "in the event of war with the United States, we know full well that there will be no chance of success without Great Britain, and it is difficult to understand how Confederation would increase our ability of resistance."[116] But it was J. C. Pope who offered the most convincing answer to the Unionists. "In the event of an invasion by the United States," he contended, "it would be necessary to retain all available strength in each of the provinces for the defence of their respective territories."[117] "Confederation," he therefore argued, "would be of no possible advantage. If every man would contribute as far as in him lies to the defense of the country in which he lives, they could trust a reasonable portion of that duty to the Mother Country, the army and the navy of which must be kept somewhere; and her experience shows that nowhere can they be maintained as cheaply as in the Colonies."[118] This argument clinched the case for the anti-Confederates, and all agreed with Pope that if they cooperated in the defense of their local hearths and remained loyal to Great Britain, they need not enter Confederation to ensure their future security.

The debate on the Quebec Resolutions engaged the House of Assembly for seven evenings. On March 31, 1865, J. C. Pope's amendment to his brother's resolutions was carried by a vote of 23-5.[119] W. H. Pope, Gray, Haviland, Whelan and Green were the five members who opposed the amendment. The Assembly then appointed J. C. Pope, Longworth, Hensley, Coles and Sinclair to prepare, in collaboration with a Committee from the Legislative Council, a Joint Address to the Queen expressive of the determination of the Legislature to refuse assent to the Quebec Resolutions.[120] The decisiveness of the Assembly vote certainly left no doubt as to the hostility of that body to Confederation.

The debate on the Quebec Resolutions in the Legislative Council was brief and halfhearted. Only one afternoon and one morning during the last two days of the session were spent on the subject. Ten of the thirteen members of the Council participated and each of them unequivocally condemned the Confederation scheme. Edward Palmer, appropriately enough, introduced the anti-Confederate case by submitting a formal resolution "that the report of the Quebec Convention is in no respect just or suitable to Prince Edward Island, and would, if accepted, prove inimical to the prosperity and happiness of its inhabitants."[121] The discussions pursuant to this resolution were similar to those in the Assembly. The Councillors maintained that Confederation would be disastrous to the Island both politically and economically. They stressed the critical aspects of the political question: representation in the Legislature, distrust of Canadian political influence, and the ultimate loss by the Island of all political significance. Edward Palmer asserted that "if anything like a desire to give us protection, or do us justice had been entertained, they would have given us equal representation in the Upper House, instead of merely a nominal representation of four members which was allowed us by that Report."[122] James McLaren maintained "that representation by population in the Lower House, even now a grave injustice to the Island would become even worse, because by the readjustments every ten years, we would probably lose one of our representatives, then another and another till in the course of time we might lose them all."[123]

The Council expressed a deep-seated distrust of Canadian political influence. Kenneth Henderson drew the attention of the members to the turmoil of Canada's political history — "the Rebellion of 1837, the perfuming of Lord Elgin with rotten eggs, the burning of the Parliament buildings, and the instability of a Parliament which had no less than five administrations in the space of the last two years."[124] He cautioned the Council that in view of their history, "the less we have to do with them, the better for ourselves."[125] James Dingwell urged the Council to remain aloof from Confederation "because Canadians had not been as well able to manage the business of their country as we have been to manage ours; and why should we trust the management of our affairs to people who have never been able to manage their own with satisfaction?"[126] He added that "if the Canadian politicians are such men as they are represented to be, they must be very corrupt."[127] Such irresistible logic was, of course, irrefutable.

The members of Council expressed their hostility to the financial arrangements. Palmer, along with many other speakers, contended that in Confederation they could expect their taxation to increase appreciably. It was obvious, moreover, that even a more generous financial settlement would not have reconciled the Council to Confederation. "Even supposing they could get more, or could get better terms," said James McLaren, "supposing they could get double as much for giving up our constitution and revenue to Canada, — I could not consent to it, for it would simply be selling ourselves for a larger sum, and I would not consent to sell ourselves at all. We have a good constitution, and let us keep it."[128] Edward Palmer handled the defense question with a single argument. "The Canadians," he said, "are right at the door of a powerful neighbor, and they must put up with their lot as we have to put up with many inconveniences here which they never feel."[129] Prince Edward Island, he maintained, need never join Confederation to enjoy security. "Nature," he calmly insisted, "defends us half the year. It is impossible, moreover, for Great Britain to have fleets on this side of the Atlantic without being in the vicinity of the Island."[130] No one was disposed to disagree with these comforting sentiments.

The debate in the Legislative Council came to a hurried close on the morning of April 3, 1865. Three of the members of Council did not have time to participate, since the Legislature was to be prorogued later in the day. They merely addressed the Chair and stated their concurrence with Edward Palmer's resolution. One of these was Andrew Archibald MacDonald who had been a delegate to both the Charlottetown and Quebec Conferences. Palmer's resolution was then placed before the Council and passed unanimously.[131] Confederation did not have a single friend in that august Chamber.

The Address to the Queen, prepared by a Joint Committee of the two Houses, left no doubt as to the attitude of Prince Edward Island to Confederation. It declared that since the "Report on the Quebec Conference would prove politically, economically and financially disastrous to the rights and best interests of the people, the Legislature humbly prayed that Her Majesty would not give Royal assent or sanction to any Act or measure founded upon this Report, that would have the effect of uniting Prince Edward Island in a federal union with Canada, or any other of Your Majesty's provinces in America."[132] The Address was carried in the Lower House by a vote or twenty-three to four, and in the Upper House, unanimously, and without a division.[133] When this Address reached the Colonial Office, Arthur Blackwood, one of the Secretaries, remarked "that Confederation seems disposed of by this Legislature in a way that leaves no doubt as to the unpopularity of the scheme."[134] His comment was a succinct and accurate analysis of the attitude of Prince Edward Island toward Confederation.

IV   THE NEVER NEVER RESOLUTIONS

The 1865 legislative session was the last occasion in which Prince Edward Island was allowed to discuss the question of Confederation free from outside influences. In subsequent years, the Maritime, Canadian and Imperial authorities exerted compelling pressures upon the Islanders. Prior to 1867 the most coercive force was the Imperial Government, which, by December of 1864, had decided to press for the accomplishment of union among the British North American Colonies. Prince Edward Island invariably revealed her vehement opposition to any form of union. But discussions continued even when both sides seemingly realized that Confederation could not be carried on the Island.

An invitation from Nova Scotia to resume negotiations on Maritime Union enabled Prince Edward Island to stage a dress rehearsal for her future performances on all forms of union. Charles Tupper, attempting to avoid a frontal attack on Confederation in Nova Scotia, revived the defunct scheme of Maritime union. In April, 1865, he formally suggested that Nova Scotia, New Brunswick and Prince Edward Island should renew negotiations on an immediate legislative union of the three provinces. The Executive Council in Prince Edward Island gave Tupper's overture brusque treatment. The formal Minute stated that "inasmuch as the people of this colony are averse as well to the union of this Island with Nova Scotia and New Brunswick as to a Federal Union of all the British North American colonies and provinces, the Board declines to renew negotiations for the

Union of Nova Scotia, New Brunswick and Prince Edward Island as proposed by the government of Nova Scotia."[135] Charles Tupper got the message from this summary rejection and Maritime Union faded even further into deep oblivion. Prince Edward Island's answer should not have been unexpected in view of her constant distaste for such a union.

The first intimation of British pressure came in February, 1865, when Edward Cardwell, the Colonial Secretary, informed Lieutenant Governor Dundas that in the event "of union being effected, Her Majesty's Government could not make provision for the salary of the Lieutenant Governor of Prince Edward Island, and that if the union did not take place, it will be equally necessary within a short time to provide for the salary of the Lieutenant Governor out of the revenue of the Colony."[136] The Assembly was bitter, and prepared an Address to the Queen stating that since "the Island had no Crown lands by virtue of the improvident alienation of these lands by the Imperial Government in 1767, the salary of the Lieutenant Governor should continue to be defrayed as a small compensation for the great injury inflicted on the Island."[137] The Colonial Secretary was unimpressed, and pointedly replied that "after averting to the very favorable representation as to the resources of the Island made by both branches of the Legislature in their Address upon Confederation there could be no departure from the British Government's decision."[138] The Imperial Government hoped that this additional charge upon the revenue of the Island would lead the the Island to have sober second thoughts on Confederation. The Islanders resentfully considered it as "a confederate screw unfairly put upon us."[139] But as yet they were not prepared to yield to such intimidation, and certainly not about to enter Confederation to avoid the painful exigency of paying the Lieutenant Governor's salary.

It was, however, on the question of defense that the British Government applied the most unrelenting pressure on Prince Edward Island. On April 28, 1865, Cardwell testily reminded the Assembly that in view of the Island's almost complete military dependence upon Great Britain, he deeply regretted the Island's "rejection of a scheme [Confederation] approved by H. M.'s Government, for this, among other reasons, that it was intended for the easier and more effective defense of all the B.N.A. provinces."[140] On June 24, Cardwell addressed an even stronger directive on defense to the Prince Edward Island government. In this despatch he ordered Dundas to inform the Legislature of Prince Edward Island of "the strong and deliberate policy of Her Majesty's Government, that it is an object much to be desired that all the British North American Colonies should agree to unite in one Government."[141] After specifying the mutual benefits that would accrue to the Colonies from Confederation, he stressed that the British Government desired to see Confederation accomplished especially for reasons of defense. "It cannot be doubted," he asserted, "that the Provinces of British North America are incapable when separate and divided from each other, of making those just and sufficient preparations for material defence which would easily be undertaken by a Province uniting in itself all the population and all the resources of the whole."[142] He concluded the despatch with the hope that Prince Edward Island would soon perceive "the advantage which, in the opinion of Her Majesty's Government the proposed union is calculated to confer upon them all."[143] This despatch announced the official policy of the British Government on Confederation. It wished to see the union accomplished. Prince Edward Island, however, remained adamant and unconvinced.

The ink was scarcely dry on Cardwell's despatch when the British Government was given an opportunity to apply additional pressure on the Island. In 1864 and 1865, many of the Island farmers had formed themselves into a "Tenants Union" with the avowed intention of withholding payment of rents until the proprietors consented to sell their estates on such terms as the union deemed just. In March, 1865, Lieutenant Governor Dundas issued a proclamation enjoining all farmers "to abstain from all such unlawful associations."[144] But the proclamation was largely ineffective. The farmers refused to disband, and when the agents and sheriffs attempted to collect the rents, much violence ensued. The disorder became so prevalent that the Administrator of the Colony, Robert Hodgson, telegraphed to Halifax for a contingent of British troops. Two companies of the Second British Battalion consisting of eight officers and one hundred and thirty men arrived in Charlottetown in August, 1865.[145] The disturbances were checked soon after the arrival of the troops, but Hodgson insisted that they must remain on the Island to deter the Tenant Leaguers from further violence.[146]

When Edward Cardwell learned of the presence of British troops on Island soil, he informed Hodgson that the Island would have to pay the expenses involved in the transport of the troops and also the cost of their maintenance while stationed on the Island.[147] The Executive Council strenuously objected to Cardwell's directive. It pointed out in a sharply worded Minute "that the feeling of discontent on the part of the tenantry owes its origin to the old Imperial error originally committed in granting the whole soil of the Colony in large tracts to individuals, an error which necessarily gave rise to an extensive leasehold system, and engendered the strife and ill-feeling between the landlord and the tenant, which from the earliest settlement of the Colony, have continued without interruption to the present time."[148] The members of Council promised that they would willingly pay the cost of the transport of the troops from Halifax, but they would not pay for their maintenance.[149] In other words, since "Imperial error" had caused the trouble, Imperial funds must pay the cost. The British Government refused to waive its demand that the Island government must defray the regimental pay for the troops. But the Island was just as refractory. The impasse lasted until March, 1867, when the British Government finally relented and agreed to meet the payment for the maintenance of the troops for the eighteen months they had served on the Island.[150] Once again, the British Government had applied pressure to make Confederation economically more appealing, but the Islanders were still unmoved.

Cardwell's despatch of June, 1865, provoked bitter resentment in the Legislature when it met in session in 1866. Premier J. C. Pope was in fighting trim when he placed his famous "no terms resolutions" before the Assembly. The first of his three resolutions maintained that a union based upon the Quebec Resolutions would "not only be unjust to the inhabitants of this Colony, but prove disastrous to their dearest and most cherished rights and interests as a free people enjoying the blessings of a priceless constitution."[151] The second resolution asserted that the Assembly could not admit that a "Federal Union of the North American Colonies, which would include Prince Edward Island, could ever be accomplished upon terms that would prove advantageous to the interests and well-being of the people of the Island."[152] And, the third stated that "while this House cannot assent to a Federal Union of this Island with the other Colonies, they recognize it to be the duty of this Colony to contribute from its local revenues towards its defense in fair and just proportion to its means."[153] J. C. Pope explained to the House of Assembly why he had introduced resolutions that "protested against anything in the shape of a Union."[154] The first reason was "the dread of being swamped by the Canadas."[155] The second was that he feared, if delegates were sent over to England, the hospitalities which had been pleaded by Coles and Palmer in extenuation of their speeches at Ottawa and Toronto might operate even more strongly in London and cause them to make commitments adverse to the views of the Island. "What has taken place once," said Pope facetiously, "may under similar influences, take place again."[156] Finally, he maintained that if the resolutions were not strongly worded, "a large majority might not support them, and stronger resolutions would be introduced and parties split up."[157] "As I believe," he contended, "that ninety-nine out of every one hundred of the people are against Confederation, I think, we as their representatives, are bound to represent or express their views."[158]

These resolutions led to a lively debate in which nineteen members participated. Fourteen speakers agreed wholeheartedly with J. C. Pope's strong stand against Union. Francis Kelly stated early in the debate that he approved "of every word of these resolutions; although if they could be made stronger, I would wish that they were."[159] Political and economic objections against Confederation were again stressed. "Considering that we would be such a small portion of the Confederacy," Cornelius Howatt argued, "our voice will not be heard in it. We would be the next thing to nothing. Are we then going to surrender our rights and liberties? It is just a question of 'self or no self'. Talk about a local Legislature. It would be a farce."[160] Frederick Brecken stated that "his greatest objection to the Confederation scheme was based on his dread of the enormous taxation to which we would, in all probability, be subjected under it."[161] And John Longworth added that "a federal grant of £48,000 per year for the relinquishment of our revenue of £70,000 a year, which in the course of a few years, would, in all probability amount to £150,000 should convince us that if we were ever to enter into Confederation on the basis of the Quebec Report, justice could never be done us."[162] All the anti-Confederates were in substantial agreement with James Duncan's contention that they "could not possibly gain anything by Confederation, and it would certainly be prejudicial to them in every particular."[163]

The discrepancy between the "no terms" resolutions and the British Government's policy announced by Edward Cardwell caused the anti-Confederates absolutely no embarrassment. They maintained that Cardwell's despatch expressed a hope or desire but did not suggest compulsion. They claimed that Great Britain had so deep a respect for constitutional rights and liberties that she would never deprive the Islanders of their constitution. Emmanuel MacEachern expressed this conviction quite forcibly. "There was, "he said, "no reason to fear that we should be driven into the projected Confederation. The people of Prince Edward Island had a constitution as well as Canada; and if they did their duty, they would never lose it."[164] "Mr. Cardwell," he admitted, "would no doubt, be glad if he found us willing to agree to the union on the terms of the Quebec scheme; but if he found we were not willing, he would not dare to force us into it."[165] It was apparent that the anti-Confederates were not prepared to yield an inch "to the strong and deliberate opinion of Her Majesty's Government that the Island should enter Confederation."[166]

The Confederates realized that they had no hope of defeating the "no terms" resolutions. They hoped, however, to amend them so as to remove the note of finality they implied. The central argument they advanced was that Prince Edward Island was placing herself in a ridiculous and absurd position by refusing to accede to the well-known desire of the British Government that she join Confederation. Edward Whelan asserted that "he could not, for one moment, suppose, that provided the other Provinces were confederated, Great Britain would allow Prince Edward Island to remain out of the Union, to be a source of weakness and annoyance to the Federation."[167] Col. J. H. Gray sarcastically claimed that J. C. Pope, in declaring that a union of the provinces could never be effected on terms favourable to Prince Edward Island was arrogating to himself "two of the grand attributes of the Deity — prescience and omniscience."[168] "Prince Edward Island," he contended, "would never be allowed to stand alone to become the resort of smugglers, and a nest of hornets in the side of Confederation."[169] T. H. Haviland claimed that the probable effect of the anti-Confederate stand would be that "while steering our vessel of state so as to avoid the rock, the *Scylla* of Confederation taxation, they would unavoidably, if not designedly, direct her course, so as to be engulfed by the *Charybdis* of American debt.[170] Colin McLennan, the last Confederate speaker in the debate, strenuously objected to the finality of J. C. Pope's resolutions. He maintained it was ridiculous to say that a scheme of union could never be a benefit to the Island. "Circumstances," he insisted, "alter cases, and circumstances have changed since last year. Then we had a flourishing trade with the United States, but now it is cut off. I would not bind myself or my children to any particular line of conduct."[171]

The advocates of Confederation staged a brave struggle but they were not able to carry their amendment designed to save the principle of union. J. C. Pope's resolutions were carried twenty-one to seven.[172] The House of Assembly then framed a vigorous Address to the Queen which stated "that any Federal Union of the North American Colonies that would embrace this Island would be as hostile to the feeling and wishes, as it would be opposed to the best and the most vital interests of its people."[173] Once again, the Island's House of Assembly had demonstrated its extreme hostility to the project of Confederation.

The Legislative Council, as usual, was even more inimical to the idea of Confederation. All the speakers insisted that the Imperial Government would never coerce them to enter union. "I say they cannot coerce us," said Kenneth Henderson, "no, the tenacious grasp with which they hold their constitutional rights and liberties of the subject prevents them. They cannot consistently with their own moral standing force us into Confederation."[174] Many speakers maintained that Edward Cardwell's despatch of June 24, 1865, was, in reality, Canadian and not Imperial pressure. "The opinions of the Colonial Minister," argued Edward Palmer, "are inspired by the wishes, the movements, and the machinations of the Ministers of Canada."[175] Henderson claimed that Cardwell's despatch was really a "trap that would pave the way for a delegation to England to help in forging chains which would forever bind us down as serfs of Canada, and make us a second Ireland."[176] James Dingwell warned the Councillors that they must avoid Confederation and never "sell the Island into the power of the most extravagant set of politicians to be found on British soil."[177] "The natural result of Confederation," George Beer insisted, "would be that the Island in a few years would be exhausted and beggared."[178] Thus, the vitriolic debate went on to its foregone conclusion. On May 10, 1866, the Council unanimously agreed to Edward Palmer's resolution that Confederation "would be opposed to the wishes, hostile to the feelings of the inhabitants, subversive of liberties, and highly detrimental to the best interests of the people of the Island."[179] The debate on Edward Cardwell's despatch certainly placed in bold relief the animosity of the Legislative Council to Confederation.

Colonel J. H. Gray and W. H. Pope found J. C. Pope's "no terms" resolutions so offensive that they recommended that the Island should be forced into Confederation. Colonel Gray wrote a long letter to his friend, John A. Macdonald, suggesting such a course of action. "I much regret," he wrote, "that all the endeavours of the friends of Confederation in this Island have been unsuccessful, and I have little hope that our people will change, and if the Imperial authorities do not legislate for us, Prince Edward Island is lost."[180] "The utterly defenseless state of the Island," he continued, "will cause it to fall at once to the hands of a United States Squadron, and it will become a starting point for their operations in the Gulf."[181] John A. Macdonald seemed convinced, and in his reply, stated that he had "little doubt that on the very strong reasons given in your letter, the Imperial Government will exercise its authority as the paramount power to annex you to Confederation."[182] W. H. Pope was so annoyed with his brother's resolutions that he resigned from the Executive Council in September, 1866. He then wrote to Lord Carnarvon and recommended that in view of the defenseless state of the Island, "Her Majesty's Ministers, when preparing the Act of Parliament for the Confederation of the British North American provinces, should include Prince Edward Island."[183] Pope and Gray were undoubtedly correct in assuming that the chances that the Island would ever voluntarily unite with Canada were very remote indeed. But the Imperial Government was not prepared to use compulsion; moral suasion and unrelenting pressure were her outside limits. Thus, the Island was allowed to remain in her chosen state of "splendid isolation."

Chapter Eight

The Coy Maiden Resists, 1867-1872

By F. W. P. BOLGER

I THE $800,000 OFFER

The next important step in the protracted Confederation negotiations in Prince Edward Island was the result of a tempting offer by the delegates to the London Conference from Nova Scotia and New Brunswick who were in England impatiently awaiting the arrival of their counterparts from Canada. It was a belated recognition of what apparently had been suggested at the Charlottetown Conference some two years before, a pledge of $800,000 to Prince Edward Island to enable it to purchase the proprietary lands. Prince Edward Island was not impressed. This proposal, far from being an inducement, caused further opposition to union with Canada, and resulted in the complete disarray of the Conservative Party in the 1867 general election. The net result was that at the end of the year 1867 Prince Edward Island was no closer to Confederation than it had been in 1864.

The proposal of the Nova Scotia and New Brunswick delegates to grant $800,000 to purchase the proprietary lands originated with J. C. Pope, the Island's Premier, who was in London at the time on business. He stayed at the *Alexandra Hotel* with the delegates and they had a number of private discussions on Prince Edward Island's attitude to Confederation. He informed them that "if they wished the people of Prince Edward Island to consider the matter [Confederation] at all, they must be prepared, in the first place, to enable us to extinguish Proprietary Rights, and to place us in as good a position as if our lands were Crown Lands.[1] Pope later claimed that his suggestions "led to the consideration of the matter by delegates from the Maritime Provinces, and the offer, so far as they were concerned, was the result."[2] Charles Tupper confirmed J. C. Pope's important role in a letter to W. H. Pope, in which he expressed "the hope that he would approve of the steps taken by us at your brother's suggestion to obtain the assent of that portion of B. N. A."[3] J. C. Pope now joined the ranks of the Island Confederates with all the enthusiasm of a recent convert.

On September 22, 1866, the Nova Scotia and New Brunswick delegates adopted a resolution pledging that if the Legislature of Prince Edward Island would authorize the appointment of delegates to the London Conference, they would support the policy of providing $800,000 for the purchase of the proprietary lands on the Island.[4] Tupper was, as usual, optimistic, and wrote to W. H. Pope that "he hoped to see you and our old friend Colonel Gray here to aid us in the completion of this work, to accomplish which you have so nobly laboured thus far."[5] Lord Carnarvon, the Colonial Secretary, forwarded a copy of this resolution to the Canadian Government for an expression of its views. The unenthusiastic Canadian Minute of Council quite effectively dampened this proposal. It pointed out that the Nova Scotia and New Brunswick delegates had no right or power to make such an offer, and the Canadian Government could not legally bind itself to pay such a sum without the previous consent of the Canadian Parliament.[6] Finally, the Government agreed "to discuss the matter with Prince Edward Island in London in a liberal spirit and to make a strong recommendation to the first Government of the United Provinces,"[7] but it would not make any commitment. This Minute did not help the cause of Confederation on the Island since it was considered to be, in effect, a veto on the $800,000 proposal.

But the attitude of the Canadian Government really had little bearing on the attitude of the Island. Even prior to this expression of opinion, the Islanders had manifested complete indifference, if not outright hostility to the suggestion. Dundas wrote to Lord Carnarvon that "in the interval between the time of the $800,000 offer by the Nova Scotia and the New Brunswick delegates, and the time I received the reply of the Canadian Government to that proposal, I had an opportunity of watching the manner in which the proposal was received by the Island, and I am bound to say that the reception was anything but favourable."[8] This was, perhaps, an understatement. Newspaper comment and resolutions passed at public meetings reveal that the proposal was indeed coldly received in Prince Edward Island.

Robert Poore Haythorne, soon to be the Island's Premier, writing in the *Islander,* expressed the hope "that the Islanders would not barter their own present, and their decendants' future independence for the paltry sum of £3 per head."[9] The *Islander* reported that "the simple mention of the offer of $800,000 induced the leading opponents of Confederation to raise the cry of bribery — 'Canada offers $10 a head, as a bribe to induce the people of Prince Edward Island to sell themselves into slavery,' was heard from one end of the Island to the other."[10] J. C. Pope wrote that the offer was styled "the bribe and gigantic swindle."[11] W. H. Pope was so disillusioned by the Islanders' reaction that he maintained that "the delegates should not make any offers in addition to those of the Quebec Report, because these would lead the people to believe that P.E.I. was necessary to the Union — would be regarded by them as an attempt to bribery — and would only intensify their opposition."[12] Edward Palmer, addressing one of the many public meetings held throughout the Island to discuss the proposal, stated "the offer made to this Island of $800,000 was an imposition to allure the people, and strongly impressed upon the audience the necessity of returning men to the new House of Assembly who would not be fickle, but would firmly carry out their views against such an offer."[13] The unbridled opposition became so vehement that the *Islander* threw in the towel and stated "that it would henceforth refrain from the advocacy of a measure, which, notwithstanding its importance, is regarded by the mass of the people as one which would render them and their children slaves to Canada."[14] It was obvious that it would take more than $800,000 to change the Islanders' hostile attitude to Confederation.

The $800,000 offer also had disastrous effects on the fortunes of the Conservative Party. In the first place, it caused a serious rift in its ranks. The sudden conversion of J. C. Pope to Confederation was bitterly resented by three members of the Executive Council, Kenneth Henderson, James McLaren and James Duncan. Henderson, for example, refused to contest the election for his seat in the Legislative Council, and instead, secured the nomination for the seat in the Assembly then held by Dr. David Kaye who was sympathetic to Confederation. J. C. Pope then forced Henderson to resign because he did not have a seat in the Legislature. Early in January, 1867, James Duncan resigned from the Executive Council. Dundas informed Carnarvon that "his resignation was mainly, if not completely, caused by the question of Confederation to which he is violently opposed."[15] Pope was perhaps relieved by the death of his third opponent, James McLaren, whom Dundas described "as a violent anti-Confederate."[16] These divisions seriously weakened the Conservatives as they prepared to contest the general election of February 26, 1867.

Early in the campaign, George Dundas wrote to Lord Carnarvon that "the opponents of Confederation are using their utmost endeavours to exclude from the new Assembly every candidate who is in favour of the Union."[17] The maneuvers of the anti-Confederates verify Dundas's statement. In several districts they used their influence to secure the nominations of anti-Confederates in seats formerly occupied by those who were sympathetic to Confederation. In Charlottetown, Edward Palmer and other anti-Confederates withdrew their support from Daniel Davies, who had voted against the "no-terms" resolutions in 1866, and nominated Thomas Dodd, a professed anti-Confederate.[18] In the fourth district of Queen's, the Conservatives campaigned against Col. J. H. Gray, and nominated David Laird, the rabid anti-Confederate editor of the *Patriot*.[19] The greatest calamity, so far as the Conservatives were concerned, was that their leader, J. C. Pope, did not contest the election. He stated that it "would afford him no pleasure to take his seat with men with whom he could not agree, and in whom he had no confidence."[20] "Neither James Pope nor William Pope," Palmer wrote to Howe, "ventured to face a constituency. James tested his constituents by meetings, but he found his late supporters most justly indignant at him for his treacherous attempt in the $800,000 bribe affair, and he did not offer. He has, therefore, become an avowed Confederate, but his influence is of no importance."[21]

These divisions within the Conservative Party ranks placed them in an unenviable position. George Coles and the Liberals took full advantage of their difficulties. They criticized them, with much success, as the "corrupt Confederate faction."[22] The *Islander,* the chief Conservative organ, clearly analysed the campaign:

Among the Conservatives, the cry is, away with every man who is so far a Confederate as to admit that there exists a possibility of devising term of union which would prove acceptable to the people of the Island, or who is disposed to find fault with the resolutions of the House of Assembly of last session which declared that any terms of Union with the other Provinces will be regarded with hostility by the people of this Island. The Liberal leaders, with few exceptions, are now more cautions in their denunciation of Confederation. They have joined in a cry which they have reason to conclude, would serve to divide their opponents. The division has been created — the Conservative Party disorganized.[23]

The Conservatives were soundly defeated. Nineteen Liberals were declared elected thereby giving George Coles's party a majority of eight.[24] Edward Palmer viewed the election as a victory for the anti-Confederates. "As anti-Confederates," he wrote glowingly to Joseph Howe, "we have triumphed at the General Election, but our Conservative section has lost the Government. . . . The number of Confederates are reduced from 8 in the old, to 5 members in the new House, and we now stand 25 against 5."[25] "As the five Confederate members," he added "are all pledged to oppose any new attempt to Confederation until the question is submitted to another General Election—we feel ourselves pretty safe on the question."[26] It was evident that Edward Palmer, the Attorney General in the Conservative government, considered the defeat of the Conservatives as being of little significance so long as the anti-Confederate cause was secure.

And that cause was indeed secure with a Liberal government with

George Coles at the helm. Next to Palmer, Coles was the most vocal and most dedicated opponent of Confederation on Prince Edward Island. Moreover, his cabinet, after the untimely death of Edward Whelan at the age of 43, did not include a single supporter of union. The Liberal victory had brought the position of Queen's Printer to Edward Whelan, but he lost the subsequent by-election by some thirty-seven votes to Edward Reilly, the staunch anti-Confederate editor of the *Herald*. Whelan's unequivocal espousal of Confederation and his harsh criticism of the Tenant League cost him the support of the constituents of St. Peter's and his only defeat in twenty-four years. Ailing since the summer, and saddened by his defeat, Confederation's most brilliant oracle on the Island died in December, 1867.[27] George Dundas could, with perfect reason, inform Lord Carnarvon that the new Liberal administration was "decidedly opposed to Confederation."[28]

In March, 1867, Lord Carnarvon forwarded to Prince Edward Island a resolution of the delegates to the London Conference, promising that "if the Colony of Prince Edward Island should hereafter desire to join the Confederation of Canada, they would urge the Government of the Confederation to deal with the question of compensation for the proprietary rights on the Island in the most liberal spirit."[29] But Prince Edward Island intended neither to join the new Dominion to be established on July 1, 1867, nor to look in Ottawa's direction for the solution of its land question. The Coles administration hoped to settle the problem outside of Confederation. Thus, in the 1867 session of the Legislature, George Coles secured the passage of a measure authorizing the government to raise a loan of £100,000 in Great Britain or elsewhere for the public service of the Island.[30] It was his intention to use this money for the purchase of the proprietary estates. When Roderick MacAulay dared to suggest in the House that "it would be better to go into Confederation, and obtain $800,000 rather than mortgage the Island,"[31] he was viciously pounced on by the anti-Confederates. Joseph Hensley claimed that the offer from Canada did not really differ from a loan "as it would be charged against us in our yearly allowance,"[32] and insisted that the approach of the Liberals "would settle the question whether we could obtain a loan outside Confederation."[33] Thus, the new administration was even more determined than its predecessor to preserve the Island's cherished independence.

II   REJECTION OF "BETTER TERMS"

As the decade of the 1860's drew to a close, the Imperial and Canadian Governments made determined efforts to induce Prince Edward Island to enter Confederation. The Colonial Office attempted to secure the Island's adherence by applying strenuous moral and financial pressure, and the Canadian Government, extremely concerned because of the Island's negotiations with the Americans, offered "better terms." The Islanders, however, stubbornly refused to yield to these new Imperial and Canadian pressures.

The refusal of the absentee proprietors to sell their lands to the Island government gave the Imperial authorities an opportunity to apply some pressure. In the year 1869, the Liberal administration, thwarted in its efforts both to secure the loan for the public service authorized in 1867 and to reach an agreement with the proprietors, prepared an Address to the Queen requesting that the sale of the proprietary lands be made compulsory, and that the Imperial Government guarantee a loan of from one hundred to one hundred and fifty thousand for the purchase of these lands.[34] Lord Granville, the Colonial Secretary of State, frigidly replied that since it was uncertain as to whether or not Prince Edward Island would enter into Confederation, he considered it was more prudent for the Imperial Government not to enter into any consideration of a question which "should as far as possible be left for the decision of those who, under the altered circumstances of the Colony would have to carry into execution any measures connected with it."[35] He stated that he would not, however, "hold out any hope that the Imperial Government would under any circumstances agree to guarantee a loan."[36] This directive implied that if Prince Edward Island wanted its land question settled, it had better look to Confederation for the solution.

Meanwhile, the Imperial Government applied pressure in another area. The Colonial Secretary informed the Island government that after the termination of Dundas's tour of duty, the salary of the Lieutenant Governor would have to be paid by the Island government.[37] Once again, the Legislature protested and asserted that such a demand was most unjust. The Colonial Office was adamant. Sir Frederic Rogers, the senior Under-Secretary, wrote on Dundas's despatch: "I feel hard-hearted. I would give P.E.I. [a most troublesome little place] no encouragement to remain outside the Dominion with a Government of its own. I would clearly tell them at the termination of Mr. Dundas's tenure of office, unless some provision is made for the payment of a Lieutenant Governor, the Island must be governed by the Governor General from Ottawa."[38] As a result, the official reply by Lord Granville simply stated that "the British Government could see no sufficient reason for exempting Prince Edward Island from the general and reasonable rule that every colony should pay the salary of its Governor."[39] Granville's despatch raised a storm of protest in the Assembly in 1869. T. H. Haviland insisted that it was "a Confederate screw unfairly put upon us."[40] Benjamin Davies maintained that the despatch intimated that "if the salary is not provided we will be annexed to a hateful Confederation."[41] "Under these circumstances," he advised the House, "I see no other course than to at once comply with the demand lest the greater evil fall on us."[42] Joseph Hensley, the House leader, agreed and easily persuaded the Assembly to assume responsibility for the salary of the Lieutenant Governor in order that "the Imperial Government will not have an excuse for forcing us into Confederation."[43] Prince Edward Island was prepared to make the monetary sacrifices necessary to keep out of Confederation.

When W. H. Pope learned of Lord Granville's despatch, he wrote in the *Islander*: "The screw is being tightened. The demand for the payment of the salary of the Lieutenant Governor was the first turn. We shall soon see the screw again in motion."[44] Pope's prognosis was not incorrect. In June, 1869, the Canadian Executive Council was authorized by Parliament to enter into negotiations with Prince Edward Island. The Canadian Government was now ready to work hand in hand with the British Government to persuade the Island to enter Confederation, or, as W. H. Pope more appropriately noted, "to put on the screws."[45] Prince Edward Island was again provided with an opportunity to teach the Canadians a well-rehearsed object lesson in Island aloofness.

The Canadian Government did not, of course, approve of the independence of this little Island situated on its doorstep. The value of its fisheries, the necessity of common tariffs and common defense plans, together with the desire to round off the Dominion, made the Canadians anxious to bring the Island into Confederation. But the desirability of reopening negotiations with Prince Edward Island assumed a new urgency in 1869. In 1868, a Congressional Committee from the United States had visited Prince Edward Island to discuss the re-establishment of reciprocity. The report presented to Congress in 1869 by this Committee caused consternation in Canadian circles and led to the new overtures to Prince Edward Island. Prince Edward Island was prepared to listen and then make its decision.

It was in March, 1868, that General Benjamin F. (Beast) Butler, a representative in the United States Congress from Massachusetts, submitted resolutions to the Congress which proposed the re-establishment of reciprocity between the United States and Prince Edward Island. These authorized the admission of the products of Prince Edward Island, duty-free, into the United States, in return for similar treatment for American products, provided that American fishermen were allowed to enter the ports of the Island to obtain supplies, to refit, and to fish within the three-mile limit in the waters surrounding the Island upon payment of a fee not exceeding five dollars per vessel.[46] Butler's resolutions were referred to a

Committee of three, which was authorized to visit the Island and to make a full report on its exports and imports as well as to recommend legislation. General B. F. Butler, Judge Luke Poland and James B. Beck were appointed to the Committee. They were not authorized to incur any expense to the United States, but they were provided with a revenue cutter for the voyage to the Island. They arrived in Charlottetown at the end of August, 1868.[47]

The Executive Council and the Charlottetown Chamber of Commerce held a series of meetings with the Butler Committee. Both sides manifested a keen desire to lay the groundwork for a reciprocal trade agreement. At a luncheon in honor of the Committee, General Butler said their delegation had come to Charlottetown "to ask as a right, to be allowed to come into the harbours of the Island whenever it might be found necessary to fish within the three-mile limit, and to exchange the productions of both countries whenever it might be found advantageous to do so."[48] The atmosphere was pleasant as toasts to the Queen, the Lieutenant Governor and the Executive Council alternated with toasts to the President, the Congress and the Congressional Committee.[49] The Islanders were extremely flattered by the remarks of the Committee. Joseph Hensley remarked "they had been treated by the Congress of the United States almost as if they were a strong nation."[50] Archibald McNeill, the final speaker at the luncheon, opined that the "Mother Country would not oppress little P. E. Island. P. E. Island was as independent as Canada, and her people were, he thought, equally as competent to enter into negotiations on the subject of reciprocity as were the people of the new Dominion."[51] On this agreeable note, the Butler Committee departed the Island on September 2, 1868.

In March, 1869, General Butler submitted a report to the House of Representatives on the visit of the Congressional Committee to Prince Edward Island. It was a very comprehensive analysis of the commercial and political potentialities of the Island. In the first place, it stressed that reciprocal free trade could very profitably be established between the United States and Prince Edward Island. "She takes our iron and produces none," the report stated. "She takes our wheat and produces none; she takes our manufactures and makes nothing of her own, but gives us in exchange cheap food by which our own manufactures may be sustained."[52] It emphasized also the benefits that would accrue to American fishermen. "The most important consideration," it maintained, "to be given us by Prince Edward Island, in return for Reciprocal legislation would be access to the fisheries around its shores . . . and we understand that the people of the Island in case of an agreement upon the legislation for reciprocal trade will be able to assure the immunity of our vessels in the waters adjacent to the Island for a nominal license only."[53]

The report did not openly suggest the desirability of annexing the Island to the United States; but it did assert that it occupied a very strategic position, and spoke of the harbour of Charlottetown as being one of the best on the continent for ease of access, capacity and safety. It noted further that "a harbour so easily fortified, and so safe, would be exceedingly valuable to any power seeking to control the bay and river of St. Lawrence."[54] The report also spoke quite glowingly of the refusal of Prince Edward Island to enter Confederation. "Most strenuous efforts," the report noted, "have been made by the Government of the Dominion to bring these colonies [P.E.I. and Newfoundland] under their jurisdiction, which have been thus far resisted with the determination of a people who know their own rights, and are determined to maintain them."[55] The concluding pages of the report were devoted to the review of the reasons why the United States would profit from a re-establishment of reciprocity with the Island. It emphasized, however, that while "it would be desirable to have a reciprocity of trade secured by legislation, with Prince Edward Island, it would be highly undesirable to have reciprocal legislation with the Dominion as an entirety."[56] The report ended with a declaration that the Committee was "deeply impressed with the desirableness of the promotion of Free Trade between the Island and the United States, that had it been within the scope of their instructions they would have reported a Bill to carry out that object."[57]

Although the United States did not act on the recommendations of the Butler report, and, seemingly, never intended to act, the report did lead the British and Canadian authorities to take precautionary steps. On March 24, 1869, Sir Edward Thornton, the Imperial Minister at Washington, sent three copies of the report to Lord Clarendon, the British Secretary of State for Foreign Affairs. "You will easily perceive," he wrote to Clarendon, "the desire which is betrayed by the tenor of this report not only to enter into isolated and destructive relations with that Island, but even to detach it and Nova Scotia from the rest of the Dominion of Canada."[58] The British authorities, realizing that the report implied that the United States was anxious to prevent further consolidation of the British North American Colonies, forwarded a copy to the Governor General of Canada. Its arrival immediately aroused consternation in Canadian Government circles.

John A. Macdonald recognized that the desire of Prince Edward Island to allow the Americans access to the fisheries in return for reciprocity was a potential danger to Canada. "Canada is directly interested in the immediate acquisition of Prince Edward Island," he wrote to Governor General Young, "from its proximity to Nova Scotia and New Brunswick, and the extent of its fisheries. Neither the Imperial Government nor Canada can carry out satisfactorily any policy in the matter of Fisheries under the present circumstances, and most unpleasant complications with the American Fishermen may ensue."[59] He also expressed the hope to Young that the British Government "would help us to conciliate the Islanders,"[60] so that the Island would not become "a rendezvous for smugglers, and, in fact, be as great a nuisance to us as the Isle of Man was in the days of old to England before its purchase from the Duke of Athol."[61] These factors prompted the Canadian Government to act immediately. Accordingly, it received authorization from the House of Commons in June, 1869, "to enter into such negotiations and to make such fiscal and other arrangements as were deemed expedient with the Government and Legislature of Prince Edward Island, with a view to its admission into the Dominion."[62] There is little reason to doubt that the offer of "better terms" made by the Canadian Government in December, 1869, was as much due to the Canadian fear of exploitation by the Americans on the Eastern seabord as it was to Canadian magnanimity.

Appropriately enough, the Governor General of Canada, Sir John Young, and three members of the Canadian Cabinet, George E. Cartier, Leonard Tilley and Edward Kenny arranged to spend a summer holiday at Charlottetown in August, 1869.[63] The Cabinet ministers discussed terms of union with the provincial government and some prominent citizens. They seemed to be well-pleased with these interviews. Tilley telegraphed to Macdonald on August 14: "Have been spending week in Island doing good service. Sir George, Kenny and I had satisfactory conversations yesterday with Island Government preparatory to sending proposals after Government meets."[64] Sir George Cartier was even more saguine: "I think," he wrote to Macdonald, "that we have made *great progress* with the P. E. Islanders for the success of Confederation."[65] But it was Sir John Young who seemed to have read the Island pulse correctly. "The ministers as well as the more educated inhabitants," he informed Lord Granville, "are inclined to join the Dominion, but the mass of the people still hold aloof. Some progress has, however, been made in disabusing their minds of various fears and prejudices."[66] The removal of "these various fears and prejudices" was destined to be a long process indeed.

Robert Poore Haythorne, the new Liberal Premier, was in charge of the negotiations for the Island. Haythorne, a wealthy land proprietor who had lived on the Island since 1842, was named Premier in 1869, after ill-health necessitated the retirement of George Coles. Haythorne gave a report to the Legislative Council in March, 1870, on the nature of the conversations between his ministers and the federal representatives. "I stated," he informed the Council, "that no overtures made to the colony would be accepted unless they embraced a full and complete settlement of the land

Robert Poore Haythorne

question—not the $800,000 from the Dominion Government—but that the question should be settled by Great Britain."[67] "I told Mr. Tilley," he added, "that the gift of $800,000 from Canada would have a demoralizing tendency—that it would compromise the independence of any members who would be elected to represent this Island in the Dominion Parliament if Confederation should ever be accomplished."[68] These conversations should have left no doubt in the minds of the Canadians as to the Islanders' principal problem and the apparent sensitivity of their political consciences.

Sir George Cartier asked the Executive Council to forward a copy to him of all the important documents bearing on the land question so that the Canadian Government could reach a full understanding of the problem. R. P. Haythorne immediately forwarded these materials to Cartier accompanied by some observations on the conditions that would determine the Island's attitude to Confederation:

The Land Question is the chief public question on Prince Edward Island. If your statesmen will grapple it, and have power and influence sufficient to wring [arracher] indemnity from Imperial Britain, that fact will go far to overcome the prejudices which still prevail in this colony against Confederation. If, moreover, you procure the passing of a compulsory law affecting the leased and wilderness lands, still subject to proprietary influence—if you deal fairly with us in the matter of public works, and give our people a pledge that the Great Dominion seeks not to enrich itself, at the expense of this small colony, and does not purpose to withdraw more money from the Island, than she expends there—then I predict the current will soon turn in favor of Confederation, and perhaps run as strongly, as it has done, hitherto in the opposite direction.[69]

These recommendations were incorporated into a report made by Cartier, Tilley and Kenny which was approved by the Canadian Privy Council on December 16, 1869, and sent to the Island Government for consideration.

These terms, corresponding in part to what had been allowed to the other Provinces by the Quebec Resolutions, offered the normal debt allowance and subsidies. The Island was granted a debt allowance of $25. per capita upon the basis of the 1861 population. If at the time of its entry into union it had not incurred debts equal to this amount, it would be entitled to interest at the rate of five per cent per annum on the difference between its debt and the amount so authorized. It was further stipulated that the Island would receive an annual per capita subsidy at the rate of eighty cents per capita upon the 1871 population; and this clause was to apply until the population reached 400,000.[70] The terms of 1869 were "better" in that they included some additional liberal features. The Dominion promised to pay an annual subsidy of $25,000 to help meet the expenses of the local government. The province was also guaranteed that "efficient Steam Service for the conveyance of Mails and Passengers was to be established and maintained between the Island and the Dominion, winter and summer, thus placing the Island in continuous communication with the Intercolonial Railway and the Railway system of the Dominion."[71] The Canadian Government also undertook to endeavour to secure adequate compensation from the Imperial Government for the Island's lack of Crown lands. It was further provided that if the Imperial Government should refuse such compensation, the Dominion would itself provide $800,000 to the Island to enable it to deal adequately with the land question. The Dominion also promised to use its influence to secure such legislation as would enable the government of the Island to purchase all the remaining proprietary lands.[72] The Canadian Government, eager to conciliate the Islanders, had adhered quite closely to the recommendations made by the Island's Executive Council.

On January 7, 1870, the Haythorne administration categorically rejected the "better terms." The Executive Council Minute simply stated that "inasmuch as the said terms do not comprise a full and immediate settlement of the Land Tenure and Indemnity from the Imperial Government for loss of Territorial Revenues, the Committee cannot recommend said terms to the consideration of their constituents and the public."[73] Robert Hodgson, the Administrator of the Island, was dissatisfied with the laconic reply of his Ministers, and persuaded them to elaborate upon it. They complied with a thoroughness which should have left no doubts in the minds of the Canadians. They pointed out that if they accepted the $800,000 gift from Canada, it would not settle the land question properly since this issue should be settled by Great Britain; and, in addition, it would compromise the independence of the Island by leaving the impression that it was bought. Union, they insisted, must depend upon "the free and unbiased consent and approval of the contracting parties," not on relations between "candidates and a bribed constituency."[74] Since Canada was not responsible for the land problem, they magnanimously maintained that "she should not be expected to assume a duty which clearly is not hers."[75] They did remind her, however, that if Canada should succeed in persuading Great Britain to redress the land grievance on the Island, "a spontaneous reaction of favorable public opinion would result, and she would then be able to look forward to a Dominion from sea to sea with more confidence."[76] They also maintained that a clause in the B. N. A. Act which placed all railways not connecting two or more provinces under the jurisdiction of the local governments, would mean that Prince Edward Island would not be able to have a much-needed railway built from Dominion funds.[77] They suggested that if the Dominion wished to recommend the question of Confederation to the serious consideration of the Islanders, "then this clause should be debarred from applying to the Island."[78] It was obvious now that any new offer of "better terms" would have to promise the construction of a railway on Prince Edward Island.

The obstinate refusal of the Islanders to accept the Canadian offer of "better terms" annoyed both the British and Canadian authorities. At the Colonial Office, Sir Frederic Rogers pungently commented that if the reply of the Island government "was more than a haggle then we must expect a revival of the old land question which we hoped to shift over to the Dominion."[79] This observation led Lord Granville to remind the members of the Island Assembly "that they would not act wisely if they allow themselves to be diverted from the practical consideration of their own real interests, for the sake of keeping alive a claim against the Imperial Government which it is quite certain will never be acknowledged."[80] He made doubly certain that the message was understood with a further letter to the Governor General of Canada informing him that the British Government would never recognize any "liability in respect of grants of land made in Prince Edward Island in 1767."[81] It was now more than obvious that Great Britain had no intention of making any atonement for the original sin committed in 1767.

The Canadian Government was also irritated with the Island administration. It was John A. Macdonald's view that the negotiations had largely been a game of humbug. "Haythorne, under pretext of desiring Union," Macdonald bitterly wrote to Rose, "humbugged Tilley and our Government into making an offer. He proved afterwards that he never had any intention of supporting union, and that his object was by getting a better offer than the terms of the Quebec Conference, to kill our friends, Haviland, Col. Gray, W. H. Pope, and others who had agreed to the original settlement."[82] This statement was not a correct analysis. Macdonald should have remembered that the Canadian offer of 1869 was not solicited, but rather initiated by the Canadians themselves. Moreover, even the friends of Confederation were not satisfied. W. H. Pope, for example, insisted that "in any negotiations between the Island and the Dominion Government, the construction of a railway at the expense of the Dominion must be stipulated for."[83] And J. C. Pope said he would "raise his voice against Confederation unless we get a railway and a fair consideration for future public works, so as to put us on a fair footing with other parts of the Dominion."[84] Haythorne's administration acted in perfect harmony with Island sentiments when it rejected the 1869 offer of "better terms."

In the Legislature in the 1870 session, the "better terms" offer was ridiculed. The failure of the Canadian Government to persuade the British authorities to settle the land question was emphasized. "Our determination," said George Howlan, "was not to surrender up the constitution of the country into other hands, until the portrait of the last landlord was hung up in the Legislative library as a memento of the past."[85] Edward Reilly realistically pointed out that the "terms were better only in a pecuniary point of view—there was no difference in constitutional points."[86] Palmer argued that in return for a grant of £25,000 per year, they were giving up a local revenue which in a few years would amount to £200,000. "Are there," he asked, "three people in the Island who can read and write who are such absolute asses as to make such a sacrifice?"[87] George Beer claimed that the Island's economic condition would be so worsened by the union with Canada that he "would rather live under the stars and stripes than under the flag of the new Dominion."[88] And Edward Reilly added the clincher by suggesting that "by holding out against union at the time the other Provinces were confederated, they had now before them much better terms than were contained in the Quebec Scheme, and he believed that better terms still would yet be offered."[89] This, in the final analysis, seemed to the Islanders to be the proper stance. They would simply wait and see, unless of course, some compelling economic crisis necessitated a different course of action. Within a few months, the Islanders unwittingly took a step that created precisely that kind of economic emergency.

III   RAILWAYS AND THE DENOUEMENT

As Prince Edward Island moved into the 1870's her people were deeply embroiled in controversies over land, religion, railways, and, of course, Confederation. The general election of July 18, 1870, was fought principally over the issues of Confederation and governmental grants to Catholic schools. The question of Confederation seemed to have been permanently settled. Robert Hodgson, the Administrator, reported to Lord Granville, "that the recent elections in no way vary the question of Confederation which has been repudiated. I believe all the candidates, even the few gentlemen favorable to Confederation who have been returned have been pledged against furthering it until it shall be submitted to the constituents at the polls and their approbation of it signified."[90] The *Islander* likewise commented that "every man, who, on the 18th, was elected to represent the people, is well aware that he was elected with the understanding that the people are opposed to Confederation, and that he is not at liberty to do any act to commit them to it without first obtaining their consent by appealing to them at the polls."[91] Thus, the offer of "better terms" left the Island in a mood of sullen silence.

The problem of financial assistance to the Catholic schools was not as easily resolved. Although the Haythorne administration had won the election by a substantial majority, it was obliged to resign because of internal conflicts over this question. The Catholic Liberal representatives, with the exception of James R. MacLean, informed Robert Haythorne that they would not support him unless he would pledge his government to make financial grants to Catholic Schools. Personally, Haythorne was favourable, but as he could not persuade the Protestant members of the Executive to agree to such grants, he tendered his resignation.[92] James C. Pope, the Conservative leader, by some adroit manipulation, managed to form a coalition government on September 10, 1870, composed of Conservatives and the Catholic Liberals who had refused to support Haythorne.[93] This maneuver was made possible only after the members of the government had signed two astonishing pledges. They agreed to leave the school question in abeyance for four years; and they pledged that "the question of Confederation was not to be agitated, nor any proposition of union to originate from the government of the Colony: and should the Imperial government or the Dominion government propose terms of union, they shall not be accepted without first appealing to the people at the polls."[94] To Prince Edward Islanders, no explanation is necessary for this kind of political craftsmanship; to others, no explanation is possible.

With Confederation and religion barred as political issues, J. C. Pope and his loosely knit supporters made the railway their politics.[95] But the railway legislation of 1871 was based not merely upon political expediency. There cannot be the slightest doubt that a mild railway mania captivated the people of the Island in the early 1870's. "A railway," W. H. Pope wrote in the *Islander* in December, 1870, "is the subject which, more completely than any other, occupies the people of this Island at the present time. Escheat, Quit Rents, Denominational Schools, and, we may add, Confederation, are subjects seldom discussed. The Railway from Alberton to Georgetown, and the immense advantage which such a road would confer upon the farmers, and upon those who buy the produce of the farmers of P.E.I. are subjects of which one hears a great deal."[96] Numerous meetings were held throughout the Island to discuss the feasibility of a railway. At Charlottetown, for example, "a representative assemblage of the people from Queen's County almost unanimously endorsed a resolution," the *Islander* noted, "that the prosperity of all classes on the Island and the value of the property, would be greatly advanced by the construction of a Trunk Line of Railway connecting Alberton, Summerside, Charlottetown, and Georgetown with each other."[97] Similar resolutions passed at many other centres suggest that the Islanders generally were in favour of a railway project. It was, therefore, with considerable justification that J. C. Pope's government sponsored railway legislation in the 1871 session of the Legislature.

In introducing the measure for the construction of a railway from Georgetown to Cascumpec, J. C. Pope emphasized its prospective earning capacity and the relatively small cost of construction. He estimated that the interest on the required capital would only amount to £30,000 per year, and that "a small additional tax would raise £15,000, while the receipts from the road would make in all probability as much more."[98] He claimed that factories would spring up in the railway centres, new land would be brought under cultivation, all of which would keep the people at home to enrich the Island by their own industry. "In every way I look at it," he said optimistically, "I see advantages which would result from the Railway—men would be more profitably employed, labor would be more in demand, while all the products of labor would unquestionably command better prices."[99] As a final touch, he predicted an influx of American tourists who would spend £300,000 a year. "In no way in which I regard the railway question," he concluded, "can I see any reason to doubt the propriety of going forward with the work."[100]

The opponents of the Bill criticized the speed with which the government had introduced the legislation. Cornelius Howatt commented "that even if a railroad should be deemed necessary, there is no need that it should be forced on us at railway speed."[101] Benjamin Davies maintained that the question should be "submitted to the people at the polls."[102] But the main thrust of the Opposition was that the construction of a railway would eventually lead to Confederation. "It strikes me very forcibly," Peter Sinclair argued, "that the intention of the government is to construct a railroad from one end of the Island to the other, saddle the Colony with a debt relatively heavier than that of the Dominion, then enter the Dominion and give up the railroad."[103] "The railway is so far beyond our means," protested Benjamin Davies, "that I am convinced that the Government are fully aware that they cannot accomplish one-third of the undertaking without aid, and that aid, I have no doubt, they expect to obtain from their friends in the Dominion, in exchange for delivering the Island into their hands."[104] "Confederation is, in my opinion, the object sought," he insisted, "and not the prosperity of the Island. It is Confederation, Mr. Chairman; it is the miserable grovelling pecuniary interests of the Government and its supporters that is sought."[105]

The promoters of the railway legislation vigorously denied that the construction of a railway would lead to Confederation. "A great many people," J. C. Pope remarked, "had been led to believe that a railroad meant Confederation, and that the present Government could not be trusted with its construction; but those who have been imposed upon had been politically duped."[106] Donald Cameron tried to soothe the anti-Confederates with the argument that "if the construction of a railway would entail a heavy debt upon the Colony, there would be less inducement for the Canadians to get us into Confederation."[107] And Edward Reilly, probably the staunchest anti-Confederate in the House, claimed like Cameron "that he was so far from believing that it would conduce to Confederation, that he felt it would be the best means of keeping us out."[108] "Under any circumstances," he added, "no pressure can be brought to bear on us for our railway indebtedness for thirty years, as the calculations will not be redeemable until the expiration of that time."[109] J. C. Pope's confirmed Confederation leanings could have made it questionable whether or not he was sincere when he maintained that the opponents of the Railway Bill were politically duped; but there cannot be the slightest doubt that his avowed anti-Confederate supporters were convinced that the building of the railway would not lead the province into Confederation.

The railway legislation was passed in the Assembly by a vote of eighteen to ten, and in the Legislative Council by a vote of eight to four. While the supporters of the legislation insisted that the construction of the railway would not lead to union, the new Lieutenant Governor, William Francis Cleaver Robinson, at least, was convinced that it would have precisely that result. On April 17, 1871, the day that he assented to the Railway Bill, he prophetically informed Lord Kimberley that "the heavy taxation which would be occasioned by railway construction would eventually lead the people to consent to enter Confederation."[110] "Because of the probable effect of the measure on the people of the Colony," he wrote, "I need hardly say that I have not assented to it with any less pleasure."[111]

The people of the Island demonstrated that they heartily approved of the railway legislation. In Charlottetown, a large torchlight procession, attended by thousands of people was held on April 19, 1871. "J. C. Pope's Railway Policy," the *Islander* commented, "so unscrupulously attacked and denounced by his political opponents, was, at all events, fully endorsed by the great bulk of the inhabitants of this metropolitan city of Charlottetown. Similar demonstrations, though on a somewhat smaller scale, have taken place in Summerside, Georgetown, Souris, Alberton, etc., etc., showing conclusively that the people of these places are fully alive to the vast importance of the immediate construction of a Grand Trunk Line of Railway in P.E.I."[112] Joseph Pope, a young clerk in the Treasury Department, and later John A. Macdonald's secretary, after watching the railway celebrations, wrote in his diary: "I suppose Uncle James is the most popular man on the Island tonight."[113] He could hardly be expected to foresee that within a year, his uncle's railway would make him very probably the most unpopular man in Prince Edward Island.

By the provisions of the Railway Act, the government was authorized to enter into a contract for the construction of a main line of railway from Alberton to Georgetown, which was to be completed within three years from the issue of the contract; and it was also authorized, upon completion of the main line, to contract for branch lines to Souris and Tignish. The cost of construction was not to exceed five thousand pounds currency per mile and the contractors must accept in payment government debentures bearing interest at six per cent per annum and payable to the contractors without discount. The construction and management of the railway was to be under the charge of three railway commissioners responsible to the Lieutenant-Governor-in-Council. A chief engineer was to be appointed by the government who would have the general superintendence of the railway construction. The public funds, revenues and securities of the Island were pledged and rendered liable for all expenses undertaken by the terms of the Railway Act.[114] The government called for tenders, and in September, 1871, the contract for construction of the railway was awarded to Collingwood Schreiber for the sum of £4,267½ per mile.[115] On October 5, Mrs. Robinson, wife of Lieutenant Governor Robinson, fittingly enough, turned the first sod, and the work of constructing roadbeds, laying narrow gauge tracks and building countless station houses commenced with great enthusiasm and speed. Prince Edward Island had taken the irretrievable step that would decide its destiny.

The railway policy of the government caused it difficulty from the start. David Laird, the editor of the *Patriot,* started the anti-government crusade. When James Duncan, a member of the Executive Council, sought re-election after his appointment as Chairman of the Railway Commissioners, he was opposed and soundly defeated by Laird. Such a storm of controversy arose that many members of Pope's party wavered in their allegiance. The popular feeling against the railway was generated first by the failure of the government to specify the length and precise route of the railway in the contract, and secondly, by the dissatisfaction over the course of the route laid out by the engineers. The railway contract, which called for a fixed cost per mile, with no limit set on actual mileage, certainly gave the opponents of the railway plenty of reasons for criticism. The contractors were thus encouraged to, and indeed did wind the railway in a serpentine fashion to avoid as many hills and estuaries as possible in order to keep the cost below the set per mile limit. The discontent eventually became so intense that in December sixteen members of the Assembly and six members of the Council petitioned Lieutenant Governor Robinson to summon a special session of the Legislature "because of the highly improper manner in which the government is carrying out the Railway Bill."[116] But Robinson disregarded their memorandum. He told Kimberley that "the carrying out of the Railway Act of the last session has caused an unusual flow of money and patrongage, and the Opposition are consequently more than ordinarily eager to place themselves at the head of affairs."[117] "I do not think," he opined, "that the Government have been guilty of any malpractice with the Railway."[118] When the Legislature met for its regular session in March, 1872, the majority of its members indicated that they were of a vastly different opinion.

In this "six day session" charges of corruption and incompetence were levelled against the Pope administration. Frederick Brecken, the Attorney General, challenged the Assembly on the opening day: "If the Government," he said, "have swerved from the proper course; done wrong; imperilled the finances of the country; played into the hands of a ring, and such sins against the public, then appoint a committee to send for persons, papers and records. If they have betrayed public confidence, and acted the part of dishonest men, then let them, one and all, be hurled from power."[119] The Opposition was able to establish that lobbyists and politicians were offering bribes to members of the Assembly to bring the railway closer to their homes. William Hooper, the member from Morell, stated that he had been offered $1,000 by Caleb Carleton of Souris if he would vote for the immediate construction of a branch line to that town.[120] When Carleton was summoned to the bar of the House, he readily admitted that he had paid $1,000 to Hooper in return for his promise to vote for the branch line. He also claimed he knew of "other parties to the eastward that would contribute pretty liberally, and help to shove along the branches."[121] Though the Opposition was not able to prove that the members of the government had been directly involved in bribery, they were able to demonstrate that they had directed the flow of patronage to places and persons that would otherwise have opposed the railway legislation.

The air in the Assembly was filled with highly personal accusations. David Laird said that the railway bill "was born in corruption and cradled in rascality;"[122] and he added that J. C. Pope was "a political blackguard . . . and a man who neither feared God nor regarded man."[123] Daniel Davies accused Pope of having carried the bill with his "d---d Brigade."[124] Pope told the Assembly that he often wondered whether Edward Reilly was "fiend or human;"[125] and Brecken maintained that he was forced to hold up Reilly's "unholy carcass for the public to look at, in order that it might be known what kind of spirit dwelt within its beautiful form."[126]

J. C. Pope made a determined attempt to save the life of his government and to defend his railway policy. He offered, in the Speech from the Throne, to change the railway policy to allow for the construction of the Souris and Tignish branches immediately, instead of waiting until the fourth year of construction as stipulated in the original Bill. He admitted that the road was lengthened, but insisted the extensions were warranted since "the traffic of the road would be increased and the general benefits thereof more equally distributed."[127] He asserted that the curvature was only 9½ per cent, and that it was necessary to avoid heavy hills and grades.[128] He assured the Assembly that the railway would pay, and that there had been no mismanagement of railway funds. "I would not wish," he concluded, "a better fortune than a lease of the line for 30 years and the Railway tax of 2½ per cent."[129]

Pope's assurances were to no avail. It was apparent that he had lost the confidence of the House. Members of his own party joined the Opposition in bitter criticism. Pope asked for and was granted a dissolution of the Assembly, and a general election ensued in April, 1872. The election campaign closely resembled the "six-day session"; personal charges and countercharges were the order of the day. The *Examiner* observed that "the result of the General Election was decided chiefly on local and personal grounds."[130] Pope and his supporters were soundly defeated, and R. P. Haythorne secured a majority of nineteen to eleven. On April 18, 1872, Haythorne's government assumed office. Next day, the Legislature assembled for the second session of that eventful year.

The change in government did not mean a reversal in railway policy. Indeed, the new administration which had so vigorously opposed the construction of the trunk railway now decided to proceed immediately with the construction of the branch lines to Souris and Tignish. But the Haythorne government really had no alternative if it wished to remain in office. The construction of the branch lines had been promised by the Pope administration; and many of Haythorne's supporters were committed to the implementation of the branch line policy. Edward Palmer, formerly a pillar of the Conservative party, and now Attorney General in Haythorne's government, explained the situation with his customary frankness:

We need not pause to consider the propriety of building these branches for the representatives of the East and North can unite and bid defiance to the whole of Queen's County. As the matter stands now, it is utterly useless to try to stop this wave which has long been forcing itself into the Legislature. If we attempt to resist it, the House will be brought to a deadlock, and another dissolution will ensue. Then these parties would be returned in greater force. There is, therefore, no alternative but to undertake those branches and add to the vast amount of debt. . . ."[131]

In these circumstances, the Haythorne administration embarked upon what seemed to be the only expedient course open to it. "I had no other course," Robert Haythorne said lamely, "but to accept a situation which was not my choice."[132] In retrospect, it seems ironic that Robert Haythorne, Edward Palmer and David Laird, the three most dedicated anti-Confederates in the province, took the final plunge that was to catapult Prince Edward Island into Union.

On December 31, 1872, the Haythorne government awarded a contract to Schreiber and Burpee to extend the railway to Tignish and Souris at a cost of $14,500 per mile.[133] This contract, together with that negotiated by the Pope administration, anticipated a financial outlay of some 3¼ million dollars.[134] It was becoming increasingly more obvious that the Island was accumulating a debt that would necessitate an almost unbearable rate of taxation. Lieutenant Governor Robinson informed Lord Kimberley "that he fully expected the increased taxation for railway purposes would reconcile the people to a change which, but for the energetically carried out policy of the late administration, would be today very far from accomplishment."[135] Robinson had stated a truism. The railway building policy of the Island government determined the Island's destiny. In December the Haythorne administration reluctantly decided it must renew negotiations with the Dominion with a view to the Island's entrance into Confederation. Prince Edward Island was almost ready to ride into Confederation on the railway.

Chapter Nine

Long Courted, Won at Last

BY F. W. P. BOLGER

I   MISSION TO CANOSSA

Lieutenant Governor Robinson, the ever-active crusader in the cause of Confederation, wrote to Lord Kimberley in December, 1872, that he fully expected "unless some hitch occurs, which I do not foresee, to hand the Island over to the Dominion within six or eight months at the latest."[1] In the latter weeks of 1872, a series of events led almost inexorably to the fulfilment of Robinson's prognosis. In the autumn of 1872, unfavorable trade conditions caused serious financial difficulties. The harvest was late and markets were unfavorable. The result was that the farmers, unable to sell their limited agricultural produce at remunerative prices, were deprived of purchasing power. This recession in the agricultural industry seriously affected the whole economy. The government found it increasingly difficult to obtain the exchange needed to meet interest payments. Moreover, this recession almost immediately had serious repercussions on the market for the government's railway securities. The government had an agreement with the railway contractors whereby they were paid in debentures redeemable at par. The contractors, in turn, sold these at the Island banks. When the economy of the Island showed serious signs of strain, these debentures could not be sold except at a discount. Moreover, the Island banks refused to purchase any more of the government debentures. The result was that the contractors refused to continue with the construction of the railway.

The banks on Prince Edward Island, large holders of the railway debentures, feared a financial crisis. Charles Palmer, the President of the Union Bank, and a brother of Edward Palmer, went to London to attempt to sell some of these debentures. His mission was an unqualified failure. He was informed that if the Island would join Canada the bonds could be sold at a good rate. It was obvious that London was putting on the pressure. "No one can shut his eyes to the fact," J. C. Pope emphasized, "that influences have been brought to bear on our paper. Baring Brothers will not take one of our bonds."[2] On his return to the Island, Charles Palmer had a number of interviews with the members of the Executive Council with a view to persuading them that Confederation was the only solution to the Island's financial crisis. He later informed Sir John Rose, Canada's unofficial agent in London, "that he was quite certain that the way is open for our joining the Dominion on fair terms, and that, as soon as the matter can be brought about without prominent advances on our part."[3] There cannot be the slightest doubt that the pressure by Palmer and other Island bankers was of considerable influence in convincing the Haythorne administration that it should reopen negotiations with Canada. While it is incontestable that these negotiations would have been initiated eventually, the pressure of the financial leaders undoubtedly hastened their beginnings.

The Island government spent a number of weeks in a fruitless attempt to save face. Prince Edward Island did not wish to make an open admission that Confederation was a necessity. Such an acknowledgment, the government correctly reasoned, would reduce its bargaining strength with the Dominion authorities. But the government's efforts to present a bold front were undermined from the very outset. Lieutenant Governor Robinson, Governor General Dufferin and Sir John Rose engaged in a triangular correspondence which eventually came across John A. Macdonald's desk. Robinson assumed the initiative with a revealing letter to Lord Dufferin:

Looking at the question fairly in the face, my Ministers see that there are only two courses open to them: either they must impose heavy additions to taxes on the people [and this, while it would be exceedingly unpopular would not get over the difficulty of exchange], or seek admission into the Union, provided that Canada would thereupon make our Railway debt her own. One or the other course will have to be adopted at the next session of the Local Parliament. Under these circumstances I shall feel greatly obliged if your Excellency will ascertain for me whether Canada will be prepared to adhere to the offer which she made to us in 1869 [commonly known as the "better terms"], and assume our Railway liabilities in addition, in the event of Prince Edward Island desiring admission into the Union.[4]

Robinson had already shown the Island's hand. The Canadian reply was cautious. Dufferin replied that "while my Ministers would not be prepared themselves to re-initiate any fresh proposals, I am authorized to assure you should your Government be disposed to make any overtures, there is no intention on the part of the Dominion Government to recede from the offer made in 1869, popularly known as "the better terms."[5] Pressed further by Robinson as to whether the Island's railway debt would be regarded as a Dominion or local debt, Dufferin replied evasively that the "railway debt was a subject for consideration and would be considered fairly."[6]

The replies of the Dominion authorities indicated that they intended to exercise extreme caution in their negotiations with the Islanders. Ever since 1864 the Canadians had taken the initiative in offering terms of union. The Islanders had invariably been unreceptive; and now that the "tight little Island" was in financial difficulties, Sir John A. Macdonald and his colleagues resolved that the overtures should come from the Islanders themselves. Sir John Rose told Macdonald of his correspondence with Charles Palmer and advised that "the present condition of things was a favorable opportunity for you to strike."[7] But Macdonald was wary and would not commit the Dominion Government. He indicated his stance in his reply to Rose in London:

Governor Robinson of P. E. Island has written privately and as if off his own bat, to Lord Dufferin, saying that he thought he could bring round his Government to consider the subject of union if Canada were still inclined in that direction. He wrote beyond a doubt, at the instigation of his Council, and, as we know from experience the style of the men, we answered guardedly. . . . You may remember how shamefully old Palmer behaved in '65. Haythorne behaved just as badly to us on the "better terms" matter in '69. He, then, under pretence of union, humbugged Tilley and our government into making an offer. He proved afterwards, that he never had any intention of supporting union, and that his object was by getting a better offer than the terms of the Quebec Conference, to kill our friends Haviland, Col. Gray, W. H. Pope, and others who had agreed to the original arrangement. This treacherous policy was successful, and our friends were for the time being politically snuffed out. Now Haythorne and Palmer are the ruling spirits of the present government, hence our caution. I have little doubt that our policy will be successful and that we will get a proposition before Parliament meets.[8]

The careful policy adopted by Macdonald made it necessary for the Islanders to swallow their pride and make the formal overture.

Robert Haythorne, pressured by Charles Palmer and Lieutenant Governor Robinson, and by now personally convinced that there was really no viable alternative, decided to ask his Executive Council to draft a series of proposals. The task which confronted Premier Haythorne was not an easy one. Robinson described the anti-Confederate complexion of his government:

My present Government, as your Lordship is aware, is an anti-Confederate one. Mr. Palmer, the Attorney General, is the same gentleman, who, as a delegate to Canada in 1864, spoke warmly in favor of Confederation and opposed it with equal warmth on his return to the Island. Mr. Haythorne, the Leader of the Government, is not personally opposed to it, but he represents an anti-Confederate constituency, is naturally of a timid disposition, and would not be a likely person to initiate successfully any important movement in opposition to the wishes of his constituents. The remaining members of the Government are personally, and as representatives, strongly anti-Confederate, and would like to remain out of the union as long as possible.[9]

The addition of David Laird to the Executive Council, in mid-December, made Haythorne's assignment even more delicate. As a result, the formal Minute, adopted by the Executive Council, on January 2, 1873, still reflected the spirit of independence which for so many years had characterized the Island's attitude to Confederation.

The Minute opened bravely with the claim that the members of the Executive Council were broaching the discussions on Confederation, because the Lieutenant Governor had initiated a correspondence on the subject with Lord Dufferin. They did acknowledge, however, that they had decided to pursue the subject because of the large railway liabilities. They admitted, moreover, that although the Islanders could undoubtedly sustain the taxation necessary to meet these liabilities, yet the economy would be adversely affected. They, therefore, felt the people of the Island should have the opportunity of choosing between increased taxation and Confederation. In order that the people might have the choice of deciding definitively between these two options at a general election, they asked the Dominion Government for a statement of the commitments it was prepared to make to the Island.[10] Specifically, the Minute requested the Dominion to concede, in addition to the proposals made by the "better terms" offer of 1869, the following terms: an additional annual allowance of $5,000 to bring the subsidy for the expenses of the local Legislature up to $30,000; that the Dominion Government take over the Prince Edward Island Railway and assume its debts, not exceeding $3,250,000; that the Dominion accept the new Law Courts Building and the Post Office, at a cost of $69,000, and the new Steam Dredge under contract, at a cost of $22,000; and that the Island be allowed to retain any sum, which might be awarded under the Washington Treaty, as an equivalent for surrendering the fisheries of the Island.[11] The Islanders managed to present a bold front despite their precarious economic situation.

Meanwhile, before the arrival of the Minute of Council in Ottawa, John A. Macdonald decided that any negotiations between the Island and Dominion Governments should be conducted by a delegation rather than by correspondence. He asked Lord Dufferin to write to Lieutenant Governor Robinson expressing these sentiments. After Robinson informed Haythorne of Macdonald's views, Haythorne replied that "he considered it unnecessary, at the present time, to send authorized agents to Ottawa, but if, hereafter, any circumstances should occur, which would render *viva voce* explanations necessary or desirable, we will not hesitate to adopt Lord Dufferin's suggestion."[12] Robert Haythorne did not have long to wait, however, before packing his luggage for Ottawa. When the Island Minute of Council arrived, it was immediately referred to Leonard Tilley, the Minister of Finance, who was placed in charge of negotiations. He informed the Privy Council "that some of the conditions are inadmissable, while others seemed reasonable, but that, in his opinion, it would be impossible to discuss fully or to settle these terms by correspondence."[13] He, therefore, suggested that the government of Prince Edward Island should send a delegation to Ottawa, and that a Committee of the Privy Council should receive it at once in conference. The Privy Council concurred, and on January 31, 1873, Lord Dufferin sent to the Island government a formal Minute incorporating these recommendations.

The Haythorne administration was disturbed by the request that a delegation should be appointed and sent to Ottawa. The authorization of such a body obviously meant that the negotiations with Canada, heretofore private, would have to be made public. The members of the Executive Council had hoped to avoid any publicity until they were in a position to announce the terms that Canada would concede. But their plan was to no avail. Robert Haythorne, when taunted in the Legislature about his mission to Ottawa, explained:

When the answer to our Minute of Council was received, it became a question whether we would accept the invitation, and send a delegation to Canada, or let the subject drop. However, the Government came to the conclusion that, having put our hand to the plough we should go forward, so that when Parliament would meet, we would be able to state what terms Canada was prepared to offer, and then the representatives of the people would be able to choose between Confederation and a large amount of increased taxation. That was the object of the Government in the first instance, and when it was shown that our object could not be attained without sending a delegation, we determined to put the matter through efficiently.[14]

Thus, since the Island administration had no other choice, Haythorne and Laird "stole away in the night by the ice-boat route to the mainland," George Howlan sarcastically noted, "and reached Ottawa on February 24, 1873."[15]

Several conferences were held between Haythorne and Laird and a sub-committee of the Canadian Privy Council, consisting of John A. Macdonald, Leonard Tilley, Hector Langevin, Joseph Howe and Charles Tupper. Although the Canadians fully realized that Prince Edward Island's financial crisis had prompted the negotiations, they did not manifest any disposition to take unfair advantage of the situation. After lengthy discussions lasting ten days, generous terms of union were mutually agreed upon.

These terms, with minor modifications, became the basis of the political union between Prince Edward Island and the Dominion of Canada.

The Island's debts and liabilities were to be assumed by the Dominion. The debt allowance, which in the other provinces had been set at approximately $25 per capita upon the population of 1861, was fixed for the Island at $45 per head on the basis of the 1871 census.[16] This clause meant that the Island, with a population of 94,021, was entitled to incur a debt of $4,230.95.[17] If the Island, at the time of its entrance into union, had not incurred debts equal to this sum, it was entitled to receive interest at the rate of 5 per cent per annum on the difference between the actual amount of its indebtedness and the amount authorized.[18] Since the debt of the Island amounted to $3,785,576, the net effect of this clause was to concede $22,218.42 annually to the Island.[19] This concession was granted in view of the limited benefits which the Island would receive from Dominion public works, the possibility of a new financial adjustment between Canada and its existing provinces, as well as the Island's "isolation during six months of the year."[20] In return for the transfer to the Dominion of the power of taxation the Island received for the support of its government and legislature an annual grant of $30,000 and a subsidy of 80 cents per capita upon the population of 1871, which was to be augmented in proportion to the increase of population until it reached 400,000.[21]

The terms contained many provisions designed to settle the Island's particular problems. All the railways under contract and in course of construction became the property of the Dominion; and the new Law Courts Building and new Steam Dredge were also transferred to the federal government.[22] "Efficient Steam Service for the conveyance of Mails and Passengers," and "continuous communication" with the mainland was also guaranteed.[23] The allotment of six members in the House of Commons, now warranted by the Island's population, met the Island's principal constitutional objections to Confederation.[24] Finally, to enable the Island to settle its contentious land tenure question, a special provision was mutually agreed upon by the Island and Federal negotiators:

The Island Government holding no lands from the Crown, and consequently enjoying no revenue from that source for the construction and maintenance of Local Works, it is agreed that the Dominion Government pay, in half-yearly instalments, and in advance, to the Government of Prince Edward Island, $45,000 per annum, less five per cent upon any sum not exceeding $800,000, that the Dominion Government may advance to the Island Government for the purchase of Lands, now held by large proprietors.[25]

Prince Edward Island certainly received generous treatment from the Canadian Government. The Dominion took over the railway that had seriously threatened the financial collapse of the Island. While its cost, naturally enough, was charged against the Island as a local debt, yet the Dominion increased the debt alowance by $20 per capita to permit the Island to derive some revenue from the debt allowance clause. The annual grant for the support of the local government and legislature was increased by some $5,000 over the amount promised in 1869. The land settlement was also liberal. The annual subsidy of $45,000 per year in consideration of the absence of Crown Lands on the Island helped to alleviate the loss the Island had suffered in this category since 1767; and, moreover, the provision of $800,000, would enable the government to purchase the proprietary estates. Since the interest on the $800,000 would amount to only $40,000, the net effect of this clause was to add $5,000 if the Island borrowed the whole amount; and if the government elected to repay the principal, it would receive the $45,000 subsidy *in toto*.

Haythorne and Laird, completely satisfied with the negotiations, telegraphed a synopsis of the terms to their colleagues on March 3, 1873, and advised a dissolution.[26] Three days later they received word that their colleagues agreed to the terms and concurred in advising an immediate appeal to the electors.[27] On the next day, March 7, the Island delegates and the sub-committee of the Privy Council formally attached their signatures to the terms; and in Charlottetown, Lieutenant Governor Robinson dissolved the Legislature. Haythorne and Laird returned immediately to defend the new terms before the perplexed and astonished electors of Prince Edward Island.

II CONFEDERATION — YES: INCREASED TAXATION — NO

Haythorne and his colleagues fully realized the formidable challenge they faced in attempting to persuade the people of Prince Edward Island to vote for Confederation. Lieutenant Governor Robinson, who now saw his objective nearing realization, lent considerable assistance to his government. "What is now to be feared," he wrote Lord Kimberley, "is intrigue, and the raising of side issues, on the part of Confederates, who are exceedingly jealous of an anti-Confederate Government having taken up the question, and will do everything to overthrow the present Government and get into office themselves."[28] With characteristic partisanship he enlisted support for the Liberals. He informed Lord Dufferin, that "the standard taken by the Opposition is that the terms are not good enough, and that if in power they could procure better."[29] In order to undermine this campaign strategy, he asked Lord Dufferin to state that "the delegates had procured terms as good as they could expect or are ever likely to receive."[30] Lord

Dufferin replied by telegraph, that his "Ministers are of opinion — an opinion in which I fully coincide — that no additonal concessions would have any chance of being adopted by the Parliament of Canada."[31] Robinson also cabled Lord Kimberley at the Colonial Office, and asked him to express the pleasure of the British Government that Prince Edward Island was considering Confederation.[32] Lord Kimberley replied on the same day, that "Her Majesty's Government learns with much satisfaction that terms are agreed upon for the admission of Prince Edward Island into the Dominion, and trust that Prince Edward Island will not lose this opportunity of union with her sister colonies."[33] Robinson immediately published these messages in all the Island newspapers with the hope that they would influence the electorate to return the Haythorne administration to power.

The political platform upon which the Haythorne Government based its appeal was outlined by David Laird at a large political rally in Charlottetown. He marshalled two principal arguments, the first of which was, that Confederation was now a financial necessity. "I care not what political party comes into power," he argued, "as sure as the sun rises in the heaven, so surely will this Island enter Confederation, whatever better political "shibboleth" pronounced at the coming election. I will tell you why I know this. It is because our debt is so great that we cannot meet the interest upon it."[34] Secondly, he maintained that the terms were generous and no additional concessions could or should be expected. "Viewing the situation from a financial standpoint," he asserted, "I conclude that the offer of the Dominion Government is very liberal, and that it should be accepted without hesitation on our part."[35] "To attempt to maintain our independence any longer," he insisted, "encumbered as we are, with a debt, so disproportionate to our resources, would be sheer folly. We would be literally dragging out a sickly and miserable existence, quarrelling among ourselves and getting more hopelessly and irretrievably involved, and in the end would have to accept the inevitable with loss of prestige and self-respect."[36] Confident that such arguments were irrefutable, the Liberals, under the leadership of Haythorne and Laird, hoped to receive a mandate for Confederation on the proposed terms.

The Conservatives, under the leadership of James C. Pope, were placed in an embarrassing position in this campaign. They realized that Confederation was the only answer to the Island's financial difficulties, and for this reason, they wanted the constituencies to declare in favor of it. "Union with Canada," said J. C. Pope, "will place our securities on a par with those of the Dominion, and our public position will be much better."[37] But the Conservatives also wanted to win the election. Their problem was to defeat a government committed to Confederation without endangering the principle of Confederation itself. Pope, their strong Confederate leader, eventually adopted a two-fold strategy. In the first place, he maintained that the people were being asked by the Haythorne administration to make an irrevocable decision without sufficient knowledge and time. "Parliament should have met," he contended, "and the terms agreed upon by our Government, should have been submitted to the Representatives of the people, as well as the financial state of the Colony. All matters, relating to the state of the Colony, should have been discussed, and then the question of Confederation could properly have been submitted to you at the polls."[38] In the second place, Pope claimed that the terms obtained by Haythorne and Laird were inadequate. He stated that if the Conservatives were elected he would immediately renew negotiations with the Dominion Government in order to obtain "proper terms." He insisted that he, as a Conservative and a close personal friend of Sir John A. Macdonald, could make a much better bargain with the Dominion.[39] Pope and the Conservatives hoped the alluring appeal of "still better terms" would be favorably received by the electorate and that they would gain power without endangering the principle of Confederation.

Although the 1873 campaign was ostensibly contested on the question of Confederation, another controversy intervened that served to cloud, to some degree, the main issue. The second problem was the school question which had been for years a prolific source of bitterness in Prince Edward Island. It seemed to be endowed with a magic charm. No matter what other problems might be raised, it was always a force to be reckoned with at every fresh appeal to the electorate. The 1873 campaign was no exception, and the education question came to the forefront. James C. Pope, in the thick of a desperate fight for office, decided to attempt to turn the school question to his advantage. He realized he could be assured of his party's victory if he could obtain the support of the Catholic electorate. What better ploy than to promise the Catholics governmental support for their separate schools? He, therefore, took counsel with his supporters, and the Conservative caucus promised that "the Opposition, as a party, was prepared to go for such a modification of the School Law, as will entitle any school, open to Government inspection, to its equitable proportion of the school-tax . . . provided a sufficient number of the supporters of the present Government, being dissatisfied with the present policy of the Government, are prepared to join us in carrying such a measure."[40] W. H. Pope even went so far as to draw up a Draft Bill embodying the principles contained in the caucus resolution.

The Draft Bill soon became public and the Conservative proposals were widely circulated in the press. The Protestant clergy, naturally enough, united against the proposals of the Draft Bill. Shortly afterwards, they published a letter in all the newspapers of the Island, in which they recommended that the "unsectarian system of education should be maintained, and that our Protestant brethern and our fellow-colonists, in general, in order to perserve in its integrity the present system, should give their support to those only who, in seeking their suffrages, shall satisfy them that such system will not be interfered with."[41] This letter proved quite effective. The Protestant electors exacted pledges from all Protestant candidates that they would not alter the existing educational system. Every Protestant candidate, even J. C. Pope, agreed to this pledge. Feelings were so embittered at this time that even the least perspicacious could realize that to refuse to do so was to court political disaster. Once again religion and politics were mixed in hopeless confusion and bitterness.

The people of Prince Edward Island, confronted with the confusing issues of "just terms" versus "proper terms," "grants" versus "no grants," went to the polls on April 2, 1873. They approved the principle of Confederation but gave a majority to J. C. Pope. L. H. Davies, commenting on the election, remarked that Confederation "was discussed in every hamlet and school house in the country, and there was hardly a man who did not understand it, in all its bearings. The result of that election, was that there is today, in this House, only one man, who opposed a Union with Canada, and he is not to the fore, while the question is being discussed."[42] Although Haythorne had lost the election, he was pleased that Confederation had been approved. He attributed the favorable response of public opinion to Confederation "not merely to the financial position of the Colony, and the heavy pecuniary obligations she has assumed, but to the fact that for the first time in the history of the question, it can be fairly argued, that the terms of Union, offered for our acceptance, by Canada, are advantageous and just."[43] James Rowe's explanation for the change of viewpoint was less altruistic: "After the terms came down," he told the Assembly, "I went among the people and laid them before them, telling them, they would have to choose these, or increased taxation. I did not try to persuade them, as to what they should do, but placed Confederation or increased taxation before them, asking them to say, which they would choose. They chose the former."[44] Considering the Islanders' previous rejections of terms not dissimilar, it seems safe to assume that their aversion to increased taxation was the impelling motive that led them to declare so unanimously in favor of Confederation.

The decision at the polls also indicated that the Islanders wished to place the direction of their public affairs in the hands of the Conservatives. This party, under J. C. Pope's leadership, won a decisive victory. It was placed in command of eighteen of the thirty seats in the Assembly. Since two of the elected Liberals, Cornelius Howatt and A. E. C. Holland, declared themselves independents, Haythorne's supporters numbered only ten. The magnitude of the Conservative victory can be attributed to two principal factors. Firstly, Pope's promise to secure "still better terms" won many votes for the Conservatives. This alluring appeal was not lost on the Islanders, who had demonstrated since 1864 that they were determined to drive a shrewd economic bargain before they would consent to union with Canada. Secondly, the Catholic electors voted almost unanimously for the Conservative party. The Draft Bill, published early in the campaign, pledging aid to Catholic schools brought the Catholics into alliance with the Conservatives; and the situation did not change appreciably when the Conservative Protestant candidates had to pledge they would not alter the school law. The Catholic electors considered that the Protestant candidates were literally forced to make this pledge so they placed their confidence in J. C. Pope's candidates. Thus, the promise of the Conservatives to redress the Catholic grievance gained Pope and five other Conservative Protestant candidates Catholic support. In addition, the twelve Catholic candidates elected were all supporters of J. C. Pope. The *Herald* remarked that "Mr. Pope came into power with a triumphant majority, and the very pith of that majority was Catholic representatives."[45] J. C. Pope had his substantial majority, but his attempts to mollify his Catholic supporters caused him many anxious moments in the next few months.

III   J. C. POPE AND PROPER TERMS

On April 15, 1873, Robert Haythorne tendered his resignation to Lieutenant Governor Robinson, and expressed his appreciation "for the frankness and courtesy,"[46] he had displayed during his term of office. In choosing Haythorne's successor, Robinson displayed considerably more frankness than courtesy. He was disappointed that Haythorne had been defeated, and extremely displeased that J. C. Pope had engaged in a criticism of the terms obtained by Haythorne and Laird. He did not like J. C. Pope personally, and would have preferred to have offered the office of Premier to T. H. Haviland.[47] But since Robinson really had no alternative but to accept Pope, he attempted to place conditions on his acceptance so as to ensure the passage of Confederation. Robinson's attempts to impose these conditions introduced an interesting constitutional conflict, in which Pope diplomatically, but firmly, reminded Robinson of the position of the Crown under responsible government.

After accepting Haythorne's resignation, Robinson informed J. C. Pope

J. C. Pope

that he intended to entrust the formation of the new government to him if he promised to do his best "to carry Confederation during the coming session, on the terms which have recently been submitted to the people, if none better can be procured from the Dominion authorities."[48] Although Pope declared that he would do all in his power "to ensure the speedy admission of the Island into the Union on terms just and equitable," he refused to accept "the honor of attempting to form a Government pledged to your Honor to pursue any definite policy. . . ."[49] "I trust that I may be pardoned," he wrote, "if I remind your Honor that the people of this Island have the right to self-government, and that as one of their representatives, I can never undertake, at the instance of the representative of the Crown, to do any act calculated to abridge this right."[50] Robinson was highly incensed by Pope's reply and said he needed such a pledge in view of his assertion during the campaign, that the delegation to Ottawa was "a conspiracy to deprive the people of self-government, *et hoc genus omne*."[51] He reminded Pope that he was perfectly aware of his constitutional position, but "it was absolutely necessary to the harmonious working of the Constitution, that the Crown shall be aware of, and have full reliance on, the personal views of the Minister, in whom it proposes to place its chief confidence."[52] Pope remained unimpressed and simply replied that he "still could not recognize the propriety of your requiring from me any pledge."[53]

J. C. Pope's second refusal convinced Robinson that he should adopt a more threatening approach. He said that some of Pope's election statements required him to make sure that his views, and those of the Assembly, on union, would not "be so wide apart as to be practically irreconcilable."[54] Without such assurance he would "have no alternative but to entrust the formation of the new Administration to some member of your party whose estimate of the relative position of the Crown and its chief adviser shall better accord with my own."[55] Such a threat to a man who had just received an overwhelming mandate, as leader of a party, was remarkably naive. Pope refused to budge. He informed Robinson that he still could not see any propriety in a pledge even if his views and those of the Legislature did not agree.[56] "As a matter of course," Pope wrote, "if I were to fail to acquiesce in the decision of the Legislature upon this or any other question, I would at once cease to be one of your Honor's constitutional advisers."[57] Robinson seemed to be completely disarmed by Pope's astute reply. He removed the condition, retreated gracefully and informed Pope he would be delighted if he would "proceed to form a Government and submit the names of your proposed colleagues with as little delay as possible."[58] The whole episode reveals not only the strange impression Robinson entertained of his function as head of the government, but also his partisanship and the extent to which he was prepared to interfere in order to bring the Island into Confederation.

J. C. Pope formed an administration at once, and the Legislature was convened on April 22, 1873. The new Conservative government was as determined as its predecessor to unite Prince Edward Island with the Dominion. "Feeling as we do," said J. C. Pope, "that all side issues should give way in order that the public credit may be maintained, and if Confederation will do this, I believe in view of all the difficulties entailed upon the country, this side of the House feels constrained to overcome their scruples against Confederation."[59] But the Conservatives insisted that they intended to seek better terms from Ottawa, and this for two principal reasons. In the first place, they maintained that the present terms were inadequate. Pope insisted that "they did not secure to this Colony a sum sufficient to defray the ordinary and indispensable requirements of its local government, and are by no means an equivalent for the Revenue, present and prospective, which it would be called upon to surrender to the Dominion."[60] "Better terms than those offered," he challenged the Assembly, "we have a right to look for. Better, I feel persuaded, we are entitled to, and if sought for, I am confident better we shall obtain."[61] In the second place, the Conservatives insisted that their mandate from the electorate required them to seek "better terms." "The late Government went to the country with these terms," A. J. Macdonald said, "and I contend that the people voted against them. But while doing so, they also voted in favor of the principle of Confederation, a majority declaring that we were justly entitled to better terms still. Such being the case, I contend that it is the duty of this side of the House to see what better terms can yet be obtained."[62] J. C. Pope then asked the Assembly to endorse a resolution authorizing the appointment of a delegation to proceed at once to Ottawa to confer with the Government of the Dominion of Canada on the securing of "just and reasonable terms."[63]

David Laird, the leader of the Liberals in the Lower House, and his colleagues vigorously maintained that the Conservatives had no justification for resuming further negotiations with the Dominion. They insisted that the terms received were just and liberal and that no additional concessions could or need be obtained. Laird contended that "by accepting the terms now offered, the Island would be placed in a superior position to any of the other Colonies that have entered the Confederacy."[64] "We have some honor and dignity to maintain in this matter," he said, "and have no right to send off a begging delegation to Canada for new Terms. The Colony has already obtained terms which the Governor General has declared cannot be increased, and I, for one, cannot stultify myself in supporting the resolution in favor of another delegation."[65] The Liberals also argued that Confederation should not be delayed in view of the financial and commercial difficulties of the Island. "The business of the country," Arthur Stewart asserted, "is now embarrassed. Trade is encumbered with many difficulties. All this would be relieved, if Confederation was effected. That is why, I am so anxious that no unnecessary delay should take place."[66] For these reasons, David Laird countered J. C. Pope's resolution with an amendment that the Assembly should prepare an Address to the Queen asking her to unite "Prince Edward Island with the Dominion of Canada on terms and conditions approved of in the Minute of the Privy Council, of the 10th March, 1873."[67]

After a spirited debate, Laird's amendment was rejected by the Assembly by a vote of fifteen to ten.[68] Cornelius Howatt and A. E. C. Holland, and two die-hard anti-Confederates, sponsored a resolution "that the best interests and future prosperity of Prince Edward Island would be secured by refusing Terms of admission into union with the Dominion of Canada."[69] This resolution was defeated by a majority of twenty-four to two, an almost complete contrast to the votes registered on similar anti-Confederate resolutions in the past.[70] Pope's original resolution was then adopted on a division of sixteen to ten.[71] In accordance with this resolution, Lieutenant Governor Robinson was requested to appoint a delegation to renew Confederation negotiations with the Dominion of Canada. The Assembly was then adjourned for ten days to await the results of the second mission to Ottawa.

When John A. Macdonald heard the results of the election on Prince Edward Island, he was highly pleased. He wrote to Lord Dufferin:

Pope's party which has triumphed was always in close alliance with us of the Dominion on the subject of Confederation. It was defeated by Mr. Haythorne and his friends who are anti-Confederates. At the last moment Mr. Haythorne took up Confederation as "une planche de salut" fearing defeat in their general policy at the approaching meeting of the Legislature. They have met the just reward of their tortuous policy. The original friends of Confederation have succeeded and will have the credit of carrying the measure.[72]

Apparently Macdonald also heard the rumor, falsely circulated in some quarters, that David Laird intended to join in a coalition with J. C. Pope, for he said in the same letter: "I understand that Laird who was here with Haythorne will join Pope's administration. I hope this is so for the sake of the cause, although it does not raise Mr. Laird in my estimation. His presence there will shield us from attempts at *still better* terms."[73] Laird, of course, did not become a member of Pope's administration, and Macdonald and his colleagues were not shielded from another delegation. On May 3, 1873, Macdonald's friend, J. C. Pope, accompanied by George

Howlan and T. H. Haviland, left for Ottawa to seek additional concessions. Prince Edward Island's financial crisis certainly did not prevent the Islanders from doing all in their power to make a shrewd bargain with the Dominion of Canada.

On May 6, the Island delegates arrived in Ottawa to initiate further negotiations with the Dominion government. For the next nine days they held several conferences with a sub-committee of the Privy Council, consisting of John A. Macdonald, Leonard Tilley, Charles Tupper and Hector Langevin. The first proposals of the Islanders were categorically denied, and they were placed in an embarrassing position. They concluded, however, that it would be more humiliating to return home without any concessions than to make further approaches. Accordingly, they submitted two additional memoranda comprising modified demands. The sub-committee relented and granted a few concessions. An agreement was formally reached on May 15, which enabled the Island delegates to return home loudly proclaiming that their mission was highly successful.

The additional concessions agreed upon by the delegations were that Prince Edward Island's debt allowance was to be raised from $45 per capita ($4,230,945) to $50 per capita ($4,701,050) and that telegraphic communications would be maintained by the Dominion Government between the Island and the mainland.[74] The $23,500 realized annually from the increased debt allowance, and the $2,000 for the telegraphic communications represented an annual increase of $25,500 to the original terms conceded to Haythorne and Laird. The additional terms were not impressive. David Laird claimed that the delegates had operated "on the principle that it was better to take half a loaf than to starve."[75] But to the Island delegates, who came so close to registering a zero in Ottawa, the new terms represented a substantial victory. They were now ready to defend their mission in the Island Legislature.

IV CONFEDERATION DEBATES

On May 22, 1873, J. C. Pope presented the terms of union to the members of the House of Assembly. Their approval was a foregone conclusion. The debates revealed that the members almost unanimously considered that Confederation was a necessity. "It has now become a self-evident proposition," said T. H. Haviland, "that we cannot any longer remain out of Confederation. Unless we accept the Terms now before us and go into Confederation, it will be utterly impossible, with the large debt now upon us, to float our debentures, and establish our public credit."[76] "I have held anti-Confederation views," admitted George W. Howlan, "but I find no other course is now open to us as a Colony, but to accept the best terms we can procure, and enter the Dominion."[77] But it was James Rowe, who, perhaps, best expressed the sentiments of most Islanders:

He believed that his constituents would not have gone in favor of the measure [Confederation] were it not for circumstances over which they had no control. Indeed he had reason to believe that his constituents regretted the circumstances which had placed them in their present position, and necessitated their acceptance of the Terms of Confederation now offered to the Colony. Had it not been for the introduction of the Railway Bill, his constituency, and he believed other constituencies also, would still have rejected any offer Canada might make to this Colony to induce us to unite with her, as the people would have preferred to manage their own affairs as in times past. But there is, under our present circumstances, a necessity for our accepting Terms of Confederation, in order to escape financial embarrassment . . . and he would most heartily support the resolution before the committee, in the interest of his constituents, and of the people of the whole Island.[78]

The argument that Prince Edward Island must enter Confederation, *ex necessitate,* was advanced by nearly all the members.

These final Confederation debates also indicated that the large majority of the members of the Assembly considered that they had acted very sagaciously in delaying the Island's entry into the union with Canada. David Laird proudly referred to the merits of the delay and the part he had played in effecting it. "If it had not been for my opposition to Confederation in years gone by," he asserted, "we would, today have the old spavined horse which the Hon. Col. Secretary [T. H. Haviland] was willing to accept, and with that old horse we would now be limping and hobbling along."[79] "The eighty cents per head," he continued, "and the debt equivalent, were all that they were granted under the Quebec Scheme, and I am today proud that I opposed the scheme. The Better Terms of 1869, I also opposed, and I am glad I did so, as the Terms secured by the former delegation were $14,000 better than they were."[80] "Perhaps it is as well," admitted Federick Brecken, "that we have been allowed our own way and time of joining with Canada. We have not married in haste. No doubt, the hon. member, the Leader of the Opposition [Laird] has rendered good service in opposing the measure so long, and, perhaps, his position and the influence he brought to bear has, more than anything else, contributed to the result now achieved."[81] W. W. Sullivan also maintained that "a great deal had been gained by resisting Confederation as long as we did, but as we now had fair and reasonable terms, we should be satisfied to accept them with good grace."[82]

The members of the Assembly did accept the terms with good grace. They expressed satisfaction with the generous treatment accorded by the

Dominion. Henry Beer said "all the members should be satisfied with the handsome sum that had been secured."[83] "It was not probable," he added, "that any additional concession would be made to this Colony for a long time to come, as we had been liberally dealt with by the Government of the Dominion."[84] "I am only too happy," Arthur Stewart informed the Assembly, "to know that Confederation is so nearly consummated on fair and reasonable terms, that our Island is to be freed from its tremendous debt, and that we shall be a free, independent, and well-governed people, retaining all our present rights and privileges."[85] Nearly all the members expressed similar sentiments in different ways.

The representatives predicted that Prince Edward Island would enjoy a prosperous future as a province of the Dominion. Peter Sinclair stated that the Island "would improve its agricultural, commercial and fishing operations, at a more rapid rate than it had ever done, and that general prosperity would be the result. The Colony would occupy a better financial position than ever before as it would be entirely free from debt, and would receive a sufficient revenue to meet its requirements for many years to come."[86] The members even asserted that the old bugbear of taxation, that had been so effectively used by anti-Confederates in the past, would not mar the brilliant future. David Laird, the inveterate anti-Confederate of former days, said with confidence: "I am free now to admit that I do not fear any bad results from Confederation. The people of the other Provinces are as afraid of taxation as we are. No increase of taxation can be levied upon us, but what must be imposed upon them, therefore, in that respect we have nothing to fear."[87] The members were so optimistic of the Island's future that it could be said John Lefurgy expressed the sentiments of all when he concluded the debate with the claim that the Assembly had "this night acted wisely for the interests of this Colony."[88]

On May 26, 1873, in the early hours of the morning, Premier J. C. Pope moved that the Address to the Queen, embodying the terms of union between Prince Edward Island and the Dominion of Canada, be accepted by the Assembly.[89] David Laird, the leader of the Opposition, magnanimously seconded Pope's motion, maintaining that "as a party we were defeated, but nevertheless the question has been sustained."[90] Only two members, A. E. C. Holland and Cornelius Howatt opposed the motion. Holland maintained that "no reason had been produced, save the glory argument, to show why we should support Confederation."[91] "We have sold our noble little ship," he continued, "and she now stands stripped of all the glory with which for one hundred years, she was adorned."[92] Howatt said facetiously: "I know, Mr. Speaker, that in this House, I occupy about the same position that our representatives will in the Dominion Parliament.

They will be left out, and have their views treated in the same way as mine are here."[93] The two anti-Confederates were indeed an insignificant minority. The resolutions in favor of Confederation were carried by a majority of twenty-seven to two.[94] Thus by an almost unanimous majority, a complete contrast to the vote on the Quebec Resolutions, the Assembly decided that Prince Edward Island should become a province of the Dominion of Canada.

The debate on Confederation followed a similar pattern in the Legislative Council. The Councillors unanimously declared themselves favorable to the new terms, but it was evident that necessity prompted their decision. The speeches of the two confirmed anti-Confederates, A. A. MacDonald and Edward Palmer illustrate this emphasis on necessity. "The only thing that induces me to come to the determination that Confederation is our destiny, if not an absolute necessity," said A. A. MacDonald, "is that our other securities, treasury warrants, etc. may become depreciated. . . . I have, therefore, reluctantly come to the conclusion that Confederation is a necessity."[95] "I have always been one of the strongest opponents of the union of this Island with Canada," Edward Palmer declared truthfully, "but I saw that the country was brought into such a state by the great railway debt that Confederation was the only expedient we could resort to so as to maintain the credit of the Colony, and carry on the Government."[96] Every member of the Council expressed similar views.

All the Councillors signified satisfaction with the generous terms conceded to them by Canada. "When Canada engaged to take $3,250,000 of railway debt off our shoulders," said Palmer, "I thought we had reason to congratulate ourselves. I cannot, therefore, have the slightest hesitation in accepting the present proposals."[97] "I was perfectly satisfied when we got $45 per head," Thomas Dodd remarked, "because it was very much more than we had been previously offered, but when the late Delegates got $5 additional, I am better satisfied still."[98] Patrick Walker, with typical Island logic, commented: "All I have to say is that the first Delegation did well, but the second did better."[99]

The members of the Council did not display the same optimism as their counterparts in the Assembly with respect to the Island's future in the Dominion. Edward Palmer was the only member who referred to the subject, and his remarks did not manifest much enthusiasm. He said:

I have been agreeably surprised at the advancement and prosperity in Canada since Confederation was first established. Her manufactures have vastly increased, and her prospects are good. She has maintained her public credit with great ease; and I am of the opinion that upon our going into the union now we will not have the disadvantages we would have had six or seven years ago.[100]

The silence of the rest of the Councillors would seem to imply that they regarded the future with mixed feelings. But they did not hesitate to accept the terms of Confederation for better or worse. On May 27, 1873, the resolutions recommending union with Canada were presented to the Council by A. A. MacDonald and carried unanimously without a division.[101] As in the Assembly, this vote was a perfect contrast to the 1865 vote on the Quebec Resolutions. The Legislative Council on Prince Edward Island had never believed in half-measures.

In Ottawa, the preparations for the entry of Prince Edward Island into Confederation went smoothly. On May 16, 1873, Leonard Tilley, on behalf of the Canadian Privy Council, submitted the terms of union for the admission of Prince Edward Island into Confederation to the Canadian House of Commons for ratification. He informed the House that the terms conceded to the Island differed from those granted to the other provinces in only two particulars. The differences were, he pointed out, a special grant of $800,000 for the settlement of the land tenure question, and a more generous debt allowance arrangement. He elaborated upon the $800,000 provision:

The Province was in a different position to that of any other Province in the Dominion. What passed to the other Provinces as Crown Lands had, in the case of Prince Edward Island, been sold to parties in England by the Imperial Government, so that they had no Crown Lands, and derived no revenue from such a source for local purposes as every other Province did. These lands being held by absentee proprietors, the only persons living on them were tenants; this was a very unsatisfactory state of things, and had prevented the Island from taking the position it would otherwise have taken. It was in consequence of this that the Legislature, in 1869, authorized the Government to make arrangements for the admission of the Island, including the purchase of the Crown Lands.[102]

Tilley went on to explain the reasons for the special debt allowance settlement:

From the fact that the Dominion Government and Parliament had undertaken the construction of the Intercolonial Railway at a cost of $20,000,000, that the Pacific Railway was to be built with a contribution on the part of the Dominion of $30,000,000, that $20,000,000, or $25,000,000, was to be expended on canals, that it was contemplated to readjust the debts of the Dominion by assuming the surplus of Ontario and Quebec, and giving sums in proportion to the other Provinces, and that the Island would not have public works after it came into the Dominion at all in proportion to the other Provinces, it was agreed to extend the Island debt to be assumed to $50 a head. At the negotiations in January last the sum was fixed at $45 a head. That had been submitted to the people of the Island and the result was that the newly elected Legislature had rejected the terms and authorized another deputation to come to Ottawa with power to enter into negotiations with the Government for the extension of the amount to $50.[103]

After making these explanations, Tilley asked the House of Commons to authorize the Canadian Government to admit "this beautiful and fertile Island into the Union."[104] He admitted that the terms were quite generous, but maintained that the Dominion would not need to spend much money on the Island after Confederation. "The great local works there having now been completed," contended Tilley, "there could never be any large local expenditure in the future, and it was in consideration of this fact that the Dominion had granted such liberal terms."[105] Alexander MacKenzie, the leader of the Liberals, graciously stated that "they were all very happy at the prospect of the Island joining the Confederation, and no member of the House, especially amongst those who were the originators of the Confederation project, would be disposed to treat the matter otherwise than in an amicable way."[106] All the members who spoke expressed the same views. On May, 1873, the Confederation resolutions were adopted without a division; and John A. Macdonald, Leonard Tilley, Hector Langevin and Charles Tupper were appointed to prepare an Address to the Queen requesting her to unite Prince Edward Island with the Dominion of Canada.

The debate in the Canadian Senate was very brief. On May 21, Senator Campbell moved that the Senate accept the Confederation resolutions in order to effect "the completion of the Union, which we have been endeavouring to bring about ever since 1861, and which remains simply to be completed by the admission of Prince Edward Island."[107] Senator Ferrier referred, with some satisfaction, to the motivation that had prompted the Island's entry into the union: "I am glad that Prince Edward Island has decided upon coming into Confederation. I have said that prosperity is not always an advantage, and, I think, if the seal fishing had been less successful for the last few years, we should have seen Newfoundland wishing to become part of the Confederation, like Prince Edward Island. It got into difficulties a short time ago, and was glad to take hold of the stronger power."[108] Senator Holmes concluded the debate stating that "he felt very glad that the Island had at least consented to enter the Union. This was the garden of the Lower Provinces, possessing a favorable climate and productive soil . . . and would be a benefit and not a burden to us, as we all knew that union was strength."[109] The Confederation resolutions were than adopted by the Upper House without a division. With the Senate's ratification of the terms, the Legislature of Canada authorized the entrance of another province into the Dominion of Canada.

While the legislative debates reveal that both Prince Edward Island and the Dominion of Canada were well pleased with the results of the

Confederation negotiations, their Governors and the Imperial Government were even more delighted. Lord Dufferin, in a congratulatory letter to Lieutenant Governor Robinson, expressed his enthusiasm. "The union of Prince Edward Island with the Dominion of Canada," he wrote, "is a most fortunate circumstance from whatever point it may be regarded, whether affecting Local, Imperial, or Canadian interests."[110] "I am well aware," he continued, "that it has been in a great measure owing to your wise and administrative counsels, that so happy a consummation has been reached, and in forwarding the duplicate copy of the enclosed Minute to Lord Kimberley, it has been an additional pleasure to me to state how highly conducive your efforts have been to the satisfactory results which have been obtained."[111] Lord Dufferin remarked facetiously to John A. Macdonald, when inviting him to the christening of the newest addition to the Dufferin family, that "this birth with Prince Edward Island's entry into Confederation makes twins."

Lord Dufferin did not need to remind the Colonial Office of Robinson's important role in the Confederation negotiations. Robinson had such a broad concept of humility that he had no hesitation in personally emphasizing the large part he had played in inducing Prince Edward Island to enter the union. "To me it is a matter of no little gratification," Robinson wrote to Kimberley, "that the Union of the Island with Canada has been accomplished during my Administration, and I shall always look back with pride to the share which it has been my good fortune to take in bringing about this beneficial and long wished for result."[112] In another letter he detailed the beneficial results of his influence:

Under these circumstances I may be pardoned, if I refer with a feeling of satisfaction to the large majority by which a question has now been carried, which, when I came here two years and a half ago there would not have been found 1,000 people out of a population of nearly 100,000 to support. The first great point gained was inducing the adoption of a Confederate policy by the then anti-confederate party, and tho' the scheming of the avowed Confederates at one moment threatened to throw everything back for a time, I never felt any real anxiety as to the result since the day Mr. Haythorne and his Colleagues consented to send delegates to Ottawa.[113]

Lieutenant Governor Robinson was such an ardent promoter of Confederation that it was quite natural that he should derive immense satisfaction from the Island's decision to unite with Canada. He had, moreover, played such a crucial role in influencing the Haythorne government to decide in favor of Confederation, that he could, with perfect justification, feel a real sense of accomplishment. However, in all his Confederation endeavors he was simply being a devoted and faithful public official of the Imperial Government. Since the year 1865 the British authorities had exerted unrelenting pressure to secure the adherence of Prince Edward Island to Confederation, and, therefore, when the Island decided to unite with Canada they were highly gratified. Kimberley expressed their sentiments in a letter to Robinson: "I take this opportunity of congratulating you on the successful result of the negotiations for union which have been carried on between the two Governments, and I have to desire you to make it publicly known that the accomplishment of this further important step towards the complete consolidation of Her Majesty's Possessions in British North America has offered Her Majesty's Government much gratification."[114] The Imperial Government, moreover, did not fail to acknowledge Robinson's faithful instrumentality. On June 30, 1873, Kimberley conveyed to him "the entire approval of Her Majesty's Government, for the ability and judgment you have displayed in this matter;"[115] and as a tangible expression of its approval the Imperial Government appointed him a "Companion of the Most Distinguished Order of St. Michael and St. George."[116]

V   JULY 1, 1873

On June 26, 1873, an Imperial Order-in-Council authorized that Prince Edward Island's union with Canada would become effective "from and after the first of July, 1873."[117] The union was proclaimed in due form on that day. The *Patriot* gave a vivid description of the proclamation ceremonies:

On Tuesday, July 1st, whether for weal or woe, Prince Edward Island became a province of the Dominion of Canada. At 12 o'clock noon, the Dominion Flag was run up on the flag staffs at Government House and the Colonial Building, and a salute of 21 guns was fired from St. George's battery and from H. M. S. *Spartan* now in port. The Church and city bells rang out a lively peel, and the Volunteers under review at the city park fired a *feu de joie*. So far as powder and metal could do it, there was for a short time a terrible din. But among the people who thronged the streets there was no enthusiasm. A few moments before 12, Mr. Sheriff Watson stepped forward on the balcony of the Colonial Building and read the Union Proclamation. He was accompanied by two ladies and about half a dozen gentlemen. The audience within hearing consisted of three persons, and even they did not appear to be very attentive. After the reading of the Proclamation was concluded, the gentlemen on the balcony gave a cheer, but the three persons below—who, like the Tooley street tailors who claimed to be "the people of England"—at that moment represented the people of Prince Edward Island responded never a word.[118]

The *Island Argus* also made some revealing comments on the Island's first Dominion Day celebrations:

Confederation has been consummated at last. For the first time the Dominion flag waved from the Colonial Building, on Tuesday last, when the inauguration drama was enacted. The roar of cannon, the sharp rattle of musketry, the reading of the proclamation, the administering of the gubernatorial oath and—presto, the thing is done. . . . There were no unseemly or extravagant demonstrations of joy. The people here are too self-possessed for that. Though they are impressed with the advantages resulting from Union and the financial relief it brings them, they are fully aware of the value of the acquisition to Canada of their fertile and prosperous Island. There was no waste of lung power, therefore, when it was announced to the people of Charlottetown by the High Sheriff of Queen's County that they were Canadians. As the proclamation was being read with due care, interrupted here and there by the reports of the guns on board H. M. S. *Spartan*, furnishing as it were, the note of admiration to the document, the people in the adjoining market place, bought and sold, apparently unmoved. . . . In the evening there was a display of fireworks from H. M. S. *Spartan*, and from the Colonial Building, which were brilliantly illuminated. Altogether the day passed quietly without any particularly noteworthy demonstrations.[119]

Thus with these low-key celebrations, Prince Edward Island became the seventh province of the Dominion.

On July 1, 1873, the people of Prince Edward Island accepted their destiny with mixed feelings of disappointment and satisfaction. They expressed disappointment because economic necessity alone had induced them to declare in favor of Confederation. The *Patriot* accurately commented that "the great majority of the people have accepted Confederation as a necessity. They did not take up the question *cum amore,* and when the day arrived that the union was a *fait accompli,* they did not have a cheer to give."[120] Yet they also displayed satisfaction because the Dominion Government, by its generous terms of admission, had removed their principal economic and political objections to Confederation. The special annual subsidy of $45,000 granted in lieu of the absence of Crown Lands, together with the guarantee of an $800,000 loan, placed the Island in a position to settle the contentious land question that had plagued it since 1767. In 1875, the Island Legislature passed a complusory Land Purchase Act whereby the system of proprietorship was ultimately extinguished. A Commission was established to evaluate the holdings of the proprietors and to determine the price at which they would be required to sell. In September, 1875, the government purchased 187,699 of the 381,720 acres still held by the proprietors at a cost of $1.63 per acre. The last legal obstacle was cleared away and the last estate purchased by the government in 1895. The Prince Edward Island government borrowed a total of $782,402.33 from the Dominion. It never repaid this loan, even though it received over $600,000 from the sale of the lands to the tenants. The $45,000 subsidy was, therefore, reduced by some $39,000[121] The settlement of the century-old land question was the greatest blessing that the Island received from the terms granted by the Dominion.

The guarantee of efficient steam service with the mainland, assured the Island that the economic weaknesses caused by isolation would be obviated. The Dominion Government's assumption of the ownership, maintenance and operation of a 200-mile railway system, provided the Island with a much-desired and very adequate means of internal communication. When this railway was finally completed, with its additional branches, more than four-fifths of the province was less than five miles from the line and less than eight miles by road from a station.[122] The Dominion provided the Island with a friendly, leisurely, community railway which each Islander could with reason feel was his very own. The *Island Argus* remarked with wry satisfaction: "That heavy cloud bearing railway indebtedness and a thousand other ills on its bosom, which lately loomed up so ominously has dispersed. The burden that threatened to break the back of the little Island has been put on the stout shoulders of vigorous young Canada, who marches off without wavering under the additional load and smiling triumphantly that he has won the *coy little maiden* at last."[123] Since the terms of the Quebec Conference guaranteed neither the settlement of the land question nor efficient communications with the mainland, and since the 1869 offer made no provision for a railway system, it is easy to appreciate the satisfaction with which the Islanders viewed the 1873 terms of union.

When Lord Dufferin visited Prince Edward Island in July, 1873, he was greeted on the Queen's wharf by an arch of welcome adorned with the words, "Courted long, but won at last."[124] These words were an appropriate admission from the newest province of the Dominion. Prince Edward Island had always viewed union with Canada in the light of the settlement that would accompany the marriage. For ten years, in spite of protestations from her mother, Great Britain, the Island had categorically rejected all proposals because she did not consider the terms of union sufficiently attractive to compensate her for her highly prized independence. And it was only when economic forces threatened to undermine her financial security that she consented to unite with Canada. During his visit, Lord Dufferin wrote to Sir John A. Macdonald, that he "found the Island in a high state of jubilation, and quite under the impression that it is the Dominion that has been annexed to Prince Edward Island, and in alluding to the subject, I have adopted the same tone."[125] His attitude must have been consoling indeed to the people of Prince Edward Island, who had so reluctantly relinquished their independent status.

Chapter Ten

The Transportation Issue, 1873-1973

By MARY K. CULLEN

The insularity and sense of distinctive identity so clearly evident in Prince Edward Island's prolonged opposition to Confederation was principally influenced by Northumberland Strait. Isolating the Island by masses of moving ice for nearly five months of the year, the strait had been a motivating reason for making such a small geographic unit into a separate British colony in 1769.[1] Until 1827, the Island's only winter link with the outside world was a lone courier who carried the mails fortnightly between Wood Islands and Pictou. Subsequently, weekly winter communication was established between Cape Traverse and Cape Tormentine where small ice boats with runners were hauled over the ice.[2] In the 1860's, private steamers were making bi-weekly summer trips to several mainland ports[3] but this frequent intercolonial service had not overcome the Island's special winter handicap. Prince Edward Island opposed Maritime legislative union because she refused to have her representatives sit in a remote parliament and impose taxes for public works from which the Island, in its insular position, could derive little benefit.[4] A similar belief that winter isolation would limit many of the advantages of federal union was instrumental in the Island decision not to join Canada in 1867.[5]

When delegates from the first Canadian Cabinet visited Charlottetown in August, 1869 to offer "better terms," lack of winter communications was put forward by the Island Government as one of its outstanding objections to union. Premier R. P. Haythorne explained the inconvenience the Island people experienced "for want of means of getting off and on" and pointed out that this obstacle to union might be obviated by the maintenance of steam navigation between the Island and mainland during the winter season.[6] George Etienne Cartier, one of the negotiators for Canada, felt a strong steamship could be constructed which would keep up year-round communication.[7] In an effort to woo the Island into Confederation, the federal delegation pledged that Canada would assume and defray all charges for "efficient Steam Service for the conveyance of Mails and Passengers, to be established and maintained between the Island and the Dominion, winter and summer, thus placing the Island in continuous communication with the Intercolonial Railway and the Railway system of the Dominion."[8] The "better terms" of 1869 were rejected since the Canadian Government did not also agree to settle the land question to the Island's satisfaction,[9] but the essential communications feature was included in future negotiations. In 1873, when the Island, in extremely straitened circumstances because of railway liabilities, applied for admission to Canada, the communication pledge was incorporated in the terms of union.[10]

The statesmen of Prince Edward Island considered the latter guarantee as a *sine qua non* of the agreement to enter Confederation. They always insisted that one of the principal motives that justified them in giving up their revenue and constitution was the clause in the terms of Confederation which provided for continuous and efficient transportation. It was not a mere matter of sectional privilege but a constitutional right. As the changing direction of the Island economy increased the importance of a mainland connection, the Islanders interpreted their "right" with the greatest imagination. The "conveyance of mails and passengers" was construed to embrace the transport of all kinds of produce and merchandise. Daily communication was the interpretation for "continuous" while "efficient" meant "the best available communication than can be had." Finally, much importance was attached to the phrase "steam service" as opposed to "steam navigation," and successive Island Governments maintained that if steam service could not be provided by boat, it should be furnished in some other way — be it by balloons over the Northumberland or a tunnel under the strait.[11]

For many years the Federal Government failed to implement the minimum requirements of the communications clause and at no time did it interpret the guarantee in the same sweeping manner as the Islanders. The efforts of the Island people to secure their constitutional right, as well as a service of increasing economic necessity form a dominant theme in the province's relations with the Canadian Government. Nearly fifty years of persistence was rewarded in 1917, when with the establishment of a car ferry service, interrupted winter communication virtually ceased and Prince Edward Island became an integral part of the transcontinental railway system of Canada. The most arduous phase of the Island's communication problem concluded with that breakthrough and yet inevitably the demands of continuity and efficiency continued to rise. After a century of Confederation, crossing Northumberland Strait continues to be a vital and contentious theme in the Island story.

*   *   *

During the 1870's, Prince Edward Island was probably more in- dependent of the economic need for a physical connection with its sister provinces than at any other time since Confederation. The abrogation of the Reciprocity Treaty in 1866 and a general expansion in western grain pro- duction had drastically reduced Island exports to the United States — but the United Kingdom, not Canada, had taken up the slack. In the immediate post-reciprocity period nearly 50 per cent of the total exports of the Island (about 2/3 in oats) were sent to the British Isles.[12] Island-built ships carried these products to the British market and were either sold with their cargoes or returned to the Island with English manufacturers.[13] With a high proportion of direct international trade and a wide coastal trade,[14] only mails and passengers required regular transportation to the mainland. Thus throughout the decade, "steam service" took second place in Island political attention to the Land Purchase Act, Free Schools and the Halifax Fishery Award.

Initial federal efforts to honor the communication agreement success- fully laid the basis for future complaint. Displaying a laissez-faire distrust of publicly owned services, the Alexander MacKenzie Government which came to office in November, 1873, hoped to place the burden of Northum- berland transportation on private shoulders. For summer service, it renewed the provincial subsidy to the Island Steam Navigation Company for opera- tion of two paddle-wheel steamers, one from Summerside to Shediac, N.B., the other from Charlottetown to Pictou, N. S.[15] In December, 1873, the Government accepted a tenure from James King of Halifax to run the *Albert* during the winter season between Georgetown and Pictou. For two succes- sive years, however, King's old wooden steamer refused to budge with the onset of ice. When hasty invitations for new tenders went unanswered, the MacKenzie administration reluctantly decided to purchase its own vessel.[16]

The *Northern Light,* the first Canadian Government steamer for the Island-mainland service, was a wooden ship of 700 indicated horsepower, designed for winter navigation on the St. Lawrence.[17] Her builder, E. W. Sewell of Levis, Quebec, suggested a revised design for the heavier ice of Northumberland Strait but the Department of Marine and Fisheries, con- tending the ship was only a trial vessel, despatched her without alterations.[18] The *Northern Light* commenced her twelve years of Island service, or more properly, disservice on December 7, 1876.[19] Year after year the departmental reports recorded her misfortunes. The first season her steering gear gave way and the following year the propeller broke.[20] Soon it was discovered that her stern was much better adapted for breaking through the ice than her stem and more than once the *Northern Light* bumped across eighteen miles of icy strait stern foremost.[21]

For the extended periods when steam power failed to reduce Island isolation, the Federal Government continued the pre-Confederation practice of contracting ice boat mail service from Cape Traverse to Cape Tormentine.[22] In 1878, a survey of the short nine mile Capes route was commissioned with a view to securing winter communication between the Island and Intercolonial railway systems. Henry F. MacLeod, a federal engineer, examined the coast and approaches in the vicinity of each Cape and interviewed men familiar with the crossing. His findings indicated that although there were good harbour facilities on either side, drifting ice moving against the board or stationary ice would frequently make it impossible for a steamer to approach closely enough to discharge passengers and mail. In the severest part of the winter the most reliable means of crossing would always be the iceboat. To make this service safe and efficient MacLeod recommended larger ice boats, boat houses, signal towers and a small screw steamer to assist the ice boats through open water stretches. He suggested that the steamer mentioned might also be used at the Capes for summer service and concluded his report with cost estimates of alternate railway connections to the Capes.[23] His report was submitted on April 23, 1879, but by that date the MacKenzie Government had been defeated at the polls and the Conservatives had taken office.

The prolonged indifference of the John A. Macdonald Government to the recommendations of the MacLeod Report or to any improvements in communication met with vigorous criticism from the Island Government in the 1880's. The incidental reason for the awakening provincial agitation was that problems lately occupying attention had been solved. Effective implementation of the Land Purchase Act of 1875 had ended the turbulent land tenure question while the coalition government, formed in 1876 to inaugurate Free Schools, had accomplished its object and was replaced in 1879 by a party government. The campaign for better communication waged by the W. W. Sullivan Conservative administration was a fresh political cause, but primarily and essentially, it was an expression of the growing importance of the Canadian economy in the lives of the Island people.

The end of the wooden sailing vessel and the beginning of Macdonald's National Policy effected a significant change in the orientation and flow of Island trade after the 1870's. It was no longer profitable to import goods directly from England when cargoes were not carried in Island-built vessels.[24] The shift from wood to iron shipping meant the decline of the small shipbuilding ports and the rise of strategic mainland terminals served by rail. International coastal trade was still important but high tariffs deluged the Maritimes with the manufactures of Upper Canada and prevented the Island from obtaining cheaper imports from other countries.[25] The same forces — a change in shipping and the building of a national economy — compelled Islanders to sell more of their exportable surpluses in the highly competitive and limited markets of the Maritimes and Quebec. If farmers were confined to fall shipment, the markets were immediately glutted and prices fell. "Efficient" and "continuous" communication took on a new value, for it meant that produce could be shipped when required by the consumer and at the best prices.[26]

The total inadequacy of existing governmental transportation facilities for the conveyance of either freight or passengers was illustrated during the winter of 1881. For months thousands of dollars worth of merchandise for Island merchants was stored at Pictou landing, while large quantities of freight waiting to be exported from the Island were locked out from mainland markets.[27] On one occasion when the *Northern Light* was ice-bound for three weeks, shortage of provisions caused the passengers, both men and women, to leave the steamer and make their way across the strait on foot and small boats. Some people were badly frozen, others nearly lost.[28] With this incident fresh in the minds of the people and freight blockage affecting business, the time was ripe for agitation.

A Joint Address of the Provincial Legislative Council and Assembly, opened an intensive six-year crusade by the Sullivan Government on the communications issue. The 1881 appeal to Ottawa set the pattern for subsequent memorials. Based squarely on the communications clause of the Confederation agreement, it suggested that transportation was neither continuous nor efficient. As a result, the Island people were labouring under enormous disadvantages: business was disrupted due to poor mail service and inadequate accommodation for freight; passenger travel was uncertain and dangerous. To add insult to injury, Islanders contributed to the Intercolonial Railway and other public works of Canada, yet isolation precluded them from enjoying the benefits of such enterprises. In consideration of these facts, the Legislature prayed that the Canadian Government "adopt vigorous and immediate measures to remedy the grievances complained of," and further that it provide compensation for the loss sustained through the non-fulfillment of the terms of Confederation.[29]

Prince Edward Island's Address was formally acknowledged by Ottawa on April 16, 1881,[30] but Premier Sullivan received nothing more concrete in 1882 than a telegram assuring "earnest consideration."[31] A pungent Minute of Council, dated January 3, 1883, reminded the Macdonald Government that two years had passed since the Joint Address of 1881 and still there was no improvement. This time the province not only reiterated its former arguments but defined its understanding of the Confederation clause to be "equal facilities for intercourse with the other provinces as those provinces enjoy between themselves." What was particularly grating was the unequal treatment the Federal Government accorded its respective Confederation obligations. The Islanders protested that to fulfill the terms of Confederation with British Columbia, Ottawa was expending millions in the construction of the Pacific Railway "yet to provide the means of communication between two provinces over a distance of scarcely nine miles, and thus fulfill an obligation equally as binding . . . the general Government have displayed a marked indifference."[32]

A Select Committee of the House of Commons,[33] appointed February 22, 1883, to consider the question of steam communication between Prince Edward Island and the mainland, revealed more specifically the conditions of the service and the expectations of the Island people. Ten witnesses,[34] each with a personal knowledge of the strait, disagreed on the feasibility of completely uninterrupted winter service but indicated that mail and passenger service was far from satisfactory and that conveyance of freight must become an integral part of the service.

The overriding concern of the witnesses was the inability of the existing steamers to handle the increased volume of interprovincial trade. The *Northern Light* was unreliable and the paddle-wheel steamers operated by the Island Steam Navigation Company were too small. If freight did not spoil from a wait on the wharf, it was damaged due to overcrowded cargoes.[35] A panacea advocated by one witness was a car ferry — a solution practically thirty-five years away. John T. Jenkins, a federal M. P. from Charlottetown, felt there should be a third rail put on the narrow gauge Island railway and a car ferry placed at the Capes so produce could be shipped by rail to the Intercolonial Railway.[36] Evidently, the idea was so novel that the Committee avoided its recommendation. On the witness's advice it was suggested that screw-steamers replace the present summer steamers,[37] that the federal subsidy be increased with the stipulation that "good substantial boats be used" and that the *Northern Light* which was "fast becoming unfit for service" be replaced.[38]

The discomfort and length of passenger travel was the other principal complaint of the current steam service. The effects of poor transportation on visitors worried Senator Carvell who told the Committee that "the entertainment of strangers and tourists is one of the largest interests in Prince

Edward Island." He prophesied that "a great many people might be induced to do down there and spend a lot of money" but he added "they will not go on board a steamer which is loaded, or has been loaded all season through with cattle and sheep and other stock."[39] Other witnesses expressed the same sentiments and further complained that the voyages from Shediac to Summerside and from Pictou to Georgetown were too long.[40] The Committee advocated that, whenever possible, passengers should be conveyed separately from freight and that a passenger-mail steamer be set up at the short Capes routes.[41]

The opinion of several witnesses that ice conditions in Northumberland Strait would always interrupt steam communication for some period[42] compelled the Committee to recommend vast improvements in the Capes ice boat service. Despite Henry F. MacLeod's report on the subject, the service in 1883 was basically the same as it had been before Confederation. Ice boat captains contracted for the service at $35 per round trip (for every two boats) which, after salaries and boat repair, left little for safety equipment.[43] The contracts were administered by the Post Office Department and conveyance of mail was the principal object, although for $2, passengers could pay the cost of passage by hauling the boat.[44] The Island men gladly suffered this inconvenience but one witness admitted they were slightly chagrined at the recent increase in their burden from the baggage of the Upper Canadian commercial traveller.[45] On the suggestion of the witnesses, the Committee advised that the Capes service should be shifted to the Marine Department and run as a government operation. They further recommended an increased number of boats and employees, boat houses for repair of the boats and accommodation of the men, stations for observation and signal service, good sized row-boats to relieve the ice boats in open water stretches, and finally, screw-steamers which could frequently assist the ice boats and be docked in the board ice when not at work.[46]

Even the modest recommendations of the Select Committee of 1883 were long ignored by the Federal Government. The Minister of Marine promised boat houses would be built but Island representatives had to remind Ottawa that no improvement had been made as of February, 1884.[47] Rather than replace the *Northern Light,* in January, 1884, the Macdonald Government announced its decision to restore and strengthen the vessel. To assist the old ship, it proposed to reinforce the *Napoleon,* a wooden screw-steamer used for lighthouse service.[48] Considering that federal inspectors had that fall condemned the summer steamers as unsafe for service,[49] Sullivan viewed this announcement of policy as no improvement at all. The opening Speech of the 1884 session stated that "our province still remains unprovided with that efficient and continuous steam service which was guaranteed by the articles of Confederation."[50]

The Joint Address of 1884 was the last official appeal the Sullivan Government made to Ottawa. It solemnly recited the barren history of federal inaction and incredulously observed "that the only improvement contemplated is the adaption in some way of a steamer intended for the lighthouse service, so as to supplement the work of the *Northern Light.*" It admitted that freight conveyance was outside the express terms of the agreement but emphasized that with respect to mails and passengers, Canadian indifference was in direct violation of the Confederation guarantee. The Island Government claimed $5,000,000 "as due to the present time" for the losses and disadvantages occurring from the non-fulfillment of the terms. Finally, it warned the Canadian Government that this was the last time the matter would be brought to its notice. If a favourable answer was not received, the Sullivan Government would lay its cause at the foot of the Throne.[51]

An appeal to England appeared inevitable in April, 1884, when Sullivan received yet another promise of due consideration.[52] Before the Island legislators convened for the session of 1885, however, a sad event occurred which was to make their appeal stronger than ever. On January 27, 1885, three ice boats bound from Cape Traverse to the mainland were caught in a blinding snowstorm. The crew of 15 and 7 passengers, (including P. A. McIntyre from Souris who had been a member of the 1883 Select Committee) became exhausted midway across the strait and were forced to camp on the ice for the night. A rude shelter was constructed out of two boats and some luggage, the third boat being used for fire along with the mail for kindling. There were but two matches, no axes, no food and two compasses pointing in different directions. The storm continued to rage all the next day; the fuel supply was exhausted and one man became delirious. About three o'clock in the afternoon the party, drifting in the direction of Charlottetown, sighted the spire of Desable Kirk five miles distant. The wearied men managed to reach shore by evening, and snow-blinded, made their way to habitation by the odour of chimney smoke. One man, who was discovered in a barn, lost both feet and the fingers of both hands, another lost his fingers and toes.[53] The news of the disaster soon spread throughout the Island and the shocked public laid the blame squarely on the shoulders of the Federal Government.

For the first time, the leading citizens and newspapers of Canada joined the Islanders in their crusade for continuous and efficient communication. Archbishop O'Brien of Halifax wrote a scathing letter to the *Halifax Herald* condemning the "inhuman weakness of the authorities" and their "ignorant flippancy in the Commons" regarding the Capes Service.[54] The *Toronto Globe* reported the great disaster,[55] and in a leading article, the *Montreal Herald* condemned the inefficiency of the ice-boat service and said that the

Federal Government "should have taken charge of the business long ago."[56]

In Ottawa, the Islanders had a vocal and influential spokesman in the person of George W. Howlan, a member of the Senate from Prince County. Speaking before the Senate, he criticized the government but also advocated a project designed to obliterate all their difficulties. He told the Senators that he had been a member of the provincial government which took the Island into Confederation and in the discussion of the terms of entry it was fully expected that the clause on continuous and efficient communication could be carried out. He no longer felt that this object could be accomplished by sailing craft or steamers, but suggested the Canadian Government might successfully meet its obligation by providing a subway under the strait.[57] This idea, then not seriously entertained by either the Canadian or Island Governments, would soon be courted by both as the answer to the communications question.

The immediate effect of the disaster, in terms of federal projects, was a substantial improvement in the safety and efficiency of the Capes Service. The Dominion announced its intention to transfer the winter boat service from the Post Office to the Marine Department and after the winter of 1885, to manage the Capes route as a government work. It stated that a steamer would probably be placed at the Capes to assist the passengers and mails to cross to the board ice and that a marine officer would make further observations as to what would make the crossing efficient. Moreover, it announced that the exact terminus of the Island railway had been ascertained and that the boat houses were being commenced.[58]

This belated federal action did not soften the anger of the Island legislators, who after the disaster, seemed doubly determined to appeal to England. On March 23, when Premier Sullivan moved for an Address to the Queen, he had to dissuade some members from threatening secession.[59] Proceeding from the premise that the Island must demonstrate loyalty to Canada with which it wanted closer physical connection, the Premier developed the Address to the Queen on the theme that his province had borne patiently with the neglect of the Dominion to fulfil the terms.[60] The *Albert* had been an "utter failure." The *Northern Light*, which was not constructed for the service, missed an average of 64 days each winter for the last four years. In 1881, the passengers had to leave the ship and make for shore over the ice floes. Yet, no effort had been made to replace the *Northern Light*. The Capes route had long remained unimproved, the Cape Traverse branch of the Island railroad was only partially opened and there was no connection from Cape Tormentine to the Intercolonial. Beyond a simple acknowledgement of each appeal from

1881 to 1884, the Federal Government produced no practical results. In view of the "unaccountable neglect" of the Canadian Government, the Sullivan administration submitted that the only avenue left to the Island to secure justice was an appeal to Her Majesty's Government.[61]

The Canadian Cabinet reacted strongly to Sullivan's embarrassing move by forwarding to London a written defense of the federal position. In its report of November 7, 1885, the Committee of the Privy Council placed the blame on the Northumberland Strait itself. It suggested that it was understood in the Confederation negotiations, and subsequently confirmed by the Select Committee of 1883, that ice conditions made it impossible to provide continuous steam service and that Canada could only provide "what science and experience might determine as the best and most efficient within the range of possibility." The Report asserted that through the Capes Service and the *Northern Light* every possible effort had been made to transport mails and passengers; by the terms of union, moreover, Canada was not obliged to transport freight "although it had at all times afforded facility for the transport of any freight offering." In one of the most classic cases of put-down in federal-provincial relations, the Islanders were reminded that their contribution to the general revenue was small and that their local interest was not comparable to the Canadian Pacific Railway. "In the one case," the Dominion declared, "it means the transport of nine passengers a day for an average period of forty-eight days a year in mid-winter, whilst in the other it is a great national work, providing a highway in common for the eastern and western Provinces, and opening up of vast areas of the richest soil upon which many settlers from the older Provinces including Prince Edward Island are finding homes . . ."[62]

The fuming Sullivan Government quickly sent a delegation to London despite Colonial Office protest that the Queen did not have power "to give decision or enforce action in this case."[63] At a meeting in London on March 1st, 1886, the Premier and his Provincial Secretary, Donald Ferguson, presented a memorandum to Colonial Secretary Lord Granville defending their crusade and protesting that the Federal Government was being entirely unfair. They answered the charge that passenger traffic was slight by the obvious retort that "so long as communication with the mainland is at all certain the traffic is large, but with the irregular movements of the *Northern Light* and the doubt that exists as to her seaworthiness it is not extraordinary that travel and traffic are limited." The Islanders refused to admit the impossibility of year-round steam communication, but even putting that aside, they renewed the recommendations of the 1883 Committee for better service and, further, brought to Granville's attention the scheme being mooted to lay a metallic subway across the Straits of Northumberland. They concluded that comparative contributions to the federal treasury was not the issue — it was "simply one of performing the terms of a most solemn compact."[64]

The Imperial Government refused to take sides, but in an endeavor to contribute its "friendly offices" towards an acceptable settlement, arranged a meeting between the Island delegates and Sir Charles Tupper, the Canadian High Commissioner. The results of this discussion and the mission at large were embodied in a dispatch, dated March 30, 1886, from Lord Granville to the Marquis of Lansdowne, Governor General of Canada. Granville noted that the Dominion Government had made considerable efforts to provide communication but that Island expectations had not been met. He hinted that a rail communication seemed desirable but added there was reason for doubting "whether any real satisfactory communication by steamship can be regularly maintained all the year round." For this reason, Granville personally hoped that the proposed metallic subway might provide the solution and he urged that this project receive "a full and, if feasible, favorable consideration on the part of the Government of the Dominion."[65]

The Downing Street dispatch virtually terminated the Sullivan crusade. The Island Premier had fought his last battle in the long war of petitions, memorials and addresses. He had taken his cause to the Queen "whose province and high perogative it is to see that justice is done to both parties who entered into Confederation."[66] Neither party won the battle, yet Sullivan accepted Granville's dispatch as an armistice between his Government and the Government of Canada — partly because he had run out of parties to petition, partly since to accept nothing would amount to defeat. Returning from England, the Premier optimistically announced to the people of Prince Edward Island that "there is every reason to believe that Sir John Macdonald's Government will carry out the terms of Union with this Province, and that we shall have either a subway or a tunnel across the Straits."[67]

Feasibility and cost studies for the projected subway were conducted at various intervals for the next 20 years. The initial plan was not for a tunnel underneath the floor of the strait but rather for a subway or submarine tunnel — an iron tube which was to rest on the bottom of the strait. Senator Howlan's personal research on the subject suggested a tunnel could be laid across the Northumberland Strait in approximately four years at a cost of from $4,000,000 to $5,000,000.[68] He wrote to Macdonald on March 10, 1886, indicating that he was prepared to form a company to undertake the work but although Macdonald incorporated the Northumberland Straits Tunnel Company[69] he refrained from committing the Government until it had undertaken its own studies. During the summer of 1886 a corps of Canadian Government engineers descended on the Island to examine the bottom of the strait from Cape Traverse to Cape Tormentine.[70] In 1887 the Prime Minister told Howlan that the government was sufficiently encouraged to make further examinations and that the results would be submitted to a Board of Civil Engineers for assessment of construction, durability, safety and cost. He trusted their report would "justify the Government in entertaining the project."[71]

Macdonald's letters lent themselves to wide interpretations, especially since they arrived on the most appropriate occasions, this time the federal election of 1887. The document was published in all the Island newspapers and read on the hustings. On February 16, Howlan held a subway meeting in Market Hall, Charlottetown and announced that a promise had come from Sir John to carry out the subway scheme.[72] Charles Tupper also declared at a meeting in Amherst that he was strongly in favour of the tunnel[73] and the Island people were doubly assured when the Liberals issued circulars in every county telling the people that if they really wanted a subway they should vote for them.[74]

The reality was that however altruistic federal intentions might be, Prince Edward Island could never afford the luxury of waiting for the benefits of a long-term project. With a decreasing revenue and mounting debt,[75] Sullivan decided to press for compensation due his province from its isolated position. After several deputations to Ottawa and a reminder that his provincial government was "solidly Conservative,"[76] on March 22, 1887, the Premier received an additional annual subsidy of $20,000 for the Island "in view of its isolated position from the great public works and railways of the Dominion."[77] But the account was not final. Preparing for future contingencies, the Island Premier noted that for its failure to provide continuous and efficient communication the Federal Government still owed an outstanding bill to his province.[78]

By 1888, transportation facilities had not substantially improved despite the Island appeal to London. When the *Northern Light,* which had faithfully carried out twelve years of irregular and inefficient service, was found on inspection to be badly strained and unworthy of repair,[79] the Macdonald Government had to turn its attention from the Northumberland tunnel in order to meet the immediate needs of communication. The sum of $150,000 was appropriated to a Glasgow shipbuilding firm to construct the first steamer designed specifically for the Northumberland service.[80] The icebreaker *Stanley* was made of high tensile steel and had a triple expansion engine of 2,300 indicated horsepower. She began service on December 18, 1888, and during the winter season of 1888-89 made 79 round trips, in striking contrast to the 21 round trips made by the *Northern Light* the previous winter.[81]

The initial success of the new steamer seriously undermined the subway project by reaffirming Cartier's belief that a strong steamboat could be constructed which would break ice under all circumstances. On the Island, where the *Stanley* was viewed as the first bona-fide attempt on the part of the Federal Government to carry out the terms of its contract,[82] tunnel agitation virtually ceased. In Ottawa, the thought of providing satisfactory communication for $150,000 instead of $4,000,000 was eminently pleasing. The Federal Government, more candidly than usual, even admitted "the project of making a tunnel across the Straits of Northumberland . . . was really in one sense impracticable — that is to say, it would cost so much as not to justify the expenditure of the sum required for the service which it was intended to perform."[83]

In the first flush of the *Stanley's* success there remained but one persistent advocate of the tunnel scheme. Senator Howlan, keeping abreast of the latest scientific advances in underwater highways, had now changed his scheme from a subway which would lie on the bottom of the strait to a tunnel which would be burrowed beneath the floor of the sea.[84] To ascertain cost he wrote Sir Douglas Fox of the British Council of Engineers who appointed his associate, Alfred Palmer, to make a preliminary inspection with the assistance of an Island geologist, Francis Bain, in October, 1890.[85] On January 30, 1891, Fox cabled Howlan a first estimate of $6,000,000 as the probable cost of a completed tunnel.[86] It was a timely and well-used figure which proved extremely valuable, for the brief honeymoon with the *Stanley* was drawing to a close.

The winter of 1890-91 was exceptionally severe and the continuity of the *Stanley's* trips was broken at various times by heavy drift ice and gales in the Northumberland Strait. Early ice caught the *Stanley* unprepared for service, and for ten days the Island had no steam service at a time when fall produce was piling up.[87] Even when the *Stanley* resumed operations, it was unable to make a crossing on 43 different days. During those periods the mail was transferred to the ice boats, but the shift from one mode of conveyance to another was so encumbered by departmental red tape that mail often travelled from Pictou to Cape Tormentine and vice versa for several days before it reached the Island.[88] In January, Premier Neil MacLeod and Provincial Secretary Donald Ferguson went to Ottawa to suggest that if $6,000,000 could build a tunnel, it would be worthwhile for Canada to undertake it.[89] The government was noncommittal but when a federal election was called for March 5, it was evident that the Macdonald administration could not point to the Stanley as the acme of regular and efficient service. The tunnel again emerged as an election issue.

The 1891 election, fought throughout Canada on the great issue of the National Policy versus unrestricted reciprocity, was locally joined with debate on the Northumberland Tunnel to provide one of the liveliest federal contests in Island history. Howlan resigned his seat in the Senate to contest Prince County declaring that upon his success at the polls depended the future of the project. Many believed him and "Howlan and the Tunnel" became the campaign cry for the Conservatives.[90] The tunnel enlisted the sympathy of Bishop Peter MacIntyre of Charlottetown who participated actively in the Prince County contest eulogizing Howlan's scheme in almost every pulpit from Tignish to Summerside.[91] Federal politicians provided ammunition for their local forces: "I regret deeply," wired Sir Charles Tupper to the government candidate in Charlottetown, "that it is impossible for me to go to the Island, as the *Stanley* cannot cross and I dare not attempt the Cape. I have satisfied myself that the tunnel can be made for $6,000,000 and you may rely upon all the aid I can give to that important and necessary work."[92] Sir John A. Macdonald told his Island friends that he had tried to carry out the Dominion obligation by the *Stanley* but "of course she cannot fight against the elements so if cost was a reasonable amount"[93] the tunnel would receive favourable consideration. Only L. H. Davies, senior Maritime Liberal who was seeking re-election in Queen's County, remained decidedly cool on the subject.[94] The new national Liberal leader, Wilfrid Laurier never mentioned the tunnel at his Charlottetown meeting but in answer to a letter from the *Charlottetown Guardian* soliciting his opinion, he incredulously wrote that "every man who has given any attention to the condition of things and the necessities involved by the entering of the Island into Confederation must admit that such a tunnel must be constructed if the thing is reasonably practicable."[95]

As always, once the dust of political oratory settled, the words "reasonable amount" and "reasonably practicable" stood out in stark relief. The "Report on the Proposed Railway Tunnel under the Northumberland Straits" submitted by Douglas Fox in May, 1891, suggested a minimum cost of $6,000,000 but nearly $12,000,000 for a tunnel which would accommodate the rolling stock of the Intercolonial Railway.[96] On Fox's recommendation, the Federal Government commissioned Alfred Palmer to make further surveys in the summer of 1892.[97] Unfortunately, his work was delayed in every possible way by the redoubtable Senator Howlan, who, having lost the election, was reappointed Senator and government agent for the project. Howlan put himself in charge of the entire operation and proceeded to instruct Palmer, who disagreed but was unable to proceed while Howlan withheld supplies, purchased the wrong equipment and acted as general banker. The conduct of the Senator created some stir in the House of Commons,[98] but the government defended Howlan and resumed the surveys once the Senator had been safely appointed Lieutenant Governor of the Island in 1894. Borings were taken again in the summers of 1894 and 1895 by private Canadian companies hired by the Federal Government but they were insufficient to establish any definite idea of cost and the Dominion abandoned further attempts.[99]

Provincial goodwill meanwhile was wearing thin as the constant surveys were seen as an excuse for inaction. During the 1896 federal election which brought the Laurier Liberals to power, the tunnel fervor was not revived and the provincial Liberal Government, re-elected the same year, pledged itself to secure immediate improvements in communication and compensation for federal negligence.[100] In private negotiations with L. H. Davies, now Minister of Marine and Fisheries, Premier Frederick Peters demanded adequate transportation facilities and an independent arbitration commission to settel claims due to the Island.[101] In 1898, the Warburton administration renewed Peters's demands and specifically recommended a second winter steamer if the service was to be performed in a "reasonably satisfactory manner."[102] The Laurier Government assiduously avoided the precedent of arbitration in federal-provincial relations, and though, it refused a commission, it approved the construction of "another steamer to assist the *Stanley* in maintaining the efficiency of the service."[103]

The new steamer *Minto,* like the *Stanley* before it, had the effect of temporarily appeasing the Islanders and removing the idea of a tunnel further from the sphere of practical politics. The ice-breaking capacity of the *Minto* was greater than that of its predecessor and its larger size afforded more accommodation for passengers and freight.[104] From 1899 the *Minto* and *Stanley* ran together on the Pictou route and the regularity and efficiency of the service was so greatly enhanced that in 1901 the Provincial Government was generously disposed to say that the Island had "actually and practically continuous communication during the winter season and the terms of our contract of Union are being carried out!"[105]

Island gratitude, as generous as it was, never prevented the province from pressing financial claims on Ottawa. On April 9, 1901, Premier Donald Farquharson addressed a lengthy memorial claiming compensation for the non-fulfillment of the terms of union until 1901. He argued that,

Crews, aided by sails, move three ice boats across Northumberland Strait

Northern Light

Courtesy Canada, Transport from
Canadian Illustrated News.

Stanley

Minto

Prince Edward Island

Charlottetown

Courtesy Canadian National Railways

Abegweit

John Hamilton Gray *Courtesy Canadian National Railways*

though the *Stanley* had greatly improved transportation, not until the *Minto* had been added to the route was the service satisfactory or the terms of union in any way practically implemented. The result was that from 1873 to 1900 the province suffered irreparably: business was demoralized, young men forced to leave home, and farms were devalued. The Dominion was held financially responsible and the memorial suggested that payment be referred to a Board of Arbitration or that an annual grant be determined by the two governments concerned.[106]

Finance Minister Fielding, replying for the Federal Government, contended the terms had been met satisfactorily since 1888. He stated the tunnel project recommended by Granville in 1886 was not a requirement of the terms but was merely intended as a compensation at a time when it was felt the terms could not be fulfilled in any other way. The provision of the *Stanley* in 1888 had changed that, and he noted that, while the *Minto* had undoubtedly improved transportation, "more satisfactory service was not to be regarded as necessary for a compliance with the terms, and therefore the Island claims could only be made for the years from 1873 to 1888." On this understanding, Fielding announced that the Canadian Government would pay to Prince Edward Island an annual grant of $30,000 as a "full and final settlement" of all the claims which the province had in respect to communication.[107]

The Island Assembly's acceptance of this subsidy "in full satisfaction of all the claims which the Province *now* has against the Dominion of Canada" did not indicate that the province considered the 1901 settlement as final.[108] In fact, the dichotomy between federal and provincial views regarding "more satisfactory" as opposed to "satisfactory" communication possessed all the elements of an interminable struggle. Given Ottawa's attitude that the requirements of the clause had been met, the Islanders, henceforth, argued for continuous and efficient communication on the basis of improving transportation between the different regions of Canada and providing an equal opportunity for the development of all. In the first decade of the twentieth century when national transportation and prosperity were so closely allied, this argument seemed particularly relevant.

A favourable combination of low interest rates, high prices and added population produced a rapid upspring in the Canadian economy in the early 1900's; national railways were the arteries of the surging prosperity. Railways brought thousands of immigrants to the Canadian West and with them the food, fuel and equipment necessary to settlement. They dispersed the increased manufactures of industrial Canada, brought foodstuffs from the countryside to growing urban centers and carried the first millions of bushels of prairie wheat to eastern seaports for export. National railways were not merely the arteries of trade, but were the politicial expression of boundless optimism in the future of Canada. Throughout the decade, the Laurier Government lavished assistance to both the Canadian Northern and Grand Trunk Railways to triple the means of all-Canadian transport.[109] That Prince Edward Island did not participate in the national prosperity, its own politicians naturally attributed to exclusion from the transcontinental lines. Isolation, they maintained, kept the Island in financial servitude for it not only prevented industries from being established, but made it impossible to tax the farmer who was already handicapped by expensive and uncertain transportation. Since 1891, the Island had experienced an absolute loss in population and a consequent reduction of federal representation from six to four.[110] The Island people contended their sons would not have left home if inefficient transportation had not hampered the natural progress of the province.[111]

The difficulties, if not the disadvantages, of winter communication were well illustrated by the two steamers *Minto* and *Stanley*, whose record service of 1901 was succeeded by lengthy and frequent interruptions. In December, 1902, an attempt was made to establish a winter service by the *Stanley* from Summerside to Cape Tormentine, but the ice was so badly rafted in Summerside Bay that the route was useable for only one month each year.[112] During the winter of 1902-3, the *Stanley* wandered about the strait for 66 days, frozen in the centre of an ice pan. The *Minto* found the *Stanley* 21 miles east of Pictou, but in attempting to set her sistership free she broke her own propeller blades, and became a second prisoner in the ice pack.[113] Between February 5 and March 24, eight ice boats were kept busy crossing the strait with 103,950 pounds of mail and 246 passengers.[114] While the steamers drifted helplessly about, a meeting of the Charlottetown Board of Trade came to the conclusion that "the *Minto* and *Stanley* lack the strength and power sufficient to maintain continuous communication."[115] The Board urged the immediate construction of a new steamer of increased power and capacity, and the Arthur Peters Government made the same suggestion in an April 30 resolution calling for a "third and more efficient steamship, one which will keep up continuous communication."[116]

The evasive attitude which the Dominion lent to these pleas was held responsible for the misfortune of the farm community in 1905. For six weeks the steamers were unable to break an ice barrier at Pictou. Such delays were considered disastrous at the best of times, but because of a shortage of crops in the previous summer, the government had arranged for the importation of hay which unfortunately was sitting on Pictou wharf. The *Minto* failed to get through by the use of dynamite partly because there was no room for the displaced ice to escape. On March 3, 1905, Premier Peters wired Raymond Prefontaine, the Minister of Marine, that 1500 tons of hay were waiting at Pictou and the cattle were suffering. The Minister advised a more determined use of dynamite but all efforts at blasting failed and from January 25 to March 21 the boats were unable to get through.[117] Again the ice boats transported passengers and mails but the inevitable depreciation in farm stock now combined with traditional exasperation to produce a pronounced agitation in favour of permanent communication.

On February 21, 1905, Rev. A. E. Burke, the influential Pastor of Sacred Heart Parish, Alberton, Prince Edward Island, wrote to Laurier: "the province, driven to desperation, is trying to assemble in General Convention at Charlottetown. Never before has it been so clearly impressed upon us that continuous steam communication with the Mainland cannot possibly be effected by vessels."[118] At a mass meeting held in Charlottetown on March 10, Father Burke and three others were delegated to wait upon the Federal Government with a memorial urging the earliest construction of a tunnel and, in the interim, a third stronger ice-breaking steamer.[119] The delegation, accompanied by Island senators and M.P.'s, presented its plea to Laurier and Fielding on April 1, 1905.[120] A month later members of the provincial government arrived in Ottawa with an Address on the Island's disabilities and in favour of a new steamship and tunnel as the remedy.[121] Boards of Trade throughout the Maritimes deluged Laurier with similar resolutions, and a joint meeting of the Toronto Board of Trade and the Canadian Manufacturers' Association endorsed the proposed tunnel.[122]

The Laurier Government emphatically denied an obligation to provide either a new ice breaker or a railway tunnel by the terms of union, but suggested that on the ground of improving transportation between the different regions of Canada, the 1905 proposals merited consideration. During the parliamentary session of 1905, the Minister of Marine and the Minister of Public Works announced that their departments would commence respective studies on the subjects of a more powerful winter steamer and a tunnel.[123] George Foster, opposition member and former Minister of Marine in the Macdonald Cabinet, had some experience of Island persistance, and he warned the Ministers that a steamer would not do. A tunnel was the only satisfactory solution and he prophetically added that "if it would only cost ten million it would be worthwhile, as Prince Edward Island would always be with us."[124]

While Ottawa engaged in studies, the injustice of existing freight rates absorbed the attention of Island businessmen and farmers. Not all Islanders paid the same rate to ship their products to the mainland since some had to pay a longer haul on the Prince Edward Island Railway to the winter steamers. At the beginning of the winter service, usually from December to January, the *Stanley* ran from Summerside to Cape Tormentine and the *Minto* from Charlottetown to Pictou; when the ice set in both ships switched to the Georgetown route. The pressure to get produce out at the best prices produced a running conflict between residents in the eastern, central and western parts of the Island to have the steamers run longer near their homes.[125] In comparison to the mainlander using the Intercolonial all the Islanders suffered, for their products were damaged materially and financially by travelling three short hauls — the P. E. I. Railway, the Government Steamers and the Intercolonial Railway. In 1907, the provincial Legislature unanimously passed a resolution demanding more reasonable freight rates in compensation for the three haul system, and the Island Boards of Trade presented their demands for revised rates at a Charlottetown hearing by the chief officials of the Intercolonial Railway.[126] The *Charlottetown Guardian,* having long since questioned whether resolutions or delegations could help the Island, requested settlement or separation.[127]

New attempts to hurry the Prime Minister on a tunnel decision were ineffectual. In response to more public meetings, letters and another provincial memorial in 1907, Laurier insisted he would not "be pushed faster than circumstances warranted."[128] Engineers of the Department of Public Works reported in 1906 that the tunnel would cost anywhere from $10,000,000 to $20,000,000; in March 1908, Laurier informed the House that information was still being compiled.[129] Meanwhile the Minister of Marine announced that his department had designed a powerful new icebreaker and tenders for its construction would be opened on March 8, 1908.[130]

The *Earl Grey* built in Furness, Great Britain, specially shaped to withstand ice pressure, measured 250 feet in length, 47.7 feet in width, and 24.1 feet in depth, and had an indicated horsepower of 6,500. She could carry 600 tons of freight and was fitted for a high standard of passenger travel with "appointments, apparel, furniture and finish . . . in all respects superior to the best channel boats in Great Britain." The *Earl Grey* commenced service between Charlottetown and Pictou on December 30, 1909, replacing the *Stanley* which was transferred to the New Brunswick Agency of the Department of Marine in September, 1909. The *Minto* continued on the Georgetown route and in their first season together, the two steamers kept up continuous communication so that the ice boats were not employed.[131]

On the eve of the 1911 federal election, the necessity for ice boat service had resumed and federal inaction on the tunnel and freight rates remained outstanding grievances to the Island people. The dominant electoral issues of reciprocity versus economic nationalism related directly to Island transportation problems, for while the one saw Island prosperity in terms of free access to United States markets, the other asserted that the Island had markets in Canada and merely required efficient communication. Standing for the latter, Robert L. Borden, the leader of the Opposition promised the Island people that his government would conduct a tunnel survey, and abolish the three short hauls.[132] The election of a Conservative Government was therefore highly significant. Although the realties of office tempered Borden's enthusiasm for a tunnel survey they did not destroy his conviction that Island transportation must be radically revised. When a provincial election was called for January 3, 1912, Borden lent his support to the local Conservative campaign by announcing the establishment of a government car ferry service that would involve the standardization of the Island narrow gauge railway and the abolition of the three short hauls.[133] The once secessionist *Charlottetown Guardian* stated on December 29, that "no more important message has come to this province since Confederation than this."[134] The local Conservative party was returned with a resounding majority of 28 to 2 and the Premier-elect, J. A. Mathieson attributed his sweeping victory to "the Car-Ferry project which was unanimously endorsed by our people."[135]

Shortly before events were put in train for the new communications system, Premier Mathieson, in accordance with indefatigable Island tradition, headed a delegation to Ottawa to claim a subsidy in view of the past default of the Canadian Government to provide efficient transportation. The claim was one of six other grounds on which the Island hoped to receive an increase in its annual subsidy, and while all the claims were rejected by the Borden Government, yet, "upon grounds of fairness and justice as between this Dominion and the smallest of the Provinces" an additional annual subsidy of $100,000 was authorized for the province on May 26, 1912.[136] With this financial settlement and a temporary economic boom fostered by the silver fox farming industry and war-time demand for foodstuffs,[137] the implementation of the car ferry project marked one of the rare periods of quiescence in the post-Confederation history of communication between Prince Edward Island and the mainland.

Nearly six years were occupied in the establishment of the system intended to connect the mainland and Island railways. Early in 1912, "the most direct route from Moncton and the most feasible crossing of the straits" was chosen from Cape Tormentine, N.B. to Carleton Head, a point situated three miles northeast of Cape Traverse.[138] On January 9, 1913, a contract was awarded to Armstrong-Whitworth Company of Newcastle, England, for a steamer of 7,000 horsepower at a cost of $590,000. The Roger Miller Company of Prince Edward Island began work on the terminals in December, 1913. The matter of rebuilding the Prince Edward Island Railway as a standard gauge line was not taken up until the end of the war, but in order to extend the transcontinental system to the Island, in 1912, the Canadian Government bought the 38 mile N.B.-P.E.I. Railway from Sackville to Cape Tormentine. On the Island a short piece of both standard and narrow gauge line was built near the car ferry slip. Standard gauge cars were to be taken over on the car ferry and freight transshipped to and from narrow gauge cars at the Island terminus, renamed Port Borden.[139]

The ferry, *Prince Edward Island,* was launched at Newcastle-upon-Tyne on October 5, 1914. She had a capacity of twelve Intercolonial railway cars and a forward propeller design which made her especially effective as an ice breaker.[140] Until the terminals were completed the *Prince Edward Island* plied between Charlottetown and Pictou keeping up winter communication with the *Stanley* which had returned to the Island service when the *Earl Grey* and *Minto* were sold to Russia at the outset of the war.[141] In 1916 the entire winter fleet including the ice boats, the *Stanley* and the *Prince Edward Island* was transferred from the Department of Marine to the Department of Railways and Canals. Both the ice boats and the *Stanley* ceased operation with the commencement of a daily car-ferry service between Cape Tormentine and Borden on October 16, 1917.[142]

A railway link had been forged between the Island and Canada, but it could never be truly effective until the P.E.I. Railway was widened to standard gauge. In April, 1918, a provincial memorial to Ottawa pointed out that, in 1911, 2,465 steamers and sailing vessels had cleared from Charlottetown, while in 1917, this number was reduced to 1,694. Since the old time fishing vessel traffic had ceased and the famous fleet of coasting vessels had vanished, the burden of transporting all classes of agricultural products from the Island fell more heavily on the railway than ever before.[143] Accordingly, in the spring of 1918, the immediate needs of the Island were met by the laying of a third rail from Borden to Charlottetown and Summerside. Until the standard road was completed further east and west throughout the 1920's, Islanders had the rare privilege of seeing curious trains of mixed large and small cars wend their way to Borden loaded with freight for Canada.[144]

The car ferry system, operating efficiently and continuously, was the realized ideal of every Island politician in the half century since Confederation. The ferry itself made possible the first regular crossings of the strait in winter, confining to history the small ice boats which had so long maintained the only life-line to the mainland. Connection with the nation's railway system revolutionized Island freight transportation and gave to the Island people, for the first time, a service mainlanders had enjoyed for several decades. The car ferry was an important watershed in the communications question — but although the issue never again achieved the critical character it possessed in the first fifty years of Confederation — changing economic conditions soon created new demands to insure the continuity and efficiency of transportation with Canada.

The increasing freight traffic handled by the *Prince Edward Island* in its first years of operation caused speculation concerning its ability to carry future business offerings and anxiety over the disastrous consequences should the boat meet with an accident.[145] To meet this local criticism, in November 1920, the federal government announced that the rail ferry *Scotia I* used on Canso Strait would provide service when required to supplement freight carriage or allow the main vessel to undergo repairs.[146] The Islanders did not regard the *Scotia I* as a suitable alternative either in size or ice-breaking capacity. The United Farmers of Prince Edward Island passed a resolution in January, 1921 pressing for a second car ferry to make safe railroad connection with the mainland.[147] The same year the provincial government claimed the Island was being charged excessive rates for rail transport and embarked on a campaign for lower freight rates on farm products.[148] Both complaints soon became part of a wider Maritime agitation for a better deal in Confederation.

Unlike the rest of the country Maritime Canada did not emerge from the brief post-war slump of 1921-1923, but seemed to settle into an almost chronic depression. Although there were complex technological and economic reasons for the regional lag, Canadian transportation policies became the primary focus of Maritime dissatisfaction in the mid-1920's. The subversion of Confederation promises to provide effective communication with Canada was held responsible for the absence of industry, high cost of living and migration of the Maritime people. While Canadian trade through Maritime ports had been one of the repeated conditions of aid to railway promoters, eastbound traffic was diverted to Portland, Maine, and Maritime ports remained stagnant. Exorbitant freight rates destroyed the potential benefit of a wider market by reducing the competitive position of the Maritime farmer. In an increasingly vocal appeal for "Maritime Rights", press, politicians and Boards of Trade everywhere, called for the honoring of Canadian trade through Canadian ports, abolition of freight rates to the central markets of Canada and more efficient transportation services between the Maritimes and Canada.[149]

The Duncan Commission, appointed in 1926 by the MacKenzie King

Government to investigate Maritime claims, reported that many of the Maritime criticisms were justified. It made two suggestions particularly applicable to Island transportation problems. Since 1912 freight rates on the Intercolonial had risen 92 per cent compared with a rise of 55 per cent in the rest of Canada, a situation clearly contrary to the spirit of Confederation obligations to afford to the Maritimes the larger market of the whole Canadian people. The Commission recommended a reduction of 20 per cent in freight rates on most rail movements within and out of the area east of Levis and south of the St. Lawrence River.[150] The Commission agreed with the Islanders that the *Scotia I* was unsuited for the Island service, and it further noted that the present car ferry was unequipped for motor vehicle traffic. The C.N.R., which operated the ferry, even admitted to the Commission that there was a need for a second ferry boat or a special freight boat, and the Commission recommended "that the matter be gone into from the point of view of placing at the disposal of the Island such satisfactory means of communication as will insure as regular and complete a service as can reasonably be made."[151]

The King Government announced its acceptance of these recommendations on March 18, 1927.[152] The Maritime Freight Rates Act, which became effective on July 1, 1927, provided for a 20% reduction in rail freight rates within and out of the select territory suggested by the Commission.[153] During the parliamentary session of 1928, one million dollars was appropriated for the start of a new car ferry.[154] The Department of Railways and Canals, facing a considerable expenditure in any event, reinvestigated the economics of a tunnel and also looked at a new idea for a causeway or "breakwater structure with a road on top and adequate facilities here and there for the passage of boats to and fro." No engineer at the time would guarantee the durability of a causeway, and, in the final analysis, the estimated cost of both, $40,000,000 to $46,000,000, was considered prohibitive. Since an additional ferry seemed to be the only practicable solution, the government announced that it would soon employ two boats on the service to handle the increased traffic.[155] However, when the *S.S. Charlottetown* was launched in 1931, the old *Prince Edward Island,* then sixteen years old and badly strained from ice, was retired.

The beginning of the Trans Canada highway and Trans Canada airlines systems in the 1930's was paralleled by new developments and new expectations for Northumberland transportation. The *S.S. Charlottetown* was the first rail ferry equipped for auto carriage, and in the early 1930's considerable work was done at the piers at Borden and Tormentine to enable cars to drive on the ferry. The Island people saw their steamer as an interprovincial bridge in the Trans Canada highway system, and in a brief presented to the Bennett Government in April 1934, Premier W. J. P. Mac-Millan argued that the motor vehicle rate of $7. return was excessive.[156] The railway administration felt that traffic did not warrant a reduction in the rates, but were persuaded to reduce the fare to $2. one way and $3. return.[157] A daily (private) air service, inaugurated between Charlottetown and Moncton in 1935 and subsidized by the Post Office Department, added a new dimension to mail and passenger communication with the mainland.[158] As a result of election promises the King Government began construction of harbour facilities at Wood Islands in 1937 to permit operation of a subsidized auto ferry service to Nova Scotia.[159] In 1938 the Thane Campbell government re-endorsed the idea of a tunnel before the Sirois Commission on Dominion-provincial relations, but the Commission reported the Island was not entitled to demand this type of continuous communication, "that a reasonable ferry service has been provided and reasonable improvements have been instituted from time to time."[160]

The important advances made in Island-mainland communication during the 1930's received a severe setback in 1941 when the magnificent *S.S. Charlottetown* was wrecked off the coast of Nova Scotia while proceeding to dry dock for her annual spring inspection. The accident prompted appeals for a new car ferry, but the federal Cabinet insisted a new boat was an impossibility in wartime and brought out the old *S.S. Prince Edward Island* for the duration of the war.[161] In 1947 a new ice breaker built in Sorel, Quebec, went into service. The *M.V. Abegweit* which was reputed to be the finest of her type in the world, could transport 19 freight cars and 69 passenger automobiles.[162] Even with this large capacity, however, the *Abegweit* was dependent on the *Prince Edward Island* during periods of congestion. Freight car traffic had more than doubled in the decade from 1938 to 1948, while in just 7 years from 1941 to 1948, the annual number of automobiles ferried had increased by 20,000.[163] In its submission to the Turgeon Commission on Transportation in July 1949, the Island government maintained that adequate and continuous communication should not be left to the uncertain prop of the old car ferry, and that a second car ferry must be provided for the Borden-Tormentine service.[164]

With the steady growth of truck and automobile traffic, railway management of the car ferry service became a highly contentious issue. The Canadian National Railway saw every vehicle it ferried across the strait as competition with its own rail route. For a long time no allowance was made for bus schedules while complaints of exorbitant trucking rates were met by the argument that the railway must make a reasonable effort to meet operating expenses.[165] In 1949 Island Premier Walter Jones proposed the abolition of all ferry tolls arguing that by the terms of Confederation, Canada had agreed to "assume and defray all charges" for "efficient steam service." His government contended that the fundamental purpose of providing transportation to the people of the province was obscured by railway attitudes and practise in administration. The suspension of the car ferry service during the railway strike of 1950 lent force to the Island demand that the ferry service should be a public utility in the hands of a government department or independent commission.[166]

The Canadian Government studiously ignored the Island proposals for a second car ferry and a federally operated service, but made some concession to traffic demands by agreeing to continue permanently the supplementary summer service of the *S.S. Prince Edward Island*.[167] Ottawa also subsidized two private non-rail ferries which ran between Wood Islands and Caribou seven months of the year, and in 1954 it financed the construction of a larger boat to replace one of these ferries.[168] During the tourist season, however, all four vessels were badly overcrowded with the result that delays in passage meant the service was really less convenient than it was years ago. This inefficiency, combined with a growing operating deficit on the Borden-Tormentine route, caused the Island government to question once again whether a permanent crossing would not be a sound investment.[169]

In 1955 the A. W. Matheson Government requested Ottawa to investigate the economic and technical feasibility of a causeway. The Island government secured a preliminary cost estimate of $50,000,000 from O. J. McCulloch, designer of the recently completed Canso causeway between Nova Scotia and Cape Breton. The obvious problem in a Northumberland Strait project was the availability of rock fill. Nearly 10 million tons of rock were needed to close the one mile Strait of Canso and, at a minimum, 40 million tons of rock would be required for the Northumberland crossing. Federal investigation of the causeway project started in 1956 when Public Works Minister Robert Winters sent geologists to Tormentine to estimate the amount of rock fill that would be readily available.[170]

During the decade from 1955 to 1965 "the causeway" dominated discussion of communication between Prince Edward Island and the mainland. Every Island government pressed for it and every federal government promised to study and start it, while political opponents seized each delay as a portent of inaction. Feasibility studies authorized by the Diefenbaker Government revealed huge problems of engineering,[171] all of which boosted the original cost estimates and dimmed hopes. On April 17, 1962, on the eve of an election call, Prime Minister Diefenbaker announced that the project was feasible, from an economic and engineering viewpoint, and that his government had decided to build the causeway at a cost of $105 million.[172] Design of the crossing was farmed out to a consortium of Canadian engineering consultants in June, and by late 1962 actual planning had begun.[173] Both Conservative and Liberal parties promised the causeway in the 1963 election[174] campaign, and planning and analysis continued under the newly elected Liberal Government. At length, on July 8, 1965, Prime Minister Pearson announced that tenders would be called for the construction of a combined tunnel, bridge and causeway, now quoted at $148 million.[175] The first sod was turned for the approaches on the New Brunswick side on November 5. Commencement of the much courted causeway was appropriately marked in a strictly partisan ceremony three days before the November 8 federal election.[176]

The projected causeway did not preclude the need for wide interim improvements in the communication service. In 1959 the Shaw Government presented a brief to the MacPherson Commission on Transportation calling for a new rail ferry and also a vehicle ferry to meet growing traffic requirements.[177] As a result of this plea the *M.V. Confederation,* a fast moving summer ferry capable of shuttling 60 automobiles, joined the fleet in 1962.[178] A year later a new ferry, the *Prince Nova,* was launched on the Wood Islands-Caribou route making a total of six ferries operating during the peak summer season.[179] Transportation costs for agricultural and fishery products remained a lively and complicated issue. The Island joined the other Maritime provinces in pressing for reduced rail freight rates and a better deal for truck carriers.[180] At the same time since 1956, the P.E.I. Potato Marketing Board and the C.N.R. had agreed on a reduced charge for volume potato shipment which, though beneficial to the producer, excluded more truck competition in that commodity.[181] Interrupted ferry service exerted the greatest impact on the Island economy. Another railway strike in August, 1966, tied up Island commerce and forced many tourists to cancel reservations or to leave.[182]

Meanwhile construction of the causeway was still proceeding at a snail's pace. The highway approaches were still uncompleted in June, 1967, when the Canadian Government announced that tenders for the first section of the crossing had been rejected because the prices were "very much higher than anticipated" and that the government must "reassess the design of the project." Ultimate action seemed assured when Colonel Edward Churchill, who had directed construction of the highly successful Expo '67, was appointed to supervise the reassessment. Then, an austerity program announced by Finance Minister Mitchell Sharp renewed speculation on the abandonment of the project.[183] Prime Minister Trudeau refrained from mentioning the causeway in the June, 1968 federal election. Throughout the summer rumor spread that P.E.I. would receive an economic development grant but no causeway, and in October, Premier Campbell and his full cabinet went to Ottawa to urge the construction of the crossing.[184]

On March 5, 1969, the long-awaited, already-started Northumberland causeway was formally shelved in favor of a 15 year Comprehensive Development Plan with a federal contribution of $125 million in the first seven years and $100 million for the remaining period. According to Prime Minister Trudeau, the decision was clearly one of "fixing the priorities of expenditure" as between the two projects. "The government should have liked to be able to assist at the same time in the construction of a causeway linking the Island to the mainland," he stated, "but there is a limitation to the resources of Canada." It was decided "to support the Development Plan as being the likeliest method of offering appreciable and lasting benefit to the economy of Prince Edward Island in the foreseeable future."[185]

In view of the prolonged agitation over the causeway project the criticism which greeted its abandonment was surprisingly mild. There was widespread editorial disappointment and political charges of a trade-off or sell-out, but the endorsation of the Campbell Government and the Plan in the 1970 provincial election seemed to discredit any popular recrimination. Part of the reason for this mild Island reaction was the extensive upgrading undertaken by the federal government with existing mainland links. The *Prince Edward Island* was formally retired in the spring of 1969[186] and the ferry capacity on the Borden-Tormentine service was subsequently doubled with the addition of the *John Hamilton Gray* and the *Lucy Maud Montgomery*. New terminal facilities, offering a wide range of public services, introduced an element of efficiency and convenience that had been lacking for many years. In 1969 the 30% Maritime Freight Rate reduction on outbound cargo was extended to commercial truckers, and in the fall of 1970 truck rates on the P.E.I. ferries were reduced substantially. Finally, two new auto vessels, the *Holiday Island* and *Vacationland,* were introduced to the Borden-Tormentine service in 1971, and a new vessel, the *Prince Edward,* was built for the Wood Islands service in 1972.[187]

On the eve of the centennial of Confederation with Canada, communication between Prince Edward Island and the mainland is no longer seen as the principal drawback to Island progress. Increasingly, economic advancement is viewed in terms of overall planning, involving effective land use, volume processing and marketing and many other factors of which transportation is simply one part. The traditional communications question itself is more often treated by federal and provincial governments in the context of a basic Atlantic transportation policy combining a wide range of waterborne and air transportation services. To preserve the mythology, entrenched by nearly a century of frustration, that prosperity would blossom if P.E.I. were given a tunnel or causeway, would be a simplistic approach for the future. And yet the vocal vigilance of the Island provincial and federal representatives which has been a forerunner of every major transportation breakthrough must continue if the smallest province is to maintain an efficient standard of communication with mainland Canada. The communications question will thus continue to be a vital issue in Island history.

Chapter Eleven

The Island and the Dominion

By F. L. DRISCOLL

The people of Prince Edward Island seem to have had an almost prophetic view of what the result of the union would be. Yet once committed to the union, there never was, nor is there now, any question of withdrawal. The citizens of this Province have borne with patience a national policy which has been distinctly not beneficial; they see the citizens of other provinces grow rich at their expense; they see the best of their youth attracted to other provinces, just as they are entering the period when they might become an asset to the community. The only protest has been an occasional request for "better terms".[1]

The above statement of Premier Thane A. Campbell before the Royal Commission on Dominion-Provincial Relations in 1938 was a remarkably accurate reflection of Prince Edward Island's experience in the Canadian federation. Having been ". . . partly cajoled and partly forced into the Union,"[2] the province never looked back. Despite continuing economic and financial difficulties, caused at least partly by national policies over which the province had little control, its people have been good federalists. Secession has never been seriously considered. Protest parties outside of Liberal and Conservative party ranks have never emerged. Provincial autonomy has never become a political issue. Instead, successive provincial governments have constantly sought within the federal and two-party system for redress of disadvantages not always of their own making.

Circumstances nourished the tendency to seek remedies from Ottawa. The province's economic difficulties followed closely the consummation of an unwanted political union. The thirty years preceding union had been a period of uninterrupted political growth and economic expansion. The population was doubling every thirty years, revenues every twelve, and there was little or no debt.[3] After union, the population soon began to decline, trade disappeared, and the debt mounted. Such a sudden change of fortune was easily attributed to the unsatisfactory terms of union and to national policies designed for the benefit of central and western Canada. Lacking the resources to overcome liabilities aggravated by national policies, its problems became national in scope, for they could only be remedied by federal action. Only the federal government could grant better terms, re-distribute the national wealth, and compensate regions disadvantaged by its own policies. Consequently, the province's dealings with Ottawa have been an important part of its political experience.

For many years the Island based its claim for larger subsidies on the inadequacy of certain terms of union and the Dominion's failure to observe others. With minor exceptions, the terms on which the province joined the union were those to which the original provinces had agreed in 1867. Like them, the Island was paid a per capita subsidy of 80 cents, and a grant for the support of the government and legislature. The Island's debt allowance was increased to fifty dollars per capita partly because it was recognized that the Island could not benefit from the heavy Dominion expenditures on railways and canals in other parts of Canada, and an annual grant of $45,000 was to be paid in lieu of public lands, since all the province's lands had been granted to the proprietors. In addition, the Dominion was to maintain steam communication between the province and the mainland.[4]

Thus, from the very beginning some of the distinctive features of the province were recognized by the Dominion. Its isolated position, its inability to benefit from federal expenditures on public works in other parts of the Dominion, and the lack of revenues from public lands were readily admitted and written into the union agreement. Island spokesmen were to return often to these conditions in the years ahead.

Although in 1873, J. C. Pope's government claimed that these were the best terms possible, they soon were not good enough. As provincial responsibilities grew and budgets increased, federal subsidies as a percentage of provincial revenues declined steadily, from 57 per cent in 1874 to 38 per cent in 1936. At the same time, federal revenues from custom duties and excise taxes expanded rapidly, so that subsidies paid to the provinces as a percentage of federal tax revenues declined steadily from about 20 per cent in 1867 to less than 5 per cent in 1930.[5] As a result, all provinces were forced to secure additional revenues from local sources.

A situation in which the Dominion government grew rich at the expense of the provinces could not long continue, and several provinces soon voiced complaints,[6] but Prince Edward Island was in a particularly difficult position. Lacking industrial enterprises and relying almost exclusively on fishing and agriculture, it lacked an adequate tax base for the raising of additional revenue. Income from crown lands was non-existent and its winter isolation hampered the development of its trade and the marketing of its products. Despite an honest tax effort,[7] and stringent economy, "the actual results which have followed in the Province as a consequence of the financial arrangements made at Confederation show that notwithstanding the Provincial taxation which has been imposed, there have been annual deficits in our Provincial Accounts during the twenty-five years up to the end of the year 1900 since Confederation of over $775,000."[8] The province soon began to demand "better terms" and charged that the agreement of 1873 was no longer just or equitable.

For many years the most pressing need was for better communications with the mainland. In the first flush of union optimism, Islanders confidently expected to develop a flourishing trade with central Canada. After all, that was one of the beliefs on which Confederation had been accepted in the province, and its false premises had not yet been exposed. For many years, Islanders argued that efficient communications with the railway system of the mainland was all that was needed to bring prosperity to its people. Besides, the transportation issue was remarkably free of partisan politics, and governments could expect unanimous support in their demands for improvements. For these reasons, the provision of adequate steam communications with the mainland absorbed the attention of Islanders for many years. So much so, that when the first provincial conference was held in 1887 to discuss the provinces' financial arrangements with the Dominion, Premier Sullivan refused to attend, at least partly because the Island was not interested in provincial autonomy and financial arrangements.[9] This attitude produced a long series of appeals for winter steamers, and later for a tunnel.[10] Only after these appeals met with limited success and the province's economic difficulties continued, did the provincial authorities address themselves to the province's "financial arrangements" with Ottawa.

One of the earliest attempts to obtain better financial terms was made in March, 1898, when a delegation headed by Premier A. B. Warburton accompanied by Attorney General H. C. MacDonald and J. W. Richards, a member of the cabinet, carried an appeal setting forth three major claims: 1. compensation for non-fulfillment of terms respecting steam communications; 2. an increase in the debt allowance for Dominion expenditures on railways and canals in other parts of Canada in excess of that anticipated in 1873; and 3. compensation for subsidies paid for the building of local and provincial railways in other provinces.[11]

To support these claims, the delegates argued that ". . . the terms upon which this province became part of the Dominion were based upon incorrect data. . . ."[12] In determining the debt allowance and subsidies to be paid Prince Edward Island, the negotiators in 1873 estimated the amounts to be spent by the Dominion on the Canadian Pacific and Intercolonial

Railways, canals, and other public works, at $79,000,000. Since it was admitted that the province would not benefit directly from these expenditures, yet would contribute its share to them, the sum of $79,000,000 was added to the Dominion debt, thereby increasing the debt allowance credited to Prince Edward Island. The Island delegates now argued that Dominion expenditures for these purposes amounted to approximately $180,000,000 and, therefore, the union agreement of 1873 was no longer a fair or just arrangement. The Island government suggested that these claims, including that of compensation for the lack of continuous steam communication, be referred to arbitration by a three-man commission, one to be appointed by the Island, one by Ottawa, and the third by Her Majesty the Queen.

Prime Minister Wilfrid Laurier made no reply, and the same claims were repeated in 1899 by Premier Donald Farquharson, Warburton's successor. This time Laurier replied rejecting the Island's claims.[13] The Prime Minister pointed out that his government had already authorized the building of a second steamer, and since the federal government had done everything possible to provide communications, it could not be expected to pay compensation for the inadequacy of the service. Laurier disposed of the Island's second claim by pointing out that negotiations were then proceeding with a view to building a branch railway across the Hillsborough River to Murray Harbour, and that the federal government would be contributing toward the payment of its cost. Consequently, his government could not consider paying compensation for the excess expenditures on railways and canals throughout the Dominion.

Despite Laurier's unnecessarily petty attitude, the province tried again in March, 1901, and this time the delegation based its case for an increased subsidy on fiscal need.[14] The claims arising from the terms of union were repeated, but emphasis was placed on the financial distress of the province, and its continually increasing debt despite stringent economy by successive governments. Having no mines, minerals, forest or other natural sources of income, the province was forced to rely almost exclusively on direct taxation to meet increasing expenditures for such things as education and roads and bridges. Consequently, the terms of union were unfavourable and the province appealed for special consideration:

We, therefore, confidently rely upon due consideration being given by your Excellency in Council to the financial condition of our province, resulting, as it does, not from any extravagance or mismanagement . . . of its affairs, but solely to the unfavourable terms upon which we entered the Union, and to the absence of those natural resources which all the other Provinces have to aid their general revenues.[15]

Here was a new approach. Without attempting to argue the legal and histor-ical intent of specific terms of the union agreement, the Island simply ad-mitted it had made a bad bargain. Because of this, and the Island's lack of adequate sources of taxation, an increase of subsidy was requested.

This, however, was not begging. At the back of the argument was the general intent of the subsidy arrangements agreed upon in 1867. It was never questioned that at Confederation the Dominion government would collect customs duties and excise taxes. At that time, these two forms of indirect taxation accounted for most of the tax revenue of all the provinces,[16] and were sufficient for most of their ordinary expenditures. Since no one contemplated the use of direct taxes, although the provinces were given power to collect them, it was necessary to devise some means of returning to the provinces sufficient funds to carry on their reduced responsibilities after Confederation. It was for this purpose that subsidies were introduced.[17] Now that subsidies no longer met provincial expenditures, the Island de-manded revision of the 1873 agreement.

Unfortunately, the effect of the appeal of March, 1901, was lost, for the following month the same government renewed its request for compensa-tion for lack of winter communication.[18] This subject once again absorbed the attention of the province, and for the next ten years individuals, farmers, Chambers of Commerce and governments brought forth a flood of petitions, memorials and resolutions for a tunnel to connect with the mainland. It was only after Robert Borden's promise of a new car ferry in 1912 that the agitation subsided, and attention was again focused on the province's finan-cial relations with Ottawa. By that time, economic and political develop-ments throughout the country made possible a new approach to the Island's difficulties.

As the nineteenth century drew to a close, Prime Minister Wilfrid Laurier predicted that the twentieth was to be "Canada's century." Sir Wilfrid, blessed by circumstances, did his best to make it so. Encouraged by the long-awaited flood of immigration to the west, and expectations of profit from newly discovered natural resources in the northern regions of western and central Canada, foreign capital, most of it British, poured into the country seeking investment in farm buildings, livestock, and machinery, the enlargement of industrial plants and equipment, the provision of urban services, and above all else, in the construction of railways. As Donald Creighton has commented:

It was an increasingly affluent society, and at its top stood the chief benefi-ciaries of the Laurier boom, the Laurier plutocracy, made up of bankers, engineers, corporation lawyers, railway builders, mining promoters, pulp and paper producers, and public utility entrepreneurs.[19]

Indeed, it appeared that the dream of Confederation — all Canadian transport, prairie settlement, and industrialization by protective tariffs — was being realized. Unfortunately, while the Maritimes helped to foot the bill for tariff protection, railway guarantees, and prairie settlement, they reaped few of the benefits. While the Dominion's population grew by 64 per cent between 1901 and 1921, it increased by 3 per cent in the Maritimes, and actually declined in Prince Edward Island. In the same period, the Maritimes received about 5 per cent of the increase in farm investment, while the prairies obtained more than half. Ontario and Quebec had 80 per cent of the increased investment in manufacturing and hydro-electric facilities, while the Maritimes had but 10 per cent.[20] Canada's century, it seemed, was about to pass the Maritimes by.

The national policy of tariff protection, which became the basis of Island and Maritime complaints until after 1945, had been introduced by the government of Sir John A. Macdonald in 1879. Failing to negotiate free trade with the United States, the Macdonald Conservatives decided to "go it alone." Tariff protection would close the Canadian market to United States manufactured goods and encourage development of domestic industry. Prairie settlement would create a domestic market and transcontinenal railways would produce an east — west flow of trade. The settlement of the west after 1896 and the building of a second and third transcontinental railway by the Laurier government brought the plan to the point of achievement.

Although the national policy served to integrate the Canadian economy, and perhaps contributed to the building of a nation, its regional effects were unfortunate. The east, as well as the west, was an exporting region, and tariff protection served only to increase the costs of production and to invite retaliatory tariffs against Maritime exports. Prince Edward Island, dependent upon the export of fish and agricultural products, with no manufactures of any kind, was particularly badly served. Several Royal Commissions and related studies have confirmed the disadvantages of the national policy on the Maritime region, although none, it should be emphasized, has held it solely responsible for the Island province's economic difficulties. Perhaps the most judicious assessment has been made by W. A. MacKintosh. While admitting that by the end of the nineteenth century export markets for Maritime goods were declining due to world conditions, and that shipbuilding was giving way to the steam vessel, he nevertheless concludes that national policies encouraged the concentration of population and metropolitan centres in Quebec and Ontario, contributed to the contraction of Maritime exports and the fall of populations, ". . . restricted the revenues of provincial governments, and increased the expenditures necessary to cope with the problems of declining industries and declining areas."[21]

Thus, while government-sponsored immigration and railways made the prairies the chief exporting region of Canada, and Ontario and Quebec increased their manufacturing capacity and developed their pulp and paper and mining regions behind a protective tariff, the Maritimes declined in economic and political importance. Prince Edward Island suffered most, for even Nova Scotia benefited from its coal and steel industry, and New Brunswick gained from the expansion of pulp and paper production. It was not long before the province began to complain of a national policy which distributed its benefits so unequally, and it was soon joined by Nova Scotia and New Brunswick.

By 1912, political as well as economic changes within the province promised to produce a new approach to Ottawa. During the Laurier years, Liberal governments had held office in Charlottetown, and although they had been successful in securing an additional $30,000 subsidy and a promise of another steamer, the Conservative Opposition condemned them for "dilatory and ineffective action in the premises whereby justice has been delayed and the interests of this province injured to an incalculable extent."[22] On December 10, 1911, the Conservatives, led by John Mathieson, took over the government after the Liberals had been placed in a minority by the loss of two by-elections. The new Premier immediately called a general election for January 3, 1912, and swept to victory with a majority of 28 to 2 in the legislature. The campaign was dominated by Prime Minister Robert Borden's promise of a new car ferry, but Mathieson also promised to obtain relief from Ottawa for the province's financial difficulties.[23]

Premier Mathieson was not long in making good his promise. In February, he headed a delegation to Ottawa, and after a series of meetings with a committee of the Canadian cabinet, including Prime Minister Borden and Thomas White, the Minister of Finance, agreement was reached to grant the province an additional $100,000 annually.[24]

The brief presented by the delegates elaborated upon earlier claims, but new arguments were introduced. The delegates demanded compensation for the enlargement, past or future, of any Canadian province, and the national policy was criticized for its effects on Island trade and industry:

It is the opinion of your memorialists, almost unanimously supported by the people of our Province, that Confederation has caused the destruction of the industries of the Island, and has driven those formerly engaged therein to other lands. Had the Island remained out of Confederation, it could have guarded these industries, and developed its trade along the lines which it had established, but by surrendering to Canada its power to regulate its tariff, its established trade routes were broken up, its business turned into Canadian channels, its industries so heavily weighted in the race with rivals who enjoyed the advantages of continuous connection with the transportation facilities of the mainland, that they have almost become extinct. . . .

The National Policy under which Canada generally has achieved such splendid development, has not extended its benefits to the industries of this Province, for the reasons above set forth. The proportionate contribution of the Province to the revenues of Canada amounted to $1,181,052 in 1911, computing it at the average rate, but your memorialists claim that it is much larger, by reason of the almost total extinction of the manufacturing industries within the Island and the consequent large importation of dutiable goods. But even at the average rate this Province now pays to Canada in taxes more than three times as much as was required for all its public services at Confederation.[25]

The federal government accepted this argument when it based the $100,000 increase, not on any specific claim, but simply on the Island's failure to prosper in Confederation. The Minister of Finance, on reading the Island's claim, had "become enthusiastic about it," and was convinced that since Confederation, the province "has been hardly treated . . ."[26] Even Sir Wilfrid Laurier, now leader of the Opposition, who had reservations about the government's policy, was moved to comment that "the one reason only which has impressed me — and it is not a constitutional reason, it is not a legal reason, it is simply a reason of equity — is the fact that Prince Edward Island has not profited by Confederation."[27]

The following year, the growing sense of grievance and disillusionment was fed by the extension of the boundaries of Quebec and Ontario, and by Prime Minister Borden's overtures to the prairie provinces for the return of their natural resources. When Manitoba, Saskatchewan and Alberta became provinces, the federal government retained control of their public lands in order that the Dominion might carry out its policy of immigration and settlement. In return, the provinces received an additional subsidy as compensation. By 1911, the western provinces were demanding the return of their lands, and while in Opposition in Parliament, Robert Borden had expressed support for their claims. Consequently, shortly after his election Borden opened discussions with the prairie provinces and asked them to present a proposal. On December 22, 1913, the prairie Premiers wrote Borden asking for both their lands and their subsidy.[28]

Such a demand was wholly unacceptable to the Maritime provinces. The Maritime Premiers had no objection to the return of the lands, but the continuance of the subsidy was "over-generous" treatment, and would require compensation to every other province.[29] As a result of the opposition of the Maritimes, Borden rejected the request of the prairie Premiers,[30] and the matter was dropped with the outbreak of the world war in 1914.

The whole question of compensation for the alienation of Dominion lands was further complicated in 1912 by the enlargement of Ontario and Quebec. The lands acquired from the Hudson's Bay Company in 1870 included large areas of present-day Ontario and Quebec. These lands were largely unsettled in 1912, but their potential wealth was unlimited. When the Dominion government handed over some of this territory to Ontario and Quebec, the Maritime provinces claimed compensation.

The Maritime provinces joined together in 1913 to voice their claims. In a meeting with the Canadian cabinet in January, 1913, Premier Mathieson and Mr. A. E. Arsenault of Prince Edward Island, and W. C. H. Grimmer, Attorney General of New Brunswick, presented the case for compensation to the Maritimes.[31] They argued that since the lands acquired from the Hudson's Bay Company had been bought and developed by the taxpayers of all the provinces, all provinces had a proprietary interest in them, and when any portion of them was given to any province, all other provinces were entitled to compensation.

The Maritimers also made a lengthy case for compensation for school lands reserved for the benefit of the prairie provinces. In 1872, the Dominion government set aside two sections in each township of Dominion lands for the support of education in the province or territory in which the lands were located.[32] In their remarks before the cabinet, the Maritime spokesmen made it clear that no claim was made for the lands granted to settlers or set aside as railway subsidies, since the settlement and development of the west was for the benefit of all Canada. But when the lands were reserved for the benefit of a particular province, a different principle was involved. As Premier Mathieson of the Island said: "It was not in the general interest to reserve these lands, but in the special interest of the provinces in which they are situate."[33]

The significance of the school lands was clearly indicated by Attorney General Grimmer when he pointed out that the revenues from their sale enabled the western provinces to pay better salaries for teachers. "We cannot keep our teachers in the Maritime Provinces," he said, "because we cannot afford to pay them the salaries that are paid in the west, and our best teachers are annually drained from us to give their services to these new provinces."[34]

Although their claim was a specific demand for compensation for the enlargement of Ontario and Quebec, and for the school lands of the west, the delegates based much of their appeal on the favourable treatment given western Canada, while the Maritimes continued to languish. In his remarks before the cabinet, Mr. Grimmer reminded its members that during all the years since Confederation, the Maritimes had willingly contributed to the

Intercolonial Railway, which served to benefit Ontario to a greater extent than the Maritimes. They had also contributed to the canal and railway systems of central and western Canada, as well as to the costs of channeling immigration into the west.[35] Premier Mathieson summed up the Maritime case:

The resources of the Maritime Provinces are varied and great, their location in relation to the markets of the world is splendid, but they have not thriven under Confederation to the extent they should. This Government is now in each of the three Maritime Provinces, carrying out splendid improvements in aid of transportation which will have far reaching beneficial results. In the early days of Confederation and up to a very short time ago, these Provinces had to bear a heavy share of the burden of developing the west, partly by their money, but more by their men. I remember being in the West when it was a wilderness and when the conditions in the East were much more favourable, but by reason of the sacrifices made by the East the advantage has shifted. The son has been made better off than the father. But the Maritime Provinces feel that the balance should now be in some measure restored — that they should be evened up with the West. The Provinces of Alberta and Saskatchewan have been so generously endowed by Canada that they are able to pay twice the salaries and even more to our teachers than can be paid at home. . . .

I trust that this Government, with its anxiety for the welfare of the Maritime Provinces, will even it up, and we will not have to wait even for a few years. No doubt the development of the West is to some extent due to a natural process, and while it is true that Providence controls and not the Government, yet we think that under Providence the Government has had a vast deal to do with bringing about the prosperous conditions in the West. We believe that the Government has it in their power to remedy the evils that now exist in the Maritime Provinces. Every man interested in the welfare of the entire Dominion would like to see prosperity in all its parts, and it is toward that end that we are now urging our case before this Privy Council.[36]

While their complaints were directed for the most part against what they considered preferred treatment of the western provinces in regard to subsidies, there was evident in the Maritime presentation a growing sense of grievance toward federal policies designed to promote western development. The discontent was becoming regional. Provincial demands for better terms were no longer adequate responses to problems caused by national policies designed for the development of whole regions. The Maritimes now felt it necessary to join together to demand an equal share in the benefits of Confederation, and to redress the balance which had been tipped against them. The movement for Maritime rights was launched.

During the war, controversial political issues were set aside, but postwar conditions led quickly to a new round of sectional rivalry. The Maritimes had to make difficult economic adjustments after 1918. Nova Scotia and Prince Edward Island faced declining populations, and the markets for lumber, fish, agricultural products, coal and iron were highly competitive and prices unsatisfactory.[37] By 1923, freight rate increases placed a heavy additional burden on Maritime traffic.[38] As a consequence, the province once again joined with Nova Scotia and New Brunswick to press its claims on Ottawa.

By 1920 the Prince Edward Island legislature was calling for a conference of the Maritime Premiers to formulate plans for joint action in pressing for a settlement of the just claims of the Maritimes against the federal government. The Premier, J. H. Bell, moved the resolution,[39] and in a long speech, reiterated the Island's claims.[40] Boards of Trade and Chambers of Commerce took an active part in the agitation of the 1920's. In 1923, the Maritime provinces Boards of Trade formed the Maritime Development Association, whose object was the co-ordination of the activities of all parties interested in Maritime progress. Its formation was prompted by the lack of progress of the Maritimes in Confederation, the declining population, the takeover of industrial concerns by central Canadian business, marketing and transportation problems, and the despair so prevalent in the region.[41] In 1925, the Dominion Boards of Trade and Chambers of Commerce lent their support by passing resolutions sympathetic to Maritime claims.[42]

Meanwhile, the political agitation picked up speed. In 1921, MacKenzie King had brought the Liberals back to power at Ottawa with strong Maritime support, including all four Island members. King, however, was preoccupied with retaining the support of the Progressive members from the west,[43] and Maritime Liberals exerted little influence on government policy. This left it to the provincial governments to lead the agitation, and Conservative governments were elected in Prince Edward Island in 1923, and in Nova Scotia and New Brunswick in 1925. In the Prince Edward Island election of 1923, the Conservatives under J. D. Stewart defeated the government by making an issue of the financial condition of the province.[44] In the federal election of 1925, King lost most of his Maritime support in a campaign dominated in Prince Edward Island by the Maritime rights issue. Although Arthur Meighen, the Conservative leader, refused to budge from his high tariff policy, he did promise lower freight rates and told his Charlottetown audiences that high tariffs would protect the price of farm products.[45] After four years in office, King's promise of lower tariffs failed to impress, and the result was more a rejection of King than support for Meighen.[46]

The result of the 1925 election left King with fewer seats than the Conservatives, but he clung to office by securing the support of the Progressives. The Speech from the Throne promised the west the return of its natural resources. King courted the east by announcing the appointment of a Royal Commission to study Maritime claims. If it did nothing else, the Royal Commission would, as E. M. MacDonald, the Liberal member for Antigonish-Guysboro, reminded King, keep the Maritimes distracted, smother Conservative agitation, and force Maritime "extremists" to be more realistic.[47]

The Commission, under the chairmanship of Sir Andrew Rae Duncan, went quickly to work. It began its investigation in April, 1926, held hearings throughout the Maritimes, received submissions from governments, Boards of Trade, and representative persons in trade, commerce, and railway administration, visited many districts to observe conditions first hand, and still managed to report in September of the same year.

In their presentation to the Commission the Island delegates reviewed earlier claims, but emphasis was placed on the Island's inability to raise sufficient tax revenues because of the harmful effects of national policies. The Canadian tariff, high freight rates and lack of winter communication had destroyed manufacturing, diverted trade and depressed agriculture. The loss of population brought about by the industrialization and urbanization of central Canada meant a loss of tax revenue. As a result, many taxes yielded far less than the Canadian average on a per capita basis,[48] and although the Island was receiving a larger per capita subsidy than any other province, a far larger proportion of its provincial revenue was raised by direct taxation.[49] The Island summed up its case as follows:

Prince Edward Island entered Confederation upon the understanding that it would receive from the Federal Government such subsidies as would enable it to carry on the public services allotted to the Provincial Government without resorting to direct taxation.

It has been forced to resort to direct taxation and notwithstanding it is unable to continue to provide for the existing services without an increase of revenue and many of the necessary public services, notably Public Health, are altogether neglected, and many others are not adequately provided for.

That this Province has no semi-indirect sources of revenue such as public lands, natural resources and large corporations, and can only increase its revenue from two sources, viz: direct taxation upon its farming population or increase of subsidy from the Federal Government. That a further increase of direct taxation upon the farms of this Province in the face of a shrinking population should not be forced upon us.

That this Province is entitled to further subsidy upon the grounds heretofore set forth, and particularly is entitled to be placed upon the same basis as the other landless provinces with respect to the subsidy for want of Public lands.[50]

The Duncan Commission represented the first attempt by the federal government to study seriously Island and Maritime claims, and from the point of view of the Maritimes, it was a considerable success. By supporting the novel idea that the Maritimes, and by inference, all areas of the Dominion, should share in the prosperity of the other regions, even if this meant the use of federal funds to achieve equalization, the Commissioners expressed their concern for what has since been termed "regional disparities."

Although the Commission did not lay the entire blame on Confederation and federal government policies, the Commission stated ". . . that the Maritime provinces have not prospered and developed, either in population, or in commercial, industrial and rural enterprise, as fully as other portions of Canada."[51] While not blaming the Dominion for this lack of development, the Commissioners ". . . are far from saying that the Dominion, within its sphere of control, has done all for the Maritime Provinces which it should have done."[52] "We believe," they continued, "that the claims which these Provinces have submitted in connection with the present condition, and the future possibilities, of their own part of the Dominion, should now be reviewed with sympathetic consideration and understanding, so that in approaching the future a better balance of territorial prosperity can be assured, and the original hope of Confederation — unity, prosperity and contentment for all the Provinces, as well as for the whole of Canada — can be made capable of realization."[53]

The Commission then went on to review the claims of the Maritimes with "sympathetic consideration and understanding." They found that subsidy payments to the Maritimes were inadequate, and suggested a complete review of financial arrangements. They found further that the Maritimes were treated differently from the western provinces and were entitled to have their debt allowances readjusted. Prince Edward Island, said the Commissioners, was entitled to have its claim for further subsidy in lieu of public lands considered, and rail service on the Island and communications with the mainland should be improved.

The Commissioners made no attempt to fix the amount of the financial payments that should be made to the Maritimes. They recognized the justice of the claims, but left detailed settlement to the governments concerned. They considered the situation sufficiently urgent, however, to recommend the immediate payment of interim subsidies while the governments took steps to secure a complete revision of financial arrangements. They therefore recommended that the Island should receive an annual subsidy increase of $125,000.[54]

The Commission dealt at some length with Maritime freight rates. Transportation in Canada has traditionally been an instrument of national policy, and railways particularly have been viewed as political instruments for the integration of the Canadian economy. This view informed the thinking of the Fathers of Confederation when they agreed to the building of the Intercolonial Railway to connect the Maritimes with central Canada. From the Maritime point of view, rail connection with the markets of central Canada was one of the essential conditions of union. The continuing importance of transportation to an isolated exporting region dependent upon markets located outside the area has made freight rates an issue of increasing importance to the province and the region.

Until 1912 the Island province made little complaint, but freight rate increases after that time added increasing burdens to Maritime traffic. The Duncan Commission came "very definitely to the conclusion that the rate structure as it has been altered since 1912 has placed upon the trade and commerce of the Maritime Provinces . . . a burden . . . it was never intended it should bear . . ."[55] Accordingly, the Commission recommended a 20 per cent reduction on most Maritime rates and urged that future railway administration be more cognizant of the political and national functions of freight rate structures.[56]

The Report was all the province could have hoped for. Not only did the Report find in favour of most of the claims of the region, but it clearly suggested that Dominion policies adversely affected Maritime trade and industry, and that the disabilities under which the region suffered should be removed. Even the Conservative Charlottetown *Guardian* thought the Report "an able and logical one" and praised the Commissioners for the "thorough and impartial manner" in which they presented their findings.[57] It was now squarely up to the federal government to decide the fate of the Report.

MacKenzie King received the Report in September, 1926, just after his re-election. Still anxious to restore national unity, King was reluctant to accept its findings in the face of western hostility. Consequently, he announced in the House of Commons on March 18, 1927, his acceptance of most of the recommendations with the reservation that the interim subsidy payments would be for one year only.[58] Before agreeing to continue the subsidies annually, King awaited the results of the Federal-Provincial Conference of 1927, where the Maritimes agreed that the federal government should deal in a "generous and liberal manner" with the claims of the western provinces.[59] As a result, King reopened negotiations with the western provinces for the return of their natural resources.

It was not until 1930 that the federal government agreed to return the public lands of the western provinces and to continue their subsidy. This settlement prompted Prince Edward Island to renew its case for an additional subsidy in lieu of public lands. The Island's claim was indeed unique. In 1873, the province was granted $45,000 annually in lieu of public lands, but it was to subtract from that sum the interest on any amount up to $800,000 that it borrowed from the Dominion to purchase lands remaining in the hands of proprietors. Within a short time, the province had borrowed almost the entire $800,000 and so was paying in interest to the federal government an amount almost equal to the $45,000. Since the lands, when bought, were resold to the tenants, the province soon found itself with no lands and very little subsidy. A petition setting forth its case in detail was prepared in 1930,[60] but it met with no success.

The return of the public lands to the west opened the way for the detailed assessment of Maritime claims recommended by the Duncan Commission. This was not attempted until 1934, when, after repeated urgings from the Maritime Premiers, the White Commission was appointed. In their presentations before this Commission, the Maritime Premiers submitted "model budgets" outlining the estimated minimum expenditures necessary to maintain an adequate level of public services.[61]

From the point of view of the Maritimes, the White Commission was a failure. The Report began by rejecting the principle of fiscal need,[62] and consequently, the model budgets submitted by the provinces ". . . cannot be regarded by us as factors entitled to material weight in our task of determining the question of what further subsidies in aid may be equitably awarded under this heading to the Maritime Provinces . . ."[63] In other words, it didn't really matter that a province went into debt or was unable to provide adequate services for its people, unless, of course, its condition affected the national credit. Then, it would be proper for the Dominion to assist a province by way of guarantees and loans, but not by additional subsidies.[64]

After this rather disappointing beginning, the Commissioners attempted to isolate those conditions peculiar to the Maritimes calling for special consideration. These were the heavy overhead expenses of small provinces, their isolated economic position, and their smaller per capita income and wealth. The Commission also admitted the special claim of Prince Edward Island for additional subsidies in lieu of public lands. With these exceptions, the Commissioners reduced Maritime claims to compensation for their failure to share proportionately ". . . with the other provinces of Canada in the economic advantages accruing to the Dominion as a whole from Confederation . . ."[65] Consequently, no detailed assessment of Maritime claims was possible, and the Commissioners were content to use their own best judgement to recommend additional annual subsidies amounting, in the case of Prince Edward Island, to $275,000 per year.[66]

Nowhere in the Report was there any suggestion that the Maritimes failed to profit from national policies designed for the development of central and western Canada, much less any recognition that Dominion tariff policy had injured the region. Having rejected the principle of fiscal need, the Commissioners placed outside their terms of reference any consideration of the effects of federal policies on the region on the grounds that such policies affected all provinces and could not, therefore, be a condition peculiar to any one of them. Unfortunately, by ignoring the possibility that special circumstances may arise from the unequal incidence of national policies, the Commissioners were unable to make a realistic assessment of Maritime claims, and their Report displayed a tendency to accept the depressed conditions of the Maritimes as an accident of geography.[67]

The findings of the Commissioners were no doubt influenced by the depressed conditions of the entire country. When the whole country was in the throes of the Great Depression it was difficult to single out any region as suffering from unequal treatment. It was especially difficult for two of the Commissioners, Sir Thomas White, the former Minister of Finance from Toronto, and Edward Walter Nesbitt, a former member of Parliament from Woodstock, Ontario. It is not surprising, therefore, that the only Maritimer on the Commission, Chief Justice John A. Mathieson of Prince Edward Island, dissented from the views of his colleagues. In a minority Report, Chief Justice Mathieson objected to the rejection of fiscal need, arguing that this principle had been accepted in the earlier revisions of union terms.[68] He also correctly pointed out that the main task of the Commission — a detailed assessment of Maritime claims — had been left unresolved.

The whole issue of Maritime claims and the White Commission was soon superseded by events. The Great Depression had created a national emergency. Faced with greatly expanded expenditures for unemployment and relief, and depressed revenues, some provinces faced a financial crisis. When federal efforts to deal with the emergency were struck down by the courts, the Dominion government appointed a Royal Commission to study the whole question of federal-provincial relations.

The appointment of the Rowell-Sirois Commission in 1937 was a landmark in the history of Canadian federalism. On the one hand, it marked the end of a period during which the existing distribution of powers and tax revenues was growing increasingly obsolete. On the other, it signalled the beginning of a new period during which federal-provincial discussions were expanded to include a growing concern for a fundamental revision of the powers and revenue sources of both levels of government. No longer were federal-provincial meetings preoccupied with arguments about the meaning of specific terms of union. The starting point of such discussions now was the inadequacy of existing arrangements and the need to seek an entirely new basis for a successful federation.

The Island brought to these new discussions considerable enthusiasm for fundamental change and an open and sympathetic attitude towards any proposals brought forth. Such an attitude, of course, reflected the Island's unhappy experiences with existing arrangements, and a sympathy, shared by the poorer provinces, for any re-adjustment which would relieve it of its most costly responsibilities and re-distribute the national wealth. Proposals to transfer provincial responsibilities and revenue sources to the federal government did not worry Prince Edward Island. Although noted ever since the union negotiations of 1864-1873 for its insular attitude and deep-seated provincialism, the demand for "provincial rights" never became a demand for more provincial autonomy. As the author of a recent study on Maritime Union, J. R. Winter, has pointed out, "Maritimers are federalist Canadians, par excellence."[69] Provincial rights has meant, in Prince Edward Island, a demand for a share of the national prosperity, and for national policies which reflect the interests and needs of all regions. If this could be best achieved through the agency of the federal government, the Island would raise no objection.

The Island enthusiasm for a re-adjustment of governmental responsibilities and revenue sources was evident in its submission to the Rowell-Sirois Commission. Admitting that changing conditions had rendered the financial provisions of the British North America Act obsolete, the province announced its readiness to explore the possibilities of new arrangements. Since the national policy of tariff protection benefited only Ontario and Quebec, and was an actual financial burden on the rest of the provinces, it was clearly necessary to seek ways of re-distributing national wealth and compensating disadvantaged regions. This, the province argued, could only be done by accepting fiscal need as a basis for federal-provincial fiscal arrangements.[70]

Fiscal need could be best established by measuring the amount of expenditure necessary to maintain an adequate minimum of public services against the tax-raising capacity of the province. By this standard, it was pointed out that despite the use of every possible tax source at rates comparable to other provinces, the Island was still unable to pay such costs as mothers' allowances, contributed almost nothing to hospitalization, health services and child welfare, and paid the lowest old age pensions of any Canadian province. In addition, the salaries paid school teachers, civil servants, and cabinet ministers were far below those of other provinces.[71] The remedy was for the federal government to assume much of the responsibility for health and welfare, as well as unemployment insurance. In return, the province would transfer to the Dominion the exclusive right to collect income taxes and succession duties, provided it was assured of adequate compensation.[72]

The Report of the Commission was a vindication of much that Island spokesmen had been saying for over fifty years. The Report stated unequivocally that federal policies had tended to benefit certain regions more than others. "It is theoretically possible," said the Commissioners, "that federal policy might so weaken the financial position of a province as to make it difficult, if not impossible for it to perform its functions on standards reasonably comparable with those of other provinces."[73] Since such inequalities were threats to national unity, it was in the national interest that the federal government take action to remove them by expressly recognizing fiscal need as a principle of federal assistance to the provinces.[74]

Regarding Prince Edward Island's financial position the Report was even more specific:

In spite of the fact that Prince Edward Island is the most perfect geographical entity of any Canadian province, it does not form a satisfactory unit from the point of view of public finance, and particularly for raising revenue. The manifest inability of a small agricultural economy, possessing no taxable surplus, to raise revenues and to finance services on the same scale as in the rest of Canada was recognized from the first in the special debt allowance, and subsidy in lieu of land, provided when Prince Edward Island entered Confederation.[75]

Because of its "manifest inability" to raise revenue, the province should be considered quite separately from all others.[76]

As a remedy for regional variations in the national economy, the Report recommended the use of national powers of taxation to transfer income from one region to another. The Dominion government should be given exclusive rights to personal income and corporation taxes, as well as succession duties, in return for the payment of National Adjustment Grants to certain provinces based on fiscal need.[77] The acceptance of the principle of fiscal need to guarantee a minimum national standard of government services was exactly what the province had been demanding, and at the Federal-Provincial Conference of 1941, Premier Thane A. Campbell expressed his government's willingness to discuss the proposals.[78] Although the Commission's Report could not be implemented at the time, owing largely to the opposition of Ontario, Alberta and British Columbia, the Tax-Rental Agreements of the post-war period incorporated some of the Commission's proposals.

During the war the provinces had agreed to vacate the personal and corporate income tax fields and to accept federal payments in return. After the war, to avoid a return to the unsatisfactory and chaotic conditions of the thirties, most provinces agreed to continue the war-time arrangements, and by 1947, all provinces but Ontario and Quebec had signed agreements.

With minor revisions in 1952, the 1947 agreements remained the basis of federal-provincial fiscal arrangements until 1957.

The Tax-Rental Agreements of 1947 provided some relief for the poorer provinces, but as payments were based on the gross national product and the population of the provinces, no provision was made for fiscal need. Consequently, the Island accepted the agreement ". . . not because it represented some recognition of fiscal need but with a hope that during the lifetime of that agreement a more satisfactory formula would be devised, which would consider our fiscal position and recognize our fiscal need."[79]

It soon became clear that a new formula was indeed necessary if Prince Edward Island was not to raise taxes to unacceptable levels or to curtail services. The rapid expansion of government services after the war placed an undue strain on provincial budgets. Between 1952 and 1967 total ordinary expenditures increased from $7,000,000 to $40,000,000, largely the result of increased expenditures for highways, social services and education. A rural farm community is heavily dependent upon adequate roads, and expenditure for this item alone increased from a little over $1,000,000 to $3,696,000 for the same period. The attempt to modernize a school system characterized by a large number of one room schools, to attract qualified teachers and expand programs, resulted in an increase of 700 per cent in the educational budget for the same years.[80]

Although all provinces faced similar increases in expenditures, none possessed such a limited tax potential. Tax potential is most accurately reflected by per capita incomes, and by this standard, the province ranked next to last, followed only by Newfoundland.[81] A recent study has shown that despite similar rates, per capita tax yield is still substantially lower in Prince Edward Island than elsewhere.[82] Consequently, despite a tax effort comparable to that of other provinces, the Island has less to spend for the maintenance of essential public services.

Successive governments did their best to impress upon the federal government the province's special needs. National policies continued to be held responsible for some of the province's difficulties. The government of Premier A. W. Matheson complained in 1955 of a national policy which worked to ". . . the great detriment and disadvantage of Prince Edward Island," and which continued to attract ". . . the best of [its] youth . . . to other provinces . . ."[83] In 1960 Premier Walter R. Shaw told the assembled Premiers that:

Since Confederation we have helped to build and make this Canada the great nation it is today. Therefore, we feel that our growth and economic problems should be the concern of every province. . . . If we are to have a united Canada the wealth must be spread from the centre to the outside. . . . If

Dominion-Provincial Conference, Ottawa, Ont. Rt. Hon. W. L. Mackenzie King with Provincial Premiers, January 14, 1941. Standing, l. to r.: W. J. Paterson, Premier of Sask.; W. J. Patullo, Premier of B.C.; J. Bracken, Premier of Man.; T. A. Campbell, Premier of P.E.I.; W. Aberhart, Premier of Alta. Seated, l. to r.: A. S. MacMillan, Premier of N.S.; M. F. Hepburn, Premier of Ont.; W. L. Mackenzie King, Prime Minister of Canada; A. Godbout, Premier of Que.; J. B. McNair, Premier of N.B.
Courtesy of the Public Archives of Canada

disadvantages created by national policies have retarded the economic development of any region of Canada then national policies must be devised that will bring prosperity to those areas so affected.[84]

But although such views were repeated, there was also a new emphasis. There was evident a reluctant acceptance of national tariff, trade and monetary policies. "We do not criticize these policies," the Matheson government said in 1955, but "the nation should see to it that the citizens of no area fall below the national average in the matter of social and educational services."[85] Instead, taking its cue from the findings of the Rowell-Sirois Commission, the province argued for national taxation policies to transfer wealth from the more prosperous to the less wealthy regions and for fiscal arrangements that would take account of the Island's special features.

Much was made of the necessity to re-distribute the national wealth. Repeating an argument made by the Rowell-Sirois Commission, the province repeatedly pointed out that many provincial services were provided ". . . to persons engaged in nationwide industries which are so organized that the revenues collected from taxes imposed upon them tend to be concentrated in certain large centres, frequently located in taxing jurisdictions, other than those in which the government services are provided."[86] This enabled certain provinces to tax incomes and wealth derived from other provinces. "Therefore, provincial revenues must be supplemented by a reasonable distribution of the national taxation in order that governmental services may be provided in every province without imposing an undue burden on the taxable capacity of those provinces below the national average."[87]

A new note was also injected as increased attention was focused on the need for positive programs to stimulate economic development. "It is equally desirable and essential, if we are to have a truly sound and well-balanced national economy," said Premier Shaw in 1960, "that the Federal Government adopt policies designed to promote the development of secondary industry in the presently less highly industrialized provinces of Canada."[88] Such a ". . . bold, comprehensive and co-ordinated approach to the underlying problems of the region . . . would substantially increase national income for the good of the country as a whole, and would broaden the base for tax raising for all levels of government."[89]

Some relief was provided in 1957 when federal payments to the provinces were based on the returns from the three standard taxes in the two provinces of highest per capita yield.[90] This formula, which was designed to compensate the provinces of lower tax yield, was refined in 1967, but the basic concept has been retained and continues to be the basis of federal

Federal-Provincial Conference — 1960. Premiers of Canada's 10 Provinces pose with Prime Minister John G. Diefenbaker in front of main entrance to the Parliament Buildings — Centre Block in Ottawa, Ont., on July 25. From left to right are: E. C. Manning, Alta.; Walter Shaw, P.E.I.; Duff Roblin, Man.; R. L. Stanfield, N.S.; L. M. Frost, Ont.; The Prime Minister; Jean Lesage, Que.; Louis Robichaud, N.B.; W. A. C. Bennett, B.C.; T. C. Douglas, Sask. and J. R. Smallwood, Nfld.

Courtesy of the Public Archives of Canada

payments to the provinces. A further adjustment was introduced in 1958, when Prime Minister John Diefenbaker, fulfilling a campaign promise, introduced the Atlantic Provinces Adjustment Grants by which the Island province received an additional $2,500,000,[91] but these payments were discontinued in 1967 when the new equalization formula was intended to replace them.

In recent years the federal government has approached the problem of regional disparities through the programs of its Department of Regional Economic Expansion, and in the case of Prince Edward Island, through the contribution of funds to a Provincial Development Plan. Although the success of this approach has not as yet been noteworthy, it is too soon to assess its full impact. It represents, however, the first real attempt to adapt national policies of economic expansion to disadvantaged regions, and to remove a grievance first complained of by Prince Edward Island in 1880. At that time, J. C. Pope, a member of Macdonald's cabinet who had campaigned for the policy of tariff protection in 1878, complained that "however much the National Policy may promote the interests of the Dominion as a whole, we cannot shut our eyes to the fact that so far as the Island individually is concerned, it means largely increased taxation with no corresponding advantages. They have no manufactures of any importance, and must necessarily import many of their manufactured articles from Montreal and Ontario, and for their English goods they have to pay in the way of duties 50 per cent more than formerly."[92]

A review of the province's dealings with Ottawa suggests that the view of J. C. Pope in 1880 was little different from that of Premier Shaw in 1960. The great Canadian enterprises — from tariff protection to canal and railway networks, prairie settlement, and the St. Lawrence Seaway, to present day visions of northern development — have not only been of little benefit, they have been irrelevant to the province. The province's concerns have been dominated by its size and location, its dependence on agriculture and fishing, its static population, and its lack of natural wealth. Its special circumstances have led one authority to suggest that a ". . . review of Prince Edward Island's financial position ought to be mainly concerned with its special features and less with comparisons between it and other provinces."[93] While the province has been well aware of the necessity of this approach, it has not been able to ignore national policies which have added to its particular difficulties.

While the concerns of the province have changed little over many years, the mechanism for the conduct of federal-provincial discussions has altered significantly. Prior to 1945, federal-provincial gatherings were dominated by politicians who were the political spokesmen for their provinces and regions. Success depended largely on a province's political influence, and this was measured by its parliamentary and cabinet representation. By either standard, the province's position has never been strong.

In 1873, the province's population entitled it to six members in the House of Commons. Owing to its declining proportion of the Dominion population, the province's representation was reduced to five in 1892, to four in 1904, and finally in 1911, it became entitled to only three members in the House of Commons. The province continually protested that the reduction of its parliamentary representation was a violation of the terms of union,[94] and even appealed to the British Privy Council, but without success. Finally, the government of John A. Mathieson agreed to a compromise by which no province should have fewer members in the House of Commons than it had in the Senate. This arrangement was embodied in an amendment to the British North America Act in 1915, and the province is thereby guaranteed a minimum of four members in the House of Commons.[95]

The province has fared little better with its representation in the federal cabinet. The selection of his cabinet is one of the most difficult tasks facing a Prime Minister. With a variety of provincial, regional, ethnic and religious interests to reconcile, he has not always been able to select a member from a province with only four members. Besides, the province has not always embarrassed the Prime Minister with a wealth of talent, and has occasionally returned a full slate of Opposition members.[96]

The attitude of successive Prime Ministers was first stated by Alexander MacKenzie in 1876. David Laird, who had been in MacKenzie's cabinet, became Governor of the North West Territories and his place in the cabinet was given to David Mills of Ontario. Island Liberals protested vigorously, but MacKenzie was adamant:

You could hardly expect a minister as a matter of local right. Ontario has seventeen times your population. Quebec twelve times, Nova Scotia four times, and New Brunswick three times your population. It is impossible to lay down a rule that all the provinces shall be represented in the Cabinet. Indeed, I think the first Minister should be at liberty to take two from the Island if the men who are most wanted should be there . . .[97]

These views, repeated by Laurier in 1902,[98] have guided successive Prime Ministers, and the Island has rarely been represented in the federal cabinet.[99]

The province's political influence measured by its parliamentary and cabinet representation has declined since Confederation, and its position is not likely to improve as federal-provincial relations become less political confrontations and more exercises in problem-solving by the professional civil servants. The rapid growth since 1945 of inter-governmental machinery for the conduct of federal-provincial negotiations has placed a premium on a staff of competent experts who man a variety of committees, sub-committees, and liaison groups. As a consequence, the province may be further disadvantaged, not by lack of competency, but by sheer lack of numbers.[100] In addition, the growth of urban centres and their emergence as a political force demanding a voice in federal-provincial decisions will not make the province's task easier. As urban problems continue to absorb more and more of the attention and budgets of governments, a small rural province may receive less, not more, attention.

There is little doubt that this small rural province, lacking political influence, has suffered many disadvantages compared to other provinces. Constitutional amendments and re-arrangements of provincial boundaries are not likely to affect any change. The recent emphasis on the problem of regional disparities, however, may improve the Island's position and lead to the adoption of national policies relevant to all regions. But Prince Edward Island's special features will remain. It is by insisting, as has been done in the past, on the rights of a partner in a federal state, that the province's interests are best served. Size, material wealth, and political influence are not everything in a federal state. When they become so, the federal system will have failed.

Chapter Twelve

Island Politics

BY MARLENE-RUSSELL CLARK

When the first Assembly of Prince Edward Island met at the Cross Keys Tavern in 1773, the authorized representatives hastened to proclaim their legal control by dismissing the doorkeeper for disrespect when he was heard to mutter: "This is a damned queer parliament!"[1] In the following years the Assembly gained sufficient maturity to attain Responsible Government in 1851, while on the very centennial of such informal birth, it officiated the change from colonial status to that of a province. The political processes have altered in two centuries, but viewed in retrospect, the transformations have more often been smooth than abrupt — evidence of a growing sophistication in government, rather than any dramatic portrayal of innovation or of radical alteration. At the same time, however, there have been a sufficient number of incidents, of precedents, of departures from the usual British traditions of parliamentary democracy in the political life of Prince Edward Island to recall the echoes of that succinct and illustrious pronouncement on the first Assembly.

The very existence of autonomous provincial government in Prince Edward Island never ceases to amaze other Canadians. Islanders adopt a defensive position in any such implied criticism of their political independence. They argue that any examination which asks an area to justify its degree of autonomy on the basis of either population statistics or geographical size — or both — rests on the unproven assumption there is an optimum size for "good government." The province's status as a single unit is also defended on grounds that Prince Edward Island has both a history of political independence and a cultural milieu not entirely analogous with that of the other Maritime provinces. Either or both of these conditions are sufficient to warrant the province's retention of those benefits which are inherent in a federal system of government, benefits which accrue mainly from any differences between regions and cultures that are permitted to flourish in an atmosphere of political autonomy. The fact that federalism works best in a society where unequal political units are joined — or so some examples of failures among federal systems would tend to indicate — lends at least theoretical support to the defence of the Island's position.

More importantly, queries about the province's right to autonomy are usually derived from an implicit assumption that, because of the economies of scale and other related factors, absorption into a larger political entity will produce, or at least aid and influence, the growth of prosperity. In view of the area's geographical isolation, lack of minerals and associated industrial potential, such an assumption may well stand on very sandy soil. Ever since Prince Edward Island entered Confederation, its posture in the political life of the nation has been conditioned by its position as the smallest and weakest sister in the family of provinces.

Yet, simultaneously, the people of Prince Edward Island are proud of their reputation: if the number of elected representatives per capita is any criterion on which to base the amount of formal government, then Islanders have perhaps more formal government than anywhere else in the world. This somewhat dubious distinction stems from the machinery and personnel contained in the tri-level administration of a federation divided among a present maximum of 113,000 people. The province's allotment of four federal Members of Parliament and an equal number of federally-appointed Senators is more than double the number to which the population is entitled on a strictly numerical basis. Add to this a provincial Assembly of 32 members sandwiched between the federal level and the municipal officials of one city, seven towns, and 24 incorporated villages — and the result is an ample cast for an active political arena.

When Prince Edward Island joined Confederation in 1873 it did not have this magnitude of political representation. In many respects, it had, in fact, more! Because the Island's population was proportionately larger in a young Canada of seven provinces, the province had an initial representation in the House of Commons of six members with an accompanying group of four voices in the Senate. The unsuccessful struggle to retain the original quota of M.P.'s and following this defeat, the renewed and more victorious battle to stabilize provincial membership in the Ottawa chambers formed a separate chapter in the continuing saga of Dominion-provincial relations.

If Prince Edward Island was to have any voice and influence in national affairs, a representation-by-population principle could not be rigidly applied at the federal level. Because membership distribution in the Senate is based on a criterion that provides fixed representation for regions, the province's share in the Upper Chamber has never presented any real difficulties. In an attempt to create a parliamentary institution that sidestepped the pitfalls while borrowing the most admirable features of the American and British Upper Houses, the Fathers of Confederation constructed an appointed Senate with equal representation from the four major regional divisions of the nation. Quebec, Ontario, the West and the Maritimes each received a block of twenty-four seats, while the addition of Newfoundland, who did not wish to infringe on the Maritime allocation of membership, increased the Senate's composition by six to its present total of 102 representatives. From the 24 seats designated for the Maritime region, Prince Edward Island received four. However, as a forum for spokesmen of provincial or regional interests, the Senate has never fulfilled the expectations held by its creators at the time of Confederation. While it does provide the Island with additional representation in Ottawa, the Senate's influence in no way compares with that of the House of Commons. Senate representation has never been a serious issue in Prince Edward Island's federal-provincial relations: the same cannot be said for the Island's representation in the House of Commons.

The province's initial endowment of six members of Parliament was based on a population of 94,021, as recorded in the 1871 census. The federal representatives, two of whom were elected in dual constituencies in each of the three provincial counties, achieved their maiden debut in the Dominion Parliament of 1873 amidst the fervid session then embroiled in the Pacific Scandal. Four of these new Members of Parliament found themselves in opposition to the government of Sir John A. Macdonald. When the first Prime Minister was forced to resign his administration in November, 1873, David Laird was invited to become Minister of the Interior, and therefore Prince Edward Island's first federal cabinet minister, in the government formed by Alexander MacKenzie. In the federal election of 1874 and its successor of 1878, the new province began its long-standing pattern of returning federal members, most or all of whom belonged to the same partisan stripe as that of the victorious party. This became a practice which remained relatively consistent until the federal victories of the Liberal party in the past decade were contrasted with the Island's simultaneous preference for Conservative representation in the House of Commons. Initially, this match between the politics of Island M.P.'s and the governing party in Ottawa was rewarded by a cabinet post for the province. Sir John A. Macdonald, for example, chose J. C. Pope for his executive after the Conservative victory of 1878. Pope, one of the original federal members of Parliament from the Island, was given the major portfolio of Marine and Fisheries. But these early cabinet appointments did not establish a firm convention by which the province could claim any right to consistent representation in the Dominion executive. The unwritten rules surrounding the selection of the Canadian Cabinet grants all provinces a claim to a minimum of one voice in this august body — all, that is, save Prince Edward Island.[2]

This option of a Cabinet seat for the Island was directly related to the measure of representation given the province in the federal second chamber, for both were an outgrowth of the area's proportionate population. The Island's original grant of six seats was gradually whittled away as the province's population did not sustain the pace of growth evident in other parts of the nation. By 1881, the provincial population had risen to 108,891 but this rate of increase was not maintained, for the following decennial count showed an increase of only 87. Redistribution in 1892 lowered the Island's representation to five seats. This was only the beginning, for the population began a sudden decline from its all-time high of 109,078 in 1892 to 103,259 in 1901.[3] Three years later, redistribution again implemented the conclusions of this numeration and Prince Edward Island was cut to four seats. The handwriting was long on the wall; now it was too noticeable to be ignored. In only 12 years the province had lost two of its federal seats. Unless the usual rules regarding the redistribution and federal representation were modified, Prince Edward Island was in danger of becoming the first province in the federation without any voice in the House of Commons. To compound the result, the penalty of decreasing representation was being extracted from the province through what was largely no fault of its own. By losing one seat when its population was increasing, the province was suffering a decreased role in the House of Commons simply because its population refused to grow at the very time when a rapid expansion rate was being set by other sectors of the nation. The second seat that was forfeited fell victim to a declining local population in the province. But, to Islanders it seemed grossly unfair that they were entitled to only four seats when their population was still 10% higher than the 1873 count by which they had merited six members.

Even before Queen's county was left as the sole dual-constituency, the Island's provincial government began appeals to stem this tide of decreasing representation. Premier Arthur Peters was unsuccessful in his negotiations with the Laurier government in 1903, when the Island delegates claimed that any reduction in federal representation was contrary to the original union bargain of 1873. Initially, none of the other provinces would support the Island's claims. However, when New Brunswick found itself in the position of losing federal members, it joined the Island in an appeal to the courts. The Supreme Court of Canada reminded the provinces that the Confederation agreement included allowances for readjustments in representation, a view upheld in the subsequent appeal to the (British) Judicial

Committee of the Privy Council. When the chief lawyer for the provinces, A. B. Aylesworth, became the federal Minister of Justice in 1905, the provinces hoped he would continue his support for their claims. But, as a cabinet minister, Aylesworth ceased to press the view he had once been paid to advocate to the judiciary.[4] When Premier Peters died in 1908, the issue of the Island's waning voice was still a sore and unsettled subject.

The province hoped by some means or miracle to revert to its original status of six federal Members of Parliament. To effect this, it urged that the British North America Act be amended so that a minimum floor on provincial membership in the House of Commons would be set at the number of representatives allocated to each province when it joined Confederation. This would not only safeguard the Island's position, for it would guarantee that no province was penalized for either a relative or an absolute decrease in its population as a proportion of the national total. At the same time, any such provision contained an inherent implication for the future composition of the Lower Chamber: the total membership of the House of Commons would increase by necessity, if any of the provinces were to be justly rewarded for a growth in population fairly reflected in federal representation. It was undoubtedly for this reason, at least in part, that the federal government vetoed such a proposal.

While the Island's new Premier, F. L. Haszard, clung to power with a shaky balance of 16 seats in the 30-member provincial Assembly, he indicated his government was prepared to fight the issue to the stage of "rebellion."[5] The province joined other provincial governments in a number of conferences which unsuccessfully attempted to resolve the problem. The Speech from the Throne, opening the 1911 session of the Island Legislature, united an expression of optimism for the outcome with a plea to federal members to consider the issue with their usual sense of justice and fairness.[6] Some compromise between justice and rebellion was needed, for the 1911 census revealed the Island's population had dropped to a new low of 93,728.

The overthrow of the Liberal government in the provincial election of January 3, 1912, did nothing to dim the significance of the new statistics. Unless a solution was reached, and reached soon, the dual-constituency of Queen's county would be shaved to one member and the Island would be sending only three representatives to Ottawa. During 1913, attempts at settlement included an unsuccessful conference between the federal government and the Maritime provinces. It was not until the eve of the fiftieth anniversary of the Charlottetown Conference, 1914, that Tory Premier J. A. Mathieson negotiated a satisfactory compromise with the Ottawa government of Sir Robert Borden. While the Island delegates clung to their demand for six federal representatives, they initially modified this stand only to the extent that they were prepared to forego a constitutional amendment if suitable guarantees were incorporated in the forthcoming representation bill. The Conservative Prime Minister bargained on the basis of four members for the Island province. The compromise settled on four seats as the minimum representation for Prince Edward Island, with an amendment made to the British North America Act in order to guarantee the agreement and, incidentally, to sweeten the bargain. By this means, Queen's County survived as one of the two remaining (federal) dual-constituencies in Canada, until the redistribution of 1965 abolished both the Queen's and Halifax (Nova Scotia) ridings. The redistribution, now in effect, has divided the Island into four constituencies which ignore county divisions in favour of population distribution within the province. The guarantee of four seats — now called Egmont, Malpeque, Hillsborough and Cardigan — is protected by the 1915 constitution amendment known as the "Senate floor." This provision enacted the resolution that no province should have fewer members in the House of Commons than it has in the Senate, a safeguard for federal representation which is now sought by several other Canadian provinces.

Even before Prince Edward Island lost this measure of its numerical status in the national capital, the province housecleaned its local institutions. In a typically political compromise, it brushed the dirt under the rug instead of sweeping it out the door! By 1856 the province's 83-year-old Assembly contained thirty members, elected on a franchise that had evolved until it corresponded closely to a universal adult male suffrage.[7] Each of the three counties returned eight members from four constituencies, all of a dual nature. The remaining six members came from the two-seat ridings of the three county capitals: Georgetown in King's County, Charlottetown in Queen's County, and Princetown in Prince County.[8] The Assembly administered the colony in conjunction with a Legislative Council, a twelve-member committee initially appointed by the Governor. With the granting of Responsible Government and a gradual change in the balance of power between Assembly, Council and Governor, together with the trend in the British parliamentary system toward elected institutions, the Council was reformed to an elected body in 1862.[9] Because the provinces, by and large, retained their original colonial constitutions on their individual entries into Confederation, Prince Edward Island's local political institutions survived this transformation in status. An elected upper house of 13 members — four from each county, sub-divided into two dual-constituencies, and one from Charlottetown — chosen by property-owning electors, governed the affairs of the new province along with the Assembly and the Governor.

Consequently, at the same time as Prince Edward Island was enjoying the status of having six representatives in the House of Commons, its more local affairs were conducted by two chambers of government at the provincial level.

When the trend in many Canadian provinces, in the 1880's and 1890's, pointed to the abolition of second chambers, Prince Edward Island hesitated. The financial pressures which made such a move desirable were countered by vested interests propounding the theory that landowners had a greater stake in political affairs than the common folk. Throughout the decade of the 1880's, attempts at reform had proven futile. To placate differences in what had become a bitterly-contested issue, a compromise was born. The result was an amalgamation of the two bodies. While some observers hailed such a solution as the death-knell of the Legislative Council, the bargain did not ensure the Assembly's survival without the ghost of the Council's demise.[10] More significantly for the future course of political events on Prince Edward Island, the bastardized Legislative Assembly, designed in 1893, began an electoral system that remained unique in the annals of Canadian politics.

From 1893 until 1963 the electoral system remained virtually untouched in substance. Prior to the provincial balloting of 1966 the political stage of the province was highlighted by the thirty members of the Legislative Assembly elected periodically by this novel scheme. In terms of electoral boundaries and the corresponding distribution of members, the practices for the Assembly were simply continued: each county returned ten members in five dual-seat constituencies, with two members in each county representing the three county towns.[11] The innovation of 1893 lay primarily in the franchise that was enacted: half of the members of this new, amalgamated Legislative Assembly were to be elected by means of the old Assembly franchise [which meant virtually universal made suffrage], while the remaining fifteen members were to be elected by the old Council requirements, the outstanding characteristic of which was a property qualification of $325. In practice, this meant that within each dual-constituency there was one candidate from each party, styled an Assemblyman, to be elected by resident males over twenty-one years of age. His teammate, the Councillor candidate, was elected by those who owned property valued at $325 or more, with the potential voter declaring what his property was worth to him in order to claim the property vote. To provide added protection to these stipulations, the Election Act of 1893 contained a further clause which forbade any future changes in the proportion of Councillors in the Legislative Assembly unless such proposed alterations received the consent of a minimum two-thirds of the Assembly's membership. Although the property-owning provisions of the franchise and this dual composition of the Assembly were novel features, the complexity and peculiarities of the system did not lie entirely in these aspects. The uniqueness of the voting system was ensured when these provisions were allowed to co-exist with multiple voting practices.[12]

Multiple or plural voting permitted the property owner to vote in any constituency where he owned property. The rationale for the weighted political voice of landowners was derived from an assumption that such owners had a vested interest in the district where their property was located, even if they themselves did not make their usual residence there. Because of this interest, the landowner was entitled to exercise suitably proportional political influence through the institution of elections, or so the theory went. The logical conclusion would seem to be a practice whereby non-resident landowners were enfranchised to vote for Councillor candidates, who were in theory the representatives of propertied interests. It would also seem logical that non-resident landowners would not be able to influence the election of Assemblyman members, for these representatives would appear to be the embodiment of a principle close to that of the "one man, one vote" philosophy. But multiple voting did not follow such logical conclusions, either in law or in practice, when Islanders went to the polls.

Under the provisions for multiple voting, the male citizen who owned property, valued at $100 or more and located outside of his constituency of residence was permitted to cast a ballot for the Assemblyman candidate in the riding where his property was located. If such property was valued at more than $325, the elector could vote for both Assemblyman and Councillor candidates in the electoral district where this property was found. Again, it was the individual elector who set the monetary value of his property. It was possible, of course, for a voter to own property in several electoral districts while not being a property owner in his constituency of residence. In such a case, the elector could cast a ballot for the Assemblyman candidate in his residency riding, as well as exercising his multiple voting rights in electoral districts where his property was located. However, multiple voting was not affected by multiple property ownership within one constituency: possession of different properties in the various polls of one constituency, for example, did not entitle the elector to more ballots. The legal maximum number of votes which any one voter could cast was therefore limited to 30 — one ballot for each seat in the province. To exercise this measure of political weight involved possession of fifteen properties, each subjectively valued at a minimum $325 and each located in one of the fifteen constituencies. The inequalities of such a system are obvious: the man with property in every electoral district, to cite the extreme example, had more opportunity to influence the outcome of elections — 15 times more, to be exact — than the man with equal-valued property located within the boundaries of a single constituency.[13]

Yet such was the electoral system of Prince Edward Island. The Election Act of 1893 was repealed less than 30 years later but the system continued in substance with the new legislation. The Election Act, 1922, was primarily a consolidation of the earlier enactments, for it contained only one major change. The addition of the female franchise was the principal reason for the electoral legislation at the time. It allowed equal voting privileges for both sexes, although further clarification of this was later required: subsequent amendments in 1926 and 1931 extended the franchise to the spouse of any landowner.[14] In one sense the effect of the 1922 legislation and these later amendments was to heighten the inequalities and absurdities of the whole franchise structure. Henceforth it was possible for a husband and wife, owning a minimum $4,875 worth of property that was suitably divided among the various ridings, to cast a total of 60 votes in each provincial election![15]

Further amendments to the electoral legislation, before its final repeal in 1963, extended the Councillor franchise to various groups of people regardless of whether or not they owned property. War veterans and clergymen with parochial responsibilities were among those affected by such provisions. While such extensions did not enlarge the potential volume of multiple voting, which remained exclusively on a property-owning basis, the effect of these amendments was to further weaken the already diluted correlation between the Councillor franchise and property. At the same time, the electoral system evolved closer and closer to the point where both types of candidates, Councillors and Assemblymen, were elected by almost universal adult suffrage. By the time the system was repealed, almost everyone of age had two votes, while some of the more affluent could still cast anywhere up to thirty ballots.

This evolution towards universal adult suffrage in the Councillor seats was undoubtedly aided by the complexities of the electoral system. Because each additional amendment enhanced the confusion and because election officials varied in their interpretation of the rules, the informally-conducted elections probably had a wider scope of voters than would have been the case if the legislation had been strictly applied, in consistency with the principles on which, supposedly, it was based. More intentional abuses of the system were widespread, their continued growth aided by the lack of electoral lists which were deemed to be a luxury the province could ill-afford to provide.[16] As for multiple voting, it offered the greatest scope for election day abuses and became the most popular game among the parties contending for all the votes they could muster.

Yet, despite these drawbacks, the electoral system stagnated in this growing chaos for seventy years. Or perhaps it would be more truthful to say that the system flourished in that period, for those most concerned with polling outcomes found it both a challenging system in which to operate and one which served the representational requirements of the province. Once elected, there was no differentiation between members except on the basis of party affiliation.[17] It is true that Councillors sometimes felt they represented a more stable electorate, for politicians were inclined to believe there was some correlation between the "floating" voter of no fixed partisan affiliation and the non-propertied voter who could only cast an Assemblyman ballot in his constituency of residence.[18] But once the Councillor or Assemblyman found himself in the Legislative Assembly, his support of or opposition to policy was based almost exclusively on his party ties. Even if an issue directly involved the vested interests of property owners, party lines did not break down in favour of any alignment by the property-representing Councillors. In large measure, this merely reflected the adhesive qualities of partisan loyalty. Yet, in another sense, it was not surprising to find that Councillors did not attempt any significant, exclusive representation for property owners because, ironically, none of the electoral legislation contained any requirement for a Councillor candidate to own property himself!

If the paramountcy of party loyalty in the Assembly suited the elected members, the distinctions between Councillors and Assemblyman were equally expedient for nominated candidates at the polls. Because separate ballots for the two categories of nominees were used, it was not possible to vote, validly, for both Assemblymen, or conversely, for both Councillors. Nor was it possible to exercise a "plumper" vote by casting all possible choices for a single candidate. By this means, the separate categories of candidates ensured that each nominee was pitted only against the partisan opponents on his ballot, and not against all competitors in the constituency including his partisan colleague. In this way, the separation created by Councillor and Assemblyman labels provided an elaborate safeguard against the potential disadvantages inherent in any one-ballot, multi-seat constituency.

The system also enabled the parties, if they wished, to practice political strategy in positioning their candidates on the ballot. In a constituency where party margins were small, the stronger candidate could be positioned against the individual most considered to be the opposition's stronger contender. Should a party conclude that the best it might win in a riding would be one of the two seats, it could place the more likely vote-getter of its two candidates against the opposition's weaker rival. Since the system offered such a potential for juggling candidates in terms of this type of subjective political analyses, it is surprising that the parties rarely attempted to jockey their candidates in this fashion. The lack of such pairing tactics, so readily implied in this type of dual-constituency franchise system, is understood only in the light of the one variable which was long of primary importance to Islanders and which the franchise dichotomy between candidates did express most vividly — religion.[19]

The role of religion in the politics of Prince Edward Island has always been a curious one. In a population that is largely homogeneous in many respects, the most contentious variables in existence were only those of religion and politics. Strangely enough, the proponents of these two variables were almost evenly divided: about 50% of the population were Roman Catholics with the remainder composed of the members of several Protestant churches, while the popular support for Liberal and Conservative parties was almost evenly balanced. Throughout Island history some of the bitterest and hottest political issues have been fought over religious questions, or at least over matters tinged with the politics of church organizations.[20] In the midst of these emotional disputes the political parties have long experienced the problem of dissociating themselves from the risks attendant to any close alliance between a specific political party and one particular religious camp. This has not always proved easy in a province where earnest and strong convictions in both religion and politics have permeated many voters and where all too often the ghostly hand of clerical influence has been attributed to political issues and decisions far removed from the politics of the pulpit. No doubt this fear of a partisan alignment motivated the long-continued legislation which excluded clergymen from elected political office in provincial politics, a legal provision that was not repealed until 1967. Certainly it was an attempt to protect themselves from all possible political inexpediencies that led the parties to place such emphasis on the religion variable in the selection and nomination of candidates.

In applying this consideration of religious affiliation to the electoral system, the parties essentially tried to ensure that the opposing contestants for each seat in the Legislative Assembly were of the same religion. This would guarantee that voters did not support a particular candidate solely on the strength of the nominee's religious adherence. This did not mean, however, that all Councillor candidates were Roman Catholics and that all Assemblymen were Protestants or vice versa. No one-to-one correspondence was ever established between the property representatives and a particular faith. Nor did this convention ensure that both religions received equal representation among the candidates of both parties, and hence, among the elected Assembly members. The pattern principally guaranteed that each candidate would face a political opponent of a compatible religious faith.

Nine of the Island's fifteen provincial constituencies attempted to provide representation for both Protestants and Roman Catholics in the elections after 1893. In order to do so, each party nominated one candidate of each faith, with the nominees suitably paired to prevent voters from splitting their ballots in favour of religious compatriots. Which religion was represented on the Councillor ticket and which on the Assemblyman ticket depended on nothing more than local traditions in each individual riding and, on occasion, the placement of candidates by the political party first nominating in the district. For example, the Roman Catholic Assemblyman incumbent who decided to further his chances for re-election by appealing solely to property owners could be nominated in the Councillor slot, but only if the other party had not yet finalized the relative position of its slate of candidates in the constituency. Should his party be first to choose their contestants and duly honour his request to seek the Councillor seat, his opponents would respond by nominating a Catholic Councillor and a Protestant Assemblyman. Such manoeuvres were rare, but even more infrequent were instances where the religion conventions were broken, for such precedents almost invariably occurred only when a party could not find a suitable candidate of the "proper" religion.

The pattern of representation for religious interests was markedly different in the six remaining constituencies. In the electoral districts of Second Prince, Fourth Prince, First Queens, Second Queens, Fourth Queens and Fourth Kings, all of which had Protestant majorities in the populations within their constituency boundaries, the nominated candidates were usually all of the Protestant faith. Occasionally, one or more of the other nine electoral districts would produce two complete slates of Roman Catholic nominees, but this was an exception. Only when all candidates in a constituency represented one religion was there any scope for a strategy of jockeying for position on the ballots. The result of this pattern was that the Assembly usually contained nine Roman Catholics and twenty-one Protestants, regardless of party standings. Any attempts to change the system, even the inadvertent disregard for these conventions occasioned by the scarcity of potential candidates, seemed doomed to failure. Whether through coincidence, a reflection of the party's desperation in such a constituency, or popular disapproval stimulating appropriate punishment for breaking tradition, the candidate who departed from the "proper" religion on the ballot was almost invariably defeated. Paradoxically, this "gentlemen's agreement," as it was so often termed, was designed to "keep religion out of politics," and yet, by its very nature, it managed to place religion in a very central and dominant role in political life.

Local concern with representation for religious interests and with the influence of religious groupings in political life did not necessarily extend to any advocacy or practise of Christian ethics during an election campaign. Since the electoral system facilitated this preoccupation with religion in political considerations, one might expect that an associated pattern of customs, consistent with certain underlying religious principles, would also permeate the conduct of elections. On the contrary, the curious elements that contributed to the novelty of the electoral system were matched by the originality of the abuses openly displayed in the applied use of this system on election day.

If nothing else, the franchise that governed provincial elections in Prince Edward Island did add colour to the conduct of political campaigns. Barring those rare occasions when controversial issues — or, better yet, full-fledged scandals — jar the relative calm of the political surface, elections are probably the most exciting time in the steady flow of events in political life. An evenly balanced match, conducted by complex rules which, nevertheless, contain vital omissions and vague provisions, promises unlimited potential for interest and expectations. Prince Edward Island's provincial elections contained all the needed ingredients for such an entertaining contest at the polls. Rarely were the pundits, the public or the politicians disappointed in the calibre of the show.

The electoral system provided a suitable mechanism to enhance the inherent stimulation of an election campaign. The novelties of the electoral legislation, particularly the franchise provisions, flavoured elections with a taste as peculiar in political life as Malpeque oysters in gourmet circles. The absence of any definition of what constitutes "property", for example, enabled candidates and voters alike to exercise the limits of their creative imaginations. Gravel pits, cranberry bogs, blueberry patches, fishing shacks and duck blinds assumed the same importance as farms, businesses and summer cottages on election day. One ingenious voter attempted to claim the property vote in a constituency where he had purchased a graveyard plot. He was refused a ballot — otherwise, he might have begun a precedent which would have stimulated the popularity of cemetery real estate.[21]

The extent to which discretion was evident in the interpretation of the electoral legislation is best illustrated by the strange rules contained in "Instructions to Liberal Agents and Workers, 1947", under the heading "Notes on Councillor Vote":

The interest in land may be either freehold or leasehold. Freehold means when the voter owns the land; leasehold means when he rents the land. But no one can vote for Councillor on rented land if the rent he pays is a fair rental value for the premises.

For instance, John Brown rents a house from James Smith by the year at $400.00 per annum. Ten percent is usually considered a reasonable rental on the value, so let us suppose the house is worth $4,000. In that case John Brown has no vote for Councillor. But suppose soon after Brown rented the house the value of the land went away up in that neighbourhood, (discovery of oil, for instance) and Brown was able to turn around and sublet or rent the house again to Tom Jones for $325 more than he had to pay Smith, then Brown (and his wife) would have a vote for Councillor. That covers the short term lease, such as a year or so, or less than a year or so.

But sometimes land is leased for a very long time, sometimes even 999 years. The longer the lease, the less would be the amount that Brown would have to be able to charge Jones per year, over and above what he had to pay Smith. And on a long term lease such as over 100 years, leasehold land is practically the same as freehold for the purpose of a councillor vote. Another point: Suppose Brown had rented the land only, from Smith, and then Brown had build [sic] a building on it, thereby raising its value by $325.00, it would give him a vote for councillor.[22]

Small wonder that party workers used individual interpretations when presented with instructions like these. Needless to say the author of such instructions allowed his imagination to range, for the electoral legislation made no mention of any "fair rental value" concept nor any distinction between leasehold and freehold property as separate components of the Councillor vote.

One of the greatest potentials for abuses was inherent in the absence of provisions concerning *intestate* property. When a property owner died without leaving a will it was not uncommon for all of his heirs to claim a property vote on the basis of this property. Should such property lie in more than one constituency the heirs and their spouses would practice multiple voting. A related abuse stemmed from joint ownership of properties, particularly recreational properties. While joint ownership did entitle all owners to property votes, in theory at least the property should have been worth at least $325 times the number of joint owners. This was not always the case, as in the instance of ten men from Charlottetown who all claimed multiple voting privileges by virtue of their joint ownership of a duck blind in the Tracadie area. While they did not compound the outrage by bringing their wives to the polls, there was nothing to stop them from doing so, for no one, save themselves, could claim they did not value their hunting hideaway at a penny less than $3,250.

Such abuses were borderline, within the letter of the law even though they violated its spirit and intention. But the trick of producing voters who professed to own property in a district when, in fact, they could make no such legitimate claim, was an offence. The fine was $16 for each such offence, a small financial slap that was insufficient to worry the most amateur ballot box stuffer. And the lack of official lists made it difficult to police the elections in any way that would curb such abuses of the system. True, the parties usually had rough voters' lists compiled by using the local school district's tax assessment rolls. But the parties were naturally adverse to using any such guides in a concerted effort to counteract the very vices which they themselves perpetrated. At the same time, such lists were often anything but completely accurate, for almost every district had its own un-used properties whose owners were long forgotten. The proof of this situation was verified by the party strategy of employing a lawyer to search out land titles just prior to an election campaign.

If property and multiple voting enhanced the opportunity for election-eering hanky-panky, the transportation of voters involved in such practices increased the efforts needed by the parties to use organized chaos to their own advantage. Each poll was supplied with an automobile network by the parties so that voters could obtain transportation to the polls. In an age where the private automobile had not become a common household adjunct, the efficient organization of transportation was a necessary prerequisite on voting day. And when some voters were in need of transportation to several districts in the province, the mileage driven on election day mounted. Nor was all election day driving in a straight line from poll to poll. Since some voters were thought to be more favourably disposed to the party who pro-vided their conveyance to the polls, there was frequently a scramble to be the first to pick up the undecided voters. The son of one candidate related his first experience at transporting electors to the ballot stations. His instruc-tions were to proceed, in company with two additional cars and drivers, to a small settlement of Indians at 5 a.m. on election day. The miniature motor-cade then drove leisurely around the province until the polls opened some four hours later. They were on route from Souris to Charlottetown at 7 a.m. when they witnessed the opposition's arrival at the vacant Indian residences. After this extended tour of the countryside, the passengers remarked on how much they loved election day, for they said it was such a wonderful opportunity to have a pleasant drive through new and different areas of the Island!

Whether or not the parties were called on to transport a voter to the polls, they were often asked to grease his palm or quench his thirst. A quart of cheap rum was the usual answer to the latter request while $5 was often the price paid for an individual's integrity. If the stakes were high, the contest close and the parties rich, the fee might be doubled to $10 or perhaps even higher. Because the parties felt it necessary to court the doubt-fuls in this fashion while simultaneously rewarding the continued support or reliable friends, election treats added up to a sizeable bill. Voters con-sidered this their due, their compensation for exercising their democratic duties. Those who rarely indulged in the drinking pastime saved their supply for Christmastime nips, while ladies of temperance promotion usually opted for straight cash.[23] Seasoned veterans of election campaigns reported they were shocked on occasion to find some staunch pillar-of-the-community refusing transportation to the polls unless compensated for his time and effort. The confidential list of "requirements" for one political party included, for example, a poll of 125 voters with party needs for the particular campaign listed as 127 quarts of rum and $30.[24] Obviously a few voters merited more than the average rum ration in that poll.

Despite such generosity, the parties had little control over whether or not their favours were actually recognized at the polls once the secret ballot was established in 1913. These practices involving the "purchase" of votes were by no means legal, of course. While candidates were usually aware of their existence, it was frequently deemed safer and more expedient to allow party supporters to handle the administration of such deals.[25] On occasion, this led to abuses of the abuses. It was not a rare practice for party workers to dilute the liquor supplies so that more would be left for themselves while the average fellow was bribed with a weakened potion.

Long overdue reform of the electoral system did not stem primarily from a conscious effort to arrest the abuses found in such polling practices. True, the reforms did end the border-line violations inherent in some of the claims for multiple voting privileges. But the renovations of the electoral system did little to halt some of the practices which attend the conduct of most, perhaps all, Canadian elections.

The main thrust of the electoral changes in the early 1960's was initially aimed at a redistribution of seats in the Legislative Assembly. The abolition of both multiple voting and the property-based franchise were secondary, incidental results of these recent alterations in election rules. While it was largely political expediency that caused the long delay in reform, it was, simultaneously, this same factor that ultimately led to innovations in the election procedures.

Because Prince Edward Island has experienced a long history of close elections, both parties were reluctant to alter the electoral system, since reform might produce adverse results for the political party responsible for any such major alterations. Most voters in the province appear to maintain, for long periods of time, a traditional adherence to one of the two major political parties. Rarely do third parties appear on the scene and, except for John A. Dewar's victory as an Independent in 1919, no successful candidate has ever campaigned on anything but a Liberal or Conservative label. At the same time, the two old-line parties appear to be almost evenly balanced in terms of their popular support.

The first-past-the-post principle, employed in Canadian elections, customarily results in a disproportionate ratio between the popular vote and the number of seats gained by a political party. In the nineteen general elections between 1893 and 1963, this was illustrated in the provincial polling outcomes.[26] Of the 570 members elected in these province-wide contests, the Liberal party had 354 winning candidates with only 51.4% of the popular vote. Although they received an average of 47.8% of the popular vote in these provincial pollings, the Conservatives seated only 215 men, less than 40% of the possible number of seats. When by-elections are included in such an analysis, the trend is not significantly altered. As is so often the case in political life, neither party wished to initiate electoral reform, for each feared that changes might ultimately favour their opponents.

Such hesitation was compounded by additional factors peculiar to the Island's situation. Uncertain as to which party benefited most from the curious franchise arrangements and uncomfortably familiar with the narrow margins of victory in many electoral districts, both Liberals and Conservatives were loath to herald any reform that might risk losses.

Some degree of natural affinity between the Conservative party and the property-owning class of society was an assumption that has long pervaded Canadian political circles. Yet, in the time span from 1893 to 1963, the Liberals elected 172 Assemblymen and 182 Councillors, while the Conservative members victorious in these 19 general elections included 112 Assemblymen and 103 Councillors. The property based candidates would seem to have had a slight greater favour with the Liberal party. The growing underrepresentation of the urban areas, particularly the Charlottetown constituency which was regarded a Conservative stronghold, was a further consideration. In view of these diverse assessments, both parties were naturally reluctant to endanger their own position by disturbing the *status quo*.

The small Island constituencies, together with the matched attractions of the political parties, frequently resulted in narrow margins in the electoral outcome, a further reason to tread cautiously whenever changes in the electoral system were proposed. Ten per cent of all elected representatives owed their seats to twenty-five votes or less. Over one-third [37%] of all provincial members had gained their seats in general elections by margins of 100 votes or less. Disregarding any members elected by acclamation, only three of the 570 successful candidates had majorities of 1,000 votes or more.[27] Because of the extensive number of close seats a very tiny shift in votes often meant a difference of several seats. For example, the Liberals won the election of 1943 with 20 of the 30 seats, but a shift in less than one hundred votes would have given the Conservatives an identical majority in the Assembly. Under such circumstances, even the smallest change in the rules of the game might affect the results, a gamble that neither party was willing to take.

Nevertheless, reform might have occurred earlier than it did had it not been for the fact that the Liberals retained power for a stretch of some twenty-four years. Since the electoral system had provided the Liberals with the reins of government in twelve of the nineteen contests, they were naturally the least likely of the contending parties to initiate measures which might ultimately disrupt the success of their past performance. However, by 1959, when Walter Shaw swept the Conservatives out of the wilderness and into office, the outmoded distribution of seats throughout the province pointed to glaring examples of disproportionate representation. The prime example was Charlottetown which claimed only two seats in the Assembly while its population was nearing 20% of the provincial total. A fair redistribution would greatly increase the proportion of urban members in the Assembly. If the Conservative edge in the Charlottetown area could be projected for future elections, wouldn't redistribution offer an inherent assistance to the Conservative party in elections yet to come? Premier Shaw's party were willing to gamble that the answer might be found in the affirmative and reform was underway.[28]

Actually, it was the Liberals who initially campaigned, halfheartedly, for electoral reform in the 1959 election trials. Liberal Premier A. W. Matheson promised to eliminate the property qualifications for electors and hinted that the end of multiple voting was in sight. He also proposed that single constituencies be established, but the electoral reform plank in the Liberal platform was not one that caught fire.[29] When the Speech from the Throne opening the session of 1961 included a proposal to investigate the existing system, *The Guardian* which "covers the Island like the dew," credited the Conservative party with fulfilling Tory electoral promises.[30]

The Shaw government originated reform procedures by first appointing a royal commission, a step that handed the Liberals sufficient ammunition for sarcastic comments on the utility — or, more accurately, the futility — of royal commissions. Disregarding these reproaches, Premier Shaw appointed an inquiring agency under the chairmanship of Judge J. S. DesRoches. The city of Charlottetown mounted a pressure campaign requesting ten seats for the capital city, while Summerside joined the bandwagon asking for four representatives. The urban centres were opposed by several individuals, each armed with briefs, comments, petitions or opinions, and by the Federation of Agriculture. The arguments raged back and forth with the local press providing the forum for debate throughout the next year.

The *Report of the Royal Commission on Electoral Reform* was made public in March of 1962. While the report urged the abolition of multiple voting, it distinguished between multiple voting and the property vote. A property qualification for Councillor electors should be retained with the value of qualifying property raised from $325 to $1,000, the Royal Commission urged. As for redistribution, the report suggested that Queen's County be given two additional seats at the expense of King's County, so that the total membership in the Assembly would remain at thirty. Nothing had been done about this report when the Assembly dissolved in 1962, so the province went to the polls again under the old rules.

But the balloting on December 1 of that year subsequently proved to be the last contest for both property qualifications and plural voting processes. The bill introduced in the session of 1963 went further than the Royal Commission had recommended: universal suffrage for all seats, the appointment of a chief electoral officer and the establishment of a system of enumeration to produce voters' lists were among the chief features of the proposed legislation. However, the initial draft made no mention of redistribution and changes in this respect were introduced by means of amendments when the bill was in the committee stage for second reading.

When Conservative Hubert MacNeil sponsored an amendment to place Summerside in the Fifth District of Prince, while the surrounding areas were divided among the Third and Fourth Districts of that county, the Liberals cried "gerrymander". The motion was passed on straight party lines, leaving the storm to descend on the second amendment. Conservative M. A. Farmer introduced the controversial measure that would give Charlottetown two additional seats while leaving total membership in the Assembly at thirty. The implication was clear: the electoral districts in King's County would be reduced by two seats. The fat was in the fire so far as King's County members were concerned.

The Guardian proceeded to add a few drops of kerosene to the blaze by suggesting the introduction of these redistribution provisions had been postponed until the federal election of April 8 had passed into history. Only in this way, charged the press, could the controversy be delayed so that it would not result in a loss of Tory votes in either of the Prince or King's county federal constituencies. If this were not so, the editorial claimed, then such important omissions were due to "a plain case of bungling in drafting the legislation."[31]

The Speaker of the Assembly John R. MacLean, told the House, assembled in committee, that he was not in agreement with the Farmer amendment and, while urging postponement, suggested his dismay over the possibility of voting against his own government. When the count was

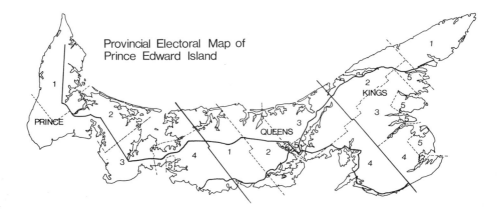

Provincial Electoral Map of Prince Edward Island

taken on the amendment — the one major recommendation by the Royal Commission that was to be followed — MacLean abstained and another King's county colleague, Walter Dingwell, joined Liberal ranks in an unsuccessful bid to defeat the motion.[32]

The 1963 Election Act modernized the system of conducting elections in the province. Dual ridings were retained but all candidates were to be elected on a universal franchise basis. "One man, one vote" — or, rather, "one man, two votes" — became the simple principle underlying the new system. With the various provisions for enumerators, voters' lists, and certain election officials, together with more realistic regulations governing the various activities associated with a campaign, elections were destined to become more formalized, sophisticated and serious in the province. Nevertheless, the legislation still retained the separate categories for Assemblymen and Councillors, even though all distinction between them apparently had been obliterated.

Three reasons might be suggested to account for this retention. The first — and certainly the least valid — reason was the one popularly expounded by the politicians and press: the old terms were being retained, even though they had been rendered meaningless, because of their "historical significance."[33] If that were the real reason it was probably the first time in history that politicians placed a priority on sentiment.

A more realistic reason for retaining the old labels and their corresponding separation of candidates was one of political expediency. So long as each group of contenders for a particular seat remained as a distinct set of candidates on one ballot, each candidate was opposing only those nominees who did not belong to his own political party. However, in a

Legislative Assembly — Prince Edward Island 1931

multiple seat constituency, whether a dual riding or larger, a single ballot for all political rivals meant that contestants would be exposed to the additional and "cut-throat" competition of their own party colleagues. In the electoral district where every voter was entitled to two votes, the placement of all candidates on a single ballot would mean that, for example, each Liberal faced competition from not only his two Conservative opponents but the more embarrassing rivalry of his own running-mate as well. A further implication of such a practice would be the confusion which this would invoke among voters. With the ever present inadequacy of knowledge relating to political matters among some members of the general public, there would no doubt be a few who would only cast one of their votes and thereby lose half of their potential influence at the polls. Others would no doubt compound personal confusion by voting for more than two candidates, particularly in any contests with a slate of more than four nominees. In addition, the dual constituency using a single ballot offered an opportunity for the "plumper" vote, where the elector could cast all his choices in favour of one individual. The "plumper" vote practice distorts the principles underlying representation, while simultaneously enhancing internal party competitions among each pair of partisan partners. Such considerations were more valid reasons for retaining the distinctions between Councillor and Assemblyman than any justification in vague terms that implied a lip-service to tradition.

Finally, the maintenance of Councillor and Assemblyman tickets meant that the religious conventions associated with the selection of proportions of religious representation in the House would not be altered in practice by any side-effects from the new legislation. While there is some evidence to indicate that this was a deliberate manoeuvre, the implications of which were fully appreciated in some political circles, no comment was made in either parliament or press when the Election Act, 1963, was debated.[34] Perhaps this omission stemmed from the feeling that geographical representation was a more vital issue than religious representation. More likely, it would seem that political discretion deemed that neither party would stand to gain by opening religious wars concurrently with urban-rural rivalries. If the continuation of the old convention to "keep religion out of politics" was the muted implication behind the vague references to "historical significance", then it has been hasty to condemn the parties for their tribute to tradition!

While the retention of the Councillor and Assemblyman categories did not cause even a murmur on the public scene, the same can not be said about the amendment that was to "deprive" the Fifth District of King's of its two-seat constituency. In the turmoil of the tempest, it seemed as if the public in the Georgetown area thought they would actually be placed outside the electorate, never again represented in the Legislative Assembly by any member whatsoever. They were losing their district, their members, their franchise. They would be treated as if they were no longer part of the Island, or so the outraged cry of these voters seemed to imply.

In actual fact, the amendment simply proposed to alter the existing boundaries of the five constituencies in King's County in such a way that four new constituencies would be formed. This would provide the decreasing population of the area with provincial representation that more closely paralleled their proportion of the Island's total number of electors. Fifth Kings would cease to exist as a separate constituency, but not just because it would be numerically extinct. In its geographical formation, the Fifth District of Kings was the most natural riding in the county to undergo absorption into the other districts, for it was a constituency composed of geographical remnants. Originally, Georgetown and Common, the capital seat of King's County, was the sole component of the district. However, as Georgetown declined in population, the constituency began to include scattered areas from the land juts between the bays and inlets of the Island's south-eastern shores. While some of the constituency's polling divisions looked to Georgetown as their urban centre, others were drawn towards the more bustling areas of Montague and Souris, both located in other electoral districts and therefore represented by different provincial members. The constituency lacked a unity of its own, but threatened with extinction as a separate entity and absorption into the other portions of King's County, the Fifth District rallied around a united cause. The prospect of reducing the county's representation from ten to eight members brought the support of fellow citizens in the other four districts. Unwilling to risk the wrath of the voters at the polls when eight seats were involved, the government relented. On the eve of the 1966 provincial election, an amendment to the Election Act of 1963 restored the Fifth District of Kings as a separate dual riding. Simultaneously, in order to retain Charlottetown's additional constituency of Sixth Queen's, the membership in the Assembly was increased to thirty-two seats.

As the initial test of the new electoral legislation, the provincial contest of May 30, 1966, was an exciting and spectacular debut. The recent attempt at redistribution had already produced a compromise. Based on the discretion of political expediency, it was reminiscent of the bargain that gave birth to the now-displaced system of 1893 and recalled the battle over federal redistribution of a half-century ago. If one of the major goals of the new legislation was the retention of existing religious balances in the Assembly, the 1963 Election Act succeeded admirably, for the sole attempt to depart from the traditional convention in the nominations of the 1966 election resulted in the defeat of the deviating candidate. But if the main thrust of the legislation was an experiment to inculcate more serious, sophisticated, honest and efficient practices into the pageant of political elections, the legislation, at best, fell short of success. The trial initiation of the new legislation demonstrated the failure of any scheme to enact suitable behavioural norms into a public cast that favoured the old ways.

Like all elections in the province, the voters found both familiar and imaginative demands to make on the candidates and their party organizations. The public wanted political jobs for themselves, their families and their friends. They wanted candidates to intervene on their behalf in order to gain pensions, allowances, grants, loans and licences. They wanted roads scraped, highways paved, public buildings constructed, and promises redeemed in practice. And some wanted liquid or monetary benefits in exchange for their support at the polls.

While the public has frequently ridiculed the pledges of politicians and the practices of politics, they would be nothing short of amazed at the ingenuity of their brethren voters if only candidates wrote memoirs on their election experiences. Consider for example, the voter who in the midst of one campaign, ordered up several weeks' supply of groceries at a local store and told the cashier that the incumbent was to receive the bill. Needless to say, it was the first the candidate knew about it! Think of the provincial member whose slumbers were disturbed by a constituent requesting assistance in locating a missing dog. Or, consider the voter who approached one nominee to ask him to co-sign a loan for money. Incidentally, this last example displayed the reciprocal skills of some candidates, for the voter was told to return after the election when they could talk business. "If it ever became known that I co-signed a loan for you the day before election," the candidate told him, "I could end up in court for trying to bribe a voter." The elector left that day, confident that his request would be fulfilled as soon as the campaign formalities concluded. He returned a few days after to see the candidate, who, by then, was a provincial Assembly member. He repeated the request about the loan, only to be told by the politician: "my dear man, I am afraid you misunderstood me. It is entirely against my judgment to co-sign a loan for anyone."

The list of such requests has often been endless and the variety of demands equally tangent on infinity. Yet this has long been the very bread-and-butter essence of grass-roots politics. Few have been the candidates to successfully fly in the face of these traditions. After every election a handful of party supporters have presented candidates with claims for automobile repairs needed as a result of their services in supplying transportation to the polls. The claims have been small: a new set of shocks, or a replaced muffler, perhaps a crumpled fender. Nine times out of ten these have been false, for the vehicle has been damaged either prior to election day or exclusive of political affairs. The politicians have been aware of such petty dishonesty if for no other reason than the fact it has usually been the same people who repeatedly experienced these personal difficulties on polling day! Yet few politicians have been prepared to alienate the good will of their supporters for the price of a few dollars.

Such nuisance expenditures have been nothing in comparison with the funds required to sponsor a full-scale political election. It has been difficult to estimate the cost of political campaigns of the past for several reasons. The amount spent by a particular party in any given election has been varied depending on the organization's affluence from preceding contests in which it has been involved. In modern elections, large portions of campaign budgets have been devoted increasingly to advertising expenditures in media that were perhaps not in existence, or at least in popular use, for earlier pollings. Even if statistics were available, comparisons would be difficult or, at least, confusing, for the value of the dollar has altered and fluctuated over the past century. But the chief reason behind the problem of analyzing campaign budgets has been the discretion practised by the political parties. No other aspect of politics has been surrounded by as much secrecy as the entire area of party financing although enough is known and can be surmised to conclude that elections have always been costly pageants to stage.

Besides protecting party clientele with financial stakes in the campaign, this cloak of silence has saved the electorate from any undue shock which might result from startling revelations that disclose the high cost of pre-election public relations. Like children who stubbornly cling to their faith in Santa Claus, many voters have persisted in a belief that campaign generosity is somewhat akin to an adult Christmas which, alas, comes less frequently than once a year.[35] Few realize that, for example, election day treats in a single constituency has often resulted in a bill in excess of $1,000 for each party. Or that newspaper advertisement alone has cost each political organization $12,000 for a provincial campaign.[36] Most active party supporters have been willing to provide transportation or act as scrutineers on election day — for a fee. Each party, if it has been able to afford it, has spent in modern elections some $50 a poll to provide this type of staff, [excluding the officials needed under the electoral legislation and given remuneration by the provincial treasury]. The paucity of statistics has resulted in an understandable hesitation to place a price tag on a province-wide election, but a total cost of $250,000 would seem to be, if anything, an underestimated guess.

Despite the reforms in the new Election Act of 1963, the subsequent provincial elections provided a continuation of many procedures, demands, abuses and expenditures long familiar from past contests. Like many previous elections, the 1966 campaign, assessed in terms of issues, could charitably be termed "dull."[37] In the midst of all possible seeds for a spectacular political scandal, the most exciting issue to surface was a tired rehash of promises to increase old-age pensions. The election, however, deserved a footnote in history for the precedents it created: this was the first time that all voters were entitled to a universal franchise for both of their representatives and it marked the initial appearance of voters' lists in a provincial campaign. Nevertheless, the election's chief claim to fame resulted not from its importance as a trial practice for a revamped electoral system, but because its unusual outcome far eclipsed any afterthoughts of campaign boredom. Not only did the results produce a tie between the two old-line political parties, but the excitement generated by this rarity was compounded by the subsequent by-election that provided an opportunity to continue or break this deadlock. At the same time, the campaign interval preceding the crucial polling in the First King's constituency focused the limelight on the full potential for excesses which any election can stimulate on a miniature stage.

This curious and unique situation sprung from the culmination of events begun several weeks before the election date of May 30, 1966. Unknown to anyone at the time, the first link in this chain of events was formed when one of the Liberal candidates in the electoral district of First King's died in the interval between the official date for nominations and the appointed day for the provincial election. Under the provisions of the electoral legislation, the death of any duly-appointed candidate prior to the polling date necessitated a postponement of the balloting in that constituency. Because of this, the voting for both seats in the riding was deferred until July 11. Little did the public realize, until after the ballots were counted on May 30, that this unexpected event was to concentrate attention on the eastern tip of Prince Edward Island for six weeks of intense political activity.

As the polling results poured in on that bright spring evening, it soon became obvious that neither party was going to sweep easily into office. The tallies teetered up and down on the television tote boards all evening. When darkness descended over the Island, even the most apathetic electors had begun to realize they were witnessing a contest with more surprise and thrills than the average race. The initial results indicated a slim victory for the Liberals with sixteen of the thirty contested seats. A total of four recounts reduced the party standings to a deadlock of fifteen members apiece, when the unofficial two-vote margin for Liberal Horace Willis in

Second Queen's was reconsidered and became a majority of three ballots for Conservative Lloyd MacPhail. The future role for both parties in the next four years rested on the outcome of the deferred elected in the First King's district. The politicians in all parts of the province accepted the challenge with an earnest dedication that gave the earlier provincial polling the appearance of being merely a dress rehearsal.

The ensuing six weeks resembled the staging of a theatrical farce. The Shaw government, which remained in power until the deferred election decided its fate, presented the first act with transparent disguise. The Minister of Public Works and Highways, Philip Matheson, resigned his portfolio. Although he had been defeated in the May balloting, his move was not duplicated by any of his three cabinet colleagues who had suffered similar losses at the hands of the voters. The Public Works and Highways department, an important key to political patronage, was placed under the jurisdiction of a First King's Candidate. The new minister has never been a member of the Legislative Assembly, so it was undoubtedly coincidence that he merited this executive post at the very time when he was seeking election in the First King's contest! Political balance seemed to be achieved when a leading Liberal, a resident of First Kings, was elevated to a vacant Senate post.

For the benefit of any voters who missed the significance of these ploys the parties had other gimmicks on hand to attract attention and favour. Some observers estimated that the crucial constituency received thirty miles of paving in the midst of the pre-election fever. One local citizen with a sense of humor was moved to erect a prominent sign which read: "PLEASE DON'T PAVE; THIS IS MY ONLY PASTURE." It was widely reported that the government was adopting the slogan: "If it moves, give it a pension; if not, pave it." The party organizations threw away their purse strings, with the price tag on votes reputed to be averaging $100 for anyone on the official lists who wanted it. Those who had more specific preferences requested gifts: a new bathroom replaced the outdoor variety for some, while paved driveways were a popular addition to the residences of the more affluent. Elsewhere in the province, Islanders looked at First King's with envy and jokingly expressed wonder that the eastern tip did not sink under the weight of road machinery. The final day of the campaign drew near amidst a current of rumors throughout the province: some residents even claimed to have witnessed long processions of trucks travelling towards Souris in the middle of the night, their cargoes composed of many cases of the finest liquor.

The parties were organized to a height of efficiency never before witnessed in any Island campaign. Lists of electors were combed and re-combed. Voters were visited and revisited. A small army of politicians and supporters from other parts of the province camped in the constituency. Both parties fully realized that every single vote counted and that each individual with the power of casting a ballot mattered, for the fate of the government rested solely on the collective wishes of less than 3,000 people. Three eligible voters had moved to the constituency of Second King's after the writ of election was issued. One Liberal party worker in that electoral district was assigned to each of these electors. Their instructions were to provide transportation to the polls in First King's. To ensure that there was no difficulty in adhering to these orders, one worker indicated that he watched the sun's appearance while parked in the driveway of the voter assigned to him. Think of the chaos that could have been injected into the deferred election had multiple voting continued to be a feature of Island politics!

After the fever pitch of the campaign was replaced by the tense waiting before the ballots were counted, it seemed almost anticlimactic to learn that the Liberals had won both seats and had consequently defeated the Shaw government.

Elections, however, tell only one segment of the political picture in any province. The conduct of government between campaigns, the substance of policies created by various administrations, and the issues floating in the stream of political events present the complementary portrait in any description of a political scene. Because of Canada's federal system of government, Prince Edward Island's political issues, like those of other provinces, have always been of two general types. Certain subjects are in part or wholly of a national composite and their particular application to the province is primarily a matter of Dominion-provincial relations. Other areas are of local concern and legally fall under the exclusive domain of the provincial government.

Three issues have long dominated or persistently recurred in the Island's relationship with the federal government. The province's representation in Ottawa has been a relatively dormant subject in recent years. It is unlikely to be revived unless the 1915 constitutional amendment is repealed or the province experiences a drastic population influx, neither of which is very probable. The same acquiescence has never been attributed to either transportation or finance. Ever since Islanders found their first railway trip was actually a journey into Canadian Confederation, transportation has been an emotional-ridden concern with sufficient capacity to make or break Island politicians and their parties. The communication-transportation issue has altered in detail the magnitude for the past century, but its fabric has been of a similar design throughout the entire period. Like transportation, the subject of finance has prevaded the Island's relationship with Ottawa since 1873. With limited resources, a small population, and the equivalent responsibilities of any larger province, the problems inherent in finance have always been integral components of the Island's political bloodstream. The province's ability to achieve its standard of living has been primarily at the mercy of federal generosity, a dependence that has dated back to 1873. Today, the federal-provincial finance issue has altered primarily in only one respect: the magnitude of money involved in the issue. From demands for a few thousand dollars, the province's need has risen to several million dollars. Because the Island must attempt to maintain a variety of services at acceptable standards, in comparison with larger and richer provinces, financial matters will no doubt continue to retain a dominant role in Prince Edward Island's federal-provincial relations.

Such issues, although a matter of federal jurisdiction, often became intricately entwined in provincial politics. Provincial political parties, on occasion, found themselves supported or obstructed by the promises, the procrastinations, or the products of their partisan federal cousins. But outside the campaign trail, it was usually the provincial government's leader and his front benchers who carried the Island banner to the negotiating tables and the legendary smoke-filled backrooms of Ottawa. While Island Premiers, and sometimes their cabinets as well, fought, argued, negotiated, pleaded and compromised with Ottawa, they were usually involved, simultaneously but primarily, with issues and concerns that fell under the domain of provincial jurisdiction. Some such matters were of importance to all provinces — education, for example — while others were of a more local interest. Some surfaced for a short time and died; others reappeared again and again; and a few never left the scene.

Up until the post-war era of today, provincial governments in Prince Edward Island were concerned primarily with health, education, agriculture, fisheries, public works and highways, although not necessarily in that order of importance. While all of these areas were necessary facets of government and administration, public works and highways long suffered the greatest potential scope for winning favour with the public. At the same time, mismanagement of institutional or highway projects contained an equally inherent possibility for political losses. A potential scandal over the management of public works in the province led to the original establishment of this administrative department, replacing the old Board of Works in 1876.

The customary concern with public institutions and government-sponsored infrastructure often had political motivations. Like the construction of the railway, the building and maintenance of roads and other capital construction offered a most suitable means to endow political patronage to both individuals and localities. Land purchases, contract awards, expenditure priorities, and other decisions implied in this aspect of political life were long governed by one fundamental rule: reward friends and punish, or at least deprive, enemies.

Apart from these necessary activities of local government, provincial administrations in the Island accomplished little that is reminiscent of governmental activities of today. It was not until after World War II that government assumed a positive role in many areas of provincial life. Until that time, the provincial politicians were happy to devote their time and attention largely to whatever limited projects would gain them greatest favour with their electorate.

It was undoubtedly this rule of thumb which led the Assembly to pass legislation banning the use of automobiles in the province. In a rare moment of non-partisan unanimity, all the elected members voted on March 26, 1908, in favour of a resolution that denounced the operation of automobiles throughout the entire province. When the substance of this resolution was framed into an Act, the few existing automobile owners on the Island challenged the constitutional validity of this measure. An appeal to the federal government brought them its refusal to intervene and veto the Act, while the Supreme Court of Prince Edward Island sustained the legislation the following year. Until the measure was repealed, the controversy continued on an annual basis.

There was substantial popular support for the ban at its initial inception. Following its introduction in the province, the automobile invoked savage hostility and opposition from many residents, particularly rural constituents who argued the new-fangled contraption frightened their cattle, horses, wives and children. Still a small minority were eager to purchase and operate a model of this intriguing invention.

An unsuccessful attempt to have the Automobile Act amended was· staged in 1910. During the ensuing debate the supporters of the law argued that good roads, a province-wide railway system, and the presence of many excellent horses rendered the new vehicle unnecessary. In the short time that automobiles had been allowed to operate, they had severely decreased the volume of trade in Charlottetown, one member claimed in defence of the ban. By 1912, however, opponents of the Act began to gain momentum. They argued that "motor prohibition" was decreasing the revenues from the tourist trade by 50% or some $90,000 annually. While the delegation that called on the Premier that year was not immediately successful in its demands, one item in the Assembly's agenda showed that the ban would not be of long duration. A private bill incorporating the Imperial Motor Company Ltd. was passed during the session. It authorized the firm to manufacture automobile engines and granted the company permission to operate demonstration vehicles in a private park, providing that the speed of such machines did not exceed six miles per hour.

Motor prohibition began to ease in 1913 when the Assembly passed legislation that would allow automobiles to operate on certain highways under very strict regulations. Included in such rules was a specification on which days driving was permitted: automobiles could run on Monday, Wednesday and Thursday of each week, but the ban continued on the other four days. Even these concessions produced considerable controversy, for five Conservatives bolted party ranks and joined the two sitting Liberals in an effort to defeat these reform measures. Soon after, one Minister without Portfolio, Murdoch Kennedy, left the cabinet because of his feelings on this issue. Under the terms of the new legislation, these revised measures did not apply to any electoral district until a majority of voters in each individual constituency signalled their favour in a plebescite. Charlottetown was soon followed by Summerside in a popular acceptance of the automobile. Local plebiscites, held at school district annual meetings, revealed considerable animosity for the new legislation among rural residents. In some constituencies, more than 90% of the voters indicated their opposition to any degree of vehicle operation. It was several years before the entire province accepted the continual operation of automobiles. Even then, rural hostility was slow to die, for older citizens have recalled motoring adventures where their progress was impeded by farmers wielding pitch forks with their wives hurling stones. No doubt automobile ambush was easy in these earlier days, for the initial regulations stipulated that operating vehicles had to be proceeded by an individual on foot bearing a red flag![38]

But the issue that regularly dominated provincial politics for more than half a century was one that still bears controversial overtones. No other legislation ever passed on the Island created more fodder for speeches, sermons, and soliloquies. And yet, no other law was every more consistently and conscientiously broken than the long succession of duly-approved Prohibition Acts.

"I know enough of the feeling of this meeting to know that you would rather have John A. drunk than George Brown sober," the first Canadian Prime Minister once told an election audience. Had he been seeking office as a provincial politician in Prince Edward Island at almost any time in the last century, Sir John A. might have deemed discretion the better part of political expediency, regardless of his personal consumption habits. Prohibition, the movement that attempted to dry out the entire country, was a raging and potent force, recognized and respected — if not wholeheartedly embraced — in Island politics on the strength of its popular acceptance locally.

Prohibition received its initial legal endorsement with the Canada

Temperance Act of 1878. Under the terms of this federal legislation, any constituency could hold a plebiscite to decide whether or not all liquor sales should cease in the area, providing at least 25% of the eligible electors in the district signed a petition to initiate this vote. When the competence of the national Parliament was challenged before the courts, the Judicial Committee of the Privy Council ultimately upheld the federal government's right to legislate on subject matters not specifically assigned to the provincial governments by the B.N.A. Act. However, in a subsequent reference case in 1896, the courts did not seek to curtail completely the powers of the provincial legislatures in promoting temperance legislation. Once the door was opened to this extent, the provinces quickly enacted prohibition measures of their own and Prince Edward Island was one of the leaders in such reforming practices.

The original Island legislation in this subject-matter, "An Act Prohibiting the Sale of Intoxicating Liquor," received the assent of Lieutenant Governor P. A. MacIntyre on June 9, 1900. The Prohibition Act, 1900, contained a specific provision that the provincial legislation would come into effect in each of the counties only when a majority of constituents voted to repeal the Canada Temperance Act. Queen's County accepted the local prohibition measures almost immediately. But it was not until 1906 that the other counties voted to end the national enactments, thus bringing the entire province under the terms of local temperance legislation. Prince Edward Island thereby became the first province to embrace prohibition throughout its whole area.

Under the terms of this legislation, no one could sell or barter any intoxicating liquor unless specifically authorized by the Act. The Lieutenant-Governor-in-Council appointed wholesale vendors, who would sell liquor to druggists, chemists, physicians and clergymen, while government-appointed inspectors would enforce the legislation. Physicians were issued with certificates that indicated alcoholic prescriptions were to be used as medicine and not as a beverage. Maximum daily dosages of such medicine were also spelled out in the law, although these ultimate limits were liberally generous. Druggists who sold liquor for these health purposes were obliged to keep records of all sales, while the government inspectors were authorized to examine the prescriptions and records of the local pharmacists. The provincial legislation also enabled local magistrates to examine any "drunkards" to determine where they obtained their liquor. Failure to satisfy the inquiries of the presiding legal officer would result in a contempt of court charge. Penalties under the law were severe, for a first offence was subject to a fine of $100, or 3 months in jail if the monetary punishment was not met. The onus of proof specifically rested on the defendant who was guilty until proven innocent. No proof that money had changed hands was needed to prove a sale had occurred. Nor did witnesses need to furnish a "precise description" of the liquor involved in order for the prosecution to obtain a conviction. Should an offence be prosecuted by any individual other than an appointed inspector, one-fourth of any fines or penalties collected were offered as a reward to such a prosecutor. Trials were conducted by stipendiary magistrates and no appeals to any other courts were permitted. If these stringent measures were designed to deter all but the very brave, then a high proportion of Island residents seemed to have been exceptionally daring souls.

Although the prohibition movement and the legislation embodying its principles were popularly supported — at least in public — its enforcement was never satisfactory, particularly in the eyes of sincere believers in the cause. Rum-running became a profitable profession, even though its dangers exceeded the boundaries of monetary and penal punishments, for law enforcers used their fire arms to impede offenders. Some medical practioners readily parted with their government-issued booklets of prescription certificates — for a suitable fee. Local bootlegging thrived in many imaginative ways. The ingenious owners of one country estate, equipped with a crude but effective plumbing system, escaped detection and inevitable prosecution for liquor trafficking: the water pipes in the barn were filled with stronger refreshments for the consumption of visitors, rather than for the resident livestock. Many were the fortunes resting on liquidy foundations. And many were the sick who called on their family doctor for the more legitimate alcohol prescription — for medicinal purposes, naturally!

In 1907 the New Brunswick Temperance Commission examined the operation and application of temperance legislation on the Island, with a view to adopting workable provisions in the mainland province. Rev. Thomas Marshall, representing the New Brunswick Temperance Federation on this Commission, told his organization that the Island legislation was favourable in its results in all aspects save one — a considerable increase in the crime of perjury appeared to exist.

Attempts to rid the legislation of its loopholes resulted in a proliferation of amendments, revised sections, and still further suggestions from prohibition advocates. Local temperance groups in 1911, for example, pressed Premier F. L. Haszard to give authorities the right to search private residences suspected of harbouring illicit liquor with the onus of proof regarding legal possession resting on the home owner. The Premier felt the measures were too extreme and refused to incorporate them as amendments to the Prohibition Act. This by no means ended the call for more stringent measures. In January of 1914, a total of 17 trials involving the unlawful sale of liquor were on the court calendars in the province. All were dismissed when both investigators and their evidence mysteriously disappeared before the judicial hearings began. In response to these events, representatives of temperance organizations called on Premier J. A. Mathieson to provide the Prohibition Act with sharper teeth: the right to search for liquor without warrants. This and other equally reactionary suggestions were not followed by the Premier who felt the existing regulations were satisfactorily enforced. Nevertheless, the legislation was revised the following year with the object of tightening controls. While the right to search for liquor without warrant was not granted, a valid warrant now authorized repeated searches within a thirty day period or until liquor was found prior to this expiration date. The Assembly simultaneously indicated its support for the cause when 24 of its 30 members signified their endorsement of the Provincial Patriotic Abstinence League.

The politicians elected to remove the troublesome enforcement of the Act from their own hands by appointing an administrative commission in 1917. The Prohibition Commission consisted of six clergymen, selected equally from the Roman Catholic and Protestant faiths. Their task was to administer the importation and distribution of liquor in the province through the use of one wholesale and several retail vendors. The object of these changes was primarily to curb the influence of druggists and physicians in the prescription of medicinal liquor. The extent of such practices was illustrated by statistics the Commission subsequently released. In the interval between July 15, 1919, and March 1, 1920, a total of 34,200 certificates were issued by doctors in the province. These authorizations to purchase liquor represented some 173 packages of beer, 1,225 cases of whiskey, 1,100 cases of rum, 250 cases of brandy, 55 cases of port wine and 94 cases of gin. Not everyone on the Island upheld a basic belief in temperance! Nonetheless, the prohibitionists still swung considerable support, for a petition by 600 Charlottetown "labouring men," calling for the sale of "stronger beer," was countered by the opposing signatures of some 867 voters and 1,647 non-voters.

The temperance cause received an unexpected blow, delivered from the Bench of the provincial Supreme Court by an ex-Premier in 1922. The local prohibition legislation contained sections which banned the possession of any liquor not purchased from a provincially authorized vendor. While the intention of such enactment undoubtedly was an attempt to regulate and control all liquor purchases by Island residents, these clauses equally applied to imported beverages, a subject with implications relating to intra-provincial commerce. The jurisdiction of the province was questioned when this portion of the Prohibition Act was challenged before the courts. Chief

Justice J. A. Mathieson presided in the case, the verdict of which deemed that legislative competence in this aspect of prohibition was *ultra vires* the provincial government. The six clergymen on the Prohibition Commission resigned following this sentence and the board was reconstructed with lay membership.

The prohibition advocates soon marshalled their forces sufficiently to demonstrate their power and influence in the political life of the province. They were later able to claim that at least one Island government collapsed at the polls by misreading public opinion on temperance. Conservative Premier J. D. Stewart fired the first shot in the 1927 election campaign when he announced that he would seek re-election on a promise to repeal the Prohibition Act. On March 15 he told a Tory banquet gathering that he was prepared to substitute government control over the sale of alcohol beverages for the existing legislation and Prohibition Commission. Strangely, his speech coincided with the opening of the Fourth Session of the Province's 40th Assembly. When Lieutenant Governor Frank R. Heartz delivered the Speech from the Throne earlier that day, any mention of the Prohibition Act was conspicuous by its absence. The Leader of the Opposition, Liberal A. C. Saunders, rebuked the Premier for choosing a feast for the faithful as the site of such a major policy announcement. Although Stewart replied to the charge by asserting that any policy which was not on the session's agenda was excluded from the Throne Speech, the Liberals had already scored a point in the shaping of the issue. With only four members in the House, the Liberal Party in Opposition had almost reached the lowest ebb in its political fortunes, but help was forthcoming.

Following the dissolution of the Assembly on April 12 and the issuance of an election writ for June 25, Saunders called for more stringent enforcement of the existing legislation on Prohibition. He also advocated lower prices for medicinal alcohol and promised, if elected, to hold a plebiscite during the month of July, 1929, in order to determine popular views on liquor prohibition. With that call to arms, various temperance organizations and other associations strongly in favour of prohibition rallied to the support of the Liberals. Their involvement was frequently active and vocal in a campaign that became heated and intense. The Women's Christian Temperance Union and the New Brunswick Temperance Alliance, together with a number of Protestant churches, were among the organizations which buttressed Liberal ranks with orators from outside the province. Their activities while successful, were illegal, for the 1922 Election Act banned any non-resident of the province from canvassing or campaigning in a provincial election — a measure implemented by an earlier Liberal government and designed to end the distorting influences of "outside" interference in local politics. The defiance of their own legislation had happy results for the Liberal Party swept back into office with 24 of the 30 Assembly seats. The new Premier fulfilled at least part of his campaign promises, for the Prohibition Act was not repealed and the plebiscite was held on July 18, 1929. The results of this vote simply echoed the election returns: 11,471 voters favoured Prohibition, while 8,080 wanted the sale of liquor under a Government-control Act.

Nevertheless, prohibition was slowly on the wane as both a popular movement and a political issue. The 1927 election was the last campaign involving the active participation of prohibition advocates. Even though the Island remained "dry" for another two decades, the tempo of reform gradually faded from the headlines in the closing years of the 1920's. A special one-day session of the Assembly was held in September, 1935, following the impressive election of July 23 when the Liberals claimed all 30 seats to become the first Commonwealth Parliament ever elected without any sitting Opposition. When the brief, initial gathering of this novel Assembly quietly abolished the Prohibition Commission and assigned its responsibilities to the Attorney General, there was scarcely a murmur.

Wartime undoubtedly sounded the death-knell for prohibition with enforcement supremely ineffective and abuses intensely magnified. Yet, events in Island politics from 1945 onwards vividly demonstrated that prohibition was not to suffer a silent demise. The Prohibition Bill, 1945, produced a split in the Cabinet, legislation that the Lieutenant Governor did not sign, and a court case to adjudicate the constitutional tangle that ensued. Horace Wright, a Minister without Portfolio, initially sponsored the government bill in the Assembly to alter the grounds for legal possession until he realized that a number of his executive colleagues, including the Premier, did not support the measure. In the midst of his performance, Wright became aware that a number of the Liberal allies actually favoured an amendment that would substantially alter the effect of the legislation he proposed. As soon as he realized that a portion of his party had deserted what he thought was government policy, the Minister without Portfolio announced his resignation to the Assembly. However, pleading that he was under pressure from his constituents to remain in the Cabinet, he never fulfilled his intentions to resign, while Premier J. Walter Jones chose to ignore Wright's proposal to relinquish his executive position. And the Prohibition Amendment Act was subsequently passed by the Assembly.

It was passed, but its ultimately legality was impeded when the Lieutenant Governor withheld his assent to the bill. Customarily, the Lieutenant Governor automatically renders his formal assent to all pieces of legislation that have been duly passed by the Assembly of the day. In rare instances, however, he may choose otherwise: the legislation may be "reserved" for the Governor General of Canada [who may then, should he wish, provide the necessary Assent], or the Lieutenant Governor may refuse to sign the bill, or he may withhold his signature. It was the last alternative that Governor B. W. LePage, without prior warning to his Government, used on April 19, 1945.

His action placed the status of prohibition legislation in question. If legislation is "reserved" for the Governor General, it becomes as valid as any other bills given the formal assent of his provincial representatives, should he decide to agree to a reserved bill. On the other hand, a reserved bill that the Governor General does not sign has the same legal status as one not passed by the Assembly. Similarly, the Lieutenant Governor's refusal to sign a bill "kills" the measure. But, what of a bill to which assent has been "withheld"? Does this indecisive gesture signify the death of the legislation or can it be revived at a later date, without passing through the Assembly again? While the constitutional and legal experts pondered such questions, Lieutenant Governor LePage finished his term of office, His Honour J. A. Bernard took office as his successor, and the Cabinet suggested to the new Governor that he sign the bill. "An Act to Amend the Prohibition Act" was duly signed in September, 1945. Except for further academic discussion, the matter should have ceased to have been relevant at that point.

It did not, for a trival quirk plummeted the tangle to further intricacies. An offence regarding the illegal possession of liquor had been committed under the terms of the Prohibition Act. If, however, the 1945 amendment was valid legislation, the charge did not apply. Chief Justice Thane A. Campbell of the Prince Edward Island Supreme Court probed the implications of a "withheld assent." He decided that the Lieutenant Governor has but one chance to consider a bill — the decision to withhold assent cannot be altered, unless the same legislation is presented to the Governor again by the Assembly. In other words, the 1945 amendment was invalid.

Prohibition, then, remained a way of life on the Island until 1948, when the Temperance Act was passed. This allowed public consumption of alcoholic beverages as refreshments under strict regulations. Administration was in the hands of a three member Temperance Commission appointed by the Lieutenant-Governor-in-Council. Retail outlets were permitted but customers had to obtain licenses in order to make purchases. Two kinds of permits were issued: "individual" permits allowed the owners to buy a maximum of one bottle of spirits or wine or one case of beer in any one week, while a "special" permit enabled druggists, dentists, physicians, clergymen and similiar professional individuals to make purchases required for the purposes specified on their permits. Consumption of liquor, except in a few unusual circumstances outlined in the Act, was confined to the individual's place of residence. The Commission had the authority to grant or refuse permits, as well as the power to cancel any existing permits. Despite these stern measures, the Temperance Act formally marked the end of the Prohibition era on the Island.[39]

Control of alcohol remained strict for more than another decade. The tone of more enlightened legislation was set in 1961 when the "Temperance Act" was amended to alter its name to the "Liquor Control Act." At the same time, the "Prince Edward Island Temperance Commission" became the "Prince Edward Island Liquor Control Commission," albeit with similar powers to its more piously-named predecessor. Not until 1964 were there legal provisions for the licencing of clubs, lounges, dining rooms, and military canteens — if such establishments complied with a variety of tight regulations. Further amendments to the renamed Temperance Act abolished the system of individual permits for liquor purchases from vending outlets in 1967. Subsequent minor alterations in the law during each of the next three years have continued to liberalize the regulations surrounding the dispensation of alcoholic beverages in the province, so that Island practices are now closely akin to those existing in other Canadian provinces.

Yet liquor laws remain a touchy issue which, on occasion, have proven to be far from latent in some circles. A recent controversy which erupted when the local University applied for a liquor licence is an illustration in point. Another example was provided as late as the autumn of 1972, when Premier Alexander B. Campbell suggested that prohibition and temperance were not synonymous terms, when he addressed a convention of Christian Women's Temperance Union members. The ladies let it be known that some individuals still supported a return to a prohibition stance. The potential for further fuss over liquor laws has been retained ever since the birth of prohibition, in part because — whether through cause or effect — the Island possesses the dubious distinction of having the highest per capita incidence of alcoholism in the nation.

Yet, it is probably fortunate that Island politicians have had controversies, like the motor and alcoholic prohibitions, on which to exercise their talents, for without these kinds of waves the waters of politics between elections would have been sufficiently calm and smooth to be readily termed dull. It was wrangles like these, which now seem in their substance occasionally to border on the absurd, that kept provincial politics not just alive but vivacious and exciting to participants and spectators alike.

Until the post-war period — indeed, until the last decade or so — provincial politics have been essentially local and uncomplicated. This was, of course, a reflection of the general characteristics of "negative" government, an acceptance of the diluted version of a *laissez-faire* role in political administration, which was evident in pre-war societies of the western world. At the same time, the provincial political stage, for many years after 1873, mirrored the specific limitations of the Island itself and its indigenous culture: a small population in an equally tiny area with restricted resources combined with an inherent native reluctance to alter the traditional Island lifestyle. Given this mixture, small wonder the local politicians were content to administer and regulate their domain with a minimum amount of public intervention in the private sphere. It is even less amazing that little attempt was made to remould the essential structure of the society as governments of today may seek to do.

Considering the calendars of other parts of Canada, it is revealing to reflect upon the evident youth of complex provincial involvement in the evolution of Island political processes. Major and intricate issues, such as the Georgetown Industries, the University Question, and the Development Plan, are of such recent vintage in political life that it can still be deemed premature to offer a comprehensive and valid assessment of their results, effects and implications. The infancy of positive government at the Island's provincial level is further demonstrated by the sudden mushrooming of the administrative machinery and other adjuncts of the provincial government. It seems incredible that the provincial civil service, for example, numbered a mere 336 full-time permanent employees, almost half of whom were in the Department of Health and Welfare, as recently as 1950.[40] Equally remarkable is the discovery that separate portfolios for the major fields of Education and Health were created only in 1935.[41] Such examples dramatically illustrate the growth and the increasing involvement of the provincial political arena, particularly when contrasted with the activities associated with the $100 million of today's annual budgetary statistics.

And yet, even as government moves into novel programs and extended regulatory control over its individual citizens, one wonders if the basic character and essence of Island politics has altered all that much throughout these intervening years. Or does a ghostly presence consider the last two centuries with the confident assertion: "I was right; it is a damn queer Parliament."

Chapter Thirteen

Economic and Social Developments Since Confederation

By LORNE C. CALLBECK

The "good old days" are apt to seem much better than they actually were to an elderly person who reflects upon them from the comfort of his rocking chair. It is natural that he should entertain a good opinion of them, for invariably his thoughts on the subject are largely influenced by nostalgia. The only accurate way to judge a previous era is to study the writings of people who wrote of it during the actual time that its conditions could be examined at first hand. Obviously, in attempting to describe the "good old days" immediately following the Island's entry into Canadian Confederation, the writer of this chapter, not having been given the opportunity to live then, has had to base his remarks on the recorded opinions of long-departed citizens.

The research we carried out has revealed, as we more or less anticipated, that the days immediately following Confederation could not be modified with the word good in many social and economic areas: which conclusion we have drawn from the attitude of the public to the proper maintenance of law and order and the exceedingly poor condition of the educational system and facilities. Gradually, however, social and economic conditions improved, and late nineteenth and early twentieth society, like our own, was a blend of good and bad, of affluence and poverty.

It was revealed that, even after the establishment of a regular police force in Charlottetown, law enforcement was a very strenuous and hazardous occupation. It became necessary, in 1874, to introduce a Bill in the Legislature imposing fines upon citizens who refused to aid the constables in quelling disturbances to the peace. This power was required, it was claimed, because it frequently happened that the police were overpowered by fishermen and sailors, in performing their duties, and it was a common thing to see crowds of people looking on, often indirectly giving encouragement. The Bill was passed on the understanding that it would apply only "to persons looking on at a row, not to persons attending to their own business."[1]

Mr. William MacPhail, a school inspector working under the benefit of the enormous salary of $200 per annum, had some interesting things to say about Charlottetown's schools in 1874, at which time there seems to have been about seventeen. After stating that they are a reproach to the whole community, he goes on to say:

"Many of the pupils are never long at one school, but keep running from school to school. As one teacher said, 'They just keep racing and chasing each other from school to school. I am sorry when they come to me, for they do harm to my school, and I am sorry when they leave me, for they do harm to themselves.' At the Temperance Hall I found pupils who had been attending at six different schools during the past six months. At the Hillsborough School, there were found pupils from four different schools in the same time. At Scott's Hall, on the day of my visit, there were 94 pupils in attendance, of whom 58 had attended nine different schools during the past six months; viz: 26 from Normal School, 4 from Hillsborough School, 2 from the Orphan School, 2 from the School in DesBrisay's Lane, 7 from Pownal School, 1 from the school in LePage's Building, 6 from the school in King's Square, 9 from the Temperance Hall School, and one from Spring Park School."[2]

Such a state of attendance of itself alone would be enough to thwart the efforts of the best teachers.

Mr. MacPhail continues his description of the Charlottetown schools as follows:

"I had some difficulty in finding Pownal School, though I had seen it before, situate as it is, in the garret of an outbuilding in a back yard. Having found the entrance to the yard, one is obliged to make the best of his way over an ash heap towards an outside flight of steps which leads to the entrance of the building on the second storey. Upon gaining this entrance and ascending the inside stairs to the garret aforesaid, I found seven children, cowering around a stove with little or no fire in it, and quarrelling very loudly, not seeming to heed the Master at the other end of the garret, who was equally loud in asking 'what's that?' Though the day (Dec. 4) was not very cold, the schoolroom was quite chilly. Upon inspecting the register, I found 27 pupils marked present for the day, whereas there were only 11 present. The attainments of those present were very low indeed. In Arithmetic, the furthest advanced were in Long Division, 8 times 4 are 27, and 8 times 4 are 36 being specimens of their knowledge in the Multiplication Table. I was assured by the boys of the Grammar Class that there were five parts of speech, that boy was an adjective and good a noun. In the Geography Class it was affirmed that there were 8 counties in P.E.I. In some of the other City Schools, too, singular answers were given. In one school it was said that a Cape is a body of water almost surrounded by land, Charlottetown was an Island, and Australia is the largest town in North America. In the same school, on two different occasions, I had to threaten to call the police, on account of insubordination."[3]

It would appear, then, that either the teaching profession was in a very sorry state in 1874 or that the scholars were exceedingly adept at "pulling an inspector's leg." We do know, however, that the teachers of the period were in general, a rather incompetent group of citizens. Mr. John MacNeil, the first provincial visitor, had this to say about them in his 1873 report:

"The little encouragement which is in most cases held out to a teacher of character and qualification, and the precarious manner in which their salaries are paid, operate most powerfully as a bar in the way of the advancement of education. Hence, it too frequently happens, that it is only persons of ship-wrecked character, and blasted prospects in life, after every other resource has failed them, who take up the important office of Schoolmaster."[4]

It seems strange that such conditions as those described by Mr. Mac-Phail and Mr. MacNeil had been allowed to develop, a Free Education Act having been passed by the Legislature in 1852. Before that year, small grants of money were provided to aid in the erection of public school buildings and in payment of teachers. Pupils' fees, however, still made up the greater part of the money earned by the teachers. Under such a weak system, the teachers practically ran their own schools and the curriculums were as varied as the knowledge [or lack of it] of the masters who conducted the miserable establishments. Because of the fees, poor parents could not afford to educate their children and illiteracy was prevalent, the signatures of numerous citizens being restricted to the making of the letter X.

The Act of 1852 was designed to change all this. Its main features were that the Board of Education of seven members, appointed by the Governor-in-Council, should have control of all public schools and should examine candidates for teachers' licences; that not more than two hundred districts should be established and that schools should be at least three miles apart; that all children over five years of age should be admitted to the school of the district in which they lived and that children outside the boundaries of any school district might attend the nearest school; that no fee should be demanded of scholars attending a school whereof the teacher received pay under the Act; and that assessment for school purposes should be on all householders residing in a district. Obviously, it took a long time for the benefits and controls provided by this Act to seep down to the grassroots level.

In 1877 a radical change was made in the educational life of the province when Premier Louis H. Davies brought the Public Schools Act before the Legislature. The Act provided that a public schools system, under the direction of a Provincial Board of Education, was to replace the haphazard and unfruitful facilities and methods described by Messrs. MacPhail and MacNeil.

The new Act was immediately successful as shown by the fact that within the first eighteen months of its operation the attendance of pupils in the public schools of the province increased by over five thousand. Its provisions, together with facilities already available at Prince of Wales College, the Provincial Normal School, and St. Dunstan's College, made the educational system of the Island quite respectable.

Two years later, in 1879, the Provincial Normal School was amalgamated with Prince of Wales College — which had been established by provincial charter in 1860 to replace the Central Academy founded by Royal Charter in 1834 — and female students were admitted to the college for the first time. In 1892 St. Dunstan's College became affiliated with Laval University in Quebec. Its campus is now that of the University of Prince Edward Island, created by amalgamating the two colleges in 1969. The Prince of Wales College buildings became Holland College.

The year 1879 also saw the beginning of necessary improvements in another public institution, the "Asylum for Insane Persons," as it was unmistakably called before the less offensive name of Falconwood Hospital was adopted, being built to succeed the old "Lunatic Asylum" which had graced the Brighton district of Charlottetown for many years. The new institution was erected near Falconwood House, the seat of Mr. John Grubbe, a fine residence in which Sir John A. Macdonald lived for a short time as an invalid. Sir John was stricken with a gallstone attack in the Council Chamber of Parliament on May 6, 1870. He arrived at Pope's Wharf, Charlottetown, in the steamer *Druid* on July 8 and spent the summer convalescing at Falconwood House, returning to Ottawa on September 16 of the same year.

Another aspect of life that could hardly be considered good during the nineteenth century was protection from fire. Charlottetown began to worry about it in 1830 and an Act was passed to provide that "within twelve months from the passing of this Act, the tenant or occupier of every house in the said Town, of the yearly value of Ten Pounds, shall be provided with, and keep, one leathern Bucket, to contain not less than two gallons, on which his name shall be painted; which Bucket shall be kept hanging up in the passage or hall of such house, under the penalty of Five Shillings for each and every time the said Bucket shall not be found so hung up in its proper place as aforesaid by the Fire Wardens when they shall visit the said house." A similar regulation was adopted in Summerside in 1858.

When a fire broke out, the man of the house was required to snatch his bucket from the peg in the hall and run to the scene as fast as his legs would carry him. At the blaze, the men formed two lines to the nearest source of water, the empty buckets being passed down one line and the full ones up the other line. It meant, of course, that a small and jerky quantity of liquid was thrown on the fire, and, very often, the best policy was to allow the burning building to be consumed and concentrate on preventing the flames from spreading to adjacent structures by throwing the contents of the buckets on them.

The worst conflagration in the history of Charlottetown was "The Great Fire" of 1866. On Sunday morning, July 16, fire broke out in an old building on the southwest corner of King and Pownal Streets and destroyed four blocks in Ward One, cutting a swath two blocks wide until it was finally checked at the Bishop's Palace on Great George Street. One hundred buildings were destroyed.

The disaster of 1866 led to the immediate re-organization of the city's fire department and, in the same year, the first steam fire engine, drawn by one horse, was purchased in England. It was known as the *Rollo*. A little later, a second, known as the *Silsby*, was brought in from Seneca Falls, New York. It was drawn by two horses.

As is the case today in many fire departments, there was considerable rivalry for glory and prestige between the men of the Rollo Company and the men of the Silsby Company. The rivalry reached its most notable height one Sunday morning when a fire was observed in John Newson's brick warehouse. The horses were out on pasture but the heroic members of the Rollo Company dragged their engine out on the street, pushed and pulled it to the warehouse, and had the fire under control before the arrival of the Silsby engine, whose company had indolently waited at the station until the horses had been fetched in from the pasture field.

Both Charlottetown and Summerside had destructive fires in 1884. In Charlottetown, the Cameron Block, Post Office, Patriot Office, and other buildings on Richmond Street were destroyed on February 20. In October, a fire started in the stable behind the *Franklin House* on Central Street in Summerside and spread from there to destroy the entire block.

The Charlottetown block contained by Kent, Prince, Fitzroy, and Hillsborough Streets was hit hard by two fires. On March 5, 1887, the Wright Furniture Factory on the corner of Kent and Hillsborough was destroyed along with all the houses up the block to the Fitzroy Street intersection. The next spring a fire broke out at the Excelsior Skating Rink on Kent Street and swept up the east side of Prince Street to the Baptist Church, then situated where the Salvation Army Citadel now stands.

Summerside's worst fire was on October 10, 1906. It started just after dark in a freight shed, hot cinders from which were carried over the town by a southeast gale, starting other fires. Within ten hours it destroyed 155 buildings over an area of nearly 50 acres and left some 2,500 people with little less than a grim outlook for the future. Included among the losses were the Anglican, Christian and Baptist Churches. The brick Court House was completely gutted.[5]

Many interesting and wonderful events took place during the period, 1863-1873, when Islanders were wrestling with the thorny issue of Confederation. The hosting of the Charlottetown Conference in 1864 was undoubtedly the most significant Island event of the century. The people of Prince Edward Island, convinced that Confederation would disastrously affect their economic, social and political structures, decided their best future lay in separatism. They maintained this stance until economic and political forces compelled them to enter Confederation in 1873.

Charlottetown was incorporated in April of 1855, at which time it boasted a population of 6,500 persons, and on August 7 the first council, with Robert Hutchinson as mayor, was elected. The Young Men's Christian Association was founded in 1856 and the first Y.M.C.A. building on the continent was erected on Richmond Street in 1863. When the city was illumined by gas lights in 1859, the probability of stepping into mud holes, hog wallows, and filth-carrying gutters was considerably reduced and Michael Doolin became the most useful and most respected resident. Michael, carrying a ladder on his shoulders, traversed the streets of the business district to ignite the lamps every evening and to extinguish them every morning. His figure became as familiar to his fellow citizens as the regular passage of the hours themselves.

The healthy condition of the economy is shown by the census data of 1861. The population of the province had almost tripled in thirty years, rising from about 32,000 in 1833 to 80,856 in 1861. There were 156 churches and 302 schools. There were 89 fishing establishments which produced 22,000 barrels of herring and gaspereaux, 7,000 barrels of mackerel, 39,000 quintals of codfish, and 17,000 barrels of fish-oils. There were 141 grist mills, 46 carding mills, 176 sawmills, 9 fulling and dressing mills, 55 tanneries. The cloth manufactured, but not fulled, totalled 303,676 yards, and the cloth fulled, 122,940 yards. The tanneries produced 143,803 pounds of leather. There were 48 lime kilns in operation and these produced 22,821 barrels of lime in 1861. Under the swamps and barrens of Prince County lay beds of brick clay. These deposits kept nine brick kilns busy making 1,331,000 bricks.

There were potteries in the old days too and they kept the farms supplied with milk bowls and butter crocks and the schools and offices with inkwells. A reminder of the days of the potter's wheel is the Lily Pond on the Charlottetown Research Station. It was formed by the removal of clay used in a pottery that was situated about three hundred yards to the north. There were two potteries near Charlottetown in the nineteenth century. The first, established in 1864, bore the name of the Spring Park Pottery — a name that probably indicates its location — and was in operation until 1885. The second, which left the Lily Pond as an attractive relic of its existence, was known as the Prince Edward Island Pottery. It was managed by Frank Hornsby and was more familiarly known to local residents as Hornsby's Pottery.

There were no welfare agencies, unemployment insurance commissions, workmen's compensation boards, local incentive programmes, youth hostels, opportunities for youth programmes, or medicare programmes. The people were happy and busy, and, taking it altogether, the Island was almost self-sufficient in the middle and third-quarter years of the nineteenth century. Perhaps the manufactured goods lacked the elegance demanded by today's more sophisticated society, but they were not flimsy and they lasted longer. They were years of plenty.

Apart from agriculture, fisheries, and their related service industries, shipbuilding was the biggest employer of labour and the greatest producer of wealth at the time of Confederation. Indeed, the industry was an important one from the very beginning of the Island's history, records showing that in 1721 the French built a vessel of 100 tons at St. Peter's for transporting codfish to Europe.

It is not certain when the first vessel was built after the Island became a British Colony. Ships were registered here as early as 1781, but whether they were built locally or built in other places and merely registered here is not certain. It is reasonably certain that a small vessel was built at Charlottetown and another at Vernon River in 1781. There is a definite record of the building of a vessel of 23 tons by Captain William Warren at Tryon in 1789. Warren's vessel, christened the *Tryon,* may have been sold far afield or lost at sea, for he registered another under the same name in 1791, but of 35 tons.

In the early years of the nineteenth century, trained shipbuilders began coming in from the Old Country and the industry started to develop. Islanders became apprentices to these men, and soon acquired the skills necessary to operate the industry themselves. From 1800 to 1810, thirty-five vessels, ranging from 31 to 242 tons, were constructed at Island yards. The next decade saw vessels of up to 400 tons sliding from the ways into our rivers and bays.

During the 1821-1830 decade two hundred and seventy-two ships were built at yards located mainly at Bedeque, Bideford, Charlottetown, Covehead, Georgetown, Hillsborough Bay, Port Hill, Rustico, Souris, and Tryon. Three hundred and sixty-six ships were registered during the 1831-1840 period, three hundred and twenty-three of which were definitely built at Island yards. The largest vessel of this period was the 643-ton *Delheli,* built at Bedeque.

Production increased to four hundred and seventy-six vessels in the 1841-1850 period. About fifty yards were now in operation, the leading ones with the number of vessels launched being: Rustico, 41; Murray Harbour, 28; Hillsborough River, 28; St. Peter's, 27; New London, 25; Orwell Bay, 23; New Glasgow, 19; Souris, 18; Port Hill, 17; Grand River, 17; Tryon River, 16; Bay Fortune, 16; Bedeque, 14; Richmond Bay, 12; Three Rivers, Rollo Bay, and Charlottetown, 11 each.

Not only was there a considerable increase in the number of vessels built but there was also a marked tendency to increase the tonnage during the 1851-1860 decade. A total of eight hundred and forty-seven ships were launched in this period and several of them approached the 1,000-ton class.

In this decade there were at least five yards along the Charlottetown waterfront between the present Sacred Heart Home and the Exhibition Grounds. The Peake yard had launched the *Fanny* which sailed for the California gold fields in 1849. The Duncan yard built two storied vessels, the *Gertrude* and the *Ethel.* The *Gertrude,* constructed of birch, pine, oak, and hackmatack, was a Liverpool transport during the Indian Mutiny and later an Australian emigrant ship. The *Ethel,* a three-decker of 1,795 tons, was the largest ship ever built on the Island. She was sold in Liverpool, England.

The most productive ten-year period was the decade of 1861-1870 and the nine hundred and fourteen vessels constructed in some sixty yards kept so many men employed felling trees, sawing and hewing lumber, fashioning blocks and pulleys, splicing ropes, caulking seams, sewing sails, and performing all the other jobs relative to the building of the huge fleet that they had little time to consider such a trivial matter as Canadian Confederation. Let the politicians worry about that. That is why we elected them and if any of them show too much enthusiasm for the scheme they had better watch themselves in the next election.

It was in this decade that Summerside came to life and started out on the development that brought it to its present position as the Island's second largest town, and it was shipbuilding that determined its future growth. In 1850, James and George Walsh moved their shipyard from the shore behind Holman's Island to the Summerside waterfront below Cedar Street and, in

November of the next year, they launched a vessel which they christened *The Two Ladies* in honour of their wives. Two years later the launching of the barque *Paxton* from a shipyard founded by James C. Pope was witnessed by the largest crowd of people that had ever assembled in the town. By the end of the 1861-1870 decade, Summerside had outstripped Georgetown in the shipbuilding race and soon became the second port in the province.

The town of Summerside was an accident. The intended seat of Prince County was to have been Princetown on the eastern side of the mouth of Malpeque Bay, the site having been chosen by Captain Samuel Holland when he surveyed the Island in 1764-65 and having been laid out by Charles Morris in 1768. That was about as far as Princetown got and old maps show the several streets but no houses of the town that was stillborn.

In 1780, Daniel Green, a Pennsylvania Quaker and United Empire Loyalist, settled his family on a 500-acre grant of land on the shore of Bedeque Bay.[6] To this piece Daniel added, by purchase, other lands on both sides, so that when he died in 1825 he possessed the land on which Summerside now stands, but which, in his day, was known as Green's Shore. The town received its present name after a grandson, Joseph Green, built an inn in 1840 and named it *Summerside House,* a name that had come to him by accident. Colonel Harry Compton, who lived on the Malpeque Bay side of the Island, came over to Green's Shore one cold March day. Here, where the hill and woods gave shelter from the north wind, the sun was more warming than it was on the bleak north side. It made the Colonel feel good and caused him to say to Joseph Green, who was splitting some stove wood in his yard: "You are a lucky fellow, Joseph; you certainly live on the summer side of the Island." This casual remark of the Colonel reposed in Joseph's mind until he finished the inn, at which time he painted the words *Summerside House* on a board and nailed it over the front door.

As time passed, other people came to build saddler's shops, tailor shops, forges, stores, houses, and stables and the little town of Summerside began to assume some importance. By 1861 the town and Lot 17 had a population of over 2,000. This had increased to 3,300 by 1871; and in 1875, when Summerside was incorporated, it boasted that number of residents itself.

But the handwriting that presaged the end of the glorious days of sail was already on the wall. Iron and steam were to replace wood and sail. The decade of 1871-1880, in which the Island entered Confederation, saw the beginning of the inevitable end of the shipbuilding industry. The period produced only five hundred and seventy-one vessels. Production dropped to one hundred and thirty-seven in 1881-1890 and fell sharply to fifty-two vessels in the decade of 1891-1900. Mount Stewart was the most productive community between 1871 and 1880, turning out one hundred and four vessels, ranging from 60 to 649 tons; Summerside came next with forty-seven ships, ranging from 200 tons to the large 1,049-ton *Gondolier*.

The dawn of the twentieth century saw most of the yards going out of business. In its first decade, only thirty-nine vessels were registered and the number dropped to eighteen for the 1911-1920 period, none being larger than 300 tons burden.

Thus the shipbuilding industry rose, reached peak production at about the three-quarters mark of the nineteenth century, and then declined rapidly to insignificance. The leading builders were Hill, Chanter, Ellis, Cambridge, LePage, Duncan, McKay, MacGill, Peake, Yeo, Richards, Douse, Owen, Orr, Bell, MacDonald, MacDougal, Pope, Heard, and numerous others. The industry had given employment to thousands of men during its many decades of existence and others had found jobs before the masts of the ships that sailed to the markets of the world. It was an insignificant community indeed that could not boast a Captain Somebody-or-Other among its citizens.

In recent years a slight comeback has been made, a shipyard at Georgetown having been set up, after many political difficulties, to build trawlers, tugs, and patrol boats out of such unromantic materials as steel and aluminum.

Agriculture has been, is, and very likely will be the backbone of our economy, the province being blessed with soils that respond well to good management and with suitable accessories of rainfall, sunshine, and temperature for most of the important crops of the temperate zone.

It was the agricultural potential that persuaded France to settle Ile St. Jean in the beginning — but it took a long time and a major war before the decision was made. Indeed, the decision was not made until 185 years after Jacques Cartier discovered this gem in the Gulf of St. Lawrence and described the land as the best quality that can be seen.

The building of the fortress of Louisbourg by the French after the 1713 Treaty of Utrecht created temporary peace with England, turned the attention of Louis XV to Ile St. Jean. It was, he and his ministers decided, to be the breadbasket of his expensive bastion at Louisbourg on the bleak Atlantic coast of Ile Royale. Agriculture developed at a steady rate until Lord Rollo's troops, after the final fall of Louisbourg in 1758, made the Island a wilderness again.[7]

Soon after settlers from England, Scotland, and Ireland came in to take over the lands that had been cleared by their predecessors and to carve new clearings out of the primeval forest, we find the first mention of our most important cash crop, the potato. In 1771, Governor Walter Patterson wrote that he had never seen such an increase in potatoes. Another writer, Walter Johnstone of Dumfries, Scotland, in describing his journey around the Island, noted that: "They export livestock of all kinds, grain and potatoes, to Newfoundland; grain, pork and potatoes to Miramichi, and grain and potatoes to Halifax. . . . The Islanders enjoy a privilege which many of the labouring classes at home cannot at present obtain; they may all be employed in cultivating the ground; and the ground, I have heard it said, is so very grateful that no man ever yet bestowed prudent labour upon it but it repaid him for his toil."[8]

For the settler the potato was an easy crop to grow and it yielded abundant food for his family. With grain it was necessary to completely clear a piece of ground but the potatoes could be grown as soon as the trees had been cut and the trash burned. Potatoes could then be planted in holes made in the ground among the stumps with a mattock or grubbing hoe and there was little more that had to be done until the crop was forked out in the autumn. There was no blight disease to destroy the leaves nor Colorado beetles to eat them. The blight fungus did not reach the Island until 1845, the same year it was causing a great famine in Ireland. The Colorado beetle, popularly known as the "potato bug," did not arrive until about thirty years later.

The early settlers ploughed their fields with one-handled ploughs and the furrows these made were never straight. Two-handled ploughs were introduced in 1810. The grain was scattered by hand and the results were often similar to those described by Jesus in the Parable of the Sower. When it ripened it was cut with scythes and sickles, gathered with wooden rakes, and threshed by beating it with flails on an earthen or wooden floor as man had been doing for thousands of years. At first it was cleaned by tossing it in the air when the wind was blowing at a rate that would carry the lighter chaff aside and allow the heavier kernels to fall: later, a machine known as a fanner was invented to clean the grain.

The first threshing machine arrived in 1828 and the first reaper in 1830. These were great technological advancements but, by modern standards, were very crude in style and performance. The reaper did not tie the grain into sheaves but merely threw it off in loose bundles which the harvesters bound with wisps of twisted straws. The thresher, driven by a tread mill, a cumbersome engine whose power was generated by one or two horses walking on an inclined and cleated belt, did not separate the chaff from the grain, the farmer still having to clean the crop by means of nature's wind or by the use of the fanner. Later, the thresher and fanner were assembled into one machine, enabling the farmer to thresh and clean the grain in a single operation. One such machine was devised and manufactured by Ambrose Monaghan of Kinkora around 1897. The Monaghan thresher was sold quite extensively in the Maritime provinces and could also be found in hundreds of wheat fields in Western Canada.

From the above description of the beginnings of agriculture in our province, we shall now return to the post-Confederation era. After the bickering and excitement generated by the Union issue had subsided, the people settled contentedly into a period of economic prosperity that lasted for about twenty-five years. Agriculture and fisheries were the foundation of the economy. The shipyards were still busy, and breweries, tanneries, carriage factories, farm implement factories, carding and weaving mills, sawmills, shingle mills, grist mills, and many other small industries provided employment for any man who wanted to work for wages. Men who wished to follow a trade of their own were blacksmiths, harness makers, saddle makers, cabinet-makers, cobblers, tailors, tinsmiths, or general tinkers. Women who failed to graduate to the status of housewife — and bore the unflattering designation of "old-maid" — were teachers, servants, dressmakers, seamstresses, milliners, clerks, or general factotums and convenient baby sitters in the homes of brothers or married sisters. Women's lib had not yet entered the female mind. But everyone was busy and few wanted to leave for far away places.

The population, through immigration and a natural propensity to raise large families, was increasing. The 1881 census showed a population of 108,891 and that of 1891, 109,078. But during the next four decades a general decline occurred and this was particularly noticeable in the 1901-1911 period, the period of rapid settlement on the western prairies. The population figure dropped to 103,259 in 1901 and to 93,728 in 1911.

The 1921 census revealed a further decrease to 88,615 but little change took place in the next decade, the figure for 1931 being but slightly less at 88,038. After that the population pendulum swung slowly in the opposite direction and by 1941 there were 95,077 people living in the province. The 1951 census showed a slight rise to 98,429. The slow upward trend brought the population to 108,835 in 1961, a figure that is almost identical with that of 1881. The 1971 census figure was 111,641.

There were several uncontrollable causes for the decline in population. The main ones were the depletion of the forests and the consequent loss suffered by the lumbering industry, the gradual outmoding of wooden ships, the opening of the Canadian West, the centralizing of commerce and industry in Quebec and Ontario and the high tariffs that the federal government applied to protect them, the great industrial expansion in the United States, and the depletion of many soils by insidious erosion. Because of these changes, young Islanders began moving away to more hopeful centres for employment and opportunity, and those who remained at home came to depend more and more on agriculture and fishing. Thus the people dependent on the lost trades and industries migrated to the centres of new development while the farm population on the Island remained at a relatively constant level.

Notwithstanding the outmoding of local industry and its resulting population shift, the people on the Island continued to make progress and to improve their style of living. The telephone came to Charlottetown in 1884, electric lights in 1885, and the water and sewage systems went into operation in 1887. Before that, the citizens got their water from pumps in their own yards, from the several public pumps that were scattered over the town, or had it delivered at the door from a stoned well in Spring Park for one cent a bucket.

Actually, there were several public wells in Charlottetown — one on Queen Square and one or two on each of the main streets — and each, as one would expect, was a popular rendezvous, for there the people would meet with their buckets and exchange the gossip of the day. It was natural, therefore, that the phasing out of these centres of communication met with considerable opposition on the part of certain die-hards, who continued to use the water from whatever wells and pumps that were still available to them. Others opposed the introduction of the system from a fear of increased taxation and still others because they missed the "flavour" of the well water.

Spring Park, which, in 1957, became part of Charlottetown's Ward Six, was a lovely place in olden times. It was a favourite resort in summer for both young and old; for through the grounds were many pretty walks, and in it rose a limpid spring whose waters meandered and rippled their way among the trees, on and on, till they flowed under Black Sam's Bridge, which crossed Brighton Road, spread out into Governor's Pond, and then passed under Christian's Bridge by Government House and so into the harbour. The spring was later walled with hewn stone and became a ready source of pure water, particularly when any town wells would go dry or there was fear of their being contaminated.

After the city water system was installed, the spring went out of use. A dam was thrown up below it to create a large pond which became a popular rink and from which a harvest of ice was gathered every winter. The pond is gone now; for men filled the depression with ashes, cans, bottles, and rubbish of all description and its grave was finally marked by a board sign which bore the epitaph NO DUMPING ALLOWED. The area of the park is now quite generally covered with houses and the Royalty Mall Shopping Centre and its parking lot have taken the place of the pond.

Some idea of life and conditions in rural communities in the 1800's is provided by an article written in the *Examiner* in 1882:

"Among the latest improvements in dairying introduced here," it says, "are the cheese factories. There are, so far, but three on the Island — one at York, one at Cornwall, and one in Lot 49; but they are certain to become more common."[9]

Dealing with a particular area of the province, the article continues:

"Crapaud is well supplied with excellent mills, having no less than four, viz: Collett's, Stordy's, Leard's, and Howatt's. They are all supplied with French Burrs and other appliances for turning out first-class flour. Messrs. Collett and Howatt have saw and carding mills fitted up in the most approved manner. Mr. Bradford Howatt, whose mill property is at Crapaud Corner, is building a fine substantial new house, and Mr. Collett is putting up a rather mysterious building a hundred feet long which has been dubbed the Station House."[10]

Reference is also made to improvements in the area:

"Besides Mr. Howatt's mill property, there are at Crapaud Corner two black-smith shops, two harness shops, two tailors, two shoemakers, and a steam carriage factory. The thriving village of Hampton, about two miles east of Crapaud Corner, contains two forges, an agricultural implement factory and a tannery."[11]

Many other mills were in operation in the same area at that time. Charles E. Stanfield started a mill for carding, spinning, and weaving at Tryon in the late 1850's. After a few years of operation, Mr. Stanfield move to Truro, Nova Scotia, where he founded the nationally-known Stanfield mill that is still in business today. The Tryon Woollen Mills continued to operate under a succession of owners and it was the largest business of its kind in the province until it was destroyed by fire. At that time, the mill was making cloth for the army of World War I.

Farther up the same stream was another mill. It was run by a man named Lewis who also moved to Truro where he continued his production of shirts and felt hats. At North Tryon there was the grist, saw, and shingle mill of Mr. Ives. Similar stories could be told of many more communities.

Thus the farmers of the region had markets close by at which they could sell their wool and hides; mills to grind wheat flour, buckwheat flour, and oatmeal; mills to saw lumber and split shingles; tailors to make their suits out of cloth manufactured in local mills; shoemakers to make their boots and shoes out of leather prepared in the tanneries; harness makers to fashion harness for their horses. Carriages and certain farm implements were manufactured close at hand and blacksmiths were available to keep them repaired. Altogether, most of the necessities of life were within easy reach back in the late years of the nineteenth century.

The Undine, *a 500-ton bark, built in Summerside in 1864 for James Colledge Pope, is illustrative of the thousands of ships built in Island shipyards in the nineteenth century.*

A typical operational base for Prince Edward Island's prosperous fishing industry.

A litter of seven silver fox pups in a ranch typical of the hundreds that existed on the Island in the first four decades of the twentieth century.
Courtesy of the Public Archives of Prince Edward Island

Potato harvesting on "Spud Island".
Courtesy of the Public Archives of Prince Edward Island

The fishing industry has always played an important, though fluctuating, role in the Island's economy. Although as much as one-tenth of the Island's working population has engaged in fishing pursuits in some years, the largest number of these people have found part, if not most, of their employment in agricultural or other activities. The seasonal nature of the industry, and the belief that subsistence was more likely to be assured upon firm mother earth rather than upon the restless and unpredictable waves, led the vast majority of islanders to opt for agriculture.

In the first half of the nineteenth century the Islanders left the fishing largely to the Americans and seemed content with the profits realized from the visits of these fishermen to their shores. After the abrogation of the Reciprocity Treaty in 1866, the Island's interest in the fisheries increased. In the decade, 1870-1880, the number employed in fishing or fish-processing rose from 1,646 to 5,792, and the number of vessels and boats from 1,183 to 2,729. The most significant development in subsequent years has been in the lobster and oyster fisheries which together have dominated the Island's fisheries ever since. The Malpeque oyster acquired a reputation not unlike that of the Island potato and has been a premium seller in sophisticated circles in America. Before the turn of the century lobsters became the leading fisheries product representing three-fifths to two-thirds of the value of the total catch.[12]

In the 1970's, lobster-fishing, which is prosecuted during a two-month period, remains the mainstay of the Island fishing industry. Mackerel, cod and related ground fish, herring, scallops, smelts and oysters are the other leading catches. Many important changes have taken place in the industry. Seining, trawling and dragging have increased production while creating conservation worries. The fisheries programme being implemented as part of the Comprehensive Development Plan, calls for the consolidation of the Island's fish-processing establishments and the reduction of protected harbours to some twenty designated centres. The fisheries seem destined to play a significant role in the future development of the Island.

In the first decade of the present century, Prince Edward Island achieved world-wide publicity as the pioneer area of the new industry of fox-farming. In the 1880's, Charles Dalton of Tignish, a trapper and fur buyer, had conceived an idea that brought a great industry to the Island and won a knighthood and the position of Lieutenant Governor for its founder. Young Dalton had occasionally bought a black fox skin from the Indians and, now and then, had caught one of the rare animals in a trap of his own. When he sold his pelts he always received higher prices for the blacks than he did for the common reds. It occurred to him that, by careful selecting and breeding, a strain of pure black foxes might be developed from the black pups that the native red animals sometimes dropped. He discussed the idea with his friend, Robert Oulton of Alberton, who was also pioneering with foxes, and, when shortly afterwards they heard of an Indian who had taken four black pups from a den, they entered upon their experiments.

Their early efforts were not particularly successful but they carried on with true research persistence. One problem lay in the fact that foxes entertained a great antipathy to being confined to small quarters, and, having very sharp teeth and claws, they often escaped back to the freedom of the woods. The problem was solved when the men learned of a firm in England that could manufacture a wire mesh that the foxes could not cut. They ordered a quantity and Mr. Oulton designed pens that spelled success for their experiments. They raised a good number of pups that year and from them they selected the clearest black types and those with the brightest silver.

Being men of intelligence and perseverance, they studied the laws of inheritance and applied what they learned to improve their basic stock. Being also very canny gentlemen, they kept their experiments as secret as possible, performing them on Savage Island in Alberton Harbour. However, other men in western Prince County became interested in the same field and in the late nineties James Tuplin, James Gordon, and Silas Raynor tried their hands at the fascinating game and they too were successful. In 1897, Mr. Dalton built a ranch of his own at Tignish but still maintained an interest in the Savage Island ranch. He soon became the chief fur merchant in the province, selling his own pelts and many of those produced by others.

Up until 1910 six concerns monopolized the domestic fox industry of the Island and, consequently, of the world; but in April of that year the public discovered what a gold mine the business was. Forty-three pelts had been sold for Dalton and Oulton by C. M. Lampson and Company of London, England, for an amount that averaged the unheard of price of one thousand dollars per pelt. One skin fetched five hundred and forty pounds sterling, equal then to over $2,500. The reason the pelts were in such demand was that Russian nobility lined their winter coats with them and titled ladies wore them for collars and neck pieces. The era of the silver black fox had dawned.

Prices now began to soar and prime pelts were bringing as high as $3,700 on the English market. It is not strange, therefore, that the six companies guarded their stock well and observed to the very letter their covenant whereby no foxes could be sold alive. This state of monopoly did not last long in the face of the demand by merchants, farmers, and professional men for breeding stock. Fabulous prices were offered to the original owners, companies were formed, and a mad rush to get rich quickly occurred. People who bought a pair of silver black animals for $10,000 were able to dispose of pairs at double that price by the end of 1913. Indeed, the choicest pairs brought as much as $35,000.

The fox boom made many people rich; and many other people who invested their life savings in fly-by-night ranches were made poor. The fox, it seems, was not the only creature that got "skinned" for profit. Once the monopoly on live animals was broken, Island breeding stock found its way to other countries with the inevitable result that prices declined as the number of pelts put on the market increased. Norway became one of the Island's main competitors and the English market was lost. Early in the 1940's the fox business fell to insignificance.

Several institutions and innovations, which have played important roles among us ever since, came into being or underwent significant changes in the latter years of the last century and the first years of the present one. The Prince Edward Island Hospital was opened in 1884 on St. Peter's Road and the building still stands on its original site [corner of Longworth Avenue and Cumberland Street], being now a tenement house. A new hospital was built in 1900 on Kensington Road. This building is now the Provincial Infirmary, having been replaced by the present hospital erected on Brighton Road in 1933.

The first Charlottetown Hospital was a small wooden building near old St. Dunstan's Cathedral. After a brief period of use it was suceeded by a larger wooden building on the corner of Haviland and Sydney Streets. In it the frostbitten men of the ice-boat disaster of 1885 had fingers and toes amputated while they slept soundly under the influence of a new and wonderful organic chemical — ether. This building became the Sacred Heart Home after a new hospital was built across the street. Later, a new Home was built south of the hospital and the old wooden structure was torn down to make a parking lot.

The precursor of our Provincial Exhibition and the several fine agricultural fairs that are held throughout the province was staged at Crapaud in 1820. The advertisement for this first fair set forth that "the inhabitants of Crapaud and surrounding country are anxious to open a market with Ramshag [now Wallace, Nova Scotia] to exchange sheep for spinning wheels and chairs." It also announced that "young cattle of the best breeds from Cumberland, Nova Scotia, would meet with purchasers for cash or barter."

Fairs were pretty modest endeavours in the old days but they helped to improve the quality of horticultural and field crops and the conformation of livestock. Every year, late in September, a fair was held on Charlottetown's Queen Square, where the Confederation Memorial Complex now stands. People from far and near came to town, bringing their fat cattle, horses, pigs, poultry, fruits, vegetables, et cetera and every available space inside and outside the market house was taken up.

Fair days were also gala ones for hucksters. Everyone who could provide the semblance of a tent, even four posts stuck in the ground and covered with patchwork quilts or old sails, went into business, selling home-made beer, cakes, apples, plums, or anything else that might appeal to the hungry crowd. And there was always at least one gentleman, with a loud voice and a good assortment of card tricks to lure the unwary to his stand, who dispensed bottles of rattle snake oil or an old Indian remedy that was guaranteed to cure any ailment of the human body from bunions up.

In the later years of the nineteenth century an annual Queen's County Exhibition was held in the armories, a large wooden building that had been erected at the beginning of Kent Street and on the east side of Governor's Pond and officially opened in 1867. It was torn down in 1967 to make way for an expansion of the Provincial Government Administrative Complex. Cattle and other livestock were judged on the grounds of Government House.

In 1888 a group of farsighted men laid plans that led to the establishment of the Charlottetown Driving Park and Provincial Exhibition Association. After a great deal of discussion and an equal amount of agitation, a Bill was passed in the Legislature, whereby the Association was granted a charter, and shares of $100 each were sold to create a capital of $25,000. Land between Kensington Road and the Hillsborough River was purchased, the trees were cut down, and the first horse race was held on the track in October of 1890. At this opening meet and in the meets for two or three years afterwards, the high-wheeled sulky was in vogue and some drivers were wont to put the butts of their whips inside the spokes, creating a noise that served to accelerate the horses and enliven the spirits of the fans.

Harness racing has always been a major sport on Prince Edward Island and, even at the time of the opening of the track at Charlottetown, there were more than a dozen ovals scattered over the province. Some of the popular places have been Montague, Georgetown, Pinette, St. Peter's, Upton, New Annan, Summerside, Northam and Kensington. These tracks, with many others that came and went over the years, gave rise to one of the many colorful nicknames that have been attached to the Island — The Kentucky of Canada.

The people who lived during the latter part of the nineteenth century and the first half of the twentieth century saw some wonderful changes, particularly in the field of agriculture. They saw the change from manual to mechanized labour as the hay mower, binder, fertilizer spreader, seed drill, hay loader, potato planter, potato sprayer, hay baler, and grain combine came into use. They saw the milking machine replace the hand of the farmer and the milkmaid. They saw old people pour milk into broad, earthen bowls set in cool cellars and watched them "skim" the cream that rose to the top. They saw the introduction of the wonderful cylindrical can known as a "creamer," which had a tap at the bottom through which the milk was carefully drawn off, leaving the upper layer of cream behind. And they saw these slow gravitational methods replaced by the centrifugal cream separator. Indeed, things are moving so fast now that the separator will soon be a museum piece too and all milk will be hauled in huge tank trucks from the farmers' cooling tanks to a few large dairy processing plants.

The Provincial Department of Agriculture was organized in 1901. The Dominion Government entered the agricultural field in 1909 when, in August of that year, it leased twenty-nine acres of land from the Provincial Government on which to establish an Experimental Station. A native Islander, J. A. Clark, was appointed superintendent, a position he held until his retirement in 1947.

The first developments were undertaken in 1910 when 100 apple trees, representing 70 varieties, and 1,259 ornamental trees and shrubs were planted. In 1912, Charlottetown No. 80 barley was selected and it was registered as a new variety in 1916, since which time it has maintained considerable popularity.

The Dominion Government gave a second impetus to agricultural development in 1915 by building a small laboratory for plant disease research on the Mount Edward Road side of the Station. Paul A. Murphy was the first officer-in-charge. He remained here until 1921 when the government's refusal of a pay increase of $100 per annum caused him to return to his native Ireland. There he continued his studies on potato diseases and became a world authority, particularly in the field of the devastating late blight disease. He was succeeded here by R. R. Hurst.

From a small beginning emerged an active programme of research, the value of which was soon reflected in the rapid development of a sound inspection service for seed potatoes, centered at the laboratory under S. G. Peppin. Later, in recognition of the necessity for an energetic attack on insect problems, an entomological laboratory was incorporated in the same building in 1937.

Seed potato certification in the province had its origin in 1916 when a few strains of Irish Cobbler and Green Mountain were found to be practically free of virus diseases. Samples of these were sent to Long Island and New Jersey for testing and produced outstanding yields and quality in those areas. Thus began the production of seed potatoes on this Island, an industry that has since made a tremendous contribution to its economy and has made the name "Spud Island" known over the world.

The first carload of seed potatoes produced in Canada was shipped from Prince Edward Island in 1918. The tubers, of the variety Irish Cobbler, were grown by farmers in Lot 16 under the leadership of Mr. W. H. McGregor, The shipment went to Leamington, Ontario. From that beginning the Island developed into Canada's leading source of high quality seed potatoes, accounting now for approximately sixty per cent of the nation's annual export of this agricultural commodity. Our seed is sold to growers in other Canadian provinces, the United States, Argentina, Bahamas, Bermuda, Cuba, Dominican Republic, Greece, Italy, Jamaica, Puerto Rico, South Africa, Trinidad, Uruguay and Venezuela.

Potato growing on the Island is a multi-million dollar business and seasonal weather conditions, the acreage planted, the prevalence of disease, yield per acre, surplus or shortage in other producing regions, and prices received by the farmers affect every citizen.[13]

It is interesting to note that three of the varieties grown here — Sebago, Kennebec, and Katahdin — were bred by an Islander. He was Dr. F. J. Stevenson who was born on a farm at Fredericton, was a pupil in the Hazel Grove School, and later studied at Prince of Wales College in Charlottetown. He obtained his advanced education in the United States, in which country he continued to work, becoming Chief of the U.S.D.A. National Potato Breeding Programme.

In the opening years of the twentieth century the introduction of the automobile upset the social structure of the Island. In 1905 a second-hand Ford was brought here by Mr. T. B. Grady and Mr. Frank Compton of Summerside and a second-hand single-cylinder Cadillac was brought in by Mr. F. R. Frost. The next year Jimmie Offer imported an Oldsmobile, Dr. Alley a three-cylinder Compound, and Mr. W. K. Rogers a two-cylinder double-opposed Russell. These five cars started the trouble.

The machines were regarded, by all sane and thoughtful citizens, as potential destroyers of life and property, creators of clouds of noxious dust raised by their passage over the clay roads at speeds of up to fifteen miles an hour, and terrifiers of horses, old ladies, and sundry other sorts of animals and people. Agitation against the cars became vehement; editors were showered with letters of protest; and politicians debated the issue in the House and on the hustings.

From letters and speeches of the time the following choice statements will illustrate the attitudes that prevailed. "Total exclusion from the public highways — $500 tax — Autos must be hung up for all time to come — We have no right to allow such a nuisance on Prince Edward Island — Only a foolish fad of millionaires and fools — It may be all right for an undertaker to support the unrestricted running of automobiles. Necessary as is the calling of undertakers, and respectable as it may be, the intelligent electors of the Province will not support this modern death producer even for their benefit." Mr. Compton of Summerside was the undertaker referred to in the last item. "The proposition that the government widen the roads for the convenience of autoists is too ridiculous to be seriously dealt with. As far as tourists are concerned we wish to encourage them in every way and for this reason automobiles should be prohibited."

Faced with such a storm of protest, the use of the automobile was prohibited by a wise and provident Legislature in 1908. The resolution was moved by John Agnew and seconded by D. P. Irving. Premier Hazard, speaking in the debate, asserted that the mover had not gone far enough, and in this contention he was ably supported by J. A. Mathieson, leader of the Opposition. Several other speakers spoke in support of the resolution and a few radicals opposed it.

Thus it came about that the famous Automobile Act, which probably cost the province a great loss in tourist dollars and gained it great publicity abroad, was passed. It provided against the use of any motor vehicle on any public street or highway, and defined motor vehicles as "any motors, automobiles, or vehicles propelled by any power other than muscular power except such vehicles as run on rails and steam road rollers." The penalty for an infraction of the Act was a fine of $500 or six months in jail.

Some inexorable citizens, however, persisted in breaking the interdict by driving their cars in by-lanes at unholy hours, and the antipathy of the farmers was gradually overcome by offers of free rides, and by the barker's cry at picnics and fairs of "Have your picture taken in a real, live automobile!" In time, permission was granted to drive cars on certain roads in certain specified hours of certain days.

Then came World War I: and the cars drove everywhere at all hours of the day and night to carry out the mobilization. After that, opposition gradually subsided and cars, raising dust, envy, and various comments relative to the ruination of the Island, increased in numbers every year. Now we can't go to the corner drug store for a package of bobby pins without one. Technological advancements were beginning to move at accelerated speeds and the experiments of the Wright brothers in the United States, Alexander Graham Bell on Cape Breton Island, and others on both sides of the Atlantic suggested the awful truth that the day of the horse-and-buggy was coming to a close.

The first plane to soar over the Island thrilled the Provincial Exhibition patrons in 1912. It was flown by a young man named Peoli, who reached the dizzy altitude of 2,500 feet in his first demonstration and 5,000 feet in his second. He took the first aerial photographs of Charlottetown, flying up the Hillsborough River as far as Falconwood Hospital and circling over the city and its suburbs. In commenting on the event, one local editor wrote:

"The Provincial Exhibition of this year will go down in history as being the first at which aeroplane flights were given, and the revolutionizing possibilities of the science of aviation were demonstrated to thousands of interested Prince Edward Islanders, who can now look forward to the day when that nine-mile strip of water which divides us from the mainland need no longer be considered a barrier in the way of continuous communication, winter or summer."[14]

The next year [1913] the Women's Institute, an organization that has since fostered and supported many forward movements, came into being, the first branch opening at Marshfield on April 1. The organization, deeply involved in programs of social action, now has 252 branches and a membership of 4,000.

In the meantime, advances in the agricultural sector were exerting a tremendous influence on the economy and sociology of the province. Indeed, some of the local research endeavours have been of great benefit to other parts of the continent. Some examples of these are the 1933 discovery that brown heart disease of turnip is caused by a soil deficiency of the element boron; the introduction of the practice of potato top killing in the early 1940's; the release of Abegweit oats in 1947, of the clubroot-resistant turnip variety York in 1963, and the oat variety Cabot in 1967 — all bred by scientists on Prince Edward Island.

In 1959 the Experimental Station and the Science Service Laboratory were amalgamated, the unit being designated an Experimental Farm. As a result of the diverse nature of its research programmes, the Farm was elevated to the rank of Research Station in 1966 and Dr. Glenn C. Russell was transferred from Lethbridge, Alberta, to be its first director. At the present time twenty-one scientists are on the staff.

In 1972, under the Prince Edward Island Development Plan, the extension, production, and veterinary services of the Provincial Department of Agriculture and Forestry were located in the Station's new office-laboratory complex built on University Avenue. This modern complex was developed by renovating the Science Service Laboratory, built in 1952, and by attaching large extensions to it. It has been financed jointly by the Research Branch of the Canada Department of Agriculture, the Department of Regional Economic Expansion, and the Prince Edward Island Department of Agriculture and Forestry.

It was considered that, by housing research and extension people under one roof, the Federal and Provincial Departments, working together, would accept, with confidence, the challenge to develop the agricultural potential of the Island according to the methods and hopes set forth by the ambitious Prince Edward Island Development Plan.

The greatest impetus to the cultural life of the province came in 1964 when Confederation Centre was opened as a national shrine to the Fathers of Confederation, whose initial meetings had been held in the old Colonial Building in September of 1864 and which eventually led to the welding of the colonies of British North America into a great nation stretching across the northern half of the continent *a mari usque ad mare.*

The huge complex of buildings had been financed by the federal government with a grant of fifteen cents per capita of the Canadian population and by the provincial governments with grants of fifteen cents per capita of their populations. At the time these commitments were made, the population of the country was calculated to be the rather odd number of 18,666,666 persons.

Forty-seven models were entered in a national architectural competition for which prize money of $30,000 was provided by Canada Council. The first prize of $7,500 was won by a group of Montreal architects and was presented by Governor General Vanier at a dinner in Ottawa. The incumbent Prime Minister, Hon. John G. Diefenbaker, delivered the address.

The sod-turning ceremony was held in the afternoon of Saturday, February 2, 1963, Hon. Robert Lorne Stanfield, then Premier of Nova Scotia, hacking a small hole in the frozen ground with a silver spade. The cornerstone was laid by Hon. Lester B. Pearson who, at that time, was Prime Minister of Canada, on August 26, 1963.

The complex stood, in the spring of 1964, a concrete colossus on Charlottetown's Queen Square, dwarfing the adjacent building in which the 1864 event it was to memorialize had taken place. It would, many people were quick to point out, become a white elephant whose appetite for funds would be a terrible drain on the provincial treasury and, consequently, on the payers of taxes. There were even some malicious individuals who suggested that it might have a useful future as a potato warehouse.

But it soon became evident that, in addition to its physical size, the most elephantine feature of the complex was the immensity of its cultural and entertainment potential. Through the summer and autumn of 1964 the Centre had maintained an almost unbroken series of events, including a Royal variety concert for Queen Elizabeth II, and people had flocked to see the exhibitions in the art gallery.

Every event staged in the theatre in 1964 had been distinctly and unmistakably Canadian — Canadian writers, composers, musicians, directors, choreographers, designers, actors, actresses, singers, dancers — and residents and tourists had filled the 946-seat theatre to see what they had to offer. An idea had been born.[15]

Mavor Moore, the artistic director of the theatre from its opening until October of 1967, decided to embark on a rash experiment — a completely Canadian summer festival through July and August of 1965. With him in the wild scheme were the incomparable team of Wayne and Shuster, assistant director and choreographer Alan Lund, music director John Fenwick, theatre director Robert Dubberley, and several other persons of talent and determination. There was to be no Shakespeare, no Shaw, no Rodgers and Hammerstein. Everything was to be Canadian from script writing to the last curtain call.

Summer Festival '65 opened with a musical based on the Island classic novel by Lucy Maud Montgomery, *Anne of Green Gables*. The show was an immediate hit and soon even the paper boys on their routes could often be heard whistling the opening bars of the title song:

> Anne of Green Gables never change,
> I like you just this way.
> Anne of Green Gables in my heart
> You are forever young.

Since its first performance, the *Anne* musical has been the leader at the box office every summer, has been staged in major Canadian cities, has thrilled audiences in London, New York, and Osaka, and, in this year of 1973, it went on an extensive tour of the provinces as the Island's centennial year gift to Canada.

The rash experiment of 1965 was an unqualified success and it was apparent that a breakthrough had been made in the Canadian entertainment field. The Summer Festival has improved annually and is now regarded as the nation's leading showcase for original musical theatre.[16]

Other major divisions of the Fathers of Confederation Memorial Building are the art gallery, archives, and library. The art gallery, under curator Moncrieff Williamson, opened in 1964 and has since brought in many exhibitions of paintings, sculptures, tapestries, and other art forms, has provided art classes for children, and has accumulated works and memorabilia of the Island's greatest artist, Robert Harris, best known for his famous painting, *The Fathers of Confederation*.[17] The gallery now has close to two hundred of his oils, water colors, drawings, and sketches in its permanent collection. In addition, there are files containing about 1,500 experimental and roughly outlined bits and pieces.

An Act to establish the Public Archives of Prince Edward Island received Royal Assent on March 24, 1964, and the task of locating the vast quantity of scattered materials and of assembling them in orderly fashion was begun. Among the primary source materials collected to date are government papers and documents, private manuscripts, photographs, pictures, maps, newspapers, and pamphlets. Secondary source material includes most standard histories, biographies, directories, almanacs, periodicals, and publications of local historical societies. As the work of collecting, sorting, indexing, and microfilming progresses, the unit will be able to offer improved services, not only to the general public, but to future writers and historians who, unlike the compilers of this book, will not be hampered and frustrated by chaos at home nor compelled to go to Ottawa to research local history.

The library, although maintained by the Provincial Department of Education, tries to have a national policy in keeping with the purpose of the Confederation Centre. At the present time there are some 40,000 books in the adult section and these are being circulated at the rate of from 1,500 to 2,000 per week. Circulation is running at 800 to 1,000 books per week in the expanding children's section. A special project for Centennial Year is to provide more circulating copies of books by Island authors, it being increasingly evident that people are discovering that, in the more than four centuries since Jacques Cartier landed on our north shore, a rich treasure of history has been laid down, interesting layer upon interesting layer.

The opening years of the 1970's have seen changes in several aspects of our social and economic structure and the beginnings of certain influences that will affect it in the future. Not being given to prophesy, the writer wisely leaves the analyses of them to future historians.

What will they have to say about our times? Will they record that the number of farmers continued to decline and the average size of farms continued to increase, that farmers remained divided into such opposing groups as the Federation of Agriculture and the National Farmers' Union, that no solution to stabilize the marketing of our farm produce was agreed upon and put into operation? Will they be able to write about the success of the Prince Edward Island Development Plan and of the recently instituted effort to save the family farm? Will they enthusiastically observe that tourism exerted tremendous pressure in raising the economy but was developed in a manner that preserved the natural charm and beauty of the Island? Will they describe the final phasing out of the railroad and the initial stages of the building of a causeway-bridge link with the mainland?

Will the history of the next hundred years be a drab account of progress or will its pages be sprinkled with some of the same old foibles, errors, bickerings, and comedies that have made the last one such an interesting period to explore?

Footnotes

Footnotes to Chapter One

1. Cartier's original manuscript was located in the Imperial Library in Paris in 1867. That section of Cartier's account that pertains to Prince Edward Island is reproduced in D. C. Harvey's *The French Regime in Prince Edward Island* (New Haven, 1926), pp. 4-6.
2. A. B. Warburton, D. C. L., K. C., *A History of Prince Edward Island* (St. John, 1923), p. 13.
3. Harvey, *op. cit.,* p. 7.
4. *Ibid.,* pp. 8-9.
5. A. H. Clark, *Three Centuries and the Island* (Toronto, 1959), p. 25.
6. Harvey, *op. cit.,* p. 16.
7. J. Henri Blanchard, *The Acadians of Prince Edward Island, 1720-1964* (Quebec, 1964), p. 16.
8. Harvey, *op. cit.,* p. 17.
9. Blanchard, *op. cit.,* p. 16.
10. Harvey, *op. cit.,* p. 25.
11. *Ibid.,* p. 28.
12. *Ibid.,* p. 33.
13. *Ibid.,* p. 37.
14. *Ibid.,* pp. 40-41.
15. Blanchard, *op. cit.,* p. 19.
16. Harvey, *op. cit.,* p. 47.
17. Clark, *op. cit.,* p. 28.
18. Blanchard, *op. cit.,* p. 22.
19. Harvey, *op. clt.,* pp. 52-53.
20. Blanchard, *op. cit.,* p. 23.
21. Harvey, *op. cit.,* p. 60.
22. For a complete listing see Blanchard, *op. cit.,* pp. 25-27.
23. Harvey, *op. cit.,* p. 63.
24. *Ibid.,* p. 65.
25. *Ibid.,* pp. 67-68.
26. *Ibid.,* pp. 73-75.
27. Blanchard, *op. cit.,* pp. 28-29.
28. Harvey, *op. cit.,* p. 91.
29. A statement formalizing the results of the archaeological investigations, conducted under the direction of the National and Historic Parks Branch of the Department of Indian Affairs and Northern Development, should be forthcoming in the near future.
30. Harvey, *op. cit.,* p. 96.
31. *Ibid.,* p. 99.
32. Blanchard, *op. cit.,* p. 31.
33. Harvey, *op. cit.,* p. 105.
34. Blanchard, *op. cit.,* p. 31.
35. *Ibid.,* p. 32.
36. The Articles of Indulgence are reprinted in Harvey, *op. cit.,* pp. 116-118.
37. *Ibid.,* pp. 121-122.
38. More complete details are provided by Harvey, *ibid.,* pp. 131-132.
39. Clark, *op. cit.,* pp. 31-32.
40. *Ibid.,* pp. 32-33.
41. *Ibid.*
42. Caven, J., "A Journey from Port La Joie to Trois Rivieres (Georgetown) in 1751" *Prince Edward Island Magazine,* vol II, No. 9, pp. 286-287.

43. *Ibid.,* p. 287.
44. This census is printed in full in the *Report of the Canadian Archives,* 1905, vol. II, pp. 77-165.
45. Harvey, *op. cit.,* pp. 170-171.
46. Clark, *op. cit.,* p. 38.
47. Reproduced in full by Harvey, *op. cit.,* p. 179.
48. *Ibid.,* pp. 181-183.

Footnotes to Chapter Two

1. Order-in-Council, May 9, 1764, *Hardwicke Papers,* vol. DXLV, British Museum, Additional Manuscripts, 35, 913,pp. 12-16.
2. Colonial Office, 217, vol. 24, 1767, pp. 3-72. There were some 166 petitioners including 63 members of Colonel Simon Fraser's Regiment who were co-signators with him. Forty-three applied directly to the Privy Council, and of these, 39 received lots.
3. *London Gazette,* June 9, 1767: Institute of Historical Research, London University, London, England.
4. Although this group deserved special consideration because of their sizeable investments on the Island, the Commissioners were, perhaps, too generous since Mure, Cathcart, Mill and Spence also participated in the lottery, and the first two received Lot 12, and the latter two Lot 36.
5. "Letter of the Lords of Trade and Plantations to the Earl of Egmont," June 5, 1767, C. O. 218, vol. 7, p. 213.
6. "Letter of the Earl of Egmont to the Lords of Trade and Plantations," June 6, 1767, C. O. 217, vol. 22, p. 57.
7. *Minute of His Majesty's Commissioners for Trade and Plantations,* July 8, 1767, pp. 6-7, Orders-in-Council (Imperial), Part 2, Sessional Papers (Canada), 1906. Public Archives of Canada.
8. *Minute of His Majesty's Commissioners for Trade and Plantations,* July 23, 1767, pp. 10-11, *ibid.*
9. John Pownall to Viscount George Townshend, July 24, 1767. *Townshend Papers,* Kelley Memorial Library, University of Prince Edward Island, Charlottetown.
10. Andrew H. Clark, *Three Centuries and the Island* (Toronto, 1959), pp. 49-50, and Appendix B, pp. 263-269.
11. *Minute of His Majesty's Commissioners for Trade and Plantations,* July 23, 1767, *ibid.,* pp. 10-11.
12. *Minute of His Majesty's Commissioners for Trade and Plantations,* July 8, 1767, *ibid.,* pp. 8-9.
13. William Campbell to the Earl of Hillsborough, April 6, 1768, C. O. 218, vol. 17, p. 51. The Earl of Hillsborough eventually had an order-in-council issued which obligated the proprietors to apply for their grants under pain of forfeiture before May 1, 1769, *ibid,* p. 54.
14. "The Petition of the Proprietors of the Island of St. John in the Gulph of St. Lawrence to the King," May 31, 1768, C. O. vol. 27, pp. 168-169.
15. Order-in-Council, June 28, 1768, *ibid.,* p. 167.
16. *Ibid.*
17. *Minute of the Commissioners for Trade and Plantations,* August 5, 1768, *Journal of the Commissioners for Trade and Plantations: January, 1768 to December 1775* (London, 1937), p. 46. All the proprietors, with the exception of eight, concurred in this arrangement.
18. *Ibid.,* May 25, 1769, p. 95.
19. *Ibid.,* pp. 136-137.
20. *Ibid.,* p. 134.
21. Order-in-Council, June 28, 1769, Privy Council II, vol. 14, pp. 67-69.
22. Earl of Hillsborough to Michael Francklin, February 26, 1768, C. O. 217, vol. 22, pp. 188-189.
23. Francklin to Hillsborough, May 29, 1768, *ibid.,* pp. 202-203.

24. *Treasury Minute,* June 15, 1769, *Treasury Papers,* T. 29, vol. 40, p. 17, P. R. O.
25. *Minutes of the Privy Council,* July 14, 1769, and August 4, 1769. *Colonial Records,* Manuscript Group II, pp. 122-128.
26. Walter Patterson to the Earl of Hillsborough, October 25, 1770, C. O. 226, vol. 1, p. 15. See also Frank MacKinnon, *The Government of Prince Edward Island* (Toronto, 1951), Chapters I and II, for an excellent analysis of early government on the Island.
27. *Journal of the Proceedings of His Majesty's Council of St. John's Island Under the Administration of His Excellency Walter Patterson,* September 19, 1770, vol. 1, p. 60.
28. *Ibid.*
29. Patterson to Hillsborough, October 24, 1770, C. O. 226, vol. 1, p. 11.
30. *Ibid.,* p. 13.
31. *Ibid.,* pp. 12-13. Sir James Montgomery, the proprietor of Lot 7, bought Lot 34 from the heirs of John Dickson, the original owner, who died in 1767.
32. Letters of John MacDonald, 1772-1805, *Captain John MacDonald Papers.* These voluminous papers of Captain John MacDonald are in the possession of Rev. A. F. MacDonald, University of Prince Edward Island, who kindly made them available to the writer. Captain MacDonald soon acquired Lot 35, and placed settlers in that lot.
33. John Stewart, *An Account of Prince Edward Island in the Gulph of St. Lawrence, North America* (London, 1806), pp. 168-170.
34. Patterson to Dartmouth, May 1, 1774, C. O. 226, vol. 6, p. 11.
35. Stewart, *op. cit.,* pp. 167-175.
36. Patterson to Hillsborough, September 3, 1771, C. O. 226, vol. 1, p. 45.
37. Duport to Hillsborough, September 3, 1771, *ibid.* pp. 86-87.
38. Ordinance and Act of Council for the Effectual Recovery of Certain of His Majesty's Quit Rents in the Island of St. John. *Council Journal,* 1771, pp. 81-82.
39. Hillsborough to Patterson, August 7, 1772, C. O. 189, vol. 10, p. 150. See also Dartmouth to Patterson, November 4, 1772, *ibid.,* p. 181. The Earl of Dartmouth replaced the Earl of Hillsborough as Secretary of State on August 14, 1772.
40. Dartmouth to Patterson, December 1, 1773, *ibid.,* p. 183. This was merely a restatement of views expressed in previous despatches. See Hillsborough to Patterson, August 7, 1772, *ibid.,* p. 180, and Dartmouth to Patterson, November 4, 1772, *ibid.,* p. 181.
41. "Memorial of Samuel Smith on behalf of the Proprietors to the Earl of Dartmouth," December 30, 1772, *Dartmouth Papers* Manuscript Group 23 Series A, vol. 15.
42. *Ibid.*
43. Patterson to Dartmouth, May 20, 1773, C. O. 226, vol. 5, p. 52.
44. Patterson to Dartmouth, February 17, 1773, *ibid.,* p. 44.
45. *Ibid.*
46. *Ibid.*
47. Dartmouth to Patterson, December 1, 1773, C. O. 189, vol. 10, pp. 183-184.
48. *Ibid.,* p. 184.
49. *Journal of the House of Assembly, St. John's Island,* 1773, vol. 1, pp. 1-2.
50. Acts of the General Assembly of Prince Edward Island, 1773, Caput XIII, *Laws of Prince Edward Island,* vol. 1, 1773-1814 (Charlottetown, 1851).
51. Patterson to Dartmouth, July 15, 1773, C. O. 226, vol. 5, p. 44.
52. *Journal of the House of Assembly,* St. John's Island, 1774, vol. 2, pp. 1-2.
53. Patterson to Dartmouth, May 20, 1773, C. O. 226, vol. 5, p. 53.
54. *Ibid.*
55. Patterson to Dartmouth, May 1, 1774, C. O. 226, vol. 6, p. 15.
56. Patterson to Dartmouth, September 2, 1774, *ibid.,* p. 32.
57. Dartmouth to Patterson, January 7, 1775, C. O. 189, vol. 10, p. 187. See also Dartmouth to Patterson, February 1, 1775, p. 188. Lord Dartmouth had tried unsuccessfully in 1774 to obtain a pariamentary grant for the Island.
58. "Memorial of Eighteen Proprietors to the King's Most Excellent Majesty in Council," February, 1776, P. C. 1./3166, P. R. O.
59. *Ibid.*
60. *Ibid.*
61. *Treasury Minute,* August 7, 1776, *Treasury Papers,* vol. 45, pp. 297-299, P. R. O.
62. Phillips Callbeck to Dartmouth, August 3, 1775, C. O. 266, vol. 6, p. 74.
63. Peter Stewart to Lord George Germain, July 10, 1779, C. O. 226, vol. 7, p. 38.
64. Callbeck to Germain, May 18, 1778, *ibid.,* p. 28.

65. DesBrisay to Germain, December 7, 1779, *ibid.,* p. 44. DesBrisay was ordered by Germain to go to the Island or vacate his post. See Germain to DesBrisay, July 23, 1779, C. O. 189, vol. 10, p. 199.
66. Callbeck to Germain, July 15, 1776, C. O. 226, vol. 6, p. 140.
67. Callbeck to Germain, January 5, 1776, *ibid.,* p. 80.
68. Germain to Callbeck, April 1, 1776, C. O. 189, vol. 10, p. 190.
69. Germain to Callbeck, May 19, 1780, C. O. 226, vol. 7, p. 64.
70. Callbeck to Germain, August 18, 1778, *ibid.,* p. 24.
71. Patterson to Germain, October 10, 1780, C. O. 226, vol. 7, p. 88.
72. Germain to Patterson, February 28, 1781, C. O. 189, vol. 10, p. 206.
73. Patterson to Germain, July 6, 1780, C. O. 226, vol. 7, p. 71.
74. *Ibid.,* p. 72.
75. DesBrisay to Germain, November 23, 1780, *ibid.,* p. 110.
76. Patterson to Germain, September 20, 1780, *ibid.,* p. 80.
77. *Journal of the House of Assembly of St. John's Island,* 1779, vol. 3, pp. 1-2.
78. Patterson to Germain, July 30, 1780, C. O. 226, vol. 7, p. 73.
79. *Ibid.*
80. Germain to Patterson, February 28, 1781, C. O. 226, vol. 189, p. 205.
81. Acts of the General Assembly of Prince Edward Island, 1798, Caput 1, *Laws of Prince Edward Island,* vol. 1, 1773-1814 (Charlottetown).
82. Patterson to Germain, July 30, 1780, C. O. 226, vol. 7, p. 74.
83. Patterson to Germain September 21, 1780, *ibid.,* p. 82.
84. *Minute of Council,* November 26, 1780, C. O. 226, vol. 3, p. 280.
85. Acts of the General Assembly of Prince Edward Island, 1781, Caput XIII, *Laws of Prince Edward Island,* 1773-1814 (Charlottetown, 1851).
86. Patterson to John Stuart, December 7, 1783, C. O. 226, vol. 9, p. 61.
87. *Ibid.*
88. *Ibid.,* p. 88.
89. Patterson to Lord North, April 10, 1784, C. O. 226, vol. 8, p. 76.
90. Patterson to John Stuart, December 7, 1783, *ibid.,* p. 57.
91. *Ibid.,* p. 58.
92. Lord North to Patterson, May 12, 1783, C. O. 189, vol. 10, p. 214.
93. *Ibid.,* pp. 214-215.
94. *Ibid.*
95. "Draft of a Bill ordered by Whitehall to be passed by the Governor of St. John's Island," C. O. 226, vol. 3, p. 69.
96. *Ibid.,* p. 72.
97. Lord North to Patterson, July 24, 1783, C. O. 189, vol. 10, p. 219.
98. Captain John MacDonald to Nelly MacDonald, July 19, 1783. *Captain John MacDonald Papers.*
99. Patterson to Lord North, April 10, 1784, C. O. 226, vol. 9, p. 72.
100. *Ibid.,* p. 73.
101. Captain John MacDonald to Nelly MacDonald, July 19, 1783. *Captain John MacDonald Papers.*
102. Walter Patterson to Lord North, April 15, 1784, C. O. 226, vol. 8, p. 82.
103. W. S. McNutt, "Fanning's Regime on Prince Edward Island," *Acadiensis,* vol. 1, No. 1, p. 38.
104. Walter Patterson to Lord North, December 12, 1784, C. O. 226, vol. 9, p. 169.
105. Walter Patterson to Lord North, April 15, 1784, C. O. 226, vol. 8, pp. 82-83.
106. *Ibid.*
107. *Ibid.,* p. 82. See also McNutt, *op. cit.,* p. 38.
108. *Ibid.,* pp. 84-85.
109. "Charges by the Assembly of the Island of St. John against Walter Patterson," C. O. 266, vol. 3, pp. 164-166. See also MacKinnon, *op. cit.,* pp. 23-24.
110. "Charges against Chief Justice Peter Stewart by Walter Patterson," *ibid.,* pp. 170-171.
111. Memorial of 17 undersigned proprietors to Lord North, June 29, 1783, C. O. 226, vol. 3, pp. 5-6. The total acreage owned by these proprietors was 436,000 acres, one-quarter of which was made available. The largest proprietors willing to participate were Lawrence Sullivan with 80,000 acres and Baron Montgomery with 60,000 acres.
112. Lord North to Walter Patterson, July, 1783, *ibid.,* p. 54.
113. Patterson to Lord North, November 20, 1784, C. O. 226, vol. 9, p. 117. Patterson

said that no more than five hundred settled on the Island. See also A. H. Clark, *op. cit.*, pp. 57-58.

114. Patterson to Lord North, November 20, 1784, *ibid.*, pp. 117-119.
115. John Stewart, *op. cit.*, pp. 194-195. Stewart, although not an unbiased witness, asserted that Patterson and his friends spent two thousand pounds in the electoral campaign.
116. *Journal of the House of Assembly of St. John's Island*, 1785, vol. 1, p. 1.
117. Walter Patterson to Lord Sydney, April 20, 1785, C. O. 226, vol. 8, p. 171.
118. "Petition of Robert Clark to the Secretary of State," August, 1784, P. C. 1./61, Bundle 13, P. R. C.
119. Lord Sydney to Patterson, September 11, 1784, C. O. 226, vol. 9, p. 106.
120. *Ibid.*, p. 107.
121. John Stuart to Lord Sydney, February 23, 1785, *ibid.*, p. 151.
122. "Report upon the Memorial of several of the proprietors on the Island of St. John against the Lieutenant Governor and others of His Majesty's Officers," April 25, 1785, P. C. 2, vol. 134, p. 155.
123. *Minute of the British Privy Council*, May 6, 1785, P. C. 2, vol. 130, pp. 211-212.
124. Patterson to Lord Sydney, May 1, 1786, *ibid.*, p. 109.
125. *Ibid.*
126. *Minutes of the Council of St. John's Island*, April 21, 1786, *ibid.*, p. 109.
127. "Evidence of John Cambridge and Others", *ibid.*, pp. 135-139.
128. Patterson to Lord Sydney, May 1, 1786, *ibid.*, p. 97.
129. "Petition of the Undersigned Proprietors to the King," March, 1786, P. C. 1./61, B 11-15, Part II.
130. Lord Sydney to Patterson, June 30, 1786, C. O. 226, vol. 10, p. 1.
131. *Ibid.*
132. Patterson to Fanning, November 7, 1786, *ibid.*, p. 128.
133. Patterson to Lord Sydney, November 5, 1786, *ibid.*, p. 18.
134. *Ibid.*, p. 19.
135. *Journal of the House of Assembly of St. John's Island*, November, 1786, *ibid.*, p. 295.
136. *Ibid.*
137. "Address of a Committee of the House of Assembly to Lieutenant Governor Walter Patterson," November 14, 1786, Assembly Journal, p. 297.
138. *Ibid.*
139. *Assembly Journal*, p. 298.
140. Enclosure in Fanning to Sydney, March 8, 1787. C. O. 226, vol. 10, pp. 73-76.
141. Patterson to Sydney, November 19, 1786, *ibid.*, p. 151. Patterson had purchased Lots 49, 57, and 67, and halves of Lots 17, 26, 48, and 65.
142. Proclamation of Edmund Fanning, April 10, 1787, *ibid.*, p. 88.
143. Proclamation of Walter Patterson, April 11, 1787, *ibid.*, p. 90.
144. Lord Sydney to Walter Patterson, April 5, 1787, C. O. 189, vol. 10, pp. 230-231.
145. Lord Sydney to Edmund Fanning, April 5, 1787, C. O. 189, vol. 10, p. 232.
146. *Minute of the British Privy Council*, July 24, 1789, P. C. 11, vol. 134, p. 186.
147. John MacDonald to Nelly MacDonald, September 12, 1789. *Captain John MacDonald Papers.*
148. *Minute of the British Privy Council*, July 24, 1789, P. C. 11, vol, 134, pp. 186-187.

Footnotes to Chapter Three

1. W. S. MacNutt, "Fanning's Regime on Prince Edward Island," *Acadiensis,* vol. 1, No. 1, pp. 37-38.
2. Patrick C. T. White, *Lord Selkirk's Diary, 1803-1804* (Toronto, The Champlain Society, 1958), p.6.
3. D. C. Harvey, "The Loyal Electors," *Proceedings and Transactions of the Royal Society of Canada,* XXIV, 1930, p. 102.
4. *Minutes of Council,* July 17, 1787, C. O. 226, vol. 11, p. 89.
5. *Ibid.*, August 20, 1787, p. 113.
6. *Journal of the House of Assembly of St. John's Island,* January 22, 1788, C. O. 226, vol. 12, p. 53.
7. Fanning to Sydney, April 16, 1788, *ibid.*, p. 32.

8. *Assembly Journal, ibid.,* p. 50.
9. Fanning to Nepean, April 30, 1788, *ibid.,* p. 95.
10. *Ibid.*
11. Fanning to Grenville, April 21, 1790, C. O. 226, vol. 13, p. 101.
12. Fanning to Grenville, November 24, 1789, *ibid.,* p. 9.
13. Fanning to Sydney, November 26, 1787, C. O. 226, vol. 12, p. 6.
14. *Ibid.,* pp. 6-7.
15. "Memorandum of John Hill on members of the House of Assembly and Legislative Council of Prince Edward Island," C. O. 226, vol. 18, p. 213.
16. *Ibid.,* p. 218.
17. Enclosure in a narrative of Prince Edward Island by John Hill, C. O. 226, vol. 17, p. 124.
18. *Ibid.*
19. *Ibid.,* p. 125.
20. *Ibid.,* p. 126.
21. "Petition to His Excellency, Major General Edmund Fanning, LL.D., Lieutenant Governor and Officer Commanding St. John's Island," March 23, 1797, C. O. 226, vol. 15, pp. 180-181. It should be noted that John Stewart was one of the three who did not sign the petition.
22. Sixth session of the Sixth General Assembly, *Journal of the House of Assembly of His Majesty's Island of St. John,* C. O. 226, *ibid.,* pp. 166-174.
23. *Ibid.,* p. 168.
24. *Ibid.,* p. 169.
25. *Ibid.,* p. 170.
26. *Ibid.,* pp. 171-172.
27. *Ibid.,* p. 172
28. *Ibid.*
29. *Ibid.*
30. *Ibid.*
31. "Colonial Office Memorandum," April 4, 1802, C. O. 226, vol. 18, p. 6.
32. *Ibid.*
33. Lord Hobart to Edmund Fanning, August 6, 1802, *ibid.,* pp. 24-25. The last class, those who had no settlers on their lots, had to pay fifteen years arrears.
34. *Ibid.,* p. 25.
35. *Ibid.,* p. 26.
36. *Ibid.,* p. 27.
37. *Ibid.*
38. *Ibid.*
39. *Ibid.,* pp. 27-28.
40. *Ibid.*
41. "Speech from the Throne by Edmund Fanning." November 2, 1802, *Journal of the House of Assembly of Prince Edward Island, 1802, ibid.,* p. 54.
42. *Ibid.,* p. 54-55.
43. Reply of Fanning to the Address of the Assembly, November 4, 1802, *ibid.,* p. 57.
44. *Assembly Journal, ibid.,* p. 62.
45. *Journal of the House of Assembly of Prince Edward Island, 1803,* C. O. 226, vol. 19, p. 81. Robert Hodgson chose to sit for Prince County and new elections were called for Georgetown and Queen's County. Ralph Brecken was returned for Queen's County and Francis Longworth for Georgetown.
46. *Ibid.,* p. 106.
47. *Ibid.,* p. 123.
48. Petition of a Joint Committee of House of Assembly and Legislative Council, April, 1803, *ibid.,* pp. 255-256.
49. William Knox to Hobart, April 26, 1803, *ibid.,* p. 253.
50. *Ibid.*
51. Stewart, *op. cit.,* p. 252. The townships sold or transferred by Stewart were as follows: 1, 10, 17, 23, 24, 31, 32. 33, 38, 39, 41, 42, 43, 54, 57, 58, 60 and 62; ½ of townships 12, 37, 40 and 47; ⅓ of townships 53 and 59.
52. Enclosure in Fanning to Hobart, March 9, 1804, C. O. 226, vol. 20, p. 5. The townships proceeded against were as follows: 2, 3, 4, 5, 6, 8, 9, 15, 52, 55; ½ of townships 12, 25, 27, 45, 46, and ⅓ of 59.

53. Robert Thorp to Sir George (Illegible), Jan. 19, 1803, C. O. 226, vol. 19, p. 202.
54. Fanning to Hobart, March 9, 1804, C. O. 226, vol, 20, p. 3.
55. *Ibid.*
56. *Ibid.*, p. 4.
57. White, *op. cit.*, p. 28.
58. Fanning to Hobart, July 30, 1804, C. O. 226, vol. 20, p. 11. The letter of recall was dated May 9, 1804. Fanning had written to Knox expressing his shock over the Greenwich paper's announcement. See Fanning to Knox, July 26, 1804, *ibid.*, p. 130.
59. Lord Hobart to Edmund Fanning, May 9, 1804, *ibid.*, p. 9.
60. G. N. D. Evans, *Uncommon Obdurate: The Several Public Careers of J. F. W. DesBarres* (Toronto, 1969). This biography is an excellent study of the life of J. F. W. DesBarres.
61. J. F. W. DesBarres to the Earl of Camden, July 1, 1805, C. O. 226, vol. 20, p. 47.
62. J. F. W. DesBarres to the Earl of Camden, Aug. 6, 1805, *ibid.*, p. 49. The census was taken in July, 1805.
63. "Reply of J. F. W. DesBarres to the Address of the Committee of the House of Assembly," November 18, 1805, *ibid.*, p. 86.
64. "Address of the House of Assembly of Prince Edward Island to the King's most Excellent Majesty," November 20, 1805, *ibid.*, p. 99.
65. *Ibid.*, pp. 99-100.
66. *Ibid.*, p. 101.
67. *Ibid.*, p. 102.
68. "Memorial of Island Proprietors to Lieutenant Governor J. F. W. DesBarres," December, 1805, *ibid.*, p. 109. The memorial was signed by William Townshend, Charles Worrell and John Cambridge.
69. *Ibid.*, p. 110.
70. J. F. W. DesBarres to Edward Cooke, December 5, 1805, *ibid.*, p. 112.
71. *Ibid.*, pp. 112-113.
72. *Ibid.*, p. 113.
73. *DesBarres Papers*, Series V, p. 2548, P. A. C.
74. *Ibid.*, p. 2567.
75. *Ibid.*, p. 2554.
76. *Ibid.*, pp. 2559-2560.
77. *Ibid.*, p. 2613.
78. *Ibid.*, p. 2619.
79. Basil Greenhill and Ann Giffard, *West Countrymen in Prince Edward's Isle* (Toronto, 1967), pp. 28-29. Hill was only slightly exaggerating when he stated that he was personally responsible for the recall of both Fanning and DesBarres.
80. "Memorial of the Undersigned Proprietors Against Escheat, 1804," C. O. 226, vol. 19, p. 170.
81. *Ibid.*
82. "Memorial of the Undersigned Proprietors to the Earl of Camden, April 13, 1805," C. O. 226, vol. 20, p. 202.
83. *Minute of the Lords Commissioners of His Majesty's Treasury*, August 31, 1808, *DesBarres Papers*, Series V, pp. 2664-2665.
84. *Journal of the House of Assembly for Prince Edward Island, 1808*, C. O. 226, vol. 21, p. 95.
85. D. C. Harvey, "The Loyal Electors," *Transactions of the Royal Society of Canada*, Section 11, 1930, pp. 101-110. Harvey's article is an excellent analysis of the *Loyal Electors*.
86. "Affidavit of William Roubel," September 17, 1811, C. O. 226, vol. 25, p. 102. William Roubel, an attorney, was a member of the society from 1809 until 1811.
87. J. F. W. DesBarres to the Earl of Liverpool, July 3, 1810, *ibid.*, p. 11.
88. *Ibid.*, p. 12.
89. *Ibid.*
90. Lord Selkirk to the Earl of Liverpool, March 2, 1811, *ibid.*, p. 80.
91. "Memorial to William Roubel," 1811, C. O. 226, vol. 28, p. 24.
92. "Affidavit of Elisha LePage," May 30, 1811, *ibid.*, p. 75.
93. Harvey, *op. cit.*, pp. 106-107.
94. "Address of the Assembly," September 26, 1812, C. O. 226, vol. 26, p. 108.
95. Colclough to Robert Montgomery, March 26, 1812, *ibid.*, p. 108.
96. Document entitled, "State of P.E.I.," *ibid.*, p. 165.

97. *Ibid.,* pp. 165-166.
98. Earl of Bathurst to DesBarres, August 4, 1812, *ibid.,* p. 12.
99. J. F. W. DesBarres to Lord Bathurst, October 5, 1812, *ibid.,* p. 39.
100. Bathurst to Smith, May 4, 1813, C. O. 226, vol. 28, p. 46.
101. Smith to Bathurst, July 29, 1813, C. O. 226, vol. 29, p. 68.
102. *Ibid.,* p. 69. Smith had reached definitive conclusions some fifteen days after his arrival on the Island.
103. "Speech from the Throne," November 7, 1813, *Journal of the House of Assembly of Prince Edward Island, 1813,* C. O. 226, vol. 28, p. 5.
104. Prorogation Speech, January 13, 1814, *ibid.,* p. 6.
105. Smith to Bathurst, January 15, 1814, *ibid.,* p. 3.
106. *Ibid.*
107. *Ibid.,* p. 4.
108. Smith to Bathurst, September 17, 1814, *ibid.,* pp. 80-81.
109. *Ibid.,* p. 4.
110. Smith to Bathurst, February 17, 1815, C. O. 226, vol. 30, p. 11.
111. Smith to Bathurst, June 13, 1815, *ibid.,* p. 42.
112. *Ibid.*
113. *Ibid.,* pp. 44-45.
114. *Ibid.,* p. 48.
115. "Memorial of the Undersigned Proprietors," 1814, *ibid.,* pp. 176-186. This memorial was signed by, among others, Lord Selkirk, Robert Montgomery, Stephen Sullivan, John Hill, Lord Westmorland, Lord Melville, and, ironically enough, by Edmund Fanning.
116. *Ibid.,* p. 185.
117. *Ibid.,* pp. 185-186.
118. *Ibid.,* p. 186.
119. Bathurst to Smith, May 16, 1816, C. O. 227, vol. 7, p. 60.
120. *Ibid.*
121. Bathurst to Smith, July 13, 1816, *ibid.,* p. 63.
122. "Statement of John Stewart, Receiver-General, on Quit Rent Receipts and Disbursements," November 15, 1816, C. O. 226, vol. 31, pp. 150-151. Most of these payments were made at the time of the Quit Rent composition. Lord Selkirk, for example, was credited with nearly £1,000.
123. Smith to Bathurst, October 31, 1816, *ibid.,* p. 126.
124. "Proclamation of Charles Douglas Smith," October 5, 1816, C. O. 226, vol. 34, p. 110.
125. *Ibid.*
126. Smith to Bathurst, October 2, 1816, C. O. 226, vol. 31, p. 113.
127. "Special Notice to all Landowners from J. E. Carmichael," January 5, 1818, C. O. 226, vol. 32, p. 277.
128. Smith to Bathurst, February 15, 1818, C. O. 226, vol. 34, p. 19.
129. Smith to Bathurst, February 14, 1818, *ibid.,* p. 18.
130. Bathurst to Smith, May 30, 1818, C. O. 227, vol. 7, p. 69.
131. *Ibid.*
132. *Ibid.*
133. *Ibid.,* p. 71.
134. *Ibid.,* p. 72.
135. *Ibid.,* p. 73.
136. Smith to Bathurst, February 13, 1818, C. O. 226, vol. 34, p. 13: See also Smith to Bathurst, May 15, 1818, *ibid.,* p. 53. It should be noted that the decision of the Colonial Office to order the escheat of Lot 55 was the result of a memorial of Captain Peter Stewart, a brother of John Stewart, requesting this lot for the establishment of a large commercial and agricultural centre.
137. "Address of the House of Assembly in Reply to the Speech from the Throne," November 5, 1818, C. O. 226, vol. 35, pp. 39-40.
138. "Message of Lieutenant Governor C. Douglas Smith to the House of Assembly," November 6, 1818, *ibid.,* p. 41.
139. *Assembly Journal,* 1818, *ibid.,* p. 58.
140. *Ibid.,* p. 61.
141. *Ibid.,* p. 70.
142. *Ibid.,* p. 75.
143. Smith to Goulburn, August 1, 1820, C. O. 226, vol. 36, pp. 52-53.

144. *Ibid.,* p. 53.
145. Smith to Goulburn, August 15, 1820, *ibid.,* p. 61.
146. *Ibid.*
147. *Prince Edward Island Register,* September 13, 1823.
148. *Ibid.*
149. Carmichael to Smith, July 5, 1825, C. O. 226, vol. 39, p. 126.
150. Carmichael to Smith, July 5, 1823, C. O. 226, vol. 41, p. 51.
151. "Requisition to John MacGregor, Esq., High Sheriff," February, 1823, C. O. 226, vol. 39, p. 16.
152. "Resolutions passed at a meeting of the Inhabitants of Queen's County," March 6, 1823; published in the *Prince Edward Island Register,* October 4, 1823.
153. *Ibid.*
154. Smith to Lord Bathurst, March 27, 1823, C. O. 226, vol. 39, p. 26.
155. *Ibid.,* p. 27.
156. Smith to Bathurst, December 11, 1823, *ibid.,* p. 19.
157. Smith to Kempt, October 29, 1823, *ibid.,* p. 159.
158. *Ibid.*
159. *Ibid.*
160. Ann Callbeck to Lord Bathurst, February 20, 1824, C. O. 226, vol. 40, p. 232.
161. "Memorial of the Proprietors to Lord Bathurst," March 5, 1824, C. O. 226, vol. 41, pp. 268-269.
162. Lord Bathurst to Smith, April 8, 1824, C. O. 227, vol. 7, p. 115.
163. Lord Bathurst to Smith, April 10, 1824, *ibid.,* p. 117.
164. *Ibid.*
165. Smith to Bathurst, June 9, 1824, C. O. 226, vol. 40, p. 93.
166. Smith to Bathurst, May 1, 1825, C. O. 226, vol. 42, p. 348.
167. James Stephen to Horton, January 6, 1826, C. O. 226, vol. 43, p. 178.
168. *Ibid,* pp. 178-180.

Footnotes to Chapter Four

1. Colonial Office memorandum on Ready to Horton, August 15, 1824, C. O. 226, vol. 41, p. 140.
2. "Address of the House of Assembly to the King's Most Excellent Majesty," March 18, 1825, C. O. 226, vol. 42, p. 47.
3. William Hill to Briscoe, October 21, 1826, *ibid.,* p. 153.
4. Ready to King, April 9, 1828, C. O. 226, vol. 45, p. 24.
5. Hay to Ready, May 24, 1828, C. O. 227, vol. 7, p. 149.
6. John Stewart to Ready, September 17, 1828, C. O. 226, vol. 45, p. 198.
7. "Petition of the Inhabitants of Prince Edward Island to the King's Most Excellent Majesty," November 18, 1828, *ibid.,* p. 216. The census of the Island, completed in 1827, showed that the Island comprised 11,976 males and 11,290 females. See *ibid.,* p. 101.
8. Hay to Stewart, January 29, 1829, C. O. 226, vol. 46, p. 153.
9. Enclosure in Ready to Murray, May 17, 1830, C. O. 226, vol. 47, pp. 48-49.
10. *Ibid.,* p. 50. It is interesting to note that Charles Worrell, a large proprietor on the Island, was the only member of the Legislature who voted against the Act.
11. "Joint Address of the House of Assembly and Legislative Council of Prince Edward Island," April 28, 1830, *ibid.,* p. 56.
12. *Ibid.*
13. *Ibid.*
14. *Ibid.,* p. 57.
15. *Ibid.*
16. Colonial Office Minute on Ready to Hay, July 26, 1831, C. O. 226, vol. 48, p. 27.
17. *Ibid.*

18. Viscount Goderich to A. W. Young, August 1, 1832, C. O. 227, vol. 8, p. 2.
19. *Ibid.*
20. Ready to Murray, June 7, 1830, C. O. 227, vol. 7, p. 169.
21. *Royal Gazette,* November 23, 1830.
22. *Royal Gazette,* January 24, 1832.
23. *Ibid.,* William Cooper was leading his opponent, Angus MacDonald, by 74 votes when the riot occurred.
24. *Royal Gazette,* April 3, 1832.
25. A. W. Young to Viscount Goderich, April 14, 1832, C. O. 226, vol. 49, pp. 83-85.
26. Viscount Godrich to A. W. Young, August 1, 1832, C. O. 227, vol. 8, pp. 1 2.
27. *Ibid.*
28. *Ibid.*
29. *Ibid.*
30. "Address of the House of Assembly to The King," March 28, 1823, C. O. 226, vol. 50, p. 49.
31. *Ibid.*
32. Viscount Goderich to A. W. Young, November 25, 1832, C. O. 227, vol. 8, p. 5.
33. "An Act to provide for the Civil Establishment of the Island and to repeal Two Certain Acts Therein Mentioned," 3rd William IV, Caput XXXIX, *Royal Gazette,* May 21, 1833.
34. *Royal Gazette,* February 26, 1833.
35. *Ibid.*
36. Robert Hodgson to Viscount Goderich, April 23, 1833, C. O. 226, vol. 50, p. 85.
37. *Ibid.,* p. 86.
38. A. W. Young to Viscount Goderich, April 27, 1833, *ibid.,* p. 68.
39. Memorial of the Undersigned Proprietors to E. J. Stanley, September, 1833, *ibid.,* p. 222.
40. *Ibid.,* p. 233.
41. *Ibid.,* p. 232.
42. Hill to Stanley, September 8, 1833, *ibid.,* p. 249.
43. E. G. Stanley to A. W. Young, May 27, 1834, C. O. 227, vol. 8, p. 25.
44. *Ibid.*
45. *Ibid.*
46. *Royal Gazette,* December 23, 1824. An Election Act was passed in 1833, requiring an election every four years.
47. *Royal Gazette,* February 10, 1835.
48. "Address of the House of Assembly of Prince Edward Island," April 7, 1835, C. O. 226, vol. 53, p. 323.
49. Young to Hay, March 20, 1835, C. O. 226, vol. 52, p. 45.
50. Lord Glenelg to Harvey, August 10, 1836, C. O. 226, vol. 53, p. 310. The House of Assembly despatch was in response to this Address as well as to the one that was forwarded by George Wright who administered the Island until the arrival of Colonel Harvey.
51. *Ibid.,* p. 311.
52. *Ibid.,* p. 317.
53. Harvey to Glenelg, October 29, 1836, *ibid.,* p. 236. It was published in the *Royal Gazette* on October 18, 1836.
54. *Royal Gazette,* January 12, 1837. The petition, signed by Cooper, MacKintosh and LeLacheur was published in the paper of this date.
55. *Ibid.*
56. "Message of Lieutenant Governor John Harvey to the House of Assembly," January 26, 1837, *Royal Gazette,* February 7, 1837.
57. *Royal Gazette,* February 28, 1837. The vote committing them to the custody of the Sergeant-at-Arms was passed by a majority of only three, indicating the House was equally divided on the question, since Cooper, LeLacheur and MacKintosh could not vote.
58. Harvey to Glenelg, February 7, 1837, C. O. 226, vol. 54, p. 42.
59. Harvey to the Proprietors, February 15, 1837, *ibid.,* pp. 62-64.
60. Harvey to Stephen, February 7, 1837, *ibid.,* pp. 48-49.
61. *Ibid.,* p. 49.

62. Glenelg to Harvey, March 30, 1837, C. O. 227, vol. 8, p. 107.
63. "Address to the King," April 21, 1837, C. O. 226, vol. 54, pp. 82-84.
64. Petition to Lieutenant Governor Sir John Harvey, *ibid.*, p. 136.
65. Harvey to Glenelg, May 6, 1837, *ibid.*, p. 135.
66. *Ibid.*, p. 137.
67. *Ibid.*, p. 138.
68. FitzRoy to Glenelg, October 3, 1837, C. O. 226, vol. 54, p. 257.
69. Enclosure in Harvey to Glenelg, April 25, 1837, *ibid.*, pp. 130-131.
70. FitzRoy to Glenelg, May 6, 1838, C. O. 226, vol. 55, p. 319.
71. FitzRoy to Glenelg, November 29, 1837, C. O. 226, vol. 54, p. 305.
72. FitzRoy to Glenelg, October 3, 1837, *ibid.*, p. 265.
73. *Ibid.*
74. *Ibid.*, p. 266.
75. A. Colville to Lord Glenelg, December 6, 1837, *ibid.*, p. 487.
76. "Memorial of the Proprietors upon the Land Assessment Act," August 30, 1837, *ibid.*, p. 444.
77. "Report of the Joint Committee of the Legislature of Prince Edward Island," January 29, 1838, C. O. 226, vol. 55, pp. 222-223.
78. *Ibid.*, p. 215.
79. *Ibid.*, p. 232.
80. FitzRoy to Glenelg, April 9, 1838, *ibid.*, p. 188.
81. *Lord Durham's Report,* ed. C. P. Lucas, vol. 11, Prince Edward Island, pp. 167-175. Lieutenant Governor FitzRoy contended that the penal tax should be higher than four shillings per one hundred acres on wilderness lands.
82. Lord Durham to Lord Glenelg, October 8, 1838, *ibid.*, p. 242.
83. *Ibid.*
84. *Ibid.*
85. *Ibid.*
86. *Ibid.*
87. *Royal Gazette,* November 13, 1838. An Election Act of 1838, had increased the membership of the House from eighteen to twenty-four.
88. *Royal Gazette,* January 29, 1839.
89. *Royal Gazette,* February 25, 1840.
90. Russell to FitzRoy, September 17, 1839, C. O. 226, vol. 58, p. 123. Cooper had been granted a short interview by the Marquis of Normandy, Russell's predecessor as Colonial Secretary.
91. *Ibid.*, p. 124.
92. *Royal Gazette,* May 12, 1840. The Bill passed on a vote of 16-4.
93. *Ibid.*
94. FitzRoy to Russell, May 4, 1840, C. O. 226, vol. 60, p. 110.
95. *Ibid.*
96. *Ibid.*, p. 111.
97. Russell to FitzRoy, September 22, 1840, *ibid.*, p. 150.
98. *Ibid.*
99. *Ibid.*
100. *Ibid.*
101. "Resolution of the House of Assembly of Prince Edward Island," February 5, 1841, C. O. 226, vol. 61, pp. 131-132.
102. *Ibid.*, p. 132.
103. FitzRoy to Russell, Confidential, May 5, 1841, C. O. 226, *ibid.*, p. 169.
104. *Ibid.*, p. 175.
105. Minute of James Stephen on Despatch of FitzRoy to Russell, June 15, 1841, *ibid.*, p. 180.
106. *Ibid.*
107. Russell to FitzRoy, June 25, 1841, *ibid.*, p. 180.
108. *Ibid.*
109. *Ibid.*
110. *Ibid.*
111. *Ibid.*
112. Huntley to Stanley, August 13, 1842, C. O. 226, vol. 64, p. 30.
113. Stanley to Huntley, July 14, 1842, C. O. 226, vol. 63, pp. 201-202.

Footnotes to Chapter Five

1. Dictionary of National Biography, *Huntley, Sir Henry Vere.*
2. Duncan Campbell, *History of Prince Edward Island, Charlottetown,* 1875, p. 96.
3. The Assembly Journal of April 23, 1841 offers a statement of the remarkably close family connections of virtually all members of the two councils. In No. 2 of *The Examiner* of 1847 Edward Whelan gave an elaborate and hostile description of the group which he labelled The Black Watch.
4. Frank MacKinnon, *The Government of Prince Edward Island,* Toronto, 1951, p. 79.
5. W. Ross Livingston, *Responsible Government in Prince Edward Island,* University of Iowa, 1931, p. 21.
6. MacKinnon, p. 79.
7. P.R.O., C.O. 226/71, Haviland to Huntley, enclosure Huntley to Grey, Jan. 19, 1847.
8. *Ibid.,* Huntley to Grey, July 13, 1847.
9. *Ibid.*
10. *Ibid.,* enclosure.
11. Livingston, p. 27.
12. P.R.O., C.O. 226/73, Campbell to Grey, June 1, 1848.
13. *Ibid.,* Grey to Campbell, January 1, 1849.
14. R. B. Stewart, a proprietor, to Lord John Russell, May 19, 1855. Letter published in *The Guardian,* Sept. 23, 1950.
15. Livingston, pp. 57-58.
16. Until recently Bannerman had been Member of Parliament for Aberdeen.
17. Livingston, pp. 79-81.
18. Members of the first administration under Responsible Government were George Coles, Charles Young, William Swabey, James Warburton, William Lord and John Jardine. Joseph Pope was added somewhat later. Salaried officers were Young as attorney general, Warburton as colonial secretary and Swabey as registrar. The outgoing administration was composed of Robert Hodgson as attorney general, Edward Palmer, solicitor general, Ambrose Lane, T. Heath Haviland, colonial secretary, George B. Goodman, C. Hensley, J. M. Holl, E. Thornton, D. Brenan.
19. D. A. MacKinnon and A. B. Warburton, eds., *Past and Present in Prince Edward Island,* Charlottetown, 1905, S. N. Robertson's account of the history of *The Public Schools,* p. 370a.
20. A. H. Clark, *Three Centuries and the Island,* Toronto, 1959. For a deep analysis of distribution of population see Chapter VI with accompanying maps.
21. According to Clark's statistics, p. 95, the number of squatters in 1841 was 734, and 879 in 1861.
22. Morpeth to Melville, March 25, 1847. From a collection of letters in possession of the author.
23. *Ibid.,* Oct. 17, 1849.
24. W. S. MacNutt, *The Atlantic Provinces,* Toronto, 1965, p. 239.
25. MacKinnon, p. 94.
26. Morpeth to Dundas, May 25, 1843.
27. Clark, p. 95.
28. Morpheth to Dundas, May 25, 1843, Campbell, p. 96, Rev. John C. MacMillan, *The Catholic Church in Prince Edward Island from 1835 to 1891,* Quebec, 1913, pp. 45-6.
29. W. S. MacNutt, *New Brunswick: A History, 1784-1867,* pp. 350-1, 358-61. For an account of the temperance movement on Prince Edward Island see McKinnon and Warburton, pp. 196-7. For an account of Catholic action, though less political, see MacMillan, pp. 81-92.
30. MacMillan, pp. 57-62.
31. The Bishop's letter is reproduced in MacMillan, pp. 123-5.
32. MacNutt, *Atlantic Provinces,* pp. 265-6.
33. MacKinnon, p. 97.
34. *Ibid.,* pp. 97-9.
35. *An Address to Prince Edward Island* by Fabius Cassius Funny Fellow — A Native, Charlottetown, 1862, p. 25. The title page gives Fabrius. A printer's eccentricity?
36. The essential portion of Cunard's letter is reproduced in Campbell, pp. 124-6.
37. John Lepage, *The Island Minstrel, II,* Charlottetown, 1867. This is taken from a poetic

satire on The Land Commission, representing a confrontation between "big-pouch Landlord Indians" and their "small-pounch tenant brothers," p. 19.

38. The report is printed in the appendix to the legislative journals of 1862. For an extended survey and comment hostile to the British Government see Campbell, pp. 131-53.
39. Lepage, p. 20.
40. Fabius Cassius, p. 10.

Footnotes to Chapter Six

1. Edward Whelan, *The Union of the British Provinces* (Charlottetown, 1865), p. 7.
2. Letter of Bartlett to Tupper, October 14, 1914, Letter 1168, *Tupper Papers*, P. A. C.
3. *Examiner,* August 22, 1864.
4. The revenue of the Island for the financial year 1863, was £62,688,14,4 and the expenditure was £55,662,3,6. The public debt was only £75,178,17,1¼. Moreover, most of this debt was due to the government's land purchases, and much of this would be repaid by tenants who had purchased these lands. *Journal of the House of Assembly,* P. E. I., 1864, Appendix G.
5. Dundas to Head, January 24, 1860, *Journal of the House of Assembly,* P. E. I., 1860, Appendix T.
6. *Journal of the House of Assembly,* P. E. I., 1862, p. 132.
7. *Islander,* June 5, 1863. The Assembly debates, on the question, were reported in full in this issue.
8. *Ibid.*
9. *Journal of the House of Assembly,* P. E. I., 1863, p. 142.
10. *Islander,* March 27, 1863.
11. Enclosure in Doyle to Dundas, February 29, 1864, *Journal of the House of Assembly,* P. E. I., 1864, Appendix A.
12. *Ibid.*
13. These were the key words in the Nova Scotia resolution. Doyle to Dundas, February 29, 1864, *Assembly Journal,* P. E. I., 1864, Appendix A.
14. These were the important words in the New Brunswick resolution. Gordon to Doyle, March 11, 1864, *Journal of the House of Assembly,* N.B., 1864, Appendix X, p. 6.
15. *Assembly Journal,* P.E.I., 1864, p. 64.
16. *Debates and Proceedings of the House of Assembly of Prince Edward Island for the year 1864,* p. 32.
17. *Ibid.,* p. 33.
18. *Ibid.*
19. *Ibid.*
20. *Ibid.,* pp. 33-34.
21. *Ibid.,* pp. 34-35.
22. *Ibid.,* p. 38.
23. *Ibid.*
24. *Ibid.*
25. *Ibid.,* p. 39.
26. *Ibid.,* p. 40.
27. *Ibid.,* p. 41.
28. *Ibid.*
29. *Ibid.*
30. *Ibid.,* pp. 41-42.
31. *Ibid.*
32. *Ibid.*
33. *Ibid.*
34. *Debates and Proceedings of the Legislative Council of Prince Edward Island for the session of 1864,* pp. 110-111.
35. *Ibid.*
36. *Ibid.,* pp. 109-110.
37. *Ibid.*

38. *Ibid.*, p. 109.
39. *Ibid.*, p. 113.
40. *Ibid.*, p. 114.
41. Gordon to Dundas, April 9, 1864, G. 8 D. vol. 69, pp. 249-250.
42. Dundas to Gordon, May 4, 1864, *Journal of the House of Assembly*, N.B., 1865, p. 7.
43. *Islander*, June 24, 1864.
44. Monck to Dundas, June 30, 1864, *Journal of the House of Assembly*, P.E.I., 1865, Appendix E.
45. MacDonnell to Dundas, July 11, 1864, *ibid.*
46. *Ibid.*
47. *Protestant*, July 30, 1864.
48. Dundas to Cole, Telegram, July 25, 1864, *Assembly Journal*, 1865, Appendix E. Cole was replacing Lieutenant Governor Gordon, who was on a visit to England.
49. Cole to Dundas, Telegram, July 25, 1864, *ibid.*
50. "Minute of the Executive Council," P.E.I., July 25, 1864, Provincial Secretary's Office, Charlottetown.
51. Dundas to Monck, July 28, 1864, *Assembly Journal*, 1865, Appendix E.
52. *Monitor*, August 25, 1864.
53. *Ibid.*
54. Letter of George Coles to the Editor of the *Examiner*, August 29, 1864, published in the *Examiner*, August 29, 1864.
55. *Examiner*, September 5, 1864, "Union Question, No. 2."
56. *Protestant*, August 27, 1864.
57. Quoted in the *Islander*, September 2, 1864.
58. *Examiner*, September 5, 1864.
59. *Monitor*, September 1, 1864.
60. *Ibid.*
61. Quoted, *ibid.*
62. *Examiner*, September 5, 1864, R. B. Dickey, one of the Nova Scotia delegates, arrived in Charlottetown on the previous morning.
63. *Ibid.*
64. Letter of George Brown to Anne Brown, September 13, 1864, *Brown Papers*, P. A. C.
65. *Vindicator*, September 7, 1864.
66. George Brown to Anne Brown, September 13, 1864, *Brown Papers*.
67. *Protestant*, September 3, 1864.
68. Saint John *Morning Telegraph*, September 5, 1864, quoted *Islander*, September 9, 1864.
69. *Ross's Weekly*, September 8, 1864. John Ross, the editor, usually made a few mistakes in spelling!
70. Saint John *Morning Telegraph*, September 5, 1864, quoted *Islander*, September 9, 1864.
71. Whelan, *op. cit.*, pp. 4-5. All were present except A. A. MacDonald, who missed the first two days of the Conference due to the serious illness of his sister. Cf. *A. C. MacDonald Diaries*, notation of September 5, 1864.
72. *Vindicator*, September 7, 1864.
73. Whelan, *op. cit.*, p. 6.
74. George Brown to Anne Brown, September 13, 1864, *Brown Papers*.
75. *Vindicator*, September 7, 1864.
76. George Brown's expression, George Brown to Anne Brown, September 13, 1864, *Brown Papers*.
77. *Ibid.*
78. D. G. Creighton, *John A. Macdonald, The Young Politician* (Toronto, 1956), p. 365.
79. George Brown to Anne Brown, September 13, 1864, *Brown Papers*.
80. *Ibid.*
81. *Ibid.*
82. *Ibid.*
83. *Ibid.*
84. Peter B. Waite, *The Life and Times of Confederation* (Toronto, 1962), pp. 77-78.
85. George Brown to Anne Brown, September 13, 1864, *Brown Papers*.
86. *Ibid.*
87. *Ibid.*

88. *Vindicator,* September 7, 1864.
89. George Brown to Anne Brown, September 13, 1864, *Brown Papers.*
90. "Charles Tupper's Minutes of the Charlottetown Conference," *Canadian Historical Review,* XLVIII, 2 (June, 1967), p. 104. A descendant of Charles Tupper presented these Minutes to Wilfred Smith, the Dominion Archivist. Dr. Smith published these hitherto unknown documents in the Review of the above date. Despite their fragmentary character, much new and worthwhile information can be gleaned from their perusal.
91. George Brown to Anne Brown, September 13, 1964, *Brown Papers.*
92. *Ibid.*
93. John LePage, the Island poet, insisted in a witty poem, that the eyes of the delegates were so blurred that the plover were quite safe.
94. *Protestant,* September 10, 1864.
95. *Ibid.*
96. *Ibid.*
97. *Monitor,* September 15, 1864.
98. *Protestant,* September 10, 1864.
99. *Ross's Weekly,* September 15, 1864.
100. George Brown to Anne Brown, September 13, 1864, *Brown Papers.*
101. *Islander,* September 23, 1864.
102. "Report of Proceedings of a Conference to consider the question of a legislative union of Nova Scotia, New Brunswick, and Prince Edward Island." *Journal of the House of Assembly,* P.E.I., 1865, Appendix E. This report was prepared by J. H. Gray, Charles Tupper and Leonard Tilley.
103. Whelan, *op. cit.,* p. 46.
104. *Ibid.,* p. 42.
105. *Ibid.,* p. 54.
106. *Ibid.,* p. 55.
107. Waite, *op. cit.,* p. 81.
108. *Assembly Journal,* 1865, Appendix E.
109. Gordon to Cardwell, Confidential, September 12, 1864. *Journal of the House of Assembly,* N. B., 1865, p. 14.
110. Tupper to Harris, May 10, 1908, *Tupper Papers,* P. A. C.
111. J. Murray Beck, *The History of Maritime Union: A Study in Frustration* (Fredericton, 1969), p. 45.
112. Charles Tupper's Minutes on the Quebec Conference, *op. cit.,* p. 106. The minutes recorded twelve brief speeches on Maritime Union.
113. *Ibid.*
114. Speech of John A. Macdonald, February 6, 1865, *Parliamentary Debates on Confederation,* 1865, p. 27.
115. *Ibid.*
116. *Ibid.*
117. "Confederation of British America," September 23, 1864, *Macdonald Papers,* Confederation, vol. 1, p. 5, P. A. C.; also in Toronto *Globe,* September 27, 1864. The author of this letter has not been established. Maurice Careless, the leading authority on George Brown, claims the style and views expressed are those of Brown. It gives us solid evidence on what happened in Charlottetown.
118. *Ibid.*
119. A. H. Gordon to Edward Cardwell, Confidential, September 22, 1864, *Journal of the House of Assembly,* N. B., p. 14.
120. Letter of Edward Palmer, December 21, 1864, *Palmer Papers.* These papers are in the possession of his grandson, Judge H. L. Palmer.
121. [A. A. MacDonald] "Notes on the Quebec Conference, 1864." A. G. Doughty, ed., *Canadian Historical Review,* I, I (March, 1920), p. 42.
122. *Ibid.*
123. "Confederation of British America," *Ibid.*
124. *Assembly Debates,* 1865, p. 67.
125. Whelan, op. cit., p. 7. These words are excerpts from a speech delivered by Premier Gray at the concluding banquet in Charlottetown.
126. Waite, *op. cit.,* p. 85.
127. *Protestant,* October 1, 1864.
128. *Vindicator,* September 28, 1864.

Footnotes to Chapter Seven

1. The delegates to the Quebec Conference were as follows:
   Canada: Sir E. P. Taché, John A. Macdonald, G. E. Cartier, George
                            Brown, Oliver Mowat, A. T. Galt, William McDougall, Thomas
                            D'Arcy McGee, Alexander Campbell, J. C. Chapais, Hector L.
                            Langevin, James Cockburn.
   Nova Scotia: Charles Tupper, William Henry, Jonathan McCully, Robert
                            B. Dickey, Adams G. Archibald.
   New Brunswick: S. L. Tilley, W. H. Steeves, J. M. Johnson, Peter Mitchell, E. B.
                            Chandler, John Hamilton Gray, Charles Fisher.
   Prince Edward Island: John Hamilton Gray, Edward Palmer, W. H. Pope, A. A.
                            MacDonald, George Coles, Edward Whelan, T. H. Haviland.
   Newfoundland: Ambrose Shea, Frederick Carter.
2. *Macdonald Papers,* "Confederation," vol. 1, p. 13, P.A.C.
3. *Ibid.,* p. 27.
4. Joseph Pope, ed., *Confederation: Being a Series of Hitherto Unpublished Documents bearing on the British North America Act* (Toronto, 1895), p. 11.
5. *Ibid.*
6. P. B. White, "Edward Whelan Reports from the Quebec Conference," *Canadian Historical Review,* XLIII, I (March, 1961), p. 35.
7. A. A. MacDonald, *op. cit.,* p. 35.
8. *Ibid.,* pp. 35-36.
9. *Ibid.,* p. 36.
10. *Ibid.,* pp. 36-37.
11. *Ibid.,* p. 37
12. Pope, *op. cit.,* p. 120. This statement was made by Macdonald at the Westminister Conference in December, 1866.
13. *Ibid.,* p. 61.
14. "Whelan Reports," p. 39.
15. Pope. *op. cit.,* p. 67.
16. *Ibid.,* p. 68.
17. *Ibid.,* p. 69.
18. *Ibid.*
19. *Ibid.*
20. *Ibid.,* p. 70.
21. *Ibid.*
22. *Ibid.*
23. *Ibid.,* pp. 70-71.
24. *Ibid.*
25. W. H. Pope to George Dundas, December 24, 1864, *W. H. Pope Papers,* P.A.C.
26. Pope, *op. cit.,* p. 70.
27. *Ibid.,* p. 72.
28. *Ibid.*
29. *Ibid.*
30. *Ibid.,* p. 73.
31. Letter to Edward Palmer, October 21, 1864, *Palmer Papers.*
32. Palmer to Laird, October 21, 1864, *Palmer Papers.* (Original Italics).
33. *Macdonald Papers,* "Confederation," vol. 1, p. 161.
34. A. A. MacDonald, *op. cit.,* p. 42.
35. *Ibid.,* p. 43.
36. *Ibid.,* p. 44., Cf. Creighton, *op. cit.,* pp. 379-380.
37. Pope, *op. cit.,* p. 26.
38. *Prince Edward Island Assembly Debates,* 1865, p. 68.
39. A. A. MacDonald, *op. cit.,* p. 46.
40. *Ibid.*
41. *Assembly Debates,* 1865, p. 5.
42. Whelan, *Union of the British Provinces,* pp. 112-113.
43. *Ibid.,* p. 113.
44. *Ibid.,* pp. 114-115.

45. *Ibid.,* p. 115.
46. *Ibid.,* p. 145.
47. *Ibid.,* p. 213.
48. *Ibid.,* pp. 137-138.
49. *Ibid.,* pp. 182-183.
50. *Ibid.*
51. Palmer to Dundas, December 22, 1864, *Palmer Papers.* A. A. MacDonald did not deliver a public speech during the tour.
52. *Islander,* December 30, 1864.
53. *Ibid.*
54. *Monitor,* November 10, 1864.
55. *Ibid.,* November 17, 1864.
56. "Letter of John Hamilton Gray to the people of Prince Edward Island," November 16, 1864, *Islander,* November 18, 1864.
57. *Ibid.*
58. *Ibid.*
59. *Ibid.*
60. "Letter of W. H. Pope to the Editor of the *Monitor,*" December 5, 1864, published in the *Protestant,* December 10, 1864.
61. *Ibid.*
62. Ambrose Shea to A. T. Galt, December 15, 1864, *Ministry of Finance Papers,* P.A.C.
63. *Ibid.*
64. *Examiner,* November 21, 1864.
65. Letter of Edward Palmer to the Editor of the *Protestant,* December 15, 1864.
66. Letter of Edward Palmer to David Laird, October 21, 1864, *Palmer Papers.*
67. Letter of Edward Palmer to the Editor of the *Protestant,* November 19, 1864.
68. Letter of J. H. Gray to Lieutenant Governor Dundas, December 16, 1864, *Palmer Papers.*
69. *Ibid.*
70. J. H. Gray to Charles Tupper, January 7, 1865, *Tupper Papers,* vol. 1, Letter 26, pp. 1-2, P.A.C.
71. "Observation of Mr. Palmer in Answer to a letter of J. H. Gray to the Lieutenant Governor in Council, December 20, 1864." *Palmer Papers.*
72. *Ibid.*
73. *Ibid.*
74. W. H. Pope to Lieutenant Governor Dundas, December 24, 1864, *W. H. Pope Papers,*
75. *Ibid.*
76. *Examiner,* January 9, 1865.
77. Letter to J. H. Gray, January 7, 1865, from James Yeo, John Longworth, David Kaye, James McLaren, and W. H. Pope, *Examiner,* January 9, 1865.
78. John A. MacDonald to J. H. Gray, March 24, 1865, *Macdonald Papers,* vol. 119, p. 8.
79. Dundas to Cardwell, February 24, 1865, C.O. 226, vol. 101, pp. 52-53.
80. *Monitor,* December 22, 1864.
81. Whelan to Galt, December 17, 1864, *Ministry of Finance Papers.*
82. *Ibid.*
83. *Examiner,* December 26, 1864.
84. *Islander,* December 16, 1864.
85. *Islander,* March 3, 1865.
86. *Islander,* February 17, 1865.
87. *Islander,* December 30, 1864.
88. Andrew Archibald MacDonald also spoke against Confederation but he was much more low-key in his remarks than was T. H. Haviland in promoting the scheme.
89. J. H. Gray to Charles Tupper. January 7, 1865, *Tupper Papers,* vol. 1, Letter 26, p. 2.
90. *Islander,* March 3, 1865.
91. *Islander,* February 24, 1865.
92. Whelan to Galt, December 17, 1864, *Minister of Finance Papers.*
93. John A. Macdonald to J. H. Gray, March 24, 1865, *Macdonald Papers,* vol. 119, p. 81.
94. "Speech from the Throne of Lieutenant Governor George Dundas," February 28, 1865, *Assembly Debates,* 1865, p. 3.
95. *Islander,* March 3, 1865.

96. *Assembly Debates,* 1865, p. 39.
97. *Ibid.,* p. 44.
98. *Ibid.,* p. 41.
99. *Ibid.,* p. 49.
100. *Ibid.,* p. 54. Edward Whelan also spoke in the debate in favor of Confederation, but his speech was not recorded because he had mislaid his notes.
101. *Ibid.,* p. 45.
102. *Ibid.,* p. 55.
103. *Ibid.,* p. 63.
104. *Ibid.,* p. 53.
105. *Ibid.,* p. 55.
106. *Ibid.,* p. 50.
107. *Ibid.,* p. 58.
108. *Ibid.,* p. 53.
109. *Ibid.,* p. 61.
110. *Ibid.,* p. 57.
111. *Ibid.,* p. 61.
112. *Ibid.,* p. 51.
113. *Ibid.,* p. 57.
114. *Ibid.,* p. 5.
115. *Ibid.,* p. 53.
116. *Ibid.,* p. 51.
117. *Ibid.,* p. 45.
118. *Ibid.*
119. *Ibid.,* p. 71.
120. *Ibid.*
121. *Debates and proceedings of the Legislative Council of Prince Edward Island for the Session of 1865,* p. 58.
122. *Ibid.,* p. 57.
123. *Ibid.,* p. 63.
124. *Ibid.,* p. 60.
125. *Ibid.,* p. 64.
126. *Ibid.,* p. 68.
127. *Ibid.,* p. 55.
128. *Ibid.,* p. 63.
129. *Ibid.,* p. 56.
130. *Ibid.*
131. *Ibid.,* p. 68.
132. *Assembly Journal,* 1865, p. 97.
133. *Ibid.* The four opponents were Whelan, Haviland, Green and W. H. Pope. It is conceivable that Colonel Gray was absent.
134. "Minute of April 26, 1865, on George Dundas's Despatch of April 3, 1865," C.O. 226, vol. 101, pp. 108-111.
135. "Minute of Executive Council," May 30, 1865, C.O. 226, vol. 101, p. 254.
136. Cardwell to Dundas, February 18, 1865, G. 34, pp. 34-37, P.A.C. (P.E.I.)
137. *Journal of the House of Assembly,* P.E.I., 1865, pp. 102-103.
138. Cardwell to Dundas, April 29, 1865, C.O. 226, vol. 101, p. 164.
139. *Assembly Debates,* 1869, p. 118. In the debates of that year on the Lieutenant Governor's salary, this expression was used.
140. Cardwell to Dundas, April 28, 1865, C.O. 226, vol. 101, p. 152.
141. Cardwell to Dundas, June 24, 1865, *ibid.,* p. 199.
142. *Ibid.,* p. 201.
143. *Ibid.,* p. 202.
144. Proclamation of George Dundas, March 22, 1865, *ibid.,* p. 97.
145. *Islander,* August 18, 1865.
146. Dundas was on a visit to England in 1865 and Robert Hodgson served as Administrator until his return.
147. Cardwell to Hodgson, August 23, 1865, C.O. 226, vol. 101, p. 365.
148. Minute of the Executive Council, October 25, 1865, *ibid.,* p. 494.
149. *Ibid.,* pp. 149-150.
150. Carnarvon to Dundas, March 4, 1867, C.O. 226, vol. 102, pp. 370-371.

151. *Debates and proceedings of the House of Assembly for the Year 1866,* p. 101.
152. *Ibid.*
153. *Ibid.*
154. *Ibid.,* p. 100.
155. *Ibid.*
156. *Ibid.,* p. 101.
157. *Ibid.,* p. 116.
158. *Ibid.*
159. *Ibid.,* p. 101.
160. *Ibid.,* p. 108.
161. *Ibid.,* p. 105.
162. *Ibid.,* p. 103.
163. *Ibid.,* p. 102.
164. *Ibid.,* p. 105.
165. *Ibid.*
166. Cardwell to Dundas, June 24, 1865, C.O. 226, vol. 101, p. 199.
167. *Assembly Debates,* 1866, p. 107.
168. *Ibid.,* p. 112.
169. *Ibid.*
170. *Assembly Debates,* 1867, Haviland's speech, omitted in the 1866 debates, was published in 1867.
171. *Assembly Debates,* 1866, p. 118.
172. *Ibid.,* p. 121.
173. *Journal of the House of Assembly,* 1866, pp. 105-106.
174. *Debates and Proceedings of the Legislative Council of Prince Edward Island for the Session of 1866,* pp. 78-79.
175. *Ibid.,* p. 55.
176. *Ibid.,* p. 39.
177. *Ibid.*
178. *Ibid.*
179. *Ibid.,* p. 79.
180. J. H. Gray to John A. Macdonald, June 27, 1866, *Macdonald Papers,* vol. 119, p. 111.
181. *Ibid.,* p. 112.
182. W. H. Pope was absent from the 1866 debates. He was the Island's representative on a trade mission in the Carribean.
183. Pope to Carnarvon, August 14, 1866, C. O. 226, vol. 102, p. 299.

Footnotes to Chapter Eight

1. "Letter of J. C. Pope to the Editor of the *Patriot,*" published in the *Islander,* January 29, 1867.
2. *Ibid.*
3. Tupper to W. H. Pope, November 8, 1866, *W. H. Pope Papers.*
4. Resolution of the Nova Scotia and New Brunswick Delegates, *Journal of the House of Assembly,* P.E.I., 1867, Appendix L.
5. Tupper to W. H. Pope, November 8, 1866, *W. H. Pope Papers.*
6. *Minute of the Canadian Executive Council,* October 22, 1866, Enclosure in Monck to Dundas, October 26, 1866, *Assembly Journal,* Appendix L.
7. *Ibid.*
8. Dundas to Carnarvon, Confidential, November 21, 1866, C. O. 226, vol. 102, p. 420.
9. "Letter of Haythorne to the Editor of the *Islander,*" October 22, 1866, *Islander,* October 22, 1866.
10. *Islander,* November 9, 1866.
11. *Islander,* January 29, 1866.
12. *Islander,* November 9, 1866.
13. Report of a Meeting at Brown's Creek, November 8, 1866, *Islander,* November 23, 1866.

14. *Islander*, November 9, 1866.
15. Dundas to Carnarvon, January 21, 1867, C. O. 226, vol. 103, p. 20.
16. Dundas to C. B. Adderley, January 25, 1867, *Macdonald Papers*, vol. 51, p. 477.
17. Dundas to Carnarvon, February 6, 1867, *Journal of the House of Assembly*, P.E.I., 1867, Appendix I.
18. *Islander*, February 1, 1867.
19. *Islander*, February 15, 1867.
20. *Islander*, February 22, 1867.
21. Edward Palmer to Joseph Howe, March 8, 1867, *Palmer Papers*.
22. *Herald*, February 6, 1867.
23. *Islander*, February 22, 1867.
24. *Islander*, March 1, 1867.
25. Edward Palmer to Joseph Howe, March 8, 1865, *Palmer Papers*.
26. *Ibid.*
27. *Examiner*, December 16, 1867.
28. Dundas to Carnarvon, March 23, 1867, *Assembly Journal*, 1867, Appendix L.
29. Enclosure in Carnarvon to Dundas, March 2, 1867, *Assembly Journal, ibid.*
30. An Act to Authorize the Government to Raise a Loan of Money for the Public Service of the Island, *Assembly Journal*, 1868, Appendix A.
31. *Assembly Debates*, 1867, p. 121.
32. *Ibid.*
33. *Ibid.*, p. 116.
34. Enclosure in Hodgson to Granville, February 15, 1869, C. O. 226, vol. 105, pp. 56-57.
35. Granville to Hodgson, March 13, 1869, *ibid.*, p. 70.
36. *Ibid.*, p. 72.
37. Buckingham and Chandos to Dundas, October 12, 1867, G. 36, P.A.C. p. 597.
38. Minute of Frederic Rogers, February 6, 1869, C. O. 226, vol. 105, p. 481.
39. Granville to Hodgson, February 15, 1869, *ibid.*, p. 47.
40. *Debates and Proceedings of the House of Assembly of Prince Edward Island for the Session of 1869*, p. 118.
41. *Ibid.*, p. 122.
42. *Ibid.*
43. *Ibid.*, p. 118.
44. *Islander*, August 16, 1869.
45. W. H. Pope to John A. Macdonald, September 18, 1870, *W. H. Pope Papers*.
46. *Journal of the House of Assembly*, P.E.I., 1869, Appendix A.
47. *Ibid.*, Appendix D.
48. *Herald*, September 16, 1868.
49. *Ibid.*
50. *Ibid.*
51. *Ibid.*
52. "Report of Mr. B. F. Butler, from a select committee on Prince Edward Island, March 2, 1869." *Journal of the House of Representatives, 1869*, 40th Congress, 3rd Session Report No. 39, p. 13.
53. *Ibid.*, pp. 6-7.
54. *Ibid.*, p. 3.
55. *Ibid.*, p. 8.
56. *Ibid.*, p. 10.
57. *Ibid.*
58. Edward Thornton to Lord Clarendon, March 29, 1869, F. O. 195, vol. 49, p. 172, P. R. O.
59. Macdonald to Sir John Young, December 8, 1869, *Macdonald Papers*, vol. 516, p. 670.
60. *Ibid.*, pp. 671-672.
61. *Ibid.*
62. *Canada, House of Commons Debate*, 1869, p. 117.
63. *Islander*, August 13, 1869.
64. Tilley to Macdonald, Telegram, August 14, 1869, *Macdonald Papers*, vol. 516, p. 317.
65. Cartier to Macdonald, August 23, 1869, *Macdonald Papers*, vol. 202, p. 269.
66. Young to Granville, Confidential, August 13, 1869, G. 21, No. 25 B, vol. 1, P.A.C.
67. *Debates and Proceedings of the Legislative Council of Prince Edward Island for the Session of 1870*, p. 35.
68. *Ibid.*

69. R. P. Haythorne to G. E. Cartier, August 20, 1869, attached to *Orders-in-Council, 945 (b)*, P. A. C.
70. *Journal of the House of Assembly*, P.E.I., 1870, Appendix F.
71. *Ibid.*
72. *Ibid.*
73. *Minute of the Executive Council*, January 7, 1870, Provincial Secretary's Office, Charlottetown.
74. *Minute of the Executive Council*, February 4, 1870, Provincial Secretary's Office, Charlottetown.
75. *Ibid.*
76. *Ibid.*
77. *Ibid.*
78. *Ibid.*
79. Minute of Rogers, February 22, 1870, C. O. 226, vol. 106, p. 29.
80. Granville to Hodgson, March 7, 1870, *ibid.*, p. 58.
81. Granville to Young, January 10, 1870, G. 21, No. 25 B, P. A. C.
82. Macdonald to Rose, December 13, 1872, *Macdonald Papers*, vol. 522, p. 321.
83. *Islander*, July 9, 1869.
84. *Islander*, February 4, 1870.
85. *Assembly Debates*, 1870, p. 127.
86. *Ibid.*, p. 39.
87. *Legislative Council Debates*, 1870, p. 136.
88. *Ibid.*, p. 98.
89. *Assembly Debates*, 1870, p. 198.
90. Hodgson to Granville, July 25, 1870, C. O. 226, vol. 106, pp. 183-184.
91. *Islander*, July 29, 1870.
92. Hodgson to Kimberley, September 6, 1870, C. O. 226, vol. 106, pp. 225-226. A. A. MacDonald and George Howlan were the Catholic cabinet ministers who championed grants to Catholic schools. Lord, Callbeck, Sinclair and Benjamin Davies objected.
93. *Islander*, September 16, 1870.
94. *Islander*, September 23, 1870.
95. Frank MacKinnon, *The Government of Prince Edward Island*, pp. 132-133.
96. *Islander*, December 23, 1870.
97. *Islander*, February 10, 1871.
98. *Debates and Proceedings of the House of Assembly of Prince Edward Island, for the Session of 1871*, p. 67.
99. *Ibid.*, p. 65.
100. *Ibid.*, p. 67.
101. *Ibid.*, p. 76.
102. *Ibid.*, p. 93.
103. *Ibid.*, p. 247.
104. *Ibid.*, p. 193.
105. *Ibid.*
106. *Ibid.*, p. 74.
107. *Ibid.*, p. 279.
108. *Ibid.*, p. 272.
109. *Ibid.*, p. 273.
110. Robinson to Kimberley, Confidential, April 17, 1871, C. O. 226, vol. 107, p. 167.
111. *Ibid.* Robinson had succeeded Dundas as Lieutenant Governor on October 7, 1870.
112. *Islander*, April 21, 1871.
113. *Diary of Sir Joseph Pope*, 1871. The diaries of Sir Joseph Pope are in the possession of his son, Lieutenant Gen. Maurice Pope of Ottawa.
114. "An Act to authorize the construction of a railroad through Prince Edward Island." *Statutes of Prince Edward Island* (1871), Provincial Archives, Charlottetown.
115. *Journal of the House of Assembly*, P.E.I., 1872, Appendix A.
116. Enclosure in Robinson to Kimberley, December 25, 1871, C. O. 226, vol. 108, pp. 224-225.
117. Robinson to Kimberley, Confidential, December 23, 1871, *ibid.*, p. 230.
118. *Ibid.*, p. 231.
119. *Debates and Proceedings of the House of Assembly of Prince Edward Island for the year 1872*, 1st session, pp. 6-7.

120. *Ibid.*, pp. 25-26.
121. *Ibid.*, p. 59.
122. *Ibid.*, p. 6.
123. *Ibid.*, p. 10.
124. *Ibid.*, p. 8.
125. *Ibid.*, p. 18.
126. *Ibid.*, p. 47.
127. *Ibid.*, p. 36. The original estimate was that the length of the line would be 120 miles. When the survey was completed and the line located it was 147 miles.
128. *Ibid.*, p. 39.
129. *Ibid.*, p. 40.
130. *Examiner*, March 18, 1872.
131. *Debates and Proceedings of the Legislative Council of Prince Edward Island for the Session of 1872*, p. 17.
132. *Ibid.*, p. 10.
133. *Journal of the House of Assembly*, P.E.I., 1873, Appendix DD.
134. *Ibid.*, Appendix O.
135. Robinson to Kimberley, Confidential, September 28, 1872, C.O. 226, vol. 110, pp. 38-39.

Footnotes to Chapter Nine

1. Robinson to Kimberley, Secret, December 23, 1872, C. O. 226, vol. 110, p. 78.
2. *Debates and Proceedings of the House of Assembly of Prince Edward Island for the year, 1873*, p. 62.
3. Palmer to Rose, November 16, 1872, *Macdonald Papers*, vol. 119, p. 133.
4. Robinson to Dufferin, Private and Confidential, November 16, 1872, C. O. 226, vol. 110, pp. 69-70.
5. Dufferin to Robinson, Private and Confidential, November 27, 1872, *ibid.*, p. 79.
6. Dufferin to Robinson, Telegraph, December 7, 1872, *ibid.*, p. 80.
7. Rose to Macdonald, November 26, 1872, *Macdonald Papers*, vol. 119, p. 134.
8. Macdonald to Rose, December 13, 1872, *Macdonald Papers*, vol. 522, p. 321.
9. Robinson to Kimberley, Confidential, September 28, 1872, C. O. 226, vol. 110, pp. 37-38.
10. *Executive Council Minute*, January 2, 1873, *Journal of the House of Assembly, P.E.I.*, 1873, Appendix A.
11. *Ibid.*
12. Haythorne to Robinson, January 6, 1873, C. O. 226, vol. 111, p. 25.
13. "Copy of a Report of the Privy Council, January 27, 1873," *Assembly Journal*, 1873, Appendix A.
14. *Legislative Council Debates*, 1873, p. 31.
15. *Assembly Debates*, 1873, p. 25.
16. "Copy of a Report of a Committee of the Honorable the Privy Council approved by his Excellency the Governor General in Council on March 10, 1873," *Assembly Journal*, 1873, Appendix A.
17. *Ibid.*
18. *Ibid.*
19. *Assembly Debates*, 1873, p. 73.
20. *Ibid.*, p. 121.
21. Privy Council Report, March 10, 1873, *Assembly Journal*, 1873, Appendix A.
22. *Ibid.*
23. *Ibid.*
24. *Ibid.* It should be noted that the Island population, having increased by some 15,000 since 1864, was actually entitled to 6 representatives in the House of Commons.
25. *Ibid.*
26. Haythorne and Laird to Edward Palmer, Telegraph, March 3, 1873, *Assembly Journal*, 1873, Appendix A.
27. Robinson to Haythorne, March 6, 1873, *ibid.*
28. Robinson to Kimberley, February 19, 1873, C. O. 537, vol. 104, pp. 12-13.

29. Robinson to Dufferin, March 10, 1873, Telegraph, *Macdonald Papers*, vol. 78, p. 240.
30. *Ibid.*
31. Dufferin to Robinson, Telegraph, March 11, 1873, G. 13, vol. 2, P.A.C.
32. Robinson to Kimberley, Cablegram, March 20, 1873, C. O. 537, vol. 104, p. 103.
33. Kimberley to Robinson, Cablegram, March 20, 1873, *ibid.*, p. 34.
34. *Patriot*, March 20, 1873.
35. *Patriot*, March 8, 1873.
36. *Ibid.*
37. *Assembly Debates*, 1873, p. 62.
38. Letter of James C. Pope to the Electors of Prince Edward Island, March 8, 1873, Published in the *Island Argus*, March 11, 1873.
39. Nomination Day Speech of J. C. Pope, *Island Argus*, April 1, 1873.
40. J. C. MacMillan, *The History of the Catholic Church in Prince Edward Island from 1835 to 1891* (Quebec, 1905), p. 349.
41. *Patriot*, March 15, 1873.
42. *Assembly Debates*, 1873, p. 97.
43. Haythorne to Robinson, April 9, 1873, C. O. 226, vol. 111, p. 86.
44. *Assembly Debates*, 1873, p. 107.
45. Quoted MacMillan, *op cit.*, p. 358.
46. Haythorne to Robinson, April 15, 1873, C. O. 226, vol. 111, p. 108.
47. Robinson to Kimberley, April 9, 1873, *ibid.*, pp. 80-81.
48. Robinson to J. C. Pope, April 15, 1873, *J. C. Pope Papers.* This correspondence is in the possession of H. R. Stewart, Ottawa.
49. J. C. Pope to Robinson, April 15, *ibid.*
50. *Ibid.*
51. Robinson to J. C. Pope, April 15, *ibid.*
52. *Ibid.*
53. J. C. Pope to Robinson, April 15, *ibid.*
54. Robinson to Pope, April 15, *ibid.*
55. *Ibid.*
56. Pope to Robinson, April 16, *ibid.*
57. *Ibid.*
58. Robinson to Pope, April 16, *ibid.*
59. *Assembly Debates*, 1873, p. 62.
60. *Ibid.*, p. 66.
61. *Ibid.*
62. *Ibid.*
63. *Ibid.*, p. 120.
64. *Ibid.*, p. 69.
65. *Ibid.*, p. 123.
66. *Ibid.*, pp. 119-120.
67. *Ibid.*, p. 126.
68. *Ibid.*, p. 149.
69. *Ibid.*
70. *Ibid.*, p. 152.
71. *Ibid.*
72. John A. Macdonald to Dufferin, April 4, 1873, *Macdonald Papers*, vol. 523 pp. 82-83.
73. *Ibid.*
74. "Minutes of Conference between the Committee of the Privy Council of Canada and the undersigned delegates from the Province of Prince Edward Island," May 15, 1873, *Assembly Journal*, 1873, Appendix O.
75. *Assembly Debates*, 1873, p. 176.
76. *Ibid.*, pp. 173-174.
77. *Ibid.*, p. 185.
78. *Ibid.*, pp. 202-203.
79. *Ibid.*, p. 182.
80. *Ibid.*
81. *Ibid.*, p. 228.
82. *Ibid.*, p. 200.
83. *Ibid.*
84. *Ibid.*

85. *Ibid.*, pp. 187-188.
86. *Ibid.*, p. 200.
87. *Ibid.*, p. 225.
88. *Ibid.*, p. 232.
89. *Ibid.*, p. 224.
90. *Ibid.*, p. 225.
91. *Ibid.*, p. 231.
92. *Ibid.*, p. 232.
93. *Ibid.*, p. 230.
94. *Ibid.*, p. 232. The Speaker, S. F. Perry, who was in favour of Confederation, was, of course, not allowed to vote.
95. *Debates and Proceedings of the Legislative Council of Prince Edward Island for the Session of 1873*, p. 35.
96. *Ibid.*, p. 88.
97. *Ibid.*
98. *Ibid.*, p. 75.
99. *Ibid.*, p. 79.
100. *Ibid.*, p. 60.
101. *Ibid.*, p. 78.
102. *House of Commons Debates*, May 17, 1873, p. 190, *Canada, Parliament, House of Commons Debates*, March 5, 1873-May 25, 1874, P. A. C.
103. *Ibid.*, pp. 189-190.
104. *Ibid.*, p. 200.
105. *Ibid.*
106. *Ibid.*, p. 190.
107. *Debates of the Senate, Canada, Parliament*, May 21, 1873, p. 202. Campbell admitted that Newfoundland still remained apart, but did not think it was "of so much importance," *ibid.*, p. 202.
108. *Ibid.*
109. *Ibid.*, p. 203.
110. Dufferin to Robinson, May 17, 1873, C. O. 226, vol. 111, p. 226.
111. *Ibid.*
112. Robinson to Kimberley, May 29, 1873, G. 8, D, vol. 55, p. 29.
113. Robinson to Kimberley, Confidential, May 29, 1873, C. O. 226, vol. 111, pp. 232-233.
114. Kimberley to Robinson, June 30, 1873, G. 8, D, vol. 42, p. 249.
115. Kimberley to Robinson, June 30, 1873, *ibid.*, p. 261.
116. Kimberley to Robinson, June 30, 1873, *ibid.*, p. 364.
117. Kimberley to Robinson, Telegraph, June 27, 1873, G. 13, vol. 2, P. A. C.
118. *Patriot*, July 3, 1873.
119. *Island Argus*, July 15, 1873.
120. *Patriot*, July 3, 1873.
121. "Precis of Correspondence relating to land tenure in Prince Edward Island," R. G. 7, G. 21, No. 63. P. A. C.
122. A. H. Clark, *op. cit.*, p. 141.
123. *Island Argus*, July 15, 1873. "Italics Mine."
124. *Patriot*, July 19, 1873.
125. Dufferin to Macdonald, July 21, 1873, *Macdonald Papers*, vol. 79, pp. 412-413.

Footnotes to Chapter Ten

1. Frank MacKinnon, *The Government of Prince Edward Island* (Toronto, 1951), pp. 6-7. Dr. MacKinnon wrote the first connected historical account of the communications question entitled "Communications Between Prince Edward Island and the Mainland," *Dalhousie Review*, vol. 29, (July, 1949), pp. 182-190.
2. The Cape Traverse—Cape Tormentine route, 9 miles wide and thickly packed with ice, was considered more expeditious and safe for walking than the Wood Islands—Pictou crossing. Neil Campbell inaugurated the ice boat system and Judge Peters

designed the craft which was used unaltered for nearly a century. Weekly service continued until 1861, when semi-weekly trips were commenced. *Prince Edward Island Register,* February 13, December 18, 1827, January 22, 1828; *The Daily Examiner,* February 9, 11, 1885. For an interesting account of the hardships of ice boat travel see Lorne C. Calbeck, "Sagas of the Strait", *Atlantic Advocate,* Vol. 49, (February, 1959).

3. Pre-confederation steam service on the Strait is traced by J. S. Martell, "Intercolonial Communications, 1840-1867", *Canadian Historical Association, Report,* 1938, pp. 41-61.

4. F. W. P. Bolger, *Prince Edward Island and Confederation 1863-1873* (Charlottetown, 1964), pp. 28, 34-35, 54.

5. *Ibid.,* pp. 80, 114, 122.

6. Canada, Senate, *Debates,* 1887, pp. 273-274 (June 8). Senator Haythorne, former Premier of the Island in the years 1869 and 1871 respectively, describes how the communications clause became embodied in the terms of Confederation.

7. Prince Edward Island, Assembly, *Debates,* 1886, p. 271 (April 30), Peter Sinclair, a member of Haythorne's Cabinet in 1869, insisted that George Cartier and Edward Kenny were chiefly instrumental in having the communications paragraph inserted in the terms.

8. Prince Edward Island, Assembly, *Journals,* 1870, Appendix F, Young to Hodgson, December 18, 1869.

9. Bolger, *Prince Edward Island and Confederation,* p. 201.

10. *Ibid.,* p. 249. The Terms of Union between Prince Edward Island and the Dominion of Canada are found in MacKinnon, *The Government of Prince Edward Island,* Appendix D, pp. 355-358.

11. See especially Prince Edward Island, Assembly, *Debates,* 1881, pp. 239, 258; (March 30); *Ibid.,* 1886, p. 266 (April 30); Canada, Senate, *Debates,* 1887, p. 275 (June 8).

12. Andrew Hill Clark, *Three Centuries and the Island* (Toronto, 1959), p. 118.

13. Although Island shipbuilding began to decline with the end of reciprocity, the greatest drop did not come until the 1880's. There were 90 wooden vessels built between 1860-1869, 63 from 1870-1879 but only 15 for the years 1880-1889. *Ibid.,* p. 143 and p. 250, n32.

14. "The activity of coastal trading vessels . . . continued to be high throughout the closing decades of the nineteenth century". *Ibid.,* p 143.

15. Prince Edward Island, Assembly, *Journals,* 1886, p. 12.

16. Canada, House of Commons, *Debates,* 1876, pp. 302-303 (February 28), David Laird, Minister of the Interior and representative from the Island, explains in detail the steps the Government had taken to secure a winter steamer for Northumberland Strait.

17. Canada, House of Commons, *Debates,* 1876, p. 1171 (April 10); *Sessional Papers,* 1878, no. 1, Appendix 36, p. 366, Tenth Annual Report of the Department of Marine and Fisheries for the fiscal year ending June 30, 1877.

18. Canada, House of Commons, *Debates,* 1883, p. 50 (19 February).

19. Canada, *Sessional Papers,* 1878, no. 1, Appendix 36, p. 366, Tenth Annual Report of the Department of Marine and Fisheries for the fiscal year ending June 30, 1877.

20. *Ibid.,* and Canada, *Sessional Papers,* 1879, no. 3, Appendix 4, p. 126. Eleventh Annual Report of the Department of Marine and Fisheries for the fiscal year ending June 30, 1878.

21. Prince Edward Island, Assembly, *Debates,* 1885, p. 113 (25 March). Also see Canada, House of Commons, *Debates,* 1883, p. 47 (19 February).

22. Prince Edward Island, Assembly, *Journals,* 1886, Appendix L, pp. 12-15, Report of a Committee of the Privy Council of Canada, 7 November, 1885.

23. Canada, House of Commons, *Journals,* 1883, Appendix No. 3, Report of a Survey of the Coast in the vicinity of Cape Traverse and Tormentine on Prince Edward Island and Mainland, and a suggested railway connection between said Capes to Intercolonial and Prince Edward Island Railways with a view to secure winter communication with the Island (hereafter cited as MacLeod Report), pp. 80-108.

24. Only 15 vessels were built on the Island from 1880 to 1889 compared with 63 in the previous decade, Clark, *Three Centuries and the Island,* p. 143.

25. L. H. Davies discusses the effects of shipping and the national policy on Island trade, Canada, House of Commons, *Debates,* 1883, pp. 69-70 (23 February).

26. Prince Edward Island Assembly, *Debates,* 1881, pp. 240-241 (30 March).

27. *Ibid.*

28. *Ibid.*
29. Canada, Sessional Papers, 1886, No. 76, pp. 34-35, Joint Address, Session of 1881.
30. *Ibid.*, p. 35, Edouard J. Langevin to T. H. Haviland, April 16, 1881.
31. Canada, House of Commons, *Debates,* 1883, p. 44 (19 February), John A. Macdonald to W. W. Sullivan, March 21, 1882; Prince Edward Island, Assembly, *Debates,* 1882, pp. 240-245 (5 April).
32. Canada, *Sessional Papers,* 1886, No. 76, pp. 36-37, Extract from the Minutes of the Executive Council of Prince Edward Island, January 31, 1883.
33. The idea of a committee originated with John T. Jenkins, M.P. for Queen's County. He believed a steamship could be constructed that would completely overcome the difficulties of winter communication on Northumberland Strait and he asked that a Committee be formed to inquire into the point, Canada, House of Commons, *Debates,* 1883, p. 68 (23 February). The five M.P.'s who composed the Committee were: Edward Hackett, Prince County, P.E.I.; Frederick De St. Croix Brecken, Queen's County, P.E.I.; P. A. McIntyre, King's County, P.E.I.; Joseph Wood, Westmorland, N.B.; and A. McIsaac, Antigonish, N.S., Canada, House of Commons, *Journals,* 1883, Appendix No. 3, Report of the Select Committee appointed by the House of Commons to consider the Question of Steam Communication between Prince Edward Island and the Mainland in Winter and Summer (hereafter cited as Report of the Select Committee, 1883), p. 1.
34. The witnesses examined by the Committee were: Samuel Prowse, M.P.P., P.E.I.; John T. Jenkins, M.P., P.E.I.; Henry Coombs, Merchant, P.E.I.; G. W. Howlan, Senator, P.E.I.; Captain McIlhinney, Department of Marine, Ottawa; Captain Irving, ice boat service, P.E.I.; R. P. Haythorne, Senator, P.E.I.; A. Finlayson, Pilot, *Northern Light,* P.E.I.; Richard Hunt, Merchant, P.E.I.; J. S. Carvell, Senator, P.E.I., *ibid.,* p. 1.
35. *Ibid.,* pp. 13-16, 26.
36. *Ibid.,* p. 14.
37. It was generally felt that screw-steamers would add three weeks to the late fall and early spring service, *ibid.,* p. 2.
38. *Ibid.,* pp. 2-3.
39. *Ibid.,* p. 77.
40. *Ibid.*
41. *Ibid.,* p. 2.
42. *Ibid.*
43. *Ibid.,* p. 37.
44. Canada, House of Commons, *Journals,* 1881, Appendix No. 3, pp. 89, 90, 94, MacLeod Report, April 23, 1879.
45. *Ibid.,* Report of the Select Committee, 1883, p. 54.
46. *Ibid.,* p. 2.
47. Canada, Senate, *Debates,* 1884, p. 104, (15 February).
48. *Ibid.*
49. Canada, *Sessional Papers,* 1884, No. 5, xxxi, Sixth Annual Report of the Department of Marine and Fisheries for the fiscal year ending, 30 June, 1883.
50. Prince Edward Island, Assembly, *Debates,* 1884, p. 2 (6 March).
51. Prince Edward Island, Assembly, *Journals,* 1884, pp. 281-289 (17 April).
52. Canada, *Sessional Papers,* 1886, No. 76, p. 38, G. Powell to T. H. Haviland, April 24, 1884.
53. *The Daily Examiner,* January 29, 30, 31, 1885; *The Daily Patriot,* January 29, 30, 31, 1885.
54. *The Halifax Herald,* January 31, 1885.
55. *The Toronto Globe,* January 30, 31, 1885.
56. Quoted in *The Daily Examiner,* February 7, 1885.
57. Canada, Senate, *Debates,* 1885, pp. 489-504 (9 April).
58. *Ibid.,* pp. 100-101 (24 February).
59. Peter Sinclair and William Hooper emphatically stated that the terms of union must be either fulfilled or cancelled. Prince Edward Island, Assembly, *Debates,* 1885, pp. 94 and 135 (24, 25 March).
60. *Ibid.,* pp. 86-87 (24 March).
61. Canada, *Sessional Papers,* 1886, No. 76, pp. 30-33, Joint Address to Her Majesty the Queen from the Legislative Council and House of Assembly of Prince Edward Island on the subject of Communication with the Mainland, March 27, 1885.
62. *Ibid.,* pp. 23-29, Report of a Committee of the Honourable Privy Council, approved by His Excellency the Governor-General in Council, November 7, 1885.

63. Prince Edward Island, Assembly, *Journals,* 1886, Appendix L, p. 8, Lord Stanley to the Lieutenant Governor of Prince Edward Island, January 26, 1886.
64. Canada, *Sessional Papers,* 1886, No. 76, pp. 5-13, W. W. Sullivan and D. Ferguson to Earl Granville, March 1, 1886.
65. *Ibid.,* p. 2, Earl Granville to Marquis of Lansdowne, March 30, 1886.
66. Prince Edward Island, Assembly, *Debates,* 1885, pp. 86-87 (24 March).
67. Prince Edward Island, Assembly, *Debates,* 1886, p. 265 (30 April).
68. Canada, Senate, *Debates,* 1887, p. 270 (8 June).
69. *Ibid.*
70. Canada, *Sessional Papers,* 1888, No. 67, pp. 1-8.
71. *The Charlottetown Herald,* February 17, 1887.
72. *Ibid.*
73. Prince Edward Island, Assembly, *Debates,* 1887, p. 12 (31 March).
74. Canada, Senate, *Debates,* 1887, p. 271 (8 June).
75. Prince Edward Island, Assembly, *Debates,* 1886, p. 394. The debt of the province by 1886 had amounted to $120,000.
76. Public Archives of Canada (hereafter cited as PAC), *Macdonald Papers,* vol. 119, W. W. Sullivan to John A. Macdonald, March 19, 1887.
77. Prince Edward Island, Assembly, *Debates,* 1887, pp. 360-361 (3 May).
78. *Ibid.,* p. 362.
79. Canada, *Sessional Papers,* 1889, No. 8, p. 22, Twenty-first Annual Report of the Department of Marine for the fiscal year ending 30 June, 1888.
80. *Ibid.*
81. Canada, *Sessional Papers,* 1890, No. 16, pp. 24-25, Twenty-second Annual Report of the Department of Marine for the fiscal year ending 30 June, 1889.
82. Prince Edward Island, Assembly, *Debates,* 1889, pp. 228-230.
83. Canada, House of Commons, *Debates,* 1891, p. 1282 (24 June).
84. *Ibid.*
85. A full account of Howlan's tunnel correspondence is printed in *The Daily Examiner,* February 12, 1891.
86. Canada, House of Commons, *Debates,* 1892, p. 405 (23 March).
87. Canada, House of Commons, *Debates,* 1891, p. 159 (12 May).
88. *The Summerside Journal,* December 31, 1890.
89. *The Daily Examiner,* February 6, 1891; also Prince Edward Island, Assembly, *Debates,* 1891, pp. 378-379 (8 July).
90. *The Daily Examiner,* February 12, 16, 18, 1891, March 4, 1891.
91. John C. MacMillan, *The History of the Catholic Church in Prince Edward Island* (Quebec, 1913), pp. 478-479.
92. Canada, House of Commons, *Debates,* 1891, p. 1287 (24 June).
93. *Ibid.,* p. 1286.
94. *The Daily Examiner,* January 23, 1891. L. H. Davies to the Editor.
95. The Charlottetown *Guardian,* February, 1891.
96. Canada, *Sessional Papers,* 1894, No. 95, pp. 1-6, Report of Sir Douglas Fox on the Proposed Railway Tunnel under the Northumberland Strait between New Brunswick and Prince Edward Island, May 5, 1891.
97. Canada, House of Commons, *Debates,* 1893, pp. 2411-2412 (15 March).
98. *Ibid.,* pp. 2403-2414.
99. Canada, House of Commons, *Debates,* 1895, p. 206 (24 April).
100. The Frederick Peters Government had announced in 1892 that any claims the province had against the Dominion would not be pressed while Ottawa was taking the tunnel under its favourable consideration. Prince Edward Island, Assembly, *Debates,* 1892, p. 453 (28 April).
101. Canada, *Sessional Papers,* 1897, No. 56, pp. 27-28, Frederick Peters to L. H. Davies, April 8, 1897.
102. In 1897, Peters was appointed leading counsel for the Dominion on the Bering Sea Commission. A. B. Warburton became the new Premier. Canada, *Sessional Papers,* 1899, No. 104, pp. 2-3, Memorial of the Province of Prince Edward Island to the Dominion of Canada, March 18, 1898.
103. Prince Edward Island, Assembly, *Journals,* 1898, Appendix N, p. 13, Wilfrid Laurier to A. B. Warburton, March 21, 1898; Canada, *Sessional Papers,* 1899, No. 104, p. 9, Wilfrid Laurier to D. Farquharson, March 28, 1899.

104. "New Winter Steamer for P.E.I.", *The Railway and Shipping World,* vol. 1 (July, 1898), p. 131.
105. Prince Edward Island, Assembly, *Journals,* 1901, Appendix K. p. 6, Memorials of the Government of Prince Edward Island to the Dominion of Canada, April 9, 1901.
106. *Ibid.,* pp. 6-9.
107. Canada, House of Commons, *Debates,* 1901, pp. 4676-4677 (8 May).
108. *Moran's Annual Register,* 1901, p. 475.
109. Donald Creighton, *Dominion of the North,* Second edition (Toronto, 1957), pp. 391-394.
110. In 1892, representation in the House of Commons dropped from six to five owing to a decrease in population; in 1904 it declined to four. MacKinnon, *Government of Prince Edward Island,* pp. 290-291.
111. The arguments summarized here are cited in newspapers, parliamentary debates and addresses throughout the decade. See especially the memorial of the P.E.I. Government to Ottawa, April 13, 1905, Prince Edward Island, Assembly, *Journals,* 1905, pp. 34-38.
112. Canada, *Sessional Papers,* 1904, No. 21, pp. 11-24, Thirty-sixth Annual Report of the Department of Marine and Fisheries, Marine Branch, December, 1903.
113. *Ibid.,* see also *The Eastern Chronicle,* January 29, March 2, 17, 1903.
114. Canada, *Sessional Papers,* 1904, No. 21, p. 24, Thirty-sixth Annual Report of the Department of Marine and Fisheries, Marine Branch, December, 1903.
115. *The Daily Patriot,* March 5, 1903.
116. Prince Edward Island, Assembly, *Journals,* 1903, pp. 116-117 (30 April).
117. *The Daily Patriot,* March 3, 1905; Canada, *Sessional Papers,* 1906, No. 21, pp. 10-11, Thirty-eighth Annual Report of the Department of Marine and Fisheries for the fiscal year ending 30 June, 1905.
118. PAC, *Laurier Papers,* vol. 356, A. E. Burke to Wilfrid Laurier, February 21, 1905.
119. *The Daily Patriot,* March 11, 1905.
120. *Canadian Annual Review,* 1905, p. 342.
121. Prince Edward Island, Assembly, *Journals,* 1905, pp. 34-38 (13 April).
122. PAC, *Laurier Papers,* vol. 365, A. T. Weldon, Secretary, Halifax Board of Trade to Wilfrid Laurier, May 13, 1905; *Canadian Annual Review,* 1905, p. 343.
123. Canada, House of Commons, *Debates,* 1905, p. 2664 (16 March); p. 6644 (26 May) and p. 2815 (21 March).
124. *Ibid.,* pp. 2811-2812 (21 March).
125. Canada, House of Commons, *Debates,* 1906, pp. 1079-1091 (18 December).
126. Prince Edward Island, Assembly, *Journals,* 1907, p. 142 (12 April); *Canadian Annual Review,* 1907, p. 629; See also Canada, House of Commons, *Debates,* 1907, pp. 3199-3201, 3218-3220.
127. The Charlottetown *Guardian,* January 12, 1907.
128. Prince Edward Island, Assembly, *Journals,* 1907, p. 142 (12 April); *Laurier Papers,* vol. 458, Laurier to A. E. Burke, March 30, 1907.
129. Canada, House of Commons, *Debates,* 1906-7, p. 3229 (18 February); *Ibid.,* 1908, p. 4654 (9 March).
130. *Ibid.,* 1908, p. 4593 (9 March).
131. Canada, *Sessional Papers,* 1911, No. 21, pp. 24-30, 34, Forty-third Annual Report of the Department of Marine for the fiscal year ending 30 June, 1910.
132. *Canadian Annual Review,* 1911, pp. 176-177.
133. Canada, House of Commons, *Debates,* 1911, pp. 1580-1581 (22 January).
134. The Charlottetown *Guardian,* December 29, 1911.
135. J. A. Mathieson, "Celebrating Confederation", *Canadian Courier,* vol. 19 (July, 1914), p. 9.
136. Prince Edward Island, Assembly, *Journals,* 1912, Appendix K, p. 10, Report of a Delegation appointed to present to the Government of Canada the claims of Prince Edward Island to further subsidy, February 17, 1912; *Canadian Annual Review,* 1912, p. 485.
137. For a discussion of the Island's economic boom during this period see, J. A. Mathieson, "Celebrating Confederation", *Canadian Courier,* vol. 19 (July, 1914), pp. 9-16.
138. A. K. Kirkpatrick, "Car-Ferry Service Between Prince Edward Island and New Brunswick", *Canadian Railway and Marine World,* vol. 15, (1912), pp. 531-534. Professor Kirkpatrick of the Kingston School of Mining was appointed by the Minister of Railways and Canals to investigate the best route and most favourable terminus for the car ferry.

139. "The Prince Edward Island Car-Ferry and Its Terminals", *Canadian Railway and Marine World*, vol. 20, (1917), pp. 447-448.
140. "Car-Ferry Steamship for Prince Edward Island", *Canadian Railway and Marine World*, vol. 17, (1914), p. 518.
141. The *Stanley* returned to the Island service in December, 1914. In October, 1914, the *Earl Grey* was sold to Russia for winter navigation at Archangel. The *Minto* followed her sistership in November, 1915. Canada, *Sessional Papers*, 1916, No. 21, pp. 11-12; Forty-eighth Annual Report of the Department of Marine for the fiscal year 1914-15; *Ibid.*, 1917, No. 21, pp. 250-252, Forty-ninth Annual Report of the Department of Marine for the fiscal year 1915-16.
142. *Ibid.*, 1918, No. 21, p. 225, Fiftieth Annual Report of the Department of Marine for the fiscal year 1916-17; *Ibid.*, 1919, No. 21; Firty-first Annual Report of the Department of Marine for the fiscal year 1917-18; "The Prince Edward Island Car-Ferry and Its Terminals", *Canadian Railway and Marine World*, vol. 20 (1917), pp. 448-449.
143. *Canadian Annual Review*, 1918, pp. 667-668.
144. The first standard train ran to Charlottetown on September 18, 1919. The road was standardized from Summerside to Tignish by August, 1923, from Charlottetown to Souris, Elmira and Georgetown by September, 1926, and to Murray Harbour on September 29, 1930. J. F. Lafferty, "Prince Edward Island Railway", *Canadian National Magazine*, vol. 37 (May, 1951), pp. 10-11, 18-19.
145. Canada, House of Commons, *Debates*, 1920, p. 1601 (23 April) and p. 2103 (6 May).
146. *Canadian Railway and Marine World*, vol. 23 (November, 1920), p. 626.
147. *Canadian Annual Review*, 1921, pp. 738-739.
148. *Ibid.*, p. 736.
149. *Ibid.*, 1924, pp. 335-337 and 1925, pp. 395-398.
150. *Report of the Royal Commission on Maritime Claims* (Ottawa, 1926), pp. 20-22.
151. *Ibid.*, pp. 27-28.
152. Canada, House of Commons, *Debates*, 1927, p. 1336 (18 March).
153. *Canadian Annual Review*, 1926-27, pp. 74-82.
154. Canada, House of Commons, *Debates*, 1928, p. 3282 (22 May).
155. *Ibid.*, 1929, p. 3078-3080 (20 May).
156. *Ibid.*, 1934, pp. 2127, 2131-2132 (13 April).
157. *Ibid.*, 1935, p. 2132 (26 March).
158. The Airways was *Maritime Central Airways*.
159. Canada, House of Commons, *Debates*, 1937, pp. 2388-2393 (31 March).
160. *Report of the Royal Commission on Dominion-Provincial Relations*, 1940, Books 1-3 reprinted in one volume (Ottawa, 1954), pp. 264-265.
161. Canada, House of Commons, *Debates*, 1943, pp. 1823-1826 (2 April).
162. Prince Edward Island, Assembly, *Journal*, 1947, pp. 11-12.
163. *Royal Commission (Turgeon) on Transportation: Submissions by the Province of Prince Edward Island* (hereafter cited as Turgeon Commission — P.E.I. Submission) (Charlottetown, July 1949), pp. 39, 66, 79-80.
164. *Ibid.*, pp. 78-80.
165. *Ibid.*, pp. 20, 58-59. Trucking rates were reduced in July, 1949. The Royal Commission on Transportation concluded that the attitude of the Canadian National Railway, with respect to trucks and buses, was "an indication of unsatisfactory conditions". See *Report of the Royal Commission on Transportation, 1951* (Ottawa, 1951), pp. 172-173.
166. Turgeon Commission, — *P.E.I. Submission*, pp. 80-81.
167. *Report of the Royal Commission on Transportation, 1951*, pp. 172-173.
168. Prince Edward Island, Assembly, *Journals*, 1956, pp. 20-21. Report of the Department of Industry and Natural Resources, Transportation Division for the period March 31, 1954 to March 31, 1955.
169. J. G. MacKay, "Causeway to P.E.I. Practical if Cost Less Than $75 Million", *Roads and Engineering Construction* (October, 1957), pp. 125-126.
170. *Ibid.* See also Michael Wardell, "Northumberland Strait Crossing," *Atlantic Advocate*, vol. 55 (August, 1965), pp. 14-18.
171. It was found a complete road crossing would change tides and alter water temperature having a disastrous effect on navigation and fishing in the area. A design had to be created which would not disturb shipping or fisheries, but at the same time resist the impact of massive ice floes which travelled through the strait at 4 miles an hour.
172. Canada, House of Commons, *Debates*, p. 3033 (17 April).

173. Wardell, "Northumberland Strait Crossing", p. 18.
174. *Canadian Annual Review*, 1963, p. 144.
175. Canada, House of Commons, *Debates*, 1965, p. 1750 (8 July).
176. *Canadian Annual Review*, 1965, pp. 173-174.
177. *Royal Commission (MacPherson) on Transportation: Submissions by the Province of Prince Edward Island* (Charlottetown, October, 1959), p. 10.
178. *Canadian Annual Review*, 1962.
179. *Ibid.*, 1963, p. 144.
180. MacPherson Commission — P.E.I. Submission, pp. 9-12. See also supplementary information supplied in letter from Premier Shaw to the Chairman, September 9, 1960.
181. Prince Edward Island, Assembly, *Journals*, 1956, pp. 20-21. Report of the Department of Industry and Natural Resources, Transportation Division, for the period March 31, 1954 to March 31, 1955.
182. *Canadian Annual Review*, 1966, p. 153.
183. *Ibid.*, p. 169.
184. *Ibid.*, 1968, p. 184.
185. Canada, House of Commons, *Debates*, 1969, p. 6227 (5 March).
186. Following a futile effort to preserve the historical vessel, the *Prince Edward Island* was later sold and reduced to scrap.
187. Canada, House of Commons, *Debates*, 1969, p. 6227 (5 March; *ibid.*, p. 10227 (17 June); Remarks on Atlantic Transportation by Transport Minister Don Jamieson, August 22, 1972.

Footnotes to Chapter Eleven

1. *The Case of Prince Edward Island; A Submission Presented to the Royal Commission on Dominion-Provincial Relations by the Government of Prince Edward Island* (Charlottetown, n.d.), p. 7.
2. *Ibid.*
3. *The Claims of Prince Edward Island Against the Dominion of Canada* (1927), p. 38. Almost the entire debt in 1873 had been incurred in the preceding two years to finance the ill-fated railway.
4. Prince Edward Island, *Assembly Journal*, 1873, Appendix A. The terms of union are fully discussed *above*, pp. 212-213, 222, 230-231.
5. Wilfred Eggleston and C. T. Kraft, *Dominion-Provincial Subsidies and Grants* (Ottawa, 1939), pp. 9-10.
6. The first Provincial Conference met in 1887 to discuss federal-provincial financial arrangements.
7. In 1894, succession duties were introduced, and in the same year, the province imposed a personal income tax, the second province to do so. See J. E. Lattimer, *Prince Edward Island, Tax Survey Report* (1946) pp. 15, 18-19.
8. Prince Edward Island, *Assembly Journal*, 1901, Appendix K., Documents Relating to Prince Edward Island's Claim against the Dominion Government re Winter Communication, etc., p. 11.
9. Prince Edward Island, *Assembly Debates*, 1888, p. 13.
10. This important aspect of the province's relations with the Dominion is dealt with elsewhere, and will not be discussed here. See *above*, Chapter X.
11. Prince Edward Island, *Assembly Journal*, 1898, Appendix N, Memorial of Prince Edward Island's Claims Respecting an Increase of Subsidy, March 18, 1898.
12. *Ibid.*, p. 3.
13. Canada, House of Commons, *Sessional Papers*, 1899, No. 104. Sir Wilfrid Laurier to Honorable D. Farquharson, March 28, 1899.
14. Prince Edward Island, *Assembly Journal*, 1901, Appendix K, Documents Relating to Prince Edward Island's Claim against the Dominion Government, re Winter Communications, etc., pp. 9-13.
15. *Ibid.*, p. 12.
16. At Confederation, customs and excise revenues accounted for 75% of the Island's total revenue. See Eggleston and Kraft, *op. cit.*, p. 1.
17. Ontario was the most strenuous opponent of subsidies although all provinces would

have preferred to avoid them. The origin of the subsidy arrangements is discussed in *Ibid.,* pp. 1-6.

18. Prince Edward Island, *Assembly Journal,* 1901, Appendix K, Documents Relating to Prince Edward Island's Claim against the Dominion Government, re Winter Communications, etc., pp. 3-9.
19. Donald Creighton, *Canada's First Century, 1867-1967* (Toronto, 1970), p. 108.
20. The economic development of the period is discussed in W. A. MacKintosh, *The Economic Background of Dominion-Provincial Relations* (Toronto, 1964), pp. 41-70.
21. MacKintosh, *op. cit.,* p. 154. At least five Royal Commissions have, in varying degrees, recognized similar effects of national policies on the Maritime region. *The Royal Commission on Maritime Claims,* (The Duncan Commission, 1926); *Royal Commission on Dominion-Provincial Relations,* (Rowell-Sirois Commission, 1940); *Royal Commission on Canada's Economic Prospects,* (The Gordon Commission, 1952); *Royal Commission, Provincial Economic Inquiry,* (The Jones Commission, 1934); *Royal Commission on Provincial Development and Rehabilitation,* (Dawson Commission, 1944). The first three were commissioned by the federal government; the last two by Nova Scotia.
22. Prince Edward Island, *Assembly Journal,* 1910, pp. 114-115.
23. See for example Mathieson's speech at Hunter River on December 19, in Charlottetown, *Daily Examiner,* December 20, 1911.
24. Prince Edward Island, *Assembly Journal,* 1912, Appendix K, Report of Delegation Appointed to Present to the Government of Canada the Claims of Prince Edward Island to further Subsidy, p. 25.
25. *Ibid.,* p. 15.
26. Canada, House of Commons, *Debates,* March 22, 1912, p. 5862.
27. *Ibid.,* p. 5860.
28. *Sir Robert Borden Papers,* Vol. 18. p. 4883, Walter Scott, R. P. Roblin and A. L. Sifton to Borden, December 22, 1913.
29. *Ibid.,* p. 4897, G. H. Murray to Sir Robert Borden, January 19, 1914; p. 4901, J. A. Mathieson to Sir Robert Borden, February 2, 1914; p. 4903, J. K. Flemming to Sir Robert Borden, February 17, 1914.
30. *Ibid.,* p. 4906, Sir Robert Borden to Premiers R. P. Roblin, A. L. Sifton and Walter Scott, March 5, 1914.
31. *Ibid.,* Vol. 57, Presentation to His Royal Highness in Council of the Claim of the Provinces of New Brunswick, Nova Scotia and Prince Edward Island for Compensation in Respect of the Public Lands of Canada, Transferred to Certain Provinces of Canada and Held in Trust for their Benefit, January 21, 1913.
32. *Ibid.*
33. *Ibid.,* Remarks of Premier Mathieson.
34. *Ibid.,* Remarks of Mr. Grimmer.
35. *Ibid.,* Remarks of Mr. Grimmer.
36. *Ibid.,* Remarks of Premier Mathieson.
37. MacKintosh, *op. cit.,* pp. 71-86.
38. *Ibid.,* pp. 62-63.
39. Prince Edward Island, *Assembly Journal,* 1920, pp. 41-42. A similar Resolution passed in the Nova Scotia legislature. See Nova Scotia, *Assembly Journal,* 1920, pp. 110-111, 312-313.
40. Charlottetown, *Patriot,* April 17, 1920.
41. *Maritime Development Committee Papers,* Accession 2223, A. E. McMahon to Hon. J. A. Robb, Acting Minister of Finance, June 10, 1924. P.E.I., Provincial Archives.
42. J. A. Maxwell, *Federal Subsidies to the Provincial Governments in Canada* (Cambridge, 1937), p. 138.
43. In the election of 1921, the west returned a large majority of Progressives as a protest against Ottawa policies, and particularly the tariff.
44. See the *Guardian* and the *Patriot* for July, 1923.
45. Charlottetown, *Guardian,* September 19, 1925. On September 18, Meighen spoke at both the Strand and the Prince Edward theatres.
46. The Island elected two Conservatives and two Liberals. In 1921, four Liberals had been elected. In the three provinces, the Liberals dropped from twenty-five to six seats.
47. The appointment of the Commission is discussed in H. B. Neatby, *William Lyon MacKenzie King, 1924-1932; The Lonely Heights* (Toronto, 1963), p. 102.

386 Canada's Smallest Province

48. *Claim of the Province of Prince Edward Island for Increase of Subsidy as Submitted to the Royal Commission Composed of Sir Andrew Rae Duncan, Hon. W. B. Wallace and Cyrus J. MacMillan* (Summerside, 1927), pp. 15-16.
49. *Ibid.,* p. 26.
50. *Ibid.,* pp. 29-30.
51. *Report of the Royal Commission on Maritime Claims* (Ottawa, 1926), p. 9.
52. *Ibid.* It should be pointed out that the Commission made no attempt to assess the regional impact of the national policy. It was less concerned with placing blame than with exposing existing conditions.
53. *Ibid.,* p. 11.
54. *Ibid.,* p. 19. The Commission made recommendations on many other subjects, such as port facilities at St. John and Halifax, export trade, and the coal and steel industry in Nova Scotia. Most of these were of more concern to Nova Scotia and New Brunswick than to Prince Edward Island.
55. *Ibid.,* p. 21.
56. *Ibid.,* pp. 23-26.
57. Charlottetown, *Guardian,* December 11, 1926.
58. Canada, House of Commons, *Debates,* March 18, 1927, pp. 1336-1337.
59. *Ibid.,* April 30, 1930, pp. 1606-1607, and *Ibid.,* February 18, 1929, p. 204. See also *Proceedings of the Dominion-Provincial Conference, 1927.*
60. Prince Edward Island, *Assembly Journal,* 1930, Appendix I, The Claim of Prince Edward Island for an Increase in its Subsidy in Lieu of Public Lands. The Dominion, of course, could claim that the province should have repaid its loan with the proceeds from the sale of the lands.
61. The Premiers had met in Charlottetown in July, 1934, to discuss the claims to be submitted. See *Accession 2524,* Item 13, Copy of Press Release of Premiers' Meeting, July 9, 1934. P.E.I., Provincial Archives.
62. Prince Edward Island, *Assembly Journal,* 1935, Appendix FFF, Report of Royal Commission on Financial Arrangements between the Dominion and the Maritime Provinces, pp. 5-6.
63. *Ibid.,* p. 12.
64. *Ibid.,* pp. 6-7.
65. *Ibid.,* p. 20.
66. This amount was to replace the $125,000 awarded by the Duncan Commission. This amounted to an additional $150,000 and was paid beginning in 1935.
67. *Ibid.,* pp. 19-20.
68. *Ibid.,* pp. 22-23. The other Commissioners admitted that earlier revisions had been made on the basis of fiscal need. But they felt that this was a dangerous principle, and so rejected it.
69. J. R. Winter, *Maritime Union Study: Federal-Provincial Fiscal Relations and Maritime Union* (1970), p. 8.
70. *The Case of Prince Edward Island; A Submission Presented to the Royal Commission on Dominion-Provincial Relations by the Government of Prince Edward Island* (Charlottetown, n.d.), p. 37.
71. *Ibid.,* pp. 29-31.
72. *Ibid.,* pp. 44-48.
73. *Report of the Royal Commission on Federal-Provincial Relations,* Book II (Ottawa, 1940), p. 232.
74. *Ibid.,* p. 233.
75. *Ibid.,* Book I, pp. 219-220.
76. *Ibid.,* p. 219.
77. *Ibid.,* Book II, p. 86.
78. *Proceedings of the Federal-Provincial Conference of 1941,* pp. 41-49.
79. *Submission by the Province of Prince Edward Island to the Federal-Provincial Conference,* October 3, 1955, p. 7.
80. *Public Accounts of Prince Edward Island,* 1952, 1967.
81. In 1971 the Island slipped into last place.
82. Touche, Ross, Bailey and Smart, *Province of Prince Edward Island, Provincial-Municipal Fiscal Study* (1969). See for example, pp. 23-24, and Table 3, p. 32.
83. *Submission by the Province of Prince Edward Island to the Federal-Provincial Conference,* October 3, 1955, pp. 3-4.

84. *Submission by the Province of Prince Edward Island to the Federal-Provincial Conference,* July 25, 1960, pp. 5-7.
85. *Submission by the Province of Prince Edward Island to the Federal-Provincial Conference,* October 3, 1955, pp. 6-7.
86. *Ibid.,* p. 5.
87. *Ibid.,* p. 6.
88. *Submission by the Province of Prince Edward Island to the Federal-Provincial Conference,* July 25, 1960, p. 30.
89. *Ibid.,* p. 30.
90. *Statutes of Canada,* 4-5 Elizabeth II, c. 29.
91. *Ibid.,* 6 Elizabeth II, c. 29.
92. *Sir John A. Macdonald Papers,* Vol. 255, p. 168, Pope to Macdonald, April 26, 1880.
93. Stewart Bates, *Financial History of Canadian Governments* (Ottawa, 1939), pp. 91-92.
94. See for example, A resolution of the Provincial Legislature in *Assembly Journal,* 1905, pp. 64-65. Also, *The Claims of Prince Edward Island Against the Dominion of Canada* (1927), pp. 37-39. In 1864 the province was entitled to only five members, but demanded six. It was now argued that the intent of the 1873 agreement was that representation should never be less than six.
95. This subject is discussed in Frank MacKinnon, *The Government of Prince Edward Island* (Toronto, 1951), pp. 289-293.
96. This happened in 1887, 1965, and 1968.
97. *Alexander MacKenzie Letterbooks,* Vol. 1, p. 760, MacKenzie to Peter Sinclair, October 26, 1876.
98. Laurier to Arthur Peters, January 20, 1902, quoted in MacKinnon, *op. cit.,* pp. 294-295.
99. The province has been represented by the following Cabinet Ministers: David Laird, Minister of the Interior, 1873-1876; James C. Pope, Minister of Marine and Fisheries, 1878-1882; Donald Ferguson, Minister without Portfolio, 1894-1896; Louis H. Davies, Minister of Marine and Fisheries, 1896-1901; John E. Sinclair, Minister without Portfolio, 1921-1925; John A. MacDonald, Minister without Portfolio, 1926; Cyrus MacMillan, Minister of Fisheries, 1930; John A. MacDonald, Minister without Portfolio, 1930-1935; J. Angus MacLean, Minister of Fisheries, 1957-1963; J. Watson MacNaught, Solicitor General, 1963-1965, changed to Minister of Mines and Technical Surveys, 1965; and Daniel J. MacDonald, Minister of Veterans' Affairs, 1972—
100. Much is made of this point for the Maritime region generally by Winter, *op. cit.,* pp. 42 ff.

Footnotes to Chapter Twelve

1. Lorne C. Callbeck, *The Cradle of Confederation* (Fredericton, 1964), pp. 70-73.
2. See also R. MacGregor Dawson, *The Government of Canada,* 2nd ed., (Toronto, 1956), p. 212; and Frank MacKinnon, *The Government of Prince Edward Island* (Toronto, 1951), pp. 293-296.
3. MacKinnon, *op. cit.,* pp 289-293 and Castell Hopkins, ed., *The Canadian Annual Review of Public Affairs* (1902-1938), (Toronto: Canadian Review Co. Ltd., 1902-1915).
4. MacKinnon, *op. cit.,* p. 292.
5. *Canadian Annual Review,* 1910, p. 474.
6. *Ibid.,* 1911, p. 535.
7. For further information, see MacKinnon, *op. cit.,* pp. 41-53.
8. The county capitals were chosen by Captain Samuel Holland when he surveyed the Island in 1764. At the same time, Charlottetown was selected as the capital city. Each of the three were referred to as "common and royalty" — for example, "Charlottetown Common and Royalty" was the correct name for the constituency. [This meant the district pertained to both crown land and common land]. For many years, these three constituencies were denoted by these formal titles; gradually, however, the county capital names for the districts were replaced by the constituency labels of Fifth Prince, Fifth Queen's and Fifth King's. The county capital of Prince was shifted to Summerside in 1876.

9. See MacKinnon, *op cit.,* pp. 34-41 and pp. 86-104 for further information on the Council and other early political institutions on the Island.

10. See also Marlene-Russell Clark, "The Franchise in Prince Edward Island and its Relation to Island Politics and Other Political Institutions", unpublished M.A. thesis, Dalhousie University, 1968, and D. C. Harvey, "The Passing of the Second Chamber in Prince Edward Island", Canadian Historical Association, *Annual Report, 1922,* pp. 22-31.

11. These constituencies were: First Prince, Second Prince, Third Prince, Fourth Prince, Fifth Prince, First Queen's, Second Queen's, Third Queen's, Fourth Queen's, Fifth Queen's [or Charlottetown common and royalty], First King's, Second King's, Third King's, Fourth King's, and Fifth King's (also known as Georgetown common and royalty).

12. Many people failed to distinguish clearly between the multiple vote and the property vote concept. However, a definite distinction is evident in both the legislation that outlined the electoral system and *The Royal Commission on Electoral Reform,* Province of Prince Edward Island, 1962.

13. In some cases, voters did not own two separate properties but were fortunate enough to find their single property sliced by a constituency boundary. Consequently, they were afforded the luxury of multiple voting, further illustration of the absurdities which the system demonstrated.

14. For a more detailed account of the provisions found in both the Election Act, 1922, and its later amendments, see Clark, unpublished thesis, pp. 19-30.

15. For a more detailed account of the extent of multiple voting, see also Clark, unpublished thesis, pp. 36-48.

16. This was the conclusion drawn by the *Royal Commission on Electoral Reform* Province of Prince Edward Island, 1962.

17. See also, Clark, unpublished thesis, pp. 62-81, for further analysis of this point.

18. *Ibid.,* pp. 39-44.

19. *Ibid.,* pp. 82-108.

20. Education, for example, has often involved controversies in which the battle lines have paralleled religious affiliations.

21. For a discussion on the conduct of elections, see Clark, unpublished thesis, pp. 33-61.

22. "Instructions to Liberal Agents and Workers", 1947, s. 30.

23. There were exceptions of course: one female voter always received a new cotton housedress and a pair of cheap shoes, both of which she consistently requested at the commencement of each campaign.

24. As in other quoted examples, it would not be expedient to identify either the district or the party involved!

25. The political candidates have not always been able to exercise control over their supporters' actions. When the participants in a recent federal campaign decided to abolish refreshment practices in their constituency, not all of the poll chairmen would agree. One candidate finally told his workers they would be required to resign if they did not accept his decision, whereupon one poll chairman tendered his resignation on the spot.

26. Clark, unpublished thesis, pp. 62-81.

27. A total of thirteen seats have been won by acclamation in the provincial elections since 1893. No election has been won by acclamation in recent years. The total number of seats contested in all elections, including by-elections, have not been included in this analysis because by-election data of earlier years can be misleading. Until recently cabinet ministers, once appointed to the Executive Council, had to resign their Assembly seat and re-test their popularity at the polls. Many such by-elections were won by acclamation; in any case, such special circumstances may unduly distort an analysis of long-term political trends in the province.

28. Clark, unpublished thesis, pp. 108-128.

29. *The Guardian,* August 13, 1959, and Liberal Platform, *Guardian,* August 17, 1959.

30. *Ibid.,* February 9, 1961.

31. *Ibid.,* April 17, 1963.

32. *Ibid.,* April 11, 1963.

33. *Ibid.,* April 4, 1963.

34. Clark, unpublished thesis, pp. 103-105.

35. One voter, for example, wrote to a candidate and suggested that her son would be

interested in adding to the party's support at the polls if he could get transportation home in time for the election and if he could be guaranteed a job once he reached the province. As time was short, she further suggested that air transportation would be the most feasible way to bring her son to the Island — from Alberta! Another elector requested a candidate intervene to get the voter's nephew into a vocational school that had earlier refused the young chap admittance. The uncle also asked if the politician would obtain employment for his son-in-law and negotiate repairs to a local wharf.

36. These statistics are based on figures for recent campaigns. The cost would be lower for earlier elections because of changes in the value of the dollar and an alteration in campaigning techniques from personal contact to more media involvement. Many individuals, groups and firms that are requested to carry out work for a political party increase their prices above normal because of an inherent, though sometimes false, assumption that political parties are rich organizations.
37. For further information, see also Clark, unpublished thesis, pp. 129-136.
38. *Canadian Annual Review,* 1908-1913.
39. MacKinnon, *op cit.,* pp. 157-160, 193-194; and *Canadian Annual Review,* 1901-1938.
40. MacKinnon, *op. cit.,* p. 197.
41. *Canadian Annual Review,* 1935-1936, p. 461.

Footnotes to Chapter Thirteen

1. In writing this chapter the author has extracted, summarized, or enlarged upon materials in his history of the Island entitled: *The Cradle of Confederation* (Fredericton, 1964).
2. L. W. Shaw, "Early Education", *Historic Highlights,* (Prince Edward Island Historical Association Booklet).
3. *Ibid.*
4. *Ibid.*
5. *Summerside Journal-Pioneer,* October 12, 1965.
6. L. C. Callbeck, "Buck's Bowpin", *The Atlantic Advocate,* July, 1961.
7. J. H. Blanchard, *The Acadians of Prince Edward Island* (Quebec, 1964).
8. Walter Johnstone, *Travels in Prince Edward Island.*
9. *The Examiner,* September 21, 1882.
10. *Ibid.*
11. *Ibid.*
12. A. H. Clark, *Three Centuries And The Island* (Toronto, 1959), pp. 148-149.
13. L. C. Callbeck, "A Faithful Friend-The Potato", *The Atlantic Advocate,* April, 1967.
14. *The Charlottetown Guardian,* September 27, 1912.
15. L. C. Callbeck, "Canada's Theatrical Showcase", *The Atlantic Advocate,* May, 1969.
16. *Ibid.*
17. Moncrieff Williamson, *Robert Harris, 1849-1919: An Unconventional Biography* (Toronto, 1970).

Index

Abbott, Sir John, 170
Abegweit, 4
Abegweit, Steamship, 250, 259
Acadia, 13, 15, 18, 22-25
Acadians: migration of, 13-14, 17-19; first census of, 18; census of (1730), 19; census of (1734), 22; census of (1735), 22; census of (1740), 23-24; 1st immigration of, 25-26; 2nd immigration of, 29-30; census of (1752), 28-29; census of (1753), 29-30; census of (1755), 30; expulsion from N.S. (1755), 30; migration to Ile St. Jean (1755-1756), 30-31; dire circumstances of, 31; deportation from Ile St. Jean (1758), 31-32; present population, 32
Act for the Effectual Recovery of certain of His Majesty's Quit Rents on the Island of Saint John, (1773-1774), 50, 55
Act Prohibiting the Sale of Intoxicating Liquor, 320
Act to Amend the Prohibition Act, 325
Act to establish the Public Archives of P.E.I., 353
Agnew, John, 350
Agricultural Exhibitions, 347
Agricultural Fairs, 346-347
Agriculture: early agriculture on P.E.I., 337-339; mechanization of, 347-348; scientific development of, 351-352
Agriculture, Provincial Department of, 348
Aichin, Graves, 49
Aix-La-Chapelle, Treaty of, 25
Albert, Steamship, 234, 240
Alberton, P.E.I., 129, 200, 202-203, 253, 345
Alexander, Ship, 47
Alexandra Hotel, London, England, 185
Algonquins Eastern, 3
Allanby, William, 46, 52
Alley, Dr., 349
American Civil War, 134, 159
American Revolutionary War, 52-53, 56, 59, 66, 68
Amherst, General Jeffrey, Lord, 33
Annapolis, Nova Scotia, 14
Anne of Green Gables, 353
Annexation of P.E.I. to Neighboring Colonies, 138
Antigonish-Guysboro, Nova Scotia, 275
Antigua, 113
Archibald, Adams G., 145, 147, 157, 370n
Argyllshire, Scotland, 47
Armstrong-Whitworth Co., 256

Arsenault, Aubin E., 272
Assemblyman, 295-311
Asylum for Insane Persons, Charlottetown, 331
Athol, Duke of, 194
Atlantic Neptune, 75
Atlantic Provinces Adjustment Grants, (1958), 286
Aubert, 16
Automain, 8
Automobile Act (1908), 318, 350; amendment to, 318-319; protests against, 318-319, 349-350
Aylesworth, A. B., 293

Bagnall, James, 80
Bagnall's Tavern, 81
Bahamas, West Indies, 127
Bain, Francis, 244
Bank of Prince Edward Island, 134
Bannerman, Sir Alexander, 126, 128; appointment, 124; grants Responsible Government, 125; recall of, 127
Baring Brothers, 208
Basin Head, P.E.I., 2
Bathurst, Lord, 83-88, 92-94
Bay Verte, New Brunswick, 15, 24, 26
Beaubassin, New Brunswick, 15, 24, 26
Beauséjour, 30
Beck, James B., 192
Beck, J. Murray, 152
Bedeque, P.E.I., 6, 116, 335-336
Beer, George, 140, 184, 199
Beer, Henry, 224
Belfast, P.E.I., 119
Belfast Riots, 118-119
Bell, Alexander Graham, 350
Bell, John Howatt, 274
Bennett, Richard Bedford, 259
Benoit, Captain, 25
Bernard, Lieutenant Governor Joseph A., 325
Berry, Walter, 54
"Better Terms": 1869 offer of, 194, 196-199; rejection of, 197-198; debate on, 198-199; J. C. Pope's promise of, 215-217; J. C. Pope negotiates to obtain, 221-222, 265
Biard, Father, 3-4, 6-9
Bible Question, 130-132
Bideford, P.E.I., 335
Bigot, François, 23, 25, 26
Binns, Charles, 104